A CULTURAL HISTORY OF IDEAS

OF IDEAS

VOLUME 2

A Cultural History of Ideas

General Editors: Sophia Rosenfeld and Peter T. Struck

Volume 1
A Cultural History of Ideas in Classical Antiquity
Edited by Clifford Ando, Thomas Habinek, and Giulia Sissa

Volume 2
A Cultural History of Ideas in the Medieval Age
Edited by Dallas G. Denery II

Volume 3
A Cultural History of Ideas in the Renaissance
Edited by Jill Kraye

Volume 4
A Cultural History of Ideas in the Age of Enlightenment
Edited by Jack R. Censer

Volume 5
A Cultural History of Ideas in the Age of Empire
Edited by James H. Johnson

Volume 6
A Cultural History of Ideas in the Modern Age
Edited by Stefanos Geroulanos

A CULTURAL HISTORY
OF IDEAS

IN THE
MEDIEVAL
AGE

Edited by Dallas G. Denery II

BLOOMSBURY ACADEMIC
LONDON · NEW YORK · OXFORD · NEW DELHI · SYDNEY

BLOOMSBURY ACADEMIC
Bloomsbury Publishing Plc
50 Bedford Square, London, WC1B 3DP, UK
1385 Broadway, New York, NY 10018, USA
29 Earlsfort Terrace, Dublin 2, Ireland

BLOOMSBURY, BLOOMSBURY ACADEMIC and the Diana logo are trademarks
of Bloomsbury Publishing Plc

First published in Great Britain 2022

Cover image: Royal 14 E.IV, f.5 © The British Library Board

A catalogue record for this book is available from the British Library.

A catalog record for this book is available from the Library of Congress.

ISBN: HB: 978-1-3500-0740-6
        Set: 978-1-3500-0755-0

Series: The Cultural Histories Series

Typeset by Integra Software Services Pvt. Ltd.
Printed and bound in Great Britain

To find out more about our authors and books visit www.bloomsbury.com
and sign up for our newsletters.

CONTENTS

ILLUSTRATIONS

GENERAL EDITORS' PREFACE

When Arthur Lovejoy introduced the field of the history of ideas to his listeners in the 1933 William James lectures, later published as *The Great Chain of Being*, he compared ideas to molecules. As he explained it, molecules combine and recombine to make compounds that vary over time. Yet the underlying stuff abides. The comparison gave him a way to capture the dynamic properties of ideas themselves and to forestall this or that thinker's eagerness to claim novelty. Further, since the periodic table has only so many elements, Lovejoy's conceit suggested that a person could, retroactively, make sensible statements about the whole.

In this book series devoted to the history of ideas, we hope to be able to make sensible judgements about the whole, but we are also convinced that the analogy needs rethinking. When Lovejoy accorded agency to the elements, with their pent-up interactive energies, he left out of focus the solution or medium in which those chemicals do their interacting. The non-noetic factors for which Lovejoy allowed come only from thinkers' internal dispositions, personal habits and preferences that might vary from person to person or from time to time. These volumes aim to widen considerably the intellectual historian's conception of how ideas emerge and move through the world.

A Cultural History of Ideas sweeps over 2,800 years of evidence. It proceeds on the premise that certain broad areas of inquiry have held humans' collective attention across a segment of the globe over all of this time. These nine topics are not presented as ideas in any simple sense. G. E. R. Lloyd's treatment of "Nature" in antiquity in volume 1 will already belie any confidence in a singular, perduring core even in this one-ninth of the terrain these volumes lay out. We propose this taxonomy instead as a set of general areas of investigation focused on comparable subjects across the ages. As historians of ideas, we aim to trace in this book series prominent lines of thought in each of these various realms—chapter by chapter, in the same order across volumes, from antiquity to the present—with close attention to constancy, change, and variation alike.

The first of these areas is "Knowledge" itself: what are we to make of the immaterial notions stored in our minds? Which ones count as true? How are such truths found, divided into new categories, conveyed, and used? After all, it is only in the twentieth century that anyone could speak meaningfully of the humanistic, social, biological, and physical sciences as distinct branches of knowledge. Many other systems came before. From "Knowledge," we turn to one of its central foci and the other starting point of this series: "The Human Self" in all its dimensions, physical, intellectual, emotional, and more. For it is the self that is the knower.

Then, moving outward from the singular self, we shift to "Ethics and Social Relations," or humans in concert with one another, and "Politics and Economies," or systems for organizing that collective existence legally and materially. "Nature" follows, including the human body, but also encompassing the earth that humans share with other animals, plants, and minerals, as well as the atmosphere and celestial bodies. Continuing to widen our lens, "Religion and the Divine" then takes the focus to the world beyond nature and to thinking about our origins, our afterlives, and our beliefs, which also means at times the limits of human knowledge.

The final categories take up, in close conversation with all of these previous domains, the realm of representation. "Language, Poetry, Rhetoric" concerns thinking about words in their many forms and uses. "The Arts" expands those questions into other symbolic systems employed in music, dance, theatre, fashion, architecture, design, and especially the visual arts, with a focus too on conceptions of beauty. Finally, "History" draws our attention to the representation of time itself, including notions of past, present, and future that simultaneously bring us full circle back to the understandings of knowledge and the self where we began.

Some specific ideas or concepts—freedom, dreams, power, difference, the environment, anger, to pick a random assortment—cross these many areas of inquiry and will appear more than once. But we take these nine broad categories to be proxies for some of the most fundamental areas to which humans in the domains of our focus—from so-called great thinkers like Plato or Locke or Einstein, to political leaders from Augustus to Charlemagne to Catherine the Great or Gandhi, to now-nameless scribes or teachers or midwives or bricklayers—have, over the centuries, applied their minds, alone and together.

But what is a *cultural* history of ideas? There are two distinguishing features of this approach, and both begin from the premise that the history of ideas is not, as some earlier historians including Lovejoy would have it, best understood as the record of a perennial conversation that largely transcends the specifics of space and time. Rather, we posit that just as the answers to big questions change depending on where and when we look, so do the questions themselves along with their stakes. "What is freedom?" means something very different to an enslaved Celt living in ancient Rome, a twelfth-century French monk, an aspiring merchant involved in transatlantic trade in seventeenth-century London, and a political theorist working in a US university in the era of late capitalism.

A cultural history of ideas is thus imagined, first, as a way to demonstrate the proposition that even the most innovative ideas to emerge from such queries, as well as the uses and impact of those ideas, have varied enormously depending on a host of contingent and contextual features extrinsic to the intellects that gave birth to them. These external features go well beyond other, competing ideas, or even competing texts in which other ideas are housed, despite the arguments of Quentin Skinner and much of what is thought of today as contextualized intellectual history. Cultural historians of ideas, to understand the thought of the past, necessarily look considerably more widely at a range of different domains of human life—or culture in the broadest sense.

Those cultural factors include changes in technology, media, and the economics of production and distribution; the authors in these volumes consider the evolution of ideas in relation to the emergence of alphabetic script and scribal culture, the printing press, photography, the computer, and other methods of communication that shaped their respective eras, as well as the commerce established around them. Our list also includes differing social structures and kinds of hierarchies and status markers, from race and gender, to estate, wealth, patronage, and credentialing, that have brought new kinds of thinkers to the fore and turned others into enemies or nonentities. In these pages we will meet, and also identify the support systems behind, philosophers, physicians, librarians, clerics, writers, artists, state officials, and only from the nineteenth century onward, "scientists," "experts," and, indeed, "intellectuals," as well as those denied these appellations. Other factors shaping ideas—including those of the most influential thinkers of every era—have been changes to laws; to religious practice and identity; to the distribution of resources; to patterns of migration, settlement, and urbanization; to notions of taste and manners; and to literacy rates, education, and intellectual life itself. So, too, do we need to study encounters between different peoples, whether through war, conquest, travel and exploration, exploitation, or peaceful cultural and commercial exchange. Then there is space in another sense. Historically specific settings, whether they be market places, monasteries, universities, salons, courts, coffee houses, medical clinics, port city docks, or think tanks, have inflected how ideas have been forged, disseminated, and debated and, ultimately, the form they have taken. So have modes of sociability. How can we understand the power of the ideas of Demosthenes or Horace or Lord Byron or Sarah Bernhardt without accounting for the social practices in which they were embedded, be that public oration, letter writing, listening to sermons or novels read out loud, or attending public performances, but also the material infrastructure behind those endeavors, from road construction to the microphone? And scaffolding everything else in the realm of ideas have, of course, always been geopolitics and the apparatuses of power: empires, nations, regions, city states, kingdoms, dioceses, and villages, but also competition about and between ideologies, factions and parties, and policies, whether established by vote, by decree, or by physical coercion.

In approaching ideas in this deeply contextual way, the cultural history of ideas could be said to be borrowing from the subfield known as the sociology of knowledge. Both share an interest in uncovering the structures, including practices and institutions, that allow for the varied means by which knowledge has been invented, organized, kept secret, exchanged, transformed, and weaponized to accomplish various goals, from acts of radical imagination and liberation to keeping people in their place. Equally, though, the approach employed in these volumes could be said to draw on histories of reading, of looking, and of hearing, that is, of interpretation and reinterpretation, or hermeneutics and textual exegesis, across genres, languages, and eras—all modes long associated with histories of the arts and literature and philosophy. Moreover, a cultural history of ideas should equally be a history of dissent and of forms of censorship and repression instituted in response. Historians also need to establish the evolving boundaries between the sayable and the unsayable, the representable and the unrepresentable, and why and how they have been enforced or not. That means paying attention to conflicts and forms of violence over just these questions as well as networks and modes of intellectual collaboration. Part of the interest in looking at the history of thought embedded in ever-shifting contexts over such a long period of time is discovering how some ideas—say, ideas about gender difference or modes of seeing others—persist across moments of social and political fracture, such as major wars. Another part is discovering how ideas are transformed by—or help transform—larger movements in the worlds that produced them; consider, for example, how much the ideas of Jean-Jacques Rousseau shaped political and religious practice in the context of the French Revolution, from republicanism to the institution of a civil religion, but also how his conceptual innovations were blamed for the revolution's excesses and thus delegitimized afterward. Some ideas, of course, fail to create any kind of traction until long after their moment of invention. Or they never do. All this is of interest to the historian of ideas too.

Yet there is a second sense in which these volumes function as a *cultural* history of ideas. Grasping this aspect requires looking more to anthropology than to sociology or literary theory. It also demands taking seriously the ideas and representations that animate everyday life, which is another meaning of culture. This approach turns our attention at least partly away from the ideas associated with philosophers, famous thinkers, or even major social movements or modern "isms" like nationalism or communism in their larger contexts. It does so in favor of a focus on collective habits, rituals, patterns of speech and behavior, and customary forms of representation operative in social, political, and economic experience, seeing them as imbued with, and productive of, a vital, culturally specific landscape of ideas. Some scholars call these ideas, taken together, folk knowledge or folk logic. From the Annaliste tradition of history writing in France, others have adopted the term *mentalité*. Included under its purview are, potentially, studies of the history of collective memory, of values, of popular and mass culture, and of the senses and emotions and decision-making in all their historical particularity.

Importantly for our purposes, sometimes the realm or realms of *mentalité* have operated to uphold the dominant ideology of the moment or to boost an ascendant one; Jack Censer and Gary Kates's introduction to the volume on the Enlightenment, for example, highlights the way eighteenth-century advertising circulars, the so-called *Affiches*, subtly bolstered the intellectual currents associated with Enlightenment philosophy without ever drawing directly on the work of any of its key thinkers. But other times folk knowledge has worked to undergird marginalized people's efforts to resist, circumvent, or revise dominant thinking, whether that has been in order to preserve traditions under pressure or to try to break free of various forms of repression. Consider craftworkers or Black revolutionaries of various eras deploying vernacular notions and forms of protest to challenge those with political and material power, including those who own the means of production. Often these commonplace and quotidian ideas, even as they structure collective life, are so routine and taken-for-granted within the culture where they exist that they go largely unremarked upon in any of the standard modes of conveying thought that are the focus of most histories of ideas. It is only when such everyday ideas collapse or get deployed in new ways that we tend to see that they belong to history too—and bear some relationship to the better-known history of explicit ideas.

What this means is that a cultural history of ideas in the second sense must extend its source base well beyond great books or texts of any kind; relevant ideas are just as likely to be embedded in visual, material, or somatic forms as they are in writing. Coin collections, garden designs, bits of code, temple complex plans, dance patterns, even habits of greeting: all become potential sites for uncovering foundational ideas in past moments and varied places. It also means thinking beyond traditional notions of thinker or audience to encompass the voices, eyes, and ears of those traditionally excluded from the tribe of "intellectuals," including women, people of color, and the nonliterate, as they can be unearthed from these varied sources. The volumes and individual chapters of this series will have succeeded if readers come away with an ability to take recognizable ideas or ideologies (i.e., those of Karl Marx and, subsequently, Marxism) or recognizable moments in intellectual history (i.e., "the Middle Ages") and see them as doubly imbricated in culture as ideational context and culture as the realm of everyday meaning-making and representation.

One risk, of course, is that this collection, with its cultural approach to ideas, ends up reinforcing an obsolete ideological construction paid lavish attention, particularly in the last century: that of "Western Civilization." The primary focus of these volumes is indeed the part of the globe, the temporal range, and much of the subject matter that scholars have inconsistently labeled and identified with "the West." But not content just to reject this terminology, we aim in these volumes to avoid the trap of its logic too, and we do so in several ways. The authors of these chapters do not take their geography to be bounded in any *a priori* way; their terrain stretches variously beyond Europe to the Near East, to China and other parts of Asia, to Russia, to Africa, and, unevenly over the last half millennium to North, Central, and South America. It is also important that every volume pushes back on the idea that the subject at hand can be described as constituting some unified cultural ethos. Radical intellectual pluralism exists in every era, and links of commonality also reach across whatever temporal and geographical boundaries we might construct. At the same time, we advocate a kind of geographical awareness that keeps us from losing sight of the fact that the histories under primary scrutiny here have been both carefully constructed and profoundly shaped by fantasies about, as well as dehumanizations of, varieties of others, whether labeled barbarians, foreigners, exotics, or heathens, whether near or far. This kind of thinking, in turn, is inseparable from an often violent history of the extraction of resources and commercial practices around the globe, of missionary activity and evangelization within and well beyond Christendom, of the enslavement of, particularly, African peoples, and of the conquest and colonization of various Indigenous peoples from the Americas to the South Seas. Advocacy for social justice is a distinct project from this one, but exposing the blinding legacies of injustice stemming from every era is very much a part of it. These volumes embrace the idea that a cultural history of ideas is necessarily a "connected history," with a focus on circulation and hybridity, along with serious attention to disparities of power.

But even more, perhaps, a cultural history of ideas potentially offers a conceptual way out of the trap of Western Civilization precisely because it historicizes, indeed "provincializes" (to borrow Dipesh Chakrabarty's term), the very categories long used to bolster it. Of particular pertinence here is "progress." Rather than treat techno-scientific or moral-political progress across time as a given, this series sees conceptions of progress, as well as those of newness and modernity, as polemical claims invented to serve different purposes at different moments (see especially the introductions to the volumes on the Enlightenment and the Age of Empire, but also the Middle Ages). The same could be said for periodization, including the very terms into which these volumes are carved up; Jill Kraye, in her volume on "the Renaissance," starts off not by guiding a tour of this arena but by showing us how this category was invented in the first place and then exposing its retrospective ideological functions. Indeed, the authors in this collection uniformly work hard to take up the intellectual pillars of standard accounts of what has been called Western Civilization and embed them, as ideas, in history. In addition to the notion of progress, these include the idea of the individual genius thinker, the advent of intellectual tolerance, the mastery of nature, secularization or the ultimate triumph of scientific reason over the enchantment of the world, and a firm distinction between past and present.

Moreover, despite the fact that this set of volumes ties ways of thinking to particular circumstances in the past, it is also designed to make the case that no one era or people or place owns those ideas going forward. Even the pointed anxieties of today, which Stefanos Geroulanos lists in the introduction to the final volume as including "dehumanization, species extinction, climate catastrophe, economic indifference to individual suffering, and artificial [forms of] intelligence," are in some sense variants of old concerns. We can thus treat previous responses to them as a storehouse from which people anywhere can continue to build new answers even as those ideas' initial relationship to particular conditions and situations remains important to understanding their full complexity. If this collection of the work of sixty-two scholars from multiple humanistic disciplines has a central goal, it is to remind us that inherited ways of thinking and our ever-changing lived experiences are constantly pushing against one another in productive ways, generating refreshed responses or, indeed, ideas as a result. We all aim to continue this endeavor.

Sophia Rosenfeld and Peter T. Struck,
General Editors

Introduction: The Sources and Circulation of Medieval Ideas

DALLAS G. DENERY II

Long-standing prejudice has it that people in the Middle Ages were gullible and superstitious illiterates, captives to religious dogma and accepting of all manner of outrageous foolishness. Renaissance humanists derided the intricate and, so they argued, pointless arguments of their scholastic predecessors and contemporaries, their allegedly crude Latin and hair-splitting logic. Petrarch, hoping for the imminent political and cultural rebirth of fourteenth-century Italian society, imagined himself standing on the brink of a new era of enlightenment, while simultaneously looking back at a thousand years of darkness, a *medium tempus*, separating him from the glories of ancient Rome.[1] The Swiss historian Jacob Burckhardt offered much the same picture in his nineteenth-century classic, *The Civilization of the Renaissance in Italy* (1860), arguing that people in the Middle Ages were like children, looking at the world as if through a veil:

> Woven of faith, illusion, and childish prepossession, through which the world and history were seen clad in strange hues. Man was conscious of himself only as a member of a race, people, party, family, or corporation—only through some general category. In Italy this veil first melted into air; an *objective* treatment and consideration of the State and of all the things of this world became possible.[2]

With the passing of the Middle Ages, so it seems, infantile fantasies gave way to mature accomplishments. The stage was set. At best the Middle Ages were little more than an interruption in the story of Western progress, at worst, they were a regression from the glories of the classical world into illiterate tribalism and violent irrationality.

As much as medieval historians would like to think they have successfully refuted this narrative of darkness to light, it persists, certainly in the popular imagination, but even among people who should know better. The influential German theorist Reinhard Koselleck, for example, who is particularly interested in problems associated with historical periodization, succumbs to typical medieval stereotypes when he describes the era as "static."[3] More telling is the United States' College Board's 2018 decision to no longer offer advanced placement tests for pre-1450 history. History effectively begins with the Renaissance as if nothing before matters or contributes to that beginning. As historians Matt Drwenski and David Eaton noted in *Perspectives on History*, "By focusing [high school European history courses] on the period defined by the rise of the West, the 'humanocentric' approach of the original course designers will be replaced by a straightforward narrative of European progress. The West acts. The rest respond."[4]

Put differently, periodization matters because periodization shapes the kinds of stories we tell about the past and the present, and however accurate they might be, these stories are always polemical and political. Long ago Thomas Carlyle, commenting on the vagaries of deciding when historical periods begin or end, observed that there is no cosmic clock whose bells announce the end of one era and the beginning of the next.[5] Much of the best recent work in the medieval cultural history of ideas has focused on this question of periodization, either explicitly raising the various agendas at work in distinguishing the medieval from the modern or questioning whether such divisions mask more than they reveal, obscuring the deeper continuities between, and the surprising rivers that flow from, the past to the present.[6] As a sort of stage-setting for the chapters that comprise this volume of the *Cultural History of Ideas*, this introduction will examine how scholars have used or misused the notion of the "Middle Ages" and how a cultural history of ideas might serve as a valuable corrective to those misuses.

One problem with raising the question "What were the Middle Ages?" or "When were the Middle Ages?" is that the mere asking seems to commit us to their existence. This was already the case with the book that, for all intents and purposes, came to define and organize medieval studies in the United States throughout the twentieth century—Charles Homer Haskins's 1927 classic, *The History of the Renaissance of the Twelfth Century*. Haskins argued that much of what Burckhardt had traced to fourteenth- and fifteenth-century Italy could be found hundreds of years earlier. Already in the twelfth and thirteenth centuries, Haskins would contend, medieval Europe had witnessed a "revival of the Latin classics and jurisprudence, the extension of knowledge by the absorption of ancient learning and by observation, and ... creative work ... in poetry and art." Burckhardt's sins, according to Haskins, were double. He not only silently suppressed evidence that the study of the arts and classics thrived in the twelfth century but also willfully ignored evidence of Renaissance irrationality and "childishness," leaving out any mention of "the alchemy and demonology which flourished throughout" the Renaissance.[7]

Whatever we want to make of these claims, they leave the historical scheme of fall and rise, darkness and light, more or less intact: two periods to be aspired to, and an intervening one to be disowned. Conceptually, the "Middle Ages" are the other, organized around negation—what is not the Renaissance, what is not classical Rome. As a period conceived through exclusion, the medieval age possess no internal principle of organization. It is simply whatever happened between the glory of Rome and Italian rebirth.

Certainly, scholars have tried to define this period in ways that give it coherence, but this has always seemed to be something of a hopeless quest. For Bloomsbury's Cultural History series and, as a result, for this book, we found it suitable to define the Middle Ages as a 950-year period extending from 500 to 1450. Why 500? Why 1450? There does not seem to be much more sense to this than a desire for round numbers and the need to chop things up somewhere. Scholars searching for dates or events to mark the end of classical Rome or the beginning of the Middle Ages have suggested, among other possibilities 312 (the Emperor Constantine's conversion to Christianity) or 476 (the deposition of the last Roman emperor).[8] Momentous as these events seem, historians such as Peter Brown and Patrick Geary have argued for a cultural and social continuity extending from the late Roman Empire well into the "Middle Ages." According to Geary, for example, "Merovingian civilization lived and died within the framework of late antiquity" and that framework only really gave way in the eighth century, with the rise of the Carolingians.[9]

Searching for the end of the Middle Ages offers no clearer answers. Petrarch may well have bemoaned the Dark Ages interfering with his inheritance of a glorious Roman past, but depending on where you look, that darkness he so despised may well have lingered on for centuries. Although the English political historian John Pocock, focusing on the rise of Florentine civic humanism, locates a sharp break between the medieval and Renaissance worlds sometime right around the year 1400, others, such as his Cambridge colleague Quentin Skinner, believe that notions of political order and organization remained unchanged between the thirteenth and late sixteenth centuries.[10] If we move from politics to religion, no doubt the Reformation seems as likely a candidate as any for marking the end of the Middle Ages. Whether we choose 1517, when Luther nailed his Ninety-five Theses to the door of Wittenberg castle church or the 1563 conclusion of the Council of Trent that forever codified the differences between Catholic and reformed religions, there seems little doubt that Europe's fragmentation into religious pluralism held momentous consequences.

Though Burckhardt proclaimed that it was during the Italian Renaissance that Europeans finally began to think about themselves as individuals, there is no shortage of writers happy to locate the origins of modern notions of individual freedom in Luther's famous statement at the Diet of Worms, "I consider myself convicted by the testimony of Holy Scripture, which is my basis. My conscience is captive to the Word of God. Thus, I cannot and will not recant anything, because acting against one's conscience is neither safe nor sound. Here I stand! I can do no other! Amen!"[11] Some locate it even later, in the 1640s when, toward the end of the first of his *Meditations on First Philosophy*, Descartes discovers that no matter how much an evil god might seek to deceive him, he still possesses the ability to withhold his assent.[12]

But even the apparent world-altering clarity of moments like these begin to fade on closer reflection. Medievalists have long called attention to various premature Reformations and reformist groups, such as the Waldensians, the Hussites, and Lollards, while also noting the continuities in daily religious practice and spiritual experience that extend from the Middle Ages well into the sixteenth century.[13] For their part, Renaissance historians have contested Burckhardt's claims about Renaissance individualism pointing to the continuing importance of group identity and ritual behavior in Florence throughout the fourteenth and fifteenth centuries.[14]

Scholars have stressed not only the religious continuity between the Middle Ages, Renaissance, and Reformation, but also the real and important similarities in their intellectual cultures. Thinkers in all three periods demonstrated an open reverence for the past. Scholastic theologians and arts masters may have preferred Aristotle, while Italian humanists often preferred Plato, nevertheless their heads were turned the same way. Writing in the twelfth century, the professionally frustrated cleric and bureaucrat Peter of Blois announced in no unclear terms his devotion to past masters:

> One only passes from the darkness of ignorance to the enlightenment of science if one re-reads with ever-increasing love the works of the ancients. Let dogs bark, let pigs grunt! I will nonetheless be a disciple of the ancients. All my care will be for them and the dawn will see me studying them.[15]

Machiavelli, writing some four hundred years later, seems to do little more than repeat Peter's praise:

When evening has come, I return to my house and go into my study. At the door I take off my clothes of the day, covered with mud and mire, and I put on my regal and courtly garments; and decently reclothed, I enter the ancient courts of ancient men, where, received by them lovingly, I feed on the food that alone is mine and that I was born for. There I am not ashamed to speak with them and to ask them the reason for their actions; and they in their humanity reply to me. And for the space of four hours I feel no boredom, I forget every pain, I do not fear poverty, death does not frighten me. I deliver myself entirely to them.[16]

Luther most certainly rejected scholastic philosophy and what he perceived to be the cult of Aristotle, but truth for him was also to be found in the past, in the primitive church and the holy words of scripture.

From this perspective, the Middle Ages, Renaissance, and Reformation seem to have much more in common with each other than with succeeding centuries, with the scientific revolution in particular. Whether or not their ideas were as novel as they claimed, there seems no denying intellectuals and artists writing in the seventeenth century considered novelty and newness to be intellectual virtues. Book titles from the time abound with proclamations of their originality, though originality need not have much truck with accuracy nor, for that matter, with actual originality—*Two New Sciences*, *New Philosophy of Human Nature*, *New and Most Curious Questions about Human Nature*, not to mention the decidedly dubiously titled *New Demonstration for the Immobility of the Earth*.[17] More importantly, looking back from our perspective, the continuing impact of the decades surrounding 1600 on our own contemporary arts, culture, and sciences seems undeniable, and perhaps even greater than anything from the preceding thousand years. Scholars generally nominate Miguel Cervantes's 1615 work *Don Quixote* as the first novel. Shakespeare, whose plays remain among the most performed works in the Western canon, composed *Hamlet* in 1603, while Monteverdi composed one of the first operas, *Orfeo*, in 1607. Contemporary philosophy traces its origins to the early seventeenth-century writings of Descartes. For his part, Galileo, who may well lay claim to being the first modern scientist, published the *Sidereus Nuncius*, in which he announced the results of his telescopic observations of the Moon and Jupiter, in 1610.

Dating the end of the Middle Ages, in other words, is a contentious muddle precisely because locating the end of the Middle Ages, the end of pre-modernity, is crucial to locating the origins of our modern world, the origins of our values and most basic assumptions about the divine, the world, and ourselves. If we locate those origins in Renaissance humanism, we end up with quite a different story about ourselves and our relation to and dependence on the past than if we locate them in the Reformation, the scientific revolution, or even, as some scholars would have it, the French Revolution or Kant's *Critique of Pure Reason*. But this suggests we need to ask our question about periodization differently. Rather than simply asking when do the Middle Ages end, we should ask what work does periodization accomplish? What contrasts does it establish and to what ends?

Unsurprisingly, the contrasts and ends that the Middle Ages are put to are many and often opposed, even when the histories written to support them are almost identical. One such narrative, a narrative of cultural and intellectual history that has achieved near canonical status over the last four or five decades, concerns developments in scholastic theology and philosophy, specifically the cultural and religious implications of debates concerning God's omnipotence. According to this story, we can trace the roots of modern secular society, the disenchantment of the world, the origins of scientific empiricism, and even the spiritual breakthrough that led to Luther's rejection of so much Catholic dogma and practice, to the bickering of theologians and arts masters at the universities of Oxford and Paris about what God can and cannot do.[18]

In its broadest terms, the story is one of fragmentation. A medieval society unified through a common faith and shared religious practices that are ultimately grounded and reflected in a set of theological and metaphysical assumptions concerning the nature of God and God's relationship to creation, finds itself questioned and then rejected. The thirteenth-century Dominican theologian Thomas Aquinas almost always serves as the representative of the "true" medieval conception of these matters. To clarify, we will look at just one aspect of Aquinas' thought and how his successors allegedly undermine it.

Early in Aquinas' *Summa of Theology*, which he composed in the 1270s, he takes up the question of God's power. What does it mean to assert that God is omnipotent, that God is all powerful? To answer these sorts of questions, Thomas asks, "Whether God can do better than he does?" For example, could God have made a better world than the world he made, that is a better world than *this* one? Aquinas answers both yes and no. He writes:

> The universe, the present creation being supposed, cannot be better, on account of the most beautiful order given to things by God; in which the good of the universe consists. For if any one thing were bettered, the proportion of order would be destroyed; as if one string were stretched more than it ought to be, the melody of the harp would be destroyed. Yet God could make other things, or add something to the present creation; and then there would be another and a better universe.[19]

As far as Aquinas sees it, what God chose to make and what God could have made are two separate questions. God is all powerful, just, wise, and perfect, and so, whatever he chooses to make is the best version of that thing possible. Despite the flaws we might perceive in ourselves as a species, for example, given the type of beings we are, God could not have made us any better. Certainly, he could improve on our species. He could have given us telepathic powers or the ability not to sin, but then we would no longer be human beings, we would be some other kind of being. We are the kind of being we are and given the kind of being we are, God could not have made us any better.

Significantly, Aquinas applies this same reasoning to the universe. Given the universe God chose to make, given the entities that make it up, it is the very best version of this universe possible. Furthermore, the perfection of this universe requires that we human beings be just the way we are, with all our apparent strengths and weaknesses, virtues and foibles. Every variety of being fits with every other being to create, in Aquinas' metaphor, a perfect "melody" of parts. Had God chosen to create a universe populated with a better version of ourselves (that is, with some kind of being different than ourselves), he would have had to adjust every other being to create a new melody that works with that new note. In other words, he would have had to create a different universe to accommodate that new version of humanity. The universe is not some random collection of tossed together parts, but an organized system, a unity built from pieces that demand one another for their existence and fulfillment. Our universe is contingent in the sense that God did not have to make it, he could have created a different universe. But given that he chose to make this universe, he had to make it the way he did. This careful balance between contingency and necessity rests on Aquinas' conception of God as utterly simple. Earlier in the *Summa*, Aquinas points out that though we talk of God's essence and existence, of his will, knowledge, justice, power, and love, God is radically simple and without distinction. He is one (even though triune), and when he acts his actions are one with his love and justice, his wisdom and benevolence.[20]

This conception of God has real consequences. It suggests that this universe has to be the way it is. It is perfectly structured given its constituent beings and that structure reflects, however distantly, God's wisdom, justice, love, and power. The Apostle Paul seems to warrant this relation between creator and created, when he writes at Romans 1:20, "The invisible things of Him are clearly seen, being understood by the things that are made." Reflecting on this passage in the first part of the *Summa*, Aquinas writes:

> From effects not proportionate to the cause no perfect knowledge of that cause can be obtained. Yet from every effect the existence of the cause can be clearly demonstrated, and so we can demonstrate the existence of God from His effects; though from them we cannot perfectly know God as He is in His essence.[21]

We may not be able to know God perfectly through his works, but we can see him dimly, as through a glass darkly, through analogies and metaphors. Aquinas' Franciscan contemporary, Bonaventure, echoed these sentiments, when, in the *Breviloquium* (c. 1257), he writes, "The first Principle created this perceptible world as a means of self-revelation so that, like a mirror of God or a divine footprint, it might lead man to love and praise his Creator. Accordingly, there are two books, one written within, inscribed by God's eternal Art and Wisdom; the other written without, and that is the perceptible world."[22]

Over the course of the late thirteenth and fourteenth centuries, this vision of a unified and meaningful world collapsed as theologians continued to investigate the consequences of God's omnipotence. Everyone accepted the idea that God could do all possible things and that "all possible things" meant anything that does not involve a logical contradiction. In other words, God could not make the same thing both exist and not exist at the same time, he could not make it that $x = -x$. But what sorts of actions constitute a logical contradiction? Much of thirteenth-century scholastic theology, much of Aquinas' theology, rested on ideas derived from Neoplatonic readings of Aristotle's natural philosophy and metaphysics. Aristotle offered an account of the cosmos as eternal and rationally ordered, the necessary consequence of the prime mover's intellectual self-reflection. There is only one cosmos, it is this one and this one cannot be different. None of this sat square with scripture, which seemed to proclaim God's absolute power, that he created the universe out of nothing. Both arts masters and theologians debated these questions, noting that while natural reason might be on Aristotle's side, scripture as the true revelation of God's word teaches something different. While Aquinas tried to balance the demands of reason and revelation through his careful arguments about what it means to say that God can do better than he did, subsequent theologians suspected he had done little more than subject God's power to Aristotle's natural philosophy.[23]

In the first decades of the fourteenth century, the Franciscan theologian William Ockham rejected major swaths of Aristotelian philosophy including his belief in the existence of universals because they seemed to impinge on God's power. Why couldn't God have made this very universe, but with a better brand of human being? To suggest He could not is to suggest that creation limits God's freedom to act and to choose. More notoriously, he took up the question of the necessity of Christ's incarnation. The eleventh-century monk, theologian, and eventual archbishop Anselm of Canterbury had famously argued in *Cur deus homo?* that given the nature of Adam and Eve's trespass in the Garden of Eden, it was necessary that a being both God and man make atonement to an aggrieved God. "Why must this be the case?" Ockham asked and he went on to assert that had he chosen, Christ could have come incarnated as an ass and our salvation would be no less assured.[24] Though no fourteenth-century theologian would claim God acts inordinately or irrationally, they increasingly laid stress on God's will, his power to choose independently of all restrictions save the principle of non-contradiction.

This emphasis on the preeminence of God's will was already present, though perhaps not recognized, within Aquinas' account of God's power. Although Aquinas claims that God always acts as a unity, his power as part of his wisdom and goodness, Aquinas' actual argument suggests something different. Aquinas admits God could have made a better world than he did, but wouldn't this apply to any world he created? Suppose he created a world better than ours. Being omnipotent, couldn't he then create a world better than that one? In consequence, no matter what world God creates, he could always create a better one. What criteria can he possibly have for choosing any world given that no such world will ever be the best of all possible worlds? Ultimately, Aquinas leaves us with a God who simply acts, simply chooses *this*, without reference to his wisdom or goodness.[25]

The implications of divine omnipotence, at least for fourteenth-century thinkers, were profound. Among other things, it suggested the radical contingency of creation. Writing in the 1340s, the English Dominican Robert Holkot, following Ockham, writes:

God can be obliged to no law but that without its observance he can be morally good, because otherwise the divine goodness would depend on creatures, and God would be less good than he is if he were to destroy every creature; and, similarly, God would begin to be better than he was before the observance of the law.[26]

There is no reason why God could not alter or do away with the Ten Commandments, change the common course of nature, command people to hate him, deceive them, or renege on his promises. No internal necessity among things requires that the cosmos be ordered in any particular way and this even applies to the practices of the church. In this particular dispensation, given this particular creation, baptism, confession, and Communion designate some of the activities necessary for our salvation, but God could have, indeed still could, change them. The only reason why baptism, for example, removes the stain of original sin is because God decided it should, and its efficacy depends entirely upon God's continuing acceptance of it. God, after all, is no man's debtor. He freely set up a covenant with human beings that if human beings do certain things, he will grant them salvation. The actions themselves have no power beyond God's willingness to accept them.[27]

Nothing about the general outline of this history of theological debate concerning God's omnipotence is controversial. There might be minor disagreements over fine points of argumentation, but most scholars agree on the overall story. Controversy arises over how this history is put to use, and what is remarkable is how often historians have put it to use in debates about periodization and the difference between the medieval and modern worlds. Is it a story of decline or beginning, waning or harvest?[28] Intellectual historians and historians of science interested in redeeming the intellectual contributions of medieval thought, have looked to these debates as central to the rise of counterfactual thinking and an increasingly empirical approach to the world so characteristic of the scientific revolution,[29] many recent writers have seen them as evidence of an epochal transformation of Western society.

Writing in the 1960s, the German historian Hans Blumenberg argued that these later medieval debates concerning God's omnipotence marked the second coming of Christianity's defining enemy, gnosticism. According to Blumenberg, the Christian attempt to reconcile God's power with his reason, to reconcile the implications of divine omnipotence with Greek philosophy, collapsed with the rise of nominalistic theologies in the fourteenth and fifteenth centuries, leaving humanity naked and helpless in a world become unintelligible before an inscrutable and capricious God. Modernity begins in all its originality in the rubble that nominalism made of an always fragile medieval culture, in the writings of men such as Nicholas of Cusa and René Descartes who constructed new accounts of nature, humanity, and God. Blumenberg sought to rescue the originality and, to use his term, "legitimacy" of the modern project of self-assertion and rational progress from critics like Karl Löwith who argued that far from marking a break with its medieval past, the modern world is really its illicit second act. We might live in a secularized world, Löwith contends, but that just means we live in a world in which medieval ideas live on, stripped of certain religious qualities, but as invidious and irrational as ever. The modern idea of progress, Marx's dream of a utopian communist society existing stable and unchanging at the end of history, to cite Löwith's most famous example, is simply a secularized version of Christian notions of eschatology and, therefore, just as fanciful.[30]

More recently, historians, philosophers, and social commentators have looked to fourteenth-century debates about God's power to diagnose and critique the perceived nihilism and fragmentation of contemporary secular society. The philosopher Charles Taylor's 2007 Templeton Prize-winning book, *A Secular Age*, is surely the subtlest of these works, even if the story he narrates pivots on a balance so weighted toward the modern condition that our premodern past becomes as homogenous and static as Reinhard Kosellek thinks it, and as Burckhardt demeaned it. To hear Taylor tell it, medieval Europe, organized around and reflected in "the ordered Aristotelian cosmos of Aquinas" in which people were always already embedded, situated, and positioned, within a meaningful or meaning-giving world gradually gives way, first under the impact of nominalism and then through its aftereffects, to a disenchanted world from which human beings become "disembedded," isolated, set adrift.[31] Rather than a triumphal tale of progress, Taylor uses his depiction of the Middle Ages to narrate a story of spiritual loss and anomie. Alistair MacIntyre's influential *After Virtue* does something similar, suggesting a past that extends from the Middle Ages back to Aristotle in which common metaphysical and communal understandings provided a unitary framework for human beings to pursue meaningful and virtuous lives. Although MacIntyre originally looked to Enlightenment deists as the source of our contemporary despair and loss of common understanding, he too has eventually come around to focus on the illness that is fourteenth-century nominalism and the holistic Thomism that it destroyed.[32]

The idea that medieval debates about God's omnipotence practically defines the very character of the modern world has even moved from the shelves of academics to the *New York Times*' bestseller list. In *The Benedict Option*, his 2017 diagnosis of the challenges facing contemporary Christians in an aggressively secularizing culture, the conservative Catholic commentator Rod Dreher looks to the fourteenth century as the source of all our modern problems. Drawing on the work of Charles Taylor and David Hart Bentley, Dreher describes William Ockham as the "theologian who did the most to topple the mighty of oak of the medieval model" and the axe he used was "nominalism." As Dreher puts it, "This sounds like angels-dancing-on-the-head of-a-pin-stuff, but its importance cannot be overstated. Medieval metaphysicians believed nature pointed to God.

Nominalists did not. They believed there is no inner meaning existing objectively within nature and discoverable by reason."[33] Further, without inner meaning, there is, he claims, no meaning at all.

Despite their intellectual heft and aspiration, all these recent works operate on the assumption of an easily known and more or less homogenized Middle Ages. Periodization locates the origins of our modern fall from a more organically and teleologically structured world in which human beings could flourish, into the hyperpluralistic nihilism of the modern world. Despite hundreds, and in Taylor's case, hundreds upon hundreds, of pages of detailed study of the last five hundred years, these authors treat the Middle Ages in deft brushstrokes as if there was little really to be said of such a transparently knowable era.

But this can hardly be right. Indeed, it is not right.

In the most historically sensitive work in this genre, *The Unintended Reformation* (2011), Brad Gregory repeatedly emphasizes the rich diversity of medieval religious, cultural, and intellectual life, while stressing that, fundamentally, the medieval Catholic Church provided an institutionalized worldview that framed and guided people's efforts to achieve moral and spiritual excellence. All this began to crumble, first, because of theological squabbles about God's nature beginning early in the fourteenth century, and second, because of the ever-expanding gap between what the church preached and how it behaved. Once again, cultural unity and ontologically grounded meaning fragments into plurality, and plurality inevitably leads to nihilism and an anything goes style of moral relativism. But Gregory may well give up the game late in his book as he wonders why the cultural and religious fragmentation of the Reformation had not occurred earlier in the Middle Ages, which had, after all, confronted its own heretical and dissident movements. "Unlike the medieval heresies that secular and ecclesiastical authorities had largely managed to suppress and control," he writes, "Lutheranism and Reformed Protestantism, including the Church of England, demonstrated their institutional staying power."[34]

For all their talk of metaphysical conceptions of order and goodness binding communities together in spiritually and emotionally satisfying ways, medieval unity (or what there was of it) was actually rooted in government-sanctioned violence and coercion. This coercion was not limited to heretics, to various and sundry disbelievers, widows, and Jews, but even extended to the medieval thinkers responsible for articulating this supposed natural and organic account of human situatedness in the world. This intellectual coercion, all in the name of maintaining some sort of metaphysical unity, took the form of academic condemnations, the burning of writings deemed heretical, voluntary or enforced exile, and the occasional execution of teachers unwilling to recant opinions deemed heretical.[35] All of which forces the question—what sort of unity was this when so many wished and wanted to wander only to be kept from doing so under threat? Can nostalgia for a nonexistent past really offer an adequate historical narrative from which to critique the present?

Whether the Dark Ages from which we escaped or the premodern Eden from which we now live in anonymous exile, scholars have used the vast and crazy sprawl of the near thousand years that encompass the medieval age to tell stories about themselves. I suspect a good case could be made that by definition histories are as much about the historian as they are about the past they purport to describe. At least one advantage of approaching the Middle Ages through the methods of a cultural history of ideas is that, while as much about ourselves as ever (as Mary Franklin-Brown emphasizes in her chapter on medieval conceptions of the self), at least such histories have a chance of upsetting long-accepted ideas and mucking up oversimplified histories put to use for contemporary religious, political, and ideological purposes. Perhaps this is the goal of most every sort of history, but as an approach to the past, the cultural history of ideas seems particularly well suited to the task. A cultural history of ideas attempts to place ideas into contexts, not just into the context of other ideas but also into the lived material contexts in which people think and hope and despair, into the religious, institutional, and political contexts that define and make possible the scope of our actions and the range of our possible self-expression.

One narrative, well known and still useful, tells the story of medieval intellectual life as it moves from monasteries to urban centers, from cathedrals to universities, while simultaneously coming to terms with two quite different cultural inheritances, pagan and Christian. These moves from one place to another had more than mere geographic significance. In the 1960s the Canadian scholar Marshall McLuhen provocatively asserted that "the medium is the message." Communications technologies are not transparent vehicles through which we transmit our thoughts. Rather, different types of technologies (mnemonics, alphabetic script, pen and paper, the printing press, the radio, the television) variously shape the kinds of thoughts we can formulate and express.[36] For quite some time now, medieval scholars have implicitly adopted McLuhen's insights, arguing, in effect, that "the institution is the medium," the monastery, the cathedral school, and the university are different forms of communications technologies, making possible different kinds of thoughts, treatises, and forms of life.

Already in 1961, Jean Leclercq demonstrated that the monastic setting, with its spiritual goals, daily rituals, and communal lifestyle, helped to shape the content and form of its intellectual practice.[37] Today, for example, we too readily abstract and examine in isolation Anselm's ontological proof for the existence of God from the treatise in which it really serves as a first step on the road to an ever-deepening meditation into the nature of divinity. But as Leclercq convincingly demonstrates, in the setting of the monastery, every action was understood as a form of prayer, a devotion to God, including philosophical inquiry. It is no wonder then, that Anselm concludes the *Prosologion* with a stirring invocation to prayer and joy:

> O, Lord, I ask what You counsel through our marvelous Counselor; may I receive what You promise through Your Truth, so that my joy may be full. O God of Truth, I ask; may I receive, so that my joy may be full. Until then, may my mind meditate upon [what You have promised]; may my tongue speak of it. May my heart love it; may my mouth proclaim it. May my soul hunger for it; may my flesh thirst for [it]; may my whole substance desire [it] until such time as I enter into the joy of my Lord, the trine and one God, blessed forever. Amen.[38]

Gorgeous as this closing prayer is, as central as it is to shaping and defining Anselm's philosophical inquiry, it never makes it into the pages of undergraduate philosophy texts.

The institutional setting of the medieval university differs profoundly from the monastery and, as a result, so does the form and content of the works that scholars produced there. Although all university members took at least minimal religious vows, the primary mission of the university was to create a professional and literate workforce of bureaucrats, lawyers, doctors, and theologians. Under these sorts of pressures, theology became a field of study with set topics to be mastered, and scholars undertook the work of creating texts in systematic theology capable of "meeting the needs of professional theological education."[39] The great age of scholastic theology commenced and, with it, the pronounced tensions between Greek philosophy and Christian revelation that motivated, among other things, debates about God's omnipotence.

This history of intellectual migration, both in space and content, certainly captures something real and true about the medieval history of ideas, but it may obscure as much as it illuminates. Amanda Power's opening chapter, "Knowledge," perfectly exemplifies the capacity of a cultural history of ideas to switch our focus from the seen to the obscured. She begins with a simple but rarely asked question about Augustine's mistress, a woman he barely mentions, never names, and eventually dismisses as he turns his thoughts toward a life of Christian chastity. Power asks, "What did she know?" It is a question that opens a vast terrain of inquiry. What sorts of knowledge, what kinds of knowing, were pushed aside, demeaned, or lost with the development of the institutional church and its proximity to secular power? Or, looked at differently, what does this process of exclusion and suppression teach us about the purpose and function of institutionally sanctioned forms of knowing?

Wesley Yu's chapter, "Language, Poetry, Rhetoric" offers a perfect complement to Power's contribution. While Power asks us to consider suppressed knowledge, Yu approaches the question of knowledge from the perspective of language itself, that is, rhetoric. Rooted in the ancient practice of oratory in which speakers needed to consider and adjust their words to the specific circumstances in which they found themselves, rhetoric provided medieval thinkers tools to think about the world and "how to comport themselves in it." Put differently, rather than consider medieval epistemology solely from the heights of the idealized metaphysical debates characteristic of the historical narratives we considered above concerning divine omnipotence, Yu asks us to consider how their rhetorical training helped medieval people to make sense of their daily, practical experience of the world, not only in works of natural philosophy but also in their civic engagements, as well as in works of poetry and autobiography.

The chapters brought together in this volume, as well as the other volumes in this collection, progress with a certain logic. Beginning with a reflection on how and what we know, they move to more specific topics of knowledge: of the world around us ("Nature"), the world within and among us ("The Human Self"), of right and wrong ("Ethics and Social Relations"), of the relations among us ("Politics and Economies"), and of the relations that will save us ("Religion and the Divine"). The final chapters dip back into each of these topics, considering what might be thought of as different modes of knowing ourselves, of expressing our relation to the world around us and to God—the literary ("Language, Poetry, Rhetoric"), the material ("The Arts"), and the retrospective ("History"). Taken together, they paint a picture of the Middle Ages as evolving and varied, different from our contemporary world, yet comprehensible. If they fail to answer the question, "What were the Middle Ages?" that may well have more to do with problems inherent to the question itself.

Mary Franklin-Brown addresses these problems in her chapter "The Human Self" when she highlights how contemporary concerns determine what we find interesting in the past. Would we care much about Guibert of Nogent's obscure twelfth-century attempt at autobiography, if we were not already interested in the autobiographical experiments of later, more influential writers, such as Montaigne and Rousseau? Present concerns may dictate our interest in the past, Franklin-Brown suggests, but we must attempt to read around our present biases to uncover a more authentic accounting of medieval selves. For example, do not read Guibert's work through the distorting concepts of Freudian psychology, but rather employ the framework of medieval moral psychology through which Guibert and his peers would have thought about themselves and others. As Franklin-Brown contends, somewhere between the two poles of individuality and group identification "stands the [medieval] subject, an individual who is fissured by conflicting roles projected upon him or her by the ideologies of the time."

Eileen Sweeney approaches medieval ethical thought through its profound differences from both the ancient philosophical traditions that preceded it and the enlightenment values that succeeded it. If Plato, Aristotle, and the Stoics promoted an ideal of self-mastery focused on the person of the great and magnanimous man, medieval thinkers organized their ethical thinking around the love of God. Likewise, while Kant grounded his ethics in the principle of rational autonomy, medieval thinkers emphasized the connection between human fulfillment and our obligations to others, to God and our neighbors. In other words, our affective lives are central to medieval conceptions of human excellence in a manner simply unimaginable in the ethical writings of ancient Greeks and Romans. In this conception of human flourishing as affective, danger arises when our affections and love are misdirected, becoming sinful passion, a topic medieval thinkers and writers explored at length, as Sweeney shows, not only in theological treatises but also in all manner of pastoral and courtly treatises.

For their chapter, "Politics and Economies," Cary Nederman and Karen Bollermann adopt a more linear approach. How did medieval thinkers respond to Europe's demographic and economic boom that began during the second half of the eleventh century, resulting in several centuries of radical social, cultural, and political transformation? Although there were moralists who warned of the spiritual dangers wealth posed to the Christian soul, others clearly took an interest in the more practical implications and functioning of the emerging market economies. Specifically, Nederman and Bollermann counter traditional histories that claim eighteenth-century thinkers such as Adam Smith founded the study of political economies. They demonstrate that medieval thinkers already began to develop "economic theories of public life, [emphasizing] the worthiness of ensuring a satisfactory arrangement of economic goods primarily for the sake of meeting the physical, temporal needs of individuals of all classes and orders."

In her chapter, "Nature," Kellie Robertson charts the competing ideas at work in medieval conceptions of nature, from the ancient Greeks to the encyclopedists Pliny and Isidore of Seville. She emphasizes this complexity as a means of countering reductive histories that emphasize Aristotle's distinction between nature and artifice as a means of aligning medieval thinking about nature with more contemporary ideas. While the encyclopedic tradition offered medieval readers a sense of nature's vast treasury of plants, animals, minerals, peoples, and wonders, Plato and Aristotle offered them theories to account for the cosmos' apparent order, interconnectedness, and purposeful direction. Thirteenth-century natural philosophers drew on Aristotle, for example, to depict "nature as an autonomous, rule-governed entity that nevertheless worked according to God's plan." If this notion of a quasi-independent nature did not sit entirely comfortably with the notion of God's omnipotence, it certainly allowed medieval intellectuals to think about our relation to the cosmos and here there were competing strains of thought. Human beings were composed of the same material elements as the rest of nature, subject to the influence of the stars and planets, but our possession of an intellectual and immaterial soul suggested our difference from the nature, so that in some sense we might be both in and outside of it.

Claire Waters focuses on a different kind of tension in "Religion and the Divine." The story of the Catholic Church, she contends, is the story of a worldly institution attempting to keep its eye on the spiritual, even as its material wealth and geographic scope increases. Is the church part of the world or merely occupying it for a time? Set against the backdrop of European demographic and economic expansion that began in the eleventh century, Waters tells a story of successive waves of spiritual and institutional reform of the church. To meet the spiritual needs of an increasingly complex society, the church fosters the formation of new religious orders (for example, the Dominicans and Franciscans) and the development of pastoral literature (such as confessional manuals and *ad status* sermons). The rise of intense affective forms of devotion among the laity throughout the later Middle Ages points to both the need for and success of the pastoral endeavors.

Medieval art was no less responsive than was the church to Europe's twelfth-century demographic and economic transformation. In "Art," Heidi Gearhart narrates a four-step history of medieval art, beginning in its earliest centuries proceeding through the Carolingian, Romanesque, and Gothic periods. While early medieval works of art were created for the elite by the Gothic era of the late twelfth and thirteenth centuries, secular craftsmen were creating books and art objects for an ever-growing literate lay audience. With the change in audience came changes in the purpose and function of art. Whereas early medieval reliquaries and jewel-encrusted Bibles were signs and testaments of power that both evoked and concealed the divine, Gothic prayer books were written to teach and inform their readers, to inspire their spiritual lives.

In the final chapter, "History," Matthew Kempshall paints a history of medieval historical practices as caught within a series of productive tensions arising from history's somewhat ill-defined disciplinary status. On the one hand, Augustine had distinguished between history and aetiology. Aetiology is the study of causes and meanings and since God wills these events, those causes and meanings are beyond the reckoning of any but preachers and prophets. History becomes the simple, but still valuable, narration of deeds done. On the other hand, thanks in large part to Cicero, historical narrative fell within the orbit of rhetorical categories and compositional strategies, particularly verisimilitude, the various techniques through which a history secures its "plausibility and trustworthiness." From the twelfth through to the fourteenth century, Kempshall contends, medieval writers grappled with the problem of "form and content, narrative and truth," in ways not so dissimilar to historians in the late twentieth century.

Taken together, these chapters tell a story about the Middle Ages that at some moments seem to confirm and at others refute Burckhardt's assertions of medieval groupthink and superstition. In certain ways the Middle Ages are profoundly different than our present world, yet in other ways we can discern the beginnings of trends, the planting of seeds, that would only reveal themselves in time. This might sound like a mere truism applicable to any age, perhaps it is. But given the incoherence and confusions lodged within the conceptualization of the Middle Ages, given its chronological, geographical, and cultural sprawl, it is a truism especially suited to this amalgamation of 950 years whose only indisputable commonality is that they do not include any years that come before 500 or after 1450. Maybe the Middle Ages cannot be all things to all people, but they can certainly be many things to many of them and it is the job of the cultural historian to question each and every one of them.

CHAPTER ONE

Knowledge: Conception and Practices, 500–1450

AMANDA POWER

In the North African city of Carthage, in the late fourth century, lived a woman who spent fifteen years of her life with an unsettled and ambitious man. She gave birth to their child. She came with him as he pursued his career as a professional teacher of rhetoric in the provincial city of his birth, Thagaste, in Carthage, and later, as he departed Africa for Rome and Milan. The man broke off their relationship in the hope of making an advantageous marriage and she went back to Carthage. She left her son with his father and swore to remain celibate for the rest of her life. We know nothing more of her, not even her name, and her son—a bright and affectionate child called Adeodatus—died before reaching adulthood.[1] Yet she played a distinctive role in the crystallization of conceptions and practices of knowledge as they run through the medieval period and into our modernity. She was the element that must be excluded for understanding to flourish. For her lover, whose name was Augustine, was subsequently baptized a Christian, ordained a priest, elevated to the bishopric of Hippo, and emerged as one of the most prolific and powerful voices of the Roman Catholic Church, shaping its discourses for more than a thousand years. He wrote only briefly of their relationship: of their mutual physical desire, which he described as "lustful," of his terrible grief over her departure, and how he could not, despite his anguish, initially follow her example and rid himself of sexual desire.[2] Even so, his rejection of what he described as loving domestic harmony was part of his journey toward his conversion to the Catholic Church, after which he "no longer desired a wife, or placed any hope in this world"— and became free to know and to serve the Christian god.[3] But what did she know, the woman who had lived with him and loved him he said; borne, nurtured, and given up a child; run a household; known the ways and peoples of different cities; thought her own thoughts, accumulated her experiences in the world as a girl and a woman? Whatever she knew, it formed no part of her culture's sense of what constituted knowledge—or, at least, knowledge that mattered enough to record—and yet it was fundamental to the fabric, daily functioning, and persistence of human society.

Some years later, as Augustine lay dying, the city of Hippo was under siege by the Vandals. They seemed to him to be deadly antagonists of civilization and its values, and indeed they have remained a byword for every kind of barbarism. Rome's frontiers had become porous to such peoples. Their languages were to be heard everywhere in the western part of the empire as migrating groups became rulers and landowners. They preserved a modicum of classical high culture and custom in their courts and the organization of their kingdoms, but they were not native to those values and were for the most part rough and recent converts to varied forms of Christianity. Yet for all the threat they posed to the empire's survival, they were not, for Augustine, by any means the enemy that mattered most. When the Visigoths sacked Rome in 410, the true danger had seemed to Augustine to be the opportunity that it gave influential pagan members of the old senatorial "elite" to blame Christianity for the humiliation. He feared that the presence in the African province of these vocal refugees from the imperial heartlands would disrupt his efforts to build Christian communities in the face of heresies and local pagan opposition. His answer was the monumental *City of God against the Pagans*, completed four years before his death in 430. It presented a dark and uncompromising vision of human history as a vast cosmological struggle between the earthly city, suffocating in the miasma of sin and death, and the city of God, whose inhabitants would find salvation through God's grace. The first half of the book critiqued pagan religion and philosophy, which—turning pagan criticisms on their head—were blamed for all the ills of the Roman past. Worse, the very splendors of pagan learning endangered human souls, for they belonged to the earthly city and to the deceptions of demons. As we will see, it was part of his achievement to open the way for their arrogation by Christian scholars.

Augustine's vigorous polemic was, from some perspectives, soon redundant. The slow unravelling of Roman imperial administration gained momentum in the decades after his death: the grasp of its governors and bureaucrats, its land-owning elites, its systems of law and taxation, its regulation of agriculture loosened, and its extensive networks of transport and trade slowly disintegrated. What remained of local governance was, increasingly, episcopal administration, and it was as Christian bishops that the residue of the Roman aristocracy now exercised power. The main institutional responsibility for the preservation of learning, the physical conservation and copying of books, and the skills of literacy and reading, came to reside with the monasteries. The landscape might be awash with barbarians and their crude, barely christianized paganisms, but the high culture of learning associated with the ancient gods of Greece and Rome now seemed to have few living representatives left to argue its cause.

Yet as we have already seen, there are strange ruptures between what might seem to be the realities and necessities of human life, and the realities and necessities around which knowledge is conceptualized and valued. For Augustine, what mattered was the renunciation of everything connected with the mortal condition to participate in something that transcended not only life, but the very earth itself: to be on his god's side in the war with the forces of evil. It is an old accusation: Rome fell because its leading men became Christian, forgot the world, neglected to have children, and did not care enough to dominate the wild landscapes and hold the wide rivers that marked civilization's edge. Yet our subject here is the way that ideas of knowledge run through the ragged incoherent millennium that stands, in European history, between two great ages of empire. For all his focus on the spiritual life, Augustine—the voice perhaps most consistently heard in the writings of the learned through all those centuries—offered little in the way of the possibility of retreat on any front. It was war between the two cities, and that meant men like him were responsible for the souls of the whole population, caught up through the generations in the turmoil that spread outward from the first sin in Eden. This was not forgotten in the martial cultures to come, when theologians and churchmen saw the spiritual life as a battleground so indistinguishable from the violence of knights and lords that the whole world could be taken over by a tangle of violent metaphors and living armies, and real blood splattered to please this Christian god. Augustine's faith was an engine of dominion tolerant of no alternative; his weapons were the tools wielded for centuries by those articulate pagan imperialists whose contemporary tongues he feared, and his rejections of earthly matters were fierce and pungent engagements with human society. There were men in his world, men whom he envied even,[4] who could make a point of turning their backs on all this, retreating to the desert for microcosmic struggles against the devil in their own minds and bodies. Their example was not forgotten in the medieval centuries—indeed, it could at times be troublesome when the humble saint critiqued the wealth and power of the church—but insofar as a conception and a practice of knowledge triumphed, it was his.

This is not to suggest that Augustine's medieval readers were always faithful to his intentions, or passive recipients of his ideas. They had reasons of their own for returning again and again to his work. His writings were part of the moral and intellectual hinterland of later innovations,[5] perhaps above all, because his formulations helped to justify the yoking together of faith and governance that was so important for medieval rule. Several closely connected ideas were required for this. The first, and one of Augustine's most useful achievements from the perspective of his readers, was to create a justification for integrating the strands of what early Christian writers had presented as the separate intellectual traditions of "pagan" antiquity and the Judeo-Christian scriptures.[6] He had done this because he feared the effects of the limitations on the resources available to educated Christians were they to follow the urgings of prominent spiritual leaders to reject the Greek high culture and the ambitious "knowledge-ordering" projects[7] of Roman imperial elites in favor of a scripture-based wisdom.[8] He had recognized that unless they took possession of cultural and political sites of power, Christians would be in no position to evangelize on a significant scale, or to draw on the cooperation of the powerful in the governance of the faithful.

While from the earliest days of the faith's emergence, there had been a powerful sense that the entirety of truth—or at least, what mattered about it—had been revealed with the death and Resurrection of Christ, all sense of ownership of other people's knowledge had been focused around this revelation and its implications for humanity. What Augustine did was to take learned texts and traditions that had nothing to do with Christianity, and claim and colonize them. He set out to show that all true and meaningful knowledge, regardless of its human provenance, originated from a single omniscient god, the god of the Christians, who had created all things and all people. Viewed in this light, material could quite legitimately be stripped out from any cultural and intellectual context and repurposed to serve the ends of Christians. Indeed, he argued, these acts of appropriation were essential for the future of the faith and therefore of human salvation. If non-Christian philosophers "have said things which are indeed true and are well accommodated to our faith," he wrote, "what they have said should be taken from them as from unjust possessors and converted to our use."[9] He was not alone in this view. In the same year, Jerome, another significant figure for medieval scholars, suggested that "worldly wisdom," with all its seductions, should be treated as a beautiful woman captured in war. Ancient Hebrew law required that before a man could have sex with a captive woman, she had to discard her own clothing, shave her head, and pare her nails. In Jerome's view, this was a process of purifying her of "idolatry, pleasure, error or lust," after which he could safely impregnate his "captive and handmaiden" with children who would serve the Christian god.[10]

Such images of divinely sanctioned theft and rape proved attractive to medieval writers and recurred throughout the period in material justifying the use of a rich variety of texts with diverse provenances. As literacy failed and books became fewer and less accessible, individual monks, against the backdrop of the preservation work undertaken by their orders, set themselves to gathering together, editing, and organizing into convenient forms what remained of Latin, and sometimes Greek, learning. Despite long-standing fantasies of indigenous superior European traditions emerging spontaneously in ancient Athens, this body of material was the product of hundreds of years of scholarly interactions back and forth among the interconnected regions of Eurasia and Africa.[11] Most of the philosophical and scientific writings of the Greeks, which would later be greatly valued, were lost to the West at this point—a notable exception was Plato's cosmological work, *Timaeus*—while priority was given to the sorts of materials that had been gathered in the service of Rome's empire, such as Pliny the Elder's voluminous *Natural History*.[12] The most influential of these early medieval compilations was Isidore of Seville's peculiar but substantial *Etymologies* (*c.* 625), not, as it happened, a monastic product (Figure 1.1).

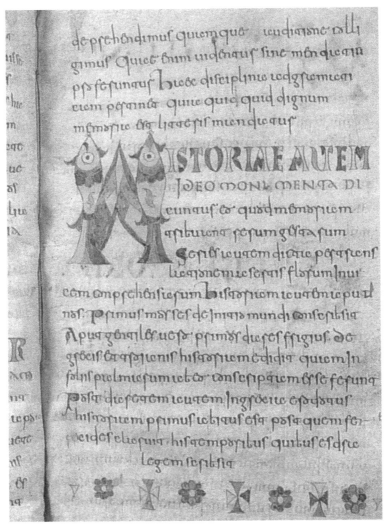

FIGURE 1.1 Isidore of Seville, *Etymologies*, *c.* 850–900, MSII 4856, Royal Albert Library, Brussels. © Wikimedia Commons (public domain).

A summary of the *Etymologies*' contents gives some notion of the subject material that seemed to him to constitute all necessary knowledge. Its twenty books covered respectively: grammar; rhetoric and dialectic; mathematics (divided into arithmetic, music, geometry, and astronomy); medicine; law; scripture, liturgical feasts and offices; God, angels, names of significant holy figures; religion and related topics (heresy, philosophy, sibyls, magicians, pagans, pagan gods); languages, nations, rulers, military, family; vocabulary; humans and portents; animals, fish, birds; the heavens; regions of the earth (including paradise); buildings and fields; minerals and metals; agriculture and plants; wars and sports; ships, building, weaving, clothing; useful equipment for food and daily life.[13] He included many suitable quotations from the poets, supplying his readers with the apparatus of the classical *literati*. He was informative, if occasionally disdainful, about such matters as Roman entertainments, notably: gymnastics, horseracing, amphitheatre games, and the theatre and its support of prostitution.[14]

Isidore's was the most extensive of the early medieval encyclopaedic compendia, but similar patterns and aspirations can be detected in all the texts that sought to transmit ancient knowledge and educational practices to medieval readers. Many elements of elite Roman education continued to be valued. There was a persistent sense that ideas could be expressed most potently when this style was adopted, even if its literary and intellectual temptations could not be wholly neutralized. The canoness Hrotswitha of Gandersheim (*c.* 935–1000) wrote, among other things, plays concerned with the conflict between flesh and spirit, many dealing with situations in which, as she put it: "it is weak women who triumph and cause strong men to retreat in confusion." She read pagan works assiduously, if, she said, with strong moral distaste, precisely so that she might imitate "the beauty of their language" but, she said, for a better purpose.[15] Even if she did not enjoy begetting children from the captive, they were fine servants of Christian ideology. Throughout these centuries, a command of formal Latin grammar, training in academic disciplines including the liberal arts, proficiency with numbers and music, and knowledge of histories, were among the skills that were urged in various combinations by writers. Despite the core continuities and agreements, each writer presented their materials in ways, and formats, and to rhetorical ends, that served local and immediate political, institutional and spiritual objectives. This remained the case as the Carolingian dynasty experimented with various ways of envisaging Christian rule in their efforts to create a "Christian empire" in the course of the ninth century, although its intellectuals operated on an entirely more ambitious scale and with considerably more focus on pastoral care, evangelization, and christianization.[16] Even so, it says a great deal about the nature of these local objectives, especially in the many relatively small, localized, and fragile kingdoms, that they believed that their needs would be well served by fragments from an empire that imagined that it commanded the known world.

Augustine's justifications for seizing wisdom from one's enemies came into their own in the course of the tenth century, as Latin scholars began, belatedly, to recognize the astonishing intensity and vigor of the intellectual life of the Muslim caliphates. The 'Abbāsid capital, Baghdad, in those days still sat amid great trade networks that spanned the world from West Africa to China, from Scandinavia and the steppe regions to the Indian Ocean. "We can compare our course across the world to the progress of the sun across the heavens," boasted the historian Mas'ūdi of his extensive travels as he sat down in 947 to write a great compendium of knowledge.[17] Scholars in that city had access to multiple bodies of knowledge, including pre-Islamic Persian, Indian, and Central Asian scholarship, and the work of the two preceding centuries in gathering and translating the corpus of ancient Greek learning. This included treatises on astrology, alchemy, and other occult sciences; arithmetic, geometry, astronomy, music; the whole of Aristotelian philosophy: metaphysics, ethics, physics, zoology, botany, and logic; medicine, pharmacology, and veterinary science; and more contemporary Byzantine works.[18] The work of translation had been carried out thoughtfully and with attention to the related priorities of accuracy, style, and relevance to the new audiences receiving the texts in a new context. An account of the methodology of one of the most prominent translators, Ḥunayn ibn Isḥāq (d.873), emphasized that he carried out his work: "with the most appropriate expression and utmost eloquence, without any defect or error, without any preference for any [particular] religious community, without any ambiguity or grammatical mistake according to the experts in Arabic style."[19] The resulting array of clear, intelligently adapted translations were part of a much wider environment in which ideas, new works, older texts, and commentaries traveled and interacted along the land and sea routes that connected Eurasia and Africa.[20]

It was chiefly from neighboring al-Andalus that Latins accessed this extraordinary wealth of learning. Some began to boast of "going among the Arabs" to benefit from what was perceived as a critical independence that contrasted sharply with Latin dependence on traditional authorities. Others set about acquiring texts and making translations, with a particular eagerness for the Aristotelian corpus and the principal Arabic commentaries (Figure 1.2). There were fruitful collaborations with scholars of other faiths and linguistic skills, especially around the richly stocked libraries of Toledo, in Christian hands after its 1085 conquest by the Castilians.[21]

The translations were soon being read all over Christendom. After a few episodes of official unease, it became clear that it was neither possible, nor desirable, to stem the tide. This was in part for the same reasons as those of Augustine, when he had feared to place Christians at a disadvantage in relation to educated pagans. By the mid-thirteenth century, the incorporation of materials and methodologies gleaned from the Muslim world was one of the most significant intellectual projects in Latin universities, engaging the attention of philosophers such as Albertus Magnus, his pupil Thomas Aquinas, and Roger Bacon. The central body of texts were the works of Aristotle, which, as Latin scholars interpreted them, proposed a radically new approach to the discovery and organization of knowledge. Of particular importance was the way in which it enabled them to organize knowledge in terms of both theory and practice; placing things into categories, and thinking in terms of universals that could be demonstrated, either through logic or, increasingly, through *scientia experimentalis*—the science "of experience."[22] This approach was perceived to be the antithesis of the blind following of authorities, although in practice, the conclusions of "experience" tended to be supported in texts with citations from recognized authorities.

The collection of materials also included many theoretical and practical texts, including treatises on arcane and magical arts, which were highly sought after in ecclesiastical and secular courts, as well as in less exalted circles.[23] One of the most popular of these was a tenth-century Arabic work, the *Secret of Secrets*, which purported to be—and was widely accepted as—a treatise of advice written by Aristotle to his pupil Alexander the Great to assist him in his rule of the territories that he had conquered. Some of the contents were in the genre of "mirrors for princes," texts of advice on everything from good health to the art of good governance. Other parts dealt with such occult subjects as astrology, alchemy, amulets, stones with mysterious powers, and an elixir for extending human life.[24] The harnessing of advanced technologies to imperial projects proved extremely appealing and a canon of literature grew up around the figure of Alexander during the medieval

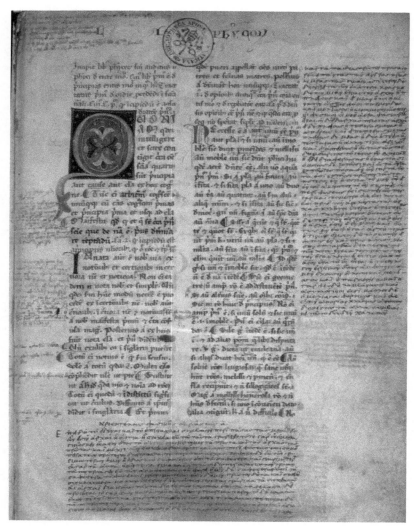

FIGURE 1.2 The beginning of the *Physics*, from Aristotle, *Libri Naturales*, *c*. 1275–1300,
Bibliotheca Apostolica Vaticana. © Wikimedia Commons (public domain).

period. He was imagined as hungry for knowledge, and skilled in creating mechanisms for
uncovering the secrets of the heavens and earth. These included a chariot that could be
lifted into the air by griffins so that he could explore "the nature of this sky that is above
us," and a "barrel of translucent glass" in which he could be lowered into the ocean "to
explore the depths of the sea and to see what sorts of creatures were there" (Figure 1.3).[25]

The widespread fascination with arcane powers could only with some difficulty be
presented as serving the proper ends of Christians. Roger Bacon drew on the Augustinian
justification in his treatise for Pope Clement IV outlining how the intellectual methods
and the substance of Aristotelian and Arabic material could be safely deployed in the
affairs of the Latin West by wise and holy members of religious orders. He considered
that they could transform the quality of Latin education and religious understanding,

FIGURE 1.3 Jansen Enikel, *Alexander the Great under Water*, c. 1405, Ms. 33, 220v. ©
Courtesy of the J. Paul Getty Museum (Open Content Programme).

assist in the conversion of non-Christians by providing a philosophical framework to
guide the rational to truth, and produce revolutionary technologies to impress, persuade,
or defeat Christendom's formidable enemies by commanding the potencies of nature.
Indeed, he rejoiced in the neatness of the way his god had planned this from time's
beginning: embedding the sacred truth in non-Christian traditions by revealing parts
of it to their greatest thinkers.[26] Yet this expanded justification for the infusion of elite
learning with an efflorescence of knowledge obtained from a rival monotheism continued
the strategic obliteration of the possibility of multiple, diversely situated, mutable, and
subjective bodies of knowledge, while laying claim to the riches of the learning and insight
of all past, present, and future societies across the globe.[27] This epistemology undoubtedly
enabled many disparate voices to be woven into the fabric of Western thought,[28] but it

also acted as a homogenizing force, since all those voices had to be made to support, or at least, not contradict, the same basic doctrines.

Given the history of relations between Christian, Muslim, and Jewish communities, these intellectual encounters can appear remarkable achievements of interfaith cooperation—as indeed, they were on the individual level. Yet they failed to offer fundamental challenges to the well-defended complacencies of Christians around the knowledge that mattered, for each in their way broadened and strengthened Latin Christian command of the terrain of both civilization and knowledge. Furthermore, this essential ease in collaboration, facilitated by shared epistemologies, throws into sharp relief the fact there was a whole realm of knowledge that was on every occasion of contact rejected, delegitimized, and where feasible, violently destroyed, by followers of all three Abrahamic faiths. This was the knowledge of the "barbarians," those other, uncivilized, "pagans." These collective nouns were used through the centuries to designate a diverse range of peoples that included migrating groups from the steppes and long-term inhabitants of the regions stretching away to the north and east of the former Roman provinces. Medieval elites, land-hungry Teutonic knights, colonialists of all kinds, and modern intellectual historians have shared the Roman conviction that everything about these people was inferior save their innate vigor and manliness, themselves indications, in this context, of barbarism. Even where pagans were presented as possessing many virtues and even worthy of imitation, they still required Christianity to become wholly admirable. This idea shaped Adam of Bremen's report on the Baltic and Scandinavian peoples in the 1070s. Of the city of Jumne on the river Oder, he wrote, "its inhabitants still blunder about in pagan rites. Otherwise, so far as morals and hospitality are concerned, a more honourable or kindly folk cannot be found." Since the formerly viking inhabitants of the cold and unproductive lands of Norway had accepted Christianity and its "better teachings," Adam noted: "they have already learned to love the truth and peace and to be content with their poverty," to abandon magical practices, and revere priests.[29] To become civilized, and to enter the kingdom of heaven, their own ideas and practices of knowing had ideally to be obliterated as if they had never been.

If we consider the matter through a different lens, away from the dichotomy of civilization and barbarism, what we see is that Latins showed very little appetite for the knowledge of non-imperial and non-universalizing societies; for knowledge that we might now describe as local, indigenous, or "state-evading";[30] for that of the neighboring peoples they conquered and subordinated to their normative Christianities. This strongly suggests that conceptions of useful and legitimate knowledge were bound up with agendas of domination. The texts from Rome, Baghdad, Toledo, and elsewhere suited colonial and militarized cultures, globalizing ideologies and universalist categories, and societies who desired to harness nature's power to civilization's ends, in the Latin West, as much as in the other powerful polities of medieval Eurasia. For these societies, it was quite simply backward—backwardness coded here as a lack of Christianity—to inhabit environments and ecosystems on anything like their own terms, or to pay any kind of respect to them. They assumed, as most people still do, that humanity's proper trajectory was from pastoralism, hunting and gathering to sedentary cereal-based agriculture to urban dwelling.[31] This was not without long-term consequences of the kind that are currently unfolding around us in a series of ecological and climate crises.[32]

Whether historians consider the fall of the Roman Empire as a catastrophic sequence of events or a period of productive transformation to a different type of social order, it has been difficult to avoid the sense that these centuries were a bad time for "knowledge," as it is conventionally defined. The sort of societies that breed and support educated elites need stability, effective taxation of the population, agricultural surpluses, infrastructure and robust communication networks: they need, in short, civilization, in the sense of complex, productive cultures.[33] Yet "civilization" engenders particular kinds of knowledge, prioritizes certain epistemologies, and empowers some groups of participants in knowledge cultures, but not others. For lack of textual records of other perspectives, the lamentations of the literate over the transfer of cultural power to "barbarians" have shaped the general view of the time for intellectual historians, even though the loosening of empire's grip on the peasantry[34] may have allowed for the flourishing of more diverse ways of knowing, thinking, and acting. Some alternative ways of envisaging the state support a different set of questions about conceptions and practices of knowledge in this context. These are critical of the assumption that the best forms of political order are complex states and that populations want to live in such states.[35] They point to the negative impacts of bureaucratic and recording cultures, state-mandated agriculture with its tendency toward mono-cropping and ecological simplification, tax systems organized through patriarchal social hierarchies, and the binding of women to heavy reproductive burdens to produce the required labor. This kind of organization seems designed to maximize the population's legibility to facilitate the state's extraction of resources, but it came at a price. Humans and animals living in these conditions were less healthy than their freer counterparts, and biodiversity suffered. It seems plausible that the majority of the inhabitants of these kinds of states may have been coerced, tied to the land as serfs or enslaved, and might rather have escaped the state if they could. Perhaps less controlled areas of complex kinds of states were "shatter zones," populated by refugees from their rule, and that the surrounding peoples, whether consciously or otherwise, developed social systems that functioned to resist and elude the nearby state, for example, through egalitarian community organization and rejection of literacy. This enabled them to engage in economic exchange without being integrated in other ways.[36] Roman Phrygia—part of Anatolia—seems a plausible example of communities adopting these strategies.[37]

When looking for the concepts and practices of knowledge in the medieval centuries, this reading of life within and without complex states is an illuminating possibility. As we have seen, Christian ideas were early synthesized with imperial and "civilizing" practices, producing the notion of a single god for all humans, to whom all humans were visible and must offer account, and whose will was administered on earth by overseeing and extractive hierarchies. The forms of knowledge labeled "pagan," on the other hand, consciously or otherwise, enabled spaces of evasive illegibility, where actions could refuse to make sense within the streamlined and simplifying world of Christian authority. Similar dynamics were at work around the peripheries of other monotheistic empires.[38] Historians have struggled to reconstruct plausible "pagan" belief systems from Christian texts, suggesting that the term was not descriptive in a precise sense,[39] but existed in the service of efforts to reshape social imaginaries. It also suggests that "pagan" peoples, or Christian individuals engaging in "pagan" practices, had considerable success in remaining at least partially opaque to observers. For example, Adam of Bremen wrote of the Sembi of Rügen, who traded much-coveted marten furs for woollen garments: "Although they share everything else with our people, they prohibit only, to this very day indeed, access to their groves and springs which, they aver, are polluted by the entry of Christians … Living, moreover, in inaccessible swamps, they will not endure a master among them."[40] It was for these reasons that conquered "pagan" communities were quickly integrated into Christian structures through "conversion," as the principal step toward reordering their societies to be legible to their conquerors and even more so to their own emerging elites. We may be seeing practices of resistance to this process in the persistence of "pagan" ideas across "Christendom" at all levels of society for so many centuries after the initiation of official and state-sponsored processes of Christianization. Even priests negotiated with and sometimes repurposed older strategies for influencing nature, such as charms, incantations, amulets, forms of magic, and predictive astrological readings.[41] Stories continued to be told, in courts, towns, and villages, of fairies and their strange ambiguous powers, of transformations and metamorphoses; of uncanny beasts, articulate monsters, and green-skinned people; of love affairs and quests that crossed into places neither of this earth nor the Christian hereafter—all of which opened up spaces for imaginative contemplation of different possibilities and different values. Clerics worked hard to tame and retell these stories to Christian ends, making werewolves desire the Eucharist (Figure 1.4), changing the fairies into demons, and their odd mysterious realms into Purgatory.[42]

While it is hard to know what "pagan" conceptions of knowledge might have been— except that Christian witnesses persistently associated them with thinking about the natural environment and the forces perceived to influence and shape it—it is easier to discern the conceptions and practices associated with "barbarism." As we have seen, the term was used in literate circles broadly to refer to populations who were not engaged in sedentary agriculture under the eye of the state, and it was moralized criticism: it

FIGURE 1.4 Gerald of Wales, Henry of Saltrey, *c.* 1196–1223, *A priest offers communion to a wolf*, (Royal 13 B VIII, f. 18, British Library). © Wikimedia Commons (public domain).

suggested inferiority in practice. Yet if we consider the conditions for life in the post-Roman period, a different view is possible—and what was at stake becomes clearer. The Roman Empire had developed in a propitious time. From around 400, this was giving way to a general cooling of the northern hemisphere, ushering in a time of colder, wetter, more erratic weather patterns, recurrent severe epidemics of plague, population stagnation, and unfolding environmental consequences, such as erosion of the soils of abandoned agricultural lands. These events were connected—if in intricate and unpredictable ways—and together with other, human, factors, they brought about the final collapse of the heartlands of the old empire.[43] The communities that survived and flourished did so by adapting to the new conditions, which meant different use of resources and practices of knowledge that came, later, to be considered "barbarian" and in many ways fit the model of state-evasion. There is evidence that during the immediately post-Roman centuries populations were physically larger and healthier, living in smaller communities with lower population density, in more diverse ecosystems that were able to supply a more varied diet, and largely free from the diseases that traveled along trade routes.[44] The Frisians, for example, developed highly specific ways of living in their tidal marshlands that were beneficial for the natural environment, less-hierarchical, resistant to individual land ownership or forced agricultural labor, and thus inimical to the practices of the encroaching Frankish state. As a new climate regime—the "medieval climate anomaly"—began around 900, bringing warmer, more stable weather patterns,[45] the situation changed. For the Frisians, a slow process of Christianization in the new millennium brought drainage, cereal crops, a new language and identity, and eventually a manorial economy.[46] The same gradual transition was repeated across the regions of westernmost Eurasia, as landscapes were colonized and physically transformed, the people "converted," and their ecologically specific forms of knowledge were made redundant, as well as being polemically derided as a justification of their suppression. Typical of the thinking behind these trends was the treatise of the high-ranking cleric Gerald of Wales, which recommended that King Henry II consolidate the English conquest of Ireland partly on the grounds that the inhabitants were little removed from barbarians, despising routine agricultural labor, mining, and industry, preferring to live "like beasts," not like "well-behaved and law-abiding people." He complained that an Irishman has "little use for the money-making of towns, contemns the rights and privileges of citizenship, and desires neither to abandon nor lose respect for, the life which it has been accustomed to lead in the woods and countryside." Significantly, he noted the fertility of what he considered to be under-cultivated lands[47]—a fertility threatened by the shift to ideologically driven "anthropogenic ecosystems."[48]

If we return now to the dominant conceptions of knowledge and its proper practice, we can see many correspondences between what was being undertaken on the ground, and how elites chose to present ideas about life in the world. "We are so created," wrote Bonaventure, the politically astute leader of a highly influential religious order, "that the material universe itself is a ladder by which we may ascend to God." "Nature avails nothing and human endeavour but little"—what must be sought is "the supremely unknown, superluminous, and most sublime height of mystical knowledge"—"all the splendours of *invisible* good things." "Let us then die and enter into this darkness," he concluded ecstatically.[49] The sense that the natural environment was suffused with Christian meaning was to be found everywhere. The most popular form of zoological compilation, the bestiary, used each animal to educate readers in approved attitudes. For example, the mole, "condemned to perpetual darkness because of its blindness" was said to be "the image of pagan idols, blind, deaf and dumb; or even their worshippers, wandering in the eternal darkness of ignorance ... The mole is also the symbol of heretics or false Christians, who, like the eyeless mole ... lack the light of true knowledge and devote themselves to earthly deeds" (Figure 1.5).[50]

These ideas were the product of a steep hierarchy of types of knowledge and ways of knowing. The arts were handmaidens of theology; the literal meaning of scripture was a mere starting point, and a person could only achieve true understanding through a process of discipline and renunciation. The world held one back from reaching true understanding. This was an old notion—idealized in descriptions of the philosophers of Athens and in many other places—and developed in specific ways as early Christian communities came to define themselves partly through their troubled sense that sexuality and human intimacy lay precisely at the rupture between their god and humanity. In the monastic environments of the early medieval period, it was perhaps inevitable that

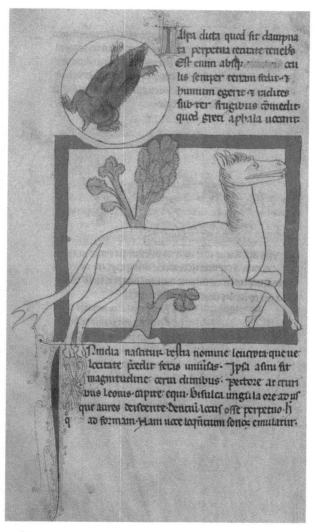

FIGURE 1.5 *Mole and Leucrota*, c. 1200–1225, Ms. 100, fol. 33v. © Getty Museum (public domain).

access to knowledge was principally reserved for literate men and women who could claim to be in the process of wresting their love away from the embodied mortal things of the world, from localities and ecologies and the people they had loved, and embracing the transcendent disembodied rationalities of the Christian revelation. They idealized the self-destructive martyrs, monks of the desert, men such as Saint Paul, Saint Anthony, and Simeon Stylites, and their imitators. For example, Elizabeth (1207–1231), a princess of Hungary, was canonized by the church and widely admired for knowing her god through the ruin of her body, will, and affections by her brutal confessor. She declared her delight that, consequently, "I do not care about my children any more than I care about my neighbours ... I love nothing purely but God alone."[51] There was a remarkable appetite, throughout the period, for graphic depictions of gaunt, tortured bodies and souls filled with the splendor of knowing their god. These figures were symbols of a very real and highly consequential way of thinking about practices of knowledge. They enacted the fierce ideology that dominated medieval voices speaking of what mattered. Such writers asserted that everything of importance was located outside the corporeal sphere of the living planet: that conversion meant renunciation of all previous ties; that the experience of enduring consciousness after death was infinitely more important than enjoyment of life before death; that the world would soon be destroyed as something evil, and replaced with a new, perfect world. They could show humane comprehension of difficulty, since difficulty was an important part of this worldview. Essentially, however, they were people who were preoccupied by drastic, simplifying visions (Figure 1.6).

It was individuals making such claims about what mattered who, throughout the period, consolidated themselves as a class of knowledge producers and gatekeepers, through schools, monasteries, and ecclesiastical and even secular administration. From the eleventh century, a vigorous narrative of "reform" was used to strengthen their societal dominance and to imbue it with a character that would prove lasting, notably, that such authority should be exercised solely by celibate men who owed as little as possible to laypeople, and who could serve their god in freedom from entangled human relations, vulnerabilities, and dependencies.[52] The prominent reforming cardinal, Peter Damian asked: "how can priests now expiate for the sins of others, when they are always intent on swelling wombs and squalling babies?"[53] The learned Heloise argued hotly against domesticity and marriage for her lover, the renounced philosopher Abelard: "What harmony can there be between scholars and servants, between desks and cradles, between books or tablets and distaffs, between pens or styluses and spindles?"[54] In 1280, Peter of Limoges wrote a manual for preachers in which he urged them to set the proper examples because they were highly visible to their parishioners, whose salvation depended upon the conviction conveyed by what they saw in their priests: the moral coherence of their lives, and the preacher's clear focus on spiritual matters.[55] This long campaign gained traction over the decades, and increasingly meant that those who were culturally enabled to produce and disseminate the central truths of society—the character and details of Christian doctrine, which set out the sole route to redemption—were the people encouraged to have the least experience of, and investment in, the realities of the human condition.

Formal education was becoming increasingly institutionalized,[56] which imposed limitations of another kind. Only a tiny minority of the population received the kind of specialized training that enabled them to participate in learned cultures. This was lightly regulated by periodic acts of scrutiny and censorship by fellow masters and ecclesiastical authorities, but more wide-ranging restrictions were, and remain, innate

FIGURE 1.6 *The Douce Apocalypse, c.* 1270–1272. Ms. Douce 180, fol. 21r, Oxford, Bodleian Library. © Wikimedia Commons (public domain).

to the whole functioning of academic study, its pedagogies and disciplinary apparatuses. A discipline is defined by its shared discourses and methodologies, and must inevitably engender broad conformities among those working within its confines. Elite knowledge production required mastery of scholarly languages, specific terminologies, core methodologies such as disputation, and other techniques to establish credibility.[57] This made it at once difficult, even risky, for insiders to think beyond disciplinary confines and virtually impossible for outsiders to contribute unless they could convincingly invoke alternative sources of authority, such as mystical or prophetic wisdom. This was also risky: in 1310 Marguerite Porete was burned at the stake for writing a mystical work, *The Mirror of Simple Souls*, and became the first of a number of women mystics to suffer such a fate.[58] Conformity was encouraged through the production of a new genre of standardized texts that supplied students with compilations of theological propositions and suitable extracts for discussing and debating them. One of the most influential was Peter Lombard's *Sentences* (*c.* 1150), put together, he wrote "from the witnesses of truth established for all eternity, and divided into four books." Its purpose was to save students trouble, so that "one who seeks [the Fathers] shall find it unnecessary to rifle through numerous books."[59] Similarly, Herrad (d. after 1196), abbess of Hohenbourg in Alsace, put together the *Garden of Delights*: over a thousand extracts from theological texts selected to facilitate her nuns' holy contemplation (Figure 1.7). The result was comparable to what would have been on offer to male students in a Parisian theological curriculum. It was to serve different practices of knowledge,[60] but the underlying

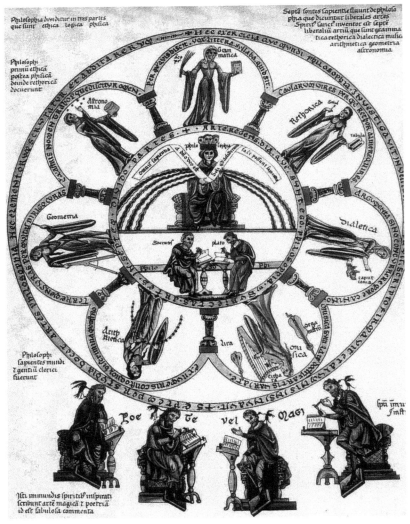

FIGURE 1.7 *Septem Artes Liberales*, from Herrad of Landsberg, *Hortus Delictarum*, *c.* 1180. © Wikimedia Commons (public domain).

conception was not significantly different. These various limitations on knowledge production did not go entirely unrecognized. As we have seen, they were part of the motivation to gather materials from Muslims. More unusual was Roger Bacon's view that as "the simple and those thought to be ignorant often know a great deal that has escaped the wise," an intelligent man should show humility toward "rustics, old women and children," and seek out areas of knowledge that were not part of the academic curriculum. Even so, he believed that only educated men in religious orders could effectively employ this knowledge.[61]

There were sharp implications for the rest of society in the various ideas around knowledge that have been discussed in this chapter. A single knowledge by its nature had to be directing, governing, and hegemonic: as universal truth, Christianity had to be accepted and internalized by all rational people.[62] The next step was to conclude, with Augustine, that there was a place for coercion in belief, although it was not until the later twelfth century that the bureaucratic and legal mechanisms of the church were robust enough to attempt it at scale. As Augustine had gained responsibility in the church and had to face down challenges from rival interpretations in his diocese, he came to feel the necessity of employing disciplinary strategies to create uniformity of belief in society along the lines prescribed by senior clergy and theologians.[63] This approach, which seemed contrary to the teaching of the scriptures, always made some Christians uneasy, but Augustine argued that it was unacceptable to abandon people to damnation. It was an act of love, he said, to force the unwilling toward salvation, including through secular legislation against "errors" in belief. Therefore, he wrote: "let the kings of the earth serve Christ even by making laws."[64]

With this idea, Christianity was on the way to becoming a viable tool of governance. Principles of coercion were made more and more central to secular and ecclesiastical governance as the centuries passed. Some people undoubtedly felt an ethical commitment to save souls through the pastoral discipline of the population, much of which was focused around making sure that the laity had the correct knowledge. Some recipients of this care seem to have welcomed the certainties and comfort it could bring. The notion of doing penance by waging papally mandated warfare and shedding the blood of God's enemies was enormously popular. Nonetheless, dominion of every kind was intensified by means of the faith. Those who rejected Christian ideas of truth, such as Jews, were increasingly held to be less rational and were eventually expelled from most latin Christian kingdoms.[65] For the baptized population, there were demands for obedience and engagement with formulaic summaries of the knowledge required of them for salvation. Intellectuals such as Hugh of Saint Victor and Peter Lombard argued that the very fact that the laity believed *without* real understanding was an act of love and faith.[66] In 1215, at a major ecumenical council, representatives of ecclesiastical and secular elites collectively mandated a regime of orthodoxy with punishments for dissent or protection of dissenters, mechanisms for monitoring the moral state of every Christian woman, man, and child through annual confession, and physical markers to distinguish Jews.[67] The procedures known as *inquisitio* were inaugurated and elaborated some short time later, and those who refused to accept orthodox doctrine on demand were put to death. This range of strategies delegitimized and criminalized the deployment of other critical epistemologies in the public sphere to the extent that historians of the later Middle Ages have had to work hard to discover evidence of the kind of rejections that could be described as doubt, unbelief, or atheism.[68]

The medieval period can seem very remote from our modernity, and particularly in the ways that it conceived of, and practiced, its bodies of knowledge. The groups of intellectuals who later described their activities as constituting a renaissance or enlightenment succeeded in creating a sense that the most recent five centuries have seen drastic discontinuities and acceleration in the progress of, at least, Western thought. Their arguments focused around the place of conventional authority and religion in knowledge. Yet as we have seen, the functioning of these elements in the knowledge of medieval societies was generally subordinate to the needs, aims, agendas, and strategies of the moment and, as ever in human history, closely associated with the requirements and ambitions of the powerful.

CHAPTER TWO

The Human Self

MARY FRANKLIN-BROWN

This tiny little newborn (*homunculus*), so pitiful and so frail, appeared to be still-born prematurely; the slender reeds growing in that region, right about mid-April, were thicker than its fingers. While I was growing up, I often heard a funny story about that day. When they were taking me to the life-giving font, a woman rolled me from hand to hand, and said, "You think he's going to live? Nature almost failed to give him any limbs; she gave him more of a rough sketch (*lineamentum*) than a body."[1]

Thus Guibert (*c.* 1060–*c.* 1125), Benedictine monk and abbot of Nogent, describes his newborn body in his autobiography, the *Monodies*. This text has drawn widespread attention among modern scholars because it reflects an interest in the self: one medieval individual's understanding of what makes himself worthy of comment, his life experience, his peculiarities. Surely (one may assume) the study of the Middle Ages must take account of the self. Surely it must determine how medieval selves were analogous to ours and how they were different. These assumptions, and the questions to which they give rise, have guided considerable research in the past hundred years. The task of the present chapter is to show the different ways scholars have responded, while also examining the assumptions themselves.

Those who have not studied premodern material before may assume that the self is stable across time, an aspect of simply being human. At first glance, the terms in which writers describe the self may appear consistent. Guibert's portrayal of the sickly infant anticipates the way Jean-Jacques Rousseau will describe his own birth in his *Confessions* (*c.* 1765), that touchstone of modern autobiography: "I was almost born dead, and they had little hope of saving me. I brought with me the seed of a disorder which has grown stronger with the years, and now gives me only occasional intervals of relief in which to suffer more painfully in some other way."[2] Beyond their hypochondria, the two autobiographers shared a willingness to link their difficult births and sickly childhoods with practices of reading and writing the self. The child Jean-Jacques formed his character in bouts of intense reading with his father,[3] and the infant Guibert's very body was a collection of swift pen strokes suggesting—but not yet filling in—a human form. Furthermore, since Guibert's word *lineamentum* suggests drawing, in combination with the other disparaging comments he makes about his newborn body ("like an abortion" and "some worthless creature"), it anticipates the comments that Michel de Montaigne makes about his first book of personal essays in 1580, when he compares his essays to the "monstrosities and *grotesques* botched together from a variety of limbs having no defined

shape" that a painter would use to fill in the border of some fine scene.⁴ For all three
authors, personal writing seems to have been an experimental, messy business.

Other readers, accustomed to thinking of modernity as the moment when the
individual or the self was born, may criticize such broad claims for disregarding the period
boundaries commonly thought to separate the Middle Ages (Guibert), the Renaissance
(Montaigne), and the Enlightenment (Rousseau). Readers may ask why a chapter devoted
to the medieval self would adopt such an opening strategy. Any careful analysis of these
authors would uncover differences as well as commonalities. Nonetheless, it is important
to acknowledge that the "discovery" of a medieval self by modern readers has always
involved recognizing some partial similarity between medieval writers and more recent
ones—from the Renaissance, the early modern period, or even the twentieth century. The
preceding paragraph represented Guibert's text as an anticipation of Montaigne's and
Rousseau's, but one could also argue that Guibert's *Monodies* would not be interesting
today were it not for the *Essays* of Montaigne and the *Confessions* of Rousseau. These
two experimental autobiographical texts that had appeared so fragile to their authors at
the moment of writing went on to acquire canonical status, and so their authors taught
generations of readers to look for selves in texts of any period.

In what follows, I shall add some definition to the self *before* Montaigne and Rousseau,
the self that medieval writers, or artists, or patrons had nursed from an inchoate outline
into durable form. The touchstone texts for this medieval self are Guibert's *Monodies*
(1115), the letters of Abelard and Heloise (*c.* 1132), and the songs of the troubadours.
These songs constitute the earliest large *corpus* of lyric in the Romance vernaculars,
whose beginnings coincide with the developments in Latin writing that have been
associated with the elaboration of a self. For this reason, troubadour lyric has proven
central to scholarly discussions of the topic. The representation of selves in all of these
genres—autobiography, epistles, and lyric—could then be traced through the later
Middle Ages, but space does not permit. I shall make only one excursus into the later
period, by devoting the final sections to questions of performance and portraiture. To
identify the portrait as the only possible rendering of the self in the graphic arts would
be to succumb to anachronism, however, so I shall end where I began, around the year
1100, with the seal.

To approach these medieval artifacts, I trace a series of resonances between them and
modern thought. I focus on the past one hundred years and consider a cluster of terms
that have been used to delineate the medieval self: individual, personality, mind, *persona*,
subject. The "self" is is so broadly employed in contemporary speech that it is of little
utility for much of the chapter, but the term will reappear when I turn to performance
and the visual arts, where it will serve as a broad umbrella for phenomena that seem to
suggest a self, but in ways that remain unclear or are contested among scholars today.
I follow the rough chronology of scholarly interests in the twentieth and twenty-first
centuries because my historical argument has as much to do with modern thought as
with medieval developments. The terms "self" and "individual" became important as
scholars of the twentieth century reacted against earlier historiography. These scholars
claimed that the Renaissance among the Italian humanists of the fourteenth century,
which was commonly believed to have rediscovered the learning of antiquity and to have
valorized the individual, was not the first such movement in Europe. It was preceded by
a "renaissance of the twelfth century" that valorized the same things. Guibert emerges as
a key figure because he was one of the first writers to sketch the outlines of a medieval
self in a genre that resembled modern autobiography, but it is also possible to discern

individuality in a range of other texts from the period. Furthermore, the emergence of psychology as an academic discipline and psychoanalysis as a therapeutic practice suggested to historians that the medieval self could be studied, not simply as possessing individuality by virtue of being different from others but also as an entity whose development, structure, and operations can be described. For example, scholars have compared medieval theories of the soul to current theories of the mind, and they have analyzed the interplay of environmental or cultural factors and individual responses. It has become clear that medieval selves (and, indeed, modern ones) were not constituted as unique, *sui generis*, and entirely autonomous entities, but rather as complex negotiations between conventional paradigms of identity made available in the wider culture and an individual agent's response. What has proven the most illuminating for understanding these negotiations are twentieth-century theories of the "subject," here understood as two things at once: an agent (as in grammar the agent is the "subject" of the verb) and the object of external constraints (as one can be the "subject of" a monarch or "subject to" forces beyond one's control).

Thus far, the sources in question have been texts, but the visual field also offers vehicles for selfhood or subjectivity. Scholars have recently emphasized performative and visual aspects of the embodied self. I shall address the issues of performance, vision, and the body in several ways. First, I shall show how physical desire occasionally exceeds conventional medieval paradigms of self-expression, eliciting—at least from Heloise— the realization that, even if she uses her gift of eloquence to convey her experience, her words will go unacknowledged by her reader, Abelard. Moreover, Heloise's description of her inability to adopt the necessary interior disposition for participating in Mass draws attention to the complexity of ritual performance: an exterior manifestation of intention and disposition whose relation to interior experience can vary. The infant Guibert was baptized before he was capable of understanding the event, but it seems important for him to depict it for his readers, and that ritual was followed by others that molded him. Between them, Guibert and Heloise show that ritual and performance can shape interior dispositions, or be at odds with them. It is visible, but enigmatic. The ritual of confession is particularly interesting in this regard. Michel Foucault has argued that practices of confession created a discourse of knowledge of the self, and Heloise's letters may partly bear this out. But as both a performance and a secret, confession creates opacity, which is suggestively represented by strategic silence in Guillaume de Berneville's *Life of St. Giles* and empty scrolls in illustrations of that text in stained glass and fresco painting. This brings us to the graphic arts, with which I shall conclude. Art historians began to address the question of the medieval individual by studying the prehistory of portraiture, but they have recently asked what other visual signs of identity might have circulated. This question has prompted an analysis of seals, which project people's identity beyond their physical presence. But because the seal is a miniature image consisting of conventional elements, scholarship on seals has thwarted research into the individual.

Time and again the study of medieval selves is caught in contradictions. Scholars' increasing awareness of these contradictions coincides with the reception of thinkers such as Jean-Luc Nancy, who call into question the notion of the modern self or subject. If, as Nancy has argued in *Ego sum* (1979), modern conceptions of the subject are tied to the metaphysics of René Descartes (1596–1650), then the medieval self has perhaps been but an effect produced in the encounter between modern scholars and medieval cultural artifacts and will recede again as we leave Cartesian metaphysics behind.[5]

THE RENAISSANCE OF THE INDIVIDUAL

Paradoxically, early modern writers are responsible, not only for prompting modern readers to search for a medieval self but also for delaying that event for so long. Thinkers of the Renaissance and Enlightenment usually disavowed kinship with medieval writers. Rousseau sweeps under the rug any literary self-portrait before his own. He opens his autobiography with the fierce claim that his enterprise of creating a "a portrait in every way true to nature" is without precedent.[6] The claim is disingenuous. He is unlikely to have known Guibert's *Monodies*, but the idea that he could have been ignorant of Augustine's *Confessions* (*c.* 400 CE), whose title he borrowed, strains credulity. Only two hundred years before Rousseau, Montaigne had created the new form of the essay in an attempt to "be seen in my simple, natural, everyday fashion, without striving or artifice."[7] Rousseau may still legitimately claim that his aspiration is distinct from Augustine's project of providing a spiritual example for readers or Montaigne's stated intention of leaving a book whereby his intimates could remember him, but the Genevan philosopher does not express himself with such nuance. If anything, it is his claim to originality that gives the self he will describe such a striking outline.

The early modern disavowal of medieval culture made possible a particular narrative of Western history that continued to be propounded through the nineteenth century. According to this story, a sophisticated classical culture was lost in the darkness of the Middle Ages and only rediscovered at the dawn of modernity, when diverse political and social factors and the encounter with antiquity created the possibility of new learning and new selves. At the close of the eighteenth century, the Romantics took a more positive view of the Middle Ages than the Renaissance or Enlightenment had done, but in reaction against the Enlightenment emphasis on the rational individual, they argued that the brilliance of the Middle Ages lay in its privileging of the community and the nation.[8]

Jacob Burckhardt's 1860 masterpiece, *The Civilization of the Renaissance in Italy*,[9] made an influential statement of the distinction between a communal Middle Ages and an individualistic Renaissance. Its six parts constitute a series of snapshots of different aspects of Renaissance culture, while their juxtaposition allows a tentative argument to emerge: the illegitimate, despotic rule of the states of Renaissance Italy encouraged in men (both the despots and their deputies and victims) a dependency on intellectual gifts and an awareness of the self.[10] This new development can be observed in the cultivation of well-rounded individuals (the "Renaissance man") and a modern idea of fame. The revival of antiquity then cultivated the artistic skills and habits of observation and description already latent in the Italian character,[11] allowing for a full understanding and expression of "man" in general, in poetry and biography (which represent the interior) and descriptions of human physiognomy. Burckhardt expresses particular admiration for the genre of biography and for the sonnet form, which condenses thoughts and emotions into "a series of pictures, clear, concise, and most effective in their brevity."[12]

Burckhardt's representation of the Middle Ages did not go without response. The insistence with which historians challenged Burckhardt's thesis was so great that Wallace Ferguson, in his 1948 study of the idea of the Renaissance, could title his final chapter "The Revolt of the Medievalists." To challenge Burckhardt, it sufficed to locate the traits he had associated with the Renaissance in the Middle Ages, but medievalists went farther, seizing the banner of "renaissance" for their own period. The most persuasive was Charles Homer Haskins, whose 1927 *The Renaissance of the Twelfth Century*[13] demonstrated the importance of classical education and culture in the 1100s. In taking classical erudition as his topic, Haskins chose a phenomenon that is easy to define and document. Individualism, on the other hand, proved elusive. Burckhardt's concept was fluid.[14] Is individualism to be found merely in the characteristics that make one person recognizably different from another, as he assumes in his treatment of biography[15] or the opening pages of his discussion of physiognomic description?[16] Or is it a willingness to ruthlessly defend one's interests, as his initial description of the Italian despots and their enablers suggests? The medievalists who wished to challenge Burckhardt on this point faced a moving target and chose to engage with him only indirectly. They located individualism, variously defined, throughout the later Middle Ages, from the year 1000 on. It was possible to demonstrate that selected poets showed signs of individuality, as Peter Dronke did in 1970,[17] or that the markers of individualism, defined as "that respect for individual human beings, their character and opinion, which has been instilled in us by our cultural tradition, and with its implications for personal relationships and beliefs,"[18] could be found in a wide range of medieval texts, as Colin Morris did in 1972.

The discussion of the individual usually involves a process of differentiation, of distinguishing one character or style of writing from another and demonstrating that medieval people valued these individual traits. But the concept of the individual remains flat; it does not delineate the structure of a personality or explain its development. Indeed, the word "personality" shifts the discussion in a new direction. At the same time, a fuller investigation of personality requires some substantial source material, a *corpus* of writing about the self. Here medievalists encountered difficulties. Especially in the English-speaking world, the writing of the self is often identified with Romantic lyric poetry. Though scholars might have hoped to discover another Keats or Wordsworth among the troubadours, they failed and so dismissed medieval lyric as a collection of rhetorical figures dressed up with artful versification. Even the most sympathetic accounts emphasized the continuity of topoi or the dominance of poetic tradition. Medieval epistles appeared no less mannered and conventional. That left the genre of autobiography as the only other source for a study of the medieval self that readers of modern literature could easily recognize. But the genre was barely practiced in the Middle Ages. Historians could point to only a few isolated examples, first among them Guibert's *Monodies*.

THE MEDIEVAL MIND

We know of the life of Guibert of Nogent almost exclusively from his *Monodies*. He was born around the middle of the eleventh century into an aristocratic family in northeastern France. When his father died, his mother refused to remarry and dedicated herself to spiritual pursuits. For her son, she engaged a private tutor whose Latin skills were not equal to the task and who caned his charge severely. Guibert struggles both to recount his own experience of the beatings and to excuse his tutor's behavior on the grounds that the man believed he was acting in the child's best interest.[19] Guibert's mother was increasingly drawn to the monastic life and eventually withdrew from the world,[20] an act that the tutor replicated, leaving the adolescent Guibert adrift. Following a brief period of self-indulgence, he took vows himself. He became a serious scholar and wrote books of biblical exegesis, theology, and history that achieved modest success among monastic readers. Eventually, he was elected abbot of the monastery at Nogent-sous-Coucy. His tenure there began poorly, and he was exiled briefly for reasons not explained in the surviving version of his autobiography, but his abbacy survived the rocky start. The text provides few details of later years. In fact, the third and final book of the *Monodies* turns away from personal narrative toward eyewitness history, an account of the communal revolt at Laon and the various personalities involved. In these events, Guibert did not distinguish himself for principles or courage, but he does not subject his own actions to lengthy analysis.

Though Guibert's other writings remained within the established genres of the day, the *Monodies* neither fit medieval literary norms nor replicate his only classical model, Augustine's *Confessions*. It should not surprise us that the text does not appear to have circulated much in the Middle Ages. The *Monodies* survived complete only in a seventeenth-century copy filled with errors and obscurities, and it is possible that a significant portion of the original text describing Guibert's early abbacy had been removed before that copy was made.[21] Nonetheless, on the basis of this damaged text scholars have introduced modern readers to the medieval self.

In the early 1970s, John Benton interpreted the *Monodies* through the lens of Freudian psychoanalysis, for which the long passages about Guibert's childhood offered much suggestive material.[22] Today Freudian psychohistory is thought anachronistic. But the emphasis on the mind and its development links this early interpretation of the *Monodies* with the work of a more recent interpreter, Jay Rubenstein. In *Guibert of Nogent: Portrait of a Medieval Mind* (2002), Rubenstein criticizes anachronistic readings of the *Monodies* and approaches Guibert's psyche through a theoretical lens contemporary to the text: moral psychology, the theory of mind elaborated by theologians of the late eleventh and early twelfth century. Guibert himself was a significant early contributor to this topic. His *Moral Commentary on Genesis*, begun in the mid-1080s, interprets the first book of the Bible according to the tropological mode, a method that spins moral lessons out of biblical stories. Moral commentary was commonly employed in sermons, which was how Guibert had first come to the project. The analysis of the mind that he would develop in the later, longer version of his commentary was initially inspired by the teaching of Anselm of Canterbury (1033/4–1109), with whom Guibert had studied when Anselm was still at Bec.

Anselm divided the mind or soul into four parts. Guibert (our principal source of Anselm's understanding of the soul) indicates that the parts were Will (*Voluntas*), Appetite (*Appetitum*), Reason (*Ratio*), and Intellect (*Intellectus*).[23] Rubenstein traces Guibert's revisions of Anselm's system, which Rubenstein illustrates with a series of triangular figures.[24] The *Moral Commentary* explicates the early stories in Genesis according to a threefold theory of the mind (Figure 2.1). Reason is associated with the paternal figure and Will with the maternal figure. Affection (*Affectus*, which is Guibert's replacement for Anselms *Appetitum*) is associated with the Serpent in the account of the Fall, and with the child figure in the subsequent stories of Genesis. The stories toward the end of Genesis, however, represent another step in the journey of the mind toward God. A higher form of intelligence, *Intellectualitas*, makes its appearance. While Reason treats of human matters, the Intellect treats of divine things, and it thus comes to occupy a place superior to Reason. However, this new version of the mind also has a tripartite structure because, in the presence of Intellect, Will and Affection are harmonized, which allows them to merge. The book of Genesis thus represents the conversion of the mind from human to spiritual concerns.

Read in parallel with the *Moral Commentary on Genesis*, the *Monodies* become legible as "a study in conversions."[25] We can see for the first time why the narratives of so many other lives are woven into Guibert's account. Further, we can read his relation to his mother and teacher as the three points of a triangle in which the Reason that

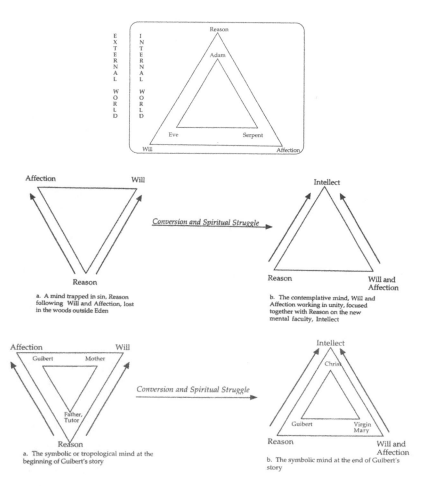

FIGURE 2.1 (a) *Guibert's three-part model of the Mind, and of Adam and Eve,* c. 1080. From Jay Rubenstein, *Guibert of Nogent: Portrait of a Medieval Mind* (Philadelphia: University of Pennsylvania Press, 2002), 46. (b) *Guibert's model of spiritual conversion, as seen in Genesis,* c. 1086–1113. From Rubenstein, *Guibert of Nogent,* 70. (c) *The plot of Guibert's Monodies,* c. 1115. From Rubenstein, *Guibert of Nogent,* 71. © Kindly reproduced with the permission of Jay Rubenstein.

should occupy the highest point has been weakened by the death of Guibert's father and the unsatisfactory substitution of his tutor as a father figure, leaving Affection (Guibert) and Will (his mother) without clear guidance and at variance with each other. Guibert's own conversion, accomplished over the course of Book 1 of the *Monodies,* will involve developing the Intellect that can perceive God and bring Will and Affection into harmony by associating both with the Mother of God.

Rubenstein has thus corrected the anachronism of Freudian psychoanalysis while preserving Benton's interest in the development of a mind. But like Benton, Rubenstein was also responding to broader developments in his own time. Cognitive theories of literature became influential in the last decades of the twentieth century. In medieval studies alone, one could point to Mary Carruthers's work on Memory.[26] Thus, even while correcting anachronism, Rubenstein's portrait of the "medieval mind" is prompted by developments in the critical thought of his own time. Furthermore, because Rubenstein's version of development must be understood in spiritual terms as conversion, Guibert becomes not a unique individual but an exemplary figure, like one of the characters in Genesis. Indeed, Rubenstein notes that Guibert's writing seems to abstract a single "psychological unity" from the disparate actors of the Genesis drama or the drama of Guibert's own day.[27] This conclusion harmonizes with that of Caroline Walker Bynum, who responded to earlier scholarship on the medieval individual by arguing that the development of the self was an interior journey toward God, in the course of which the individual's soul becomes more like God, while his or her outer life is made to conform to models of religious life and fit into a community of like individuals. Although Rubenstein emphasizes the importance and—to some degree—originality of Guibert's contribution to the intellectual and literary work of his day, the individualism that scholars had felt the need to highlight in reaction against Burckhardt recedes. At the remove of a century and a half, it has become possible to speak of a medieval self without insisting that some genius or neurosis must set one self apart from others.

PERSONAS AND SUBJECTS

Autobiography offers insights into the medieval self, but its rarity in the Middle Ages may suggest that medieval selves were equally rare, and the male, monastic origins of the few texts would exclude women and the laity from selfhood. To gain insight into other selves, scholars had to begin seeking them in other kinds of texts. "Intimate biography," as Richard Southern dubbed the genre exemplified by Eadmer's *Life of Anselm* (*c.* 1125), could be read as a recognition of the remarkable individual's journey through life. Epistles had to be read anew, to discern the lineaments of the self among the formulaic elements. For this task, the epistolary exchange of Abelard and Heloise has proven particularly revealing, and we shall return to it. Scholars had to begin considering the way reading itself, and the reflection on reading made possible by the genre of the *meditatio*, allowed medieval selves to be constituted.[28] But to discern lay selves, scholars also had to look beyond monastic milieux and Latin writing, to court cultures and the burgeoning vernacular literatures. Some of the most effective interventions in this area have directly challenged the old assessment that courtly lyric poetry is purely conventional.

This task has required a different paradigm, one that takes account of how the self is shaped by social roles and fleshly desires. In *The Loving Subject: Desire, Eloquence, and Power in Romanesque France*,[29] Gerald Bond elaborates this paradigm through two concepts: the *persona*, derived from Roman literature, and the subject, theorized in the twentieth century. The term *persona* had a wide range of senses in the Middle Ages, but it still preserved the classical Ciceronian sense of a public self constituted through verbal performance. Prompted by Horace's emphasis on the figure of *prosopopoeia*, Bond emphasizes the act of "impersonation," but he applies it not only to the assumption of someone else's character but also to the performance of one's own.[30] The application is apt because, when Cicero described the individual's *persona* in his treatise *On Obligations*, he spoke of it as possessing specific traits that would make certain gestures or actions appropriate to it, others less so. Like actors on the stage, people should strive to know what roles suit them; only thus can they attain the aesthetic dimension of human action that Cicero refers to as *decorum*.[31] Bond argues, however, that as a paradigm of the self in history, the *persona* proves inadequate because "it remains blind, often intentionally so, to the constraining forces," which originate outside the individual and shape the constitution of particular selves at particular moments.[32]

Thus the *persona* must always be considered in relation to the "subject," which is called into being by those constraining forces. For his model of the subject, Bond relies upon an influential 1970 essay by the Marxist philosopher Louis Althusser, "Ideology and Ideological State Apparatuses."[33] Althusser had argued that ideology, the imaginary relationship that individuals entertain with the real world they inhabit, imposes an identity upon them. That is, it creates subjects in the same way that a police officer subjects a suspect by hailing him or her. With "hey you!" the officer "interpellates" the suspect *as* a suspect. While Althusser's paradigms of ideology and interpellation had remained abstract, universal, and ahistoric, Bond argues that we can derive a model for understanding historically specific individuals if we acknowledge that in a given period various historically specific ideologies compete with each other to interpellate the same individual as different kinds of subject, and each develops a vocabulary for hailing those subjects. This plethora of potential subjects allows an individual to make a choice. It elicits a performance, an "impersonation" (*persona*), which we should not take as superficial or hypocritical, but instead as the espousal of a role that has been offered to the individual.

Bond's study of these "loving subjects" reveals negotiations between historical individuals and the expectations directed at them by the powerful institutions of a church in the throes of reform and worldly rulers in conflict with the church and each other. Scholars have likewise illuminated the creation of medieval subjects in other moments when individuals faced a choice between roles or social or linguistic codes. Sarah Kay argues in *Subjectivity in Troubadour Poetry*[34] that the hesitations of the troubadour subject between shared poetic codes and individual experience render its autonomy fragile. Peter Haidu's *The Subject Medieval/Modern*,[35] a rereading of all the key texts of medieval French literature, commences with the choice imposed on soldiers by the Strasbourg Oaths of 842, which committed them to choose between supporting their king and holding him accountable for the oath he himself had taken. Thus scholarship on medieval subjects has proven attentive both to the specificities of medieval language and literature, and to the politics of medieval communities.

The above summaries remain abstract. Let us trace the subject through a troubadour who has been neglected in discussions of the medieval subject: Bertran de Born (*c.* 1140–1215). Bertran was a castellan in the Limousin region during the tumultuous early years of Richard Lionheart's tenure as Duke of Aquitaine, when shifting factions of barons attempted revolts against the Duke and the Duke himself revolted against his father, King Henry II of England. Unlike most of this troubadour contemporaries, who preferred to compose love songs with little reference to contemporary events, Bertran devoted many songs to these wars. His choice of subject matter earned him a reputation for troublemaking that quickly became legend and encouraged a simplistic reading of his lyrics.[36] However, a more careful reading allows us to recognize sophisticated poetry that meditates on the ethos of men of his social position, obliged to make war or at least put on a good appearance of it to maintain their status in the face of increasingly grasping overlords.[37]

The song *Belh m'es quan vey camjar lo senhoratge* provides a programmatic statement of what traits are considered noble and what are not, organized around the opposition between youth and age. It begins by converting the traditional spring opening of a love song into the declaration that the speaker finds the passing of the guard from the old to the young even more beautiful than budding flowers or tweeting birds:

> I like it (*Belh m'es*) when I see power changing hands, and when the old leave their houses to the young ... I like it, because the world is renewed better than by flowers and birdsongs. And whoever can change his lady or his lord, old for young, really ought to.[38]

The insistence on individual judgment, which appears in the first-person pronoun, opens the song and will be repeated in the next strophe with the declaration "I think" (*tenc*):

> Old is a lady, I think, when she has ugly skin, and she's old when she doesn't have a knight. I think she's old if she satiates herself with two lovers, and she is old if a base man does it to her .... I consider her old when minstrels annoy her, and she is old when she wants to talk too much.[39]

In the opening strophe, it was possible to imagine that youth and age were understood biologically, but the subsequent strophes will instead shift these words into metaphor, whereby a woman who takes two lovers (or a base lover or none at all) is old, but one who honors nobility is young:

> Young is a lady who knows how to honor nobility, and she is young from good deeds, when she does any. She stays young when she has a nimble heart, and does not use base schemes to gain good repute; she stays young when she keeps her body beautiful, and a lady is young when she behaves properly.[40]

The song will go on to describe the attributes of youth and age among men (a true "youth" spends all his income on hospitality, gifts, tournaments, and war, lines 25–32, 298). As the cited strophes show, the first person is not expressed as frequently later in the song, and statements of the form "I consider her" (*la tenc*) are largely replaced by statements about how men or women can keep themselves young (*joves se te*, *joves es*) or make themselves old (*vielhs es*). This modification in the way youth and age are ascribed to individuals, the disappearance of first-person statements in favor of the third person, indicates that youth and age are more than ordinary metaphors. Instead, they express a dominant ideology of which the troubadour has made himself the mouthpiece by assuming the *persona* of an arbiter of nobility.

Is there anything specific to the historical individual Bertran de Born in this song, then? There is if one reads it in parallel with Bertran's other songs. The inversion of the commonplace spring opening from love songs is a characteristic technique. It appears for example in his most popular song, *Be·m plai lo gais temps*, where the flowers in the meadow are replaced by tents and shining armor.[41] This inversion is one marker of Bertran's poetic individuality. As an individual, he inscribes himself in history through the common troubadour practice of addressing songs to other individuals identified by given name or pseudonym. The song of youth and age ends with an *envoi* to Richard Lionheart: "Arnaut the joglar, carry my sirventes both old and new to Richard, that it may guide him; he should not try to pile up old treasure, for with young treasure he can win merit."[42] The song thus attempts to interpellate the ruler himself and remind him that he too is subject to the noble ideology. No one is more aware than Bertran that Richard, like every other listener, can choose whether or not to assume this *persona*. Bertran makes witticisms elsewhere about his inability to influence the barons to whom he sings.[43] In his fraught relationship with these other barons and their overlord, he is subject to the same ideology that he sings. Bertran's explicit awareness of the choices other individuals make reflects back upon himself and makes him a subject as well.

CONFESSING DESIRE

The vigorous definitions of women's roles in Bertran's song raise the question of how women might assume a subject position. There were women troubadours, but let us instead return to Latin literature and consider the letters that Heloise (c. 1090–1164) wrote to Peter Abelard (c. 1079–1142), which elaborate the nexus of sexual desire, religious devotion, literary convention, and gender performance.

Heloise's letters were prompted by Abelard's story of his "calamities," which recounts his life, from his childhood as the eldest son of a Breton knight to his brilliant career as a scholar and teacher in Paris. This narrative introduces Heloise as the adored niece of a canon of the city, who had spared no pains to give her the best education. Abelard's own words on this point suffice to sketch his character, Heloise's accomplishments, and the importance of writing to their relationship from the beginning:

> In looks she did not rank least, while in the abundance of her learning she was supreme. A gift for letters is so rare in women that it added greatly to her charm and had made her very famous throughout the realm. I considered all the usual attractions for a lover and decided she was the one to bring to my bed, confident that I should have an easy success, for at the time I had youth and exceptional good looks as well as my great reputation to recommend me, and feared no rebuff from any woman by whom I might be honoured in sharing love. Knowing her knowledge and love of letters I thought she would be all the more ready to consent, and that even when separated we could enjoy each other's presence by exchange of written messages in which we could write many things more boldly than we could say them, and so never lack the pleasures of conversation.[44]

Abelard convinced Heloise's uncle to take him as a lodger, with the understanding that the former would provide her lessons as well. Everything seems to have gone according to plan, and soon the two were exchanging "more kissing than ideas."[45] Inevitably, the lovers were discovered and the household thrown into chaos. The recital of the ensuing events—their child, their secret marriage, and the attack by Heloise's family that left Abelard a eunuch—consumes many pages. He then proceeds to the calamities that followed, his persecution by various highly placed personages and even by the monks of the Breton community that had elected him abbot. Heloise, meanwhile, had taken her vows as a nun and would go on to become the abbess of the Paraclete, a foundation first established by Abelard and later given over to Heloise and her community.

Abelard addressed his epistolary autobiography to an unnamed friend, but a copy was delivered to Heloise. She replied, begging Abelard to write to her and her community, paying them the same debt of consolation that he had paid to his friend by reassuring them of his safety—a consolation, she claims, he had never offered her in their years of separation.[46] Abelard's response leaves much to be desired. A comparison of the two letters' salutations amply represents their difference in tone. Heloise reworks the conventional salutation according to rank and relationship to demonstrate their complex bonds: "To her lord or rather her father, husband or rather brother; from his handmaid or rather his daughter, wife or rather sister; to Abelard from Heloise."[47] Abelard responds: "To Heloise, his dearly beloved sister in Christ, from Abelard her brother in Him."[48] The terse salutation reduces their relationship to the one defined by their current roles, and by placing her name ahead of his he elevates her status in a way she is not prepared to accept. Their subsequent letters debate this matter of etiquette with sufficient urgency to make it clear that they are negotiating more than an epistolary convention. What is at stake here are the roles that they ask of each other. Her inability to cease grieving over the manner of their separation frustrates him while his refusal to acknowledge that grief frustrates her, driving her to ever more explicit descriptions of her inner turmoil.

Heloise uses the epistolary exchange that the youthful Abelard had imagined for precisely the purpose he had imagined: to write things to him more boldly than she could speak them. But her interlocutor is no longer willing to accept the intimacy he had once fantasized. To try to pierce his deafness, she cites ethical philosophy common at the time, which focuses on the intention behind any action. Thus, penance cannot be effective unless it is undertaken with remorse for the sin in question, and participation in the rites of the church should reflect a devout frame of mind. This allows her to explain her torment:

> Even during the celebration of Mass, when our prayers should be purer, lewd visions of those pleasures take such hold on my most unhappy soul that my thoughts are on their wantonness rather than on prayer. I, who should be grieving for the sins I have committed, am sighing rather for what I have lost .... Sometimes my thoughts are betrayed in a movement of my body, or they break out in an unguarded word. In my utter wretchedness, that cry from a suffering soul could well be mine: "Miserable creature that I am, who will free me from the body of this death?" Would that I could truthfully go on: "The grace of God through Jesus Christ our Lord."[49]

Heloise distinguishes the performance of sacred ritual and her participation in it—her own performance—from her disposition, which makes it impossible for her to fully assume the words of Paul that she quotes, his statement of confidence that Christ will deliver him from temptation. Her disposition is both moral and physical: her desiring body makes involuntary movements. But they remain so well hidden that she can be praised for her chastity. The division of her self from her outward performance and from models offered her by preexisting texts or demanded of her by the ideologies of her time is complete.

Perhaps it is the perception of this split that drove Heloise to commit to parchment this unique description of interior experience at a time when the most intimate examinations of conscience were reserved for oral confession and so proved ephemeral. The best she can do is to write a confession of dubious efficacy to her former lover and husband, who is also her bother in Christ and spiritual father, and who refuses to make any substantive response to what she states so eloquently. The increasing clarity of her analysis of her body's desire would seem to confirm Michel Foucault's understanding of the link between confession, sexuality, and subjectivity. Desire is transformed into a discourse of truth about the self, producing a "knowledge of the subject; a knowledge not so much of his form but of that which divides him, determines him perhaps, but above all causes him to be ignorant of himself."[50] Yet we must recognize that knowledge is not what Heloise seeks. She seems little interested in the mystery of her selfhood and does not seek the recognition that her experience is unique. This exchange of letters is above all about relationship and community. Heloise seeks the shared experience of absolution or, failing that, companionship in suffering and damnation. At the very least, she seeks a reader who will hear her, but she does not find him. Not Abelard. Not many of their contemporaries. Not even some modern scholars, who long persisted in classifying her letters as an elaborate forgery.[51]

RITUAL SELVES

Heloise's anguishing experience of the disjunction between personal experience, interior or embodied, and exterior performance raises important issues for the study of the medieval self. She cannot be at peace because she expects a continuity between inner disposition and visible performance. The importance of her testimony on this matter must not be underestimated. As Susan Crane has argued, the Reformation taught modern thinkers to assume a disjunction between interior and exterior and to view ritual performance as dissimulation.[52] Heloise's letters reveal that dissimulation in ritual was possible in the Middle Ages, but it exacted a great emotional toll. Only recently, in response to probing studies of ritual and performance and to Judith Butler's argument that gender is performative, have scholars come to accept what medieval people such as Heloise took for granted: that exterior manifestations, gestures, and bodily comportments should help to constitute the self.

We have already seen some of the fruits of this realization in Bond's use of the notion of *persona* to understand medieval texts, but scholars have also attended to nonverbal aspects of performance, such as clothing and gesture. Framed as a reaction against what she considers an undue focus on interiority among earlier scholars, Crane's *The Performance of Self: Ritual, Clothing, and Identity During the Hundred Years War* reveals the complexity and significance of such courtly rituals as the three days of elaborate ceremonies for the wedding of Richard II of England and Isabel of France in 1396. Crane does not claim that visual manifestations are unambiguous: as she acknowledges, clothing both reveals and conceals.[53] But she does argue that "what people manifest and articulate is what counts about them, not what is hidden and unexpressed. Performance is a reliable measure of who one actually is."[54]

This claim has occasioned some discomfort among other scholars,[55] and it does not entirely fit with Heloise's letters. Although the articulate and audacious abbess did record her experience, how many other medieval people made such statements only in the secrecy of confession—or of their own thoughts? The study of medieval selves through the lens of ritual and performance in fact draws attention to a very specific kind of opacity: that created by confession. Although confession is a ritual, it is not public or manifest, and the myriad details that made up each confession have left little trace in the historical record. It is possible to carry out broad studies of the practice of confession, but the individual particulars are mostly lost. This does not mean that confessions did not matter. Quite the opposite. This paradox, confession's importance and its opacity, was even represented artistically. In Guillaume de Berneville's *Life of St. Giles*, an Anglo-French text from the late twelfth century, the emperor Charlemagne (who is here more a legendary than a historical figure) has a terrible sin on his conscience, and so he summons the saint. But despite multiple intimate meetings, the emperor cannot bring himself to speak the sin. One day, as Giles is murmuring a prayer during a quiet moment of the Mass, an angel discreetly delivers a letter to him. The narrator tells us that Giles saw the sin written out in the letter, with nothing omitted.[56] Giles and Charlemagne go on to discuss it. But in a remarkable narratorial sleight of hand, the *Life of St. Giles* never says what the sin was. In subsequent visual representations of this scene, in the "Charlemagne window" of Chartres Cathedral (*c.* 1200–1220) and a fresco on the wall of a church in Poitou (1300s), the letter is represented without writing. While empty scrolls appear elsewhere in medieval art as representations of speech, the blank scroll delivered by the silent angel to Saint Giles is likely a direct allusion to the secret shared by Charlemagne and his confessor.

While recognizing the importance of performance for the constitution of the self, we should also acknowledge the realms of interior experience that were never recorded. The angel's empty scroll provides an image of that opacity.

PICTURING THE INDIVIDUAL

The reservations in the previous section about what may be seen and what may not should not be taken as a dismissal of the possibility of visualizing selves. On the contrary, this chapter would be incomplete if it failed to consider the representation of individuals in the visual arts, not least because I began with Burkhardt's study of Renaissance Italy, which valorized the portrait as a sign of modern individuality. So we find ourselves facing another version of what should by now be a familiar question: was the Renaissance portrait indeed the first representation of the individual in the visual arts after classical antiquity?

At first glance, the answer would appear to be yes. Increasing attempts at verisimilitude in the visual arts in the thirteenth century, which Villard de Honnecourt referred to as "imitating the living" (*contrefaire al vif*), coincided with the ascendancy of Aristotelian natural history and its emphasis on observation and description, but it did not immediately inspire a fashion for portraits.[57] It would be easy, when admiring the august cheekbones and curly beard of a stone head sculpted for a line of kings of Judah on the façade of a Gothic church, to imagine that this is the portrait of some individual the sculptor had encountered in the street, but such a conclusion would overlook two important facts. First, the sculpted figures in Gothic churches, be they biblical characters or saints, represent the idealization of the human form, whose physical aspect takes on some of the glory of the resurrected body or else imitates the angels—to cite the title of C. Steven Jaeger's book on educational ideals, with its excursus on the wise and foolish virgins of Reims Cathedral, sculpted about 1290.[58] Jaeger argues that this idealization could also be the aspiration of individuals, who might cultivate gestures and expressions that would imitate the angels, and in this way we could locate a self in such portrayals, or at least a mind, the visual analogy of the mind fully converted to God as Guibert represents it. But that still does not make these sculptures portraits in the way the word is commonly used, and that for a practical reason. The discipline of representing the traits of a sitting human model was not a part of medieval artistic training—in fact, it is a rarity in the history of artistic training. Markers of age and traits that failed to conform to standards of beauty have often been thought irrelevant in the representation of the individual, while the mimetic ideal of art is only one of a range of possibilities. In fact, art schools ceased to include the practice in their curricula in the second half of the twentieth century.[59]

Portraiture has therefore been associated with European modernity, its ascendancy coinciding with the "discovery of the individual" in the early modern period, its decadence, with the advent of photography. The response of the historians of medieval art to this common narrative has followed a familiar path. They began by identifying medieval precursors to modern portraiture and tracing the transition from idealized representations to mimetic ones, which began at the end of the thirteenth century.[60] The first examples seem to have been the various sculptural depictions of Pope Boniface VIII (r. 1294–1303) produced in Rome, Orvieto, Florence, and Bologna, some apparently done from sketches that circulated for that purpose. Isolated examples of portraiture in sculpture or painting appear in the century that followed: relatively small paintings of King John II of France (r. 1350–1364) and Rudolf IV, archduke of Austria (r. 1358–1365) (Figure 2.2), and the sculptures of King Charles V of France (r. 1364–1380) and his queen Jeanne de Bourbon that were commissioned to flank the eastern gate of the Louvre palace (Figure 2.3). While Andrew Martindale has argued that medieval portraiture (which he associates more with paintings than sculpture) served principally as portable, private mementos,[61] Georgia Sommers Wright associates it with "the creation of new and forceful characterizations of the dead."[62]

FIGURE 2.2 *Rudolf IV of Austria, c.* 1365. Photograph by Ludwig Schneider, 2013. © Wikimedia Commons (public domain).

FIGURE 2.3 *Charles V of France and Jeanne de Bourbon, c.* 1370. Photograph by Miniwark, 2006. © Wikimedia Commons (public domain).

Yet historians have now begun to question the *a priori* that the portrait is the only possible visual representation of a self. They were always aware that other visual representations of persons had been common from the 1000s: first seals, then tomb monuments. Could these representations also manifest personal identity? A seal is too small to reveal much of a physiognomy. The reliance of such representations upon attributes, markers of identity that had nothing to do with physiognomy (such as crowns, clothing, armorials, scepters, or swords), seems to distinguish them from the portrait. However, the insight of literary historians that the historical agent chooses among conventional roles or figures of speech, and that the self or the subject plays a game of hide and seek while sorting among such external representations, could be relevant in the visual domain as well. In *Queens in Stone and Silver: The Creation of a Visual Imagery of Queenship in Capetian France*,[63]

Kathleen Nolan has argued that the creation of tomb effigies and personal seals (the silver die or matrix being the "queen in silver") allowed royal women over the course of the twelfth century to develop a visual imagery of queenship that is also a form of "visual identity."[64] For seals, they borrowed the attributes of their husbands, such as the scepter and orb, but adapted the ovoid format and the standing posture of the human figure employed by bishops and abbots to communicate a kind of power distinct from that of their husbands (Figure 2.4).[65] Their individual agency expressed itself in this power: agency in the governance of their dower lands, in their decisions as regent for an absent husband or minor son,[66] in their role as intercessors between supplicants and

FIGURE 2.4 *Seal of Matilda of Scotland, c.* 1100. From Walter de Gray Birch, *History of Scottish Seals from the Eleventh to the Seventeenth Century*, 1905. © Wikimedia Commons (public domain).

their husbands, in their commissioning of works of visual art or literature. In the seal, their patronage activities and their political role converged, and royal women innovated, adapting existing models to their own needs and desires.

Nolan is cautious in stating her case for "visual identity," since she is most interested in queenship. She avoids being drawn into philosophical debates about the individual. For the philosophical import of seals, we must turn to the work of Brigitte Bedos-Rezak, who has shown that the use of seals in the chancery (the group of clerks charged with drawing up and archiving legal documents) was closely connected to the theology of the cathedral schools. Particularly in Paris, there was considerable overlap between the schoolmen and the chancery, and so theologians of the late eleventh and twelfth centuries could be thought of as "chancery-scholars." The parallel roles inspired reflection on the metaphor of the seal in discussions of theology and philosophy. Reciprocally, these learned discourses provide a theorization of the seal contemporary to the practice. A closer look at this theological discourse raises doubts about too simple an association between the use of seals and the notion of the individual. The issues are too complex to enter into fully here, but when discussions of the Eucharist take the seal as an analogy, they suggest that the physical contact between the silver matrix and the wax transmits a presence that will remain with the seal; that the signified remains immanent in the signifier, a presence that was sometimes embodied by imprints of the human body itself, fingerprints or tooth marks, or even hair.[67] Seals work, then, not by validating documents but by transmitting the authority of the person who originates the seal. Yet the person thus transmitted is not, for Bedos-Rezak, an individual, but rather a "category," someone who fits within the established social order, as the different elements of the visual program indicate.[68] Here is where Bedos-Rezak's work tends in a different direction from that of Nolan. For the person is conceptualized through the very practice of *replication* that creates seal imprints, and it should aspire principally to be remolded in the true image of God. She writes:

> The individual consequently appears to have been a casualty of the eleventh and twelfth centuries, reduced to rule-referential roles, and retreating behind representation and representational signs whose operational principles lay not in individualization but classification, not in differentiation but replication, not in identification but verification.[69]

In a study of the late eleventh-century tomb effigy of Rudolf von Schwaben in Merseberg Cathedral, Thomas E. A. Dale has extended this argument from the practice of sealing to that of cast-metal sculpture, used to create a new kind of tomb effigy. The material elements—wax and metal—are the same, and the processes that created them shared certain analogies. In juxtaposition to the body lying within the tomb, the cast-metal effigy "should be understood as representing not so much the deceased lying in state, but rather the potential body, perfected in the image and likeness of God and the saints at the general resurrection."[70]

It is possible that the potential dissonance between Nolan's work and that of Bedos-Rezak and Dale can be explained by the fact that the last two focus on a slightly earlier period than Nolan. It is also possible that Bedos-Rezak and Dale do not take full account of the agency behind the invention of new practices or the modification of existing ones, and that is where Nolan's study of royal women's seals in comparison to those of royal men and bishops is particularly valuable. Nonetheless, once again this chapter has circled back to a self that may not be an individual. Yet this self responds to an interpellation by

FIGURE 2.5 *Tomb effigy of Rudolf von Schwaben, c.* 1080. Photograph by Michail Jungierek, 2007. © Wikimedia Commons (public domain).

the ideologies of its time. It assumes a role that is offered to it and even innovates in how it plays that role, by commissioning artisans to experiment with their materials and make something new. This self may not be an individual, but it is a *persona* and a subject.

AFTERWARD: A TURN AWAY FROM THE SUBJECT MEDIEVAL/MODERN?

This survey of theories of the medieval self has oscillated between the general and the particular, the group and the individual, likeness and difference. The chapter has moved from the early modern claim that there were no medieval individuals, only groups, to the mid-twentieth-century insistence on differentiating one medieval writer from another, to the study of the medieval mind or person conceived by analogy with the seal, a person who is not an individual at all. Somewhere between the poles of the group and the individual stands the subject, who is fissured by conflicting roles projected upon him by the ideologies of the time, or else, like Heloise, faces the deafness of her most intimate interlocutor and stands apart, an unwilling spiritual exile from her community. If this chapter has demonstrated anything, it is how the self eludes us when we attempt to define it rigorously or locate it securely in texts of the past. Its lineaments—to recall Guibert's expression—are not the confident lines of an expert artist, not the basis of a clear portrait, but a sketch that can look like a self only if that is what the viewer seeks.

CHAPTER THREE

Ethics and Social Relations

EILEEN C. SWEENEY

Philosophers trained in the history of Western thought are prone to dismiss medieval ethical thought as inferior to the Greek virtue ethics aimed at self-mastery, a theme common to Plato, Aristotle, and the Stoics, and/or by contrast to Kant for whom the only authentic ethics is founded in the principle of autonomy over heteronomy. This chapter is a small contribution to push back on this view, not by asserting the ways in which medieval thought actually exhibits the values of Plato, Aristotle, or Kant (though there are ways it does), but by pointing out some of the ideas and practices in which it is different than both ancient Greek and modern ethics, and which have continued to exert influence on Western culture down to this day. It is in a basic sense an ethics grounded on heteronomy—obligation to God and, hence, others, ultimately based on love more than reason.

The chapter is divided into two main portions, the first on love, and the second on the failure of love: sin. Part one traces the developments in the understanding of love of God and others from Augustine's identification of moral worth with the direction of one's affections: our actions are good when what we love is good, and thus when the love of God orders our actions. As we shall see in the eleventh and twelfth centuries, the attributes of love of God and the longing for and experience of divine love are transferred to human relationships, in the monastic community for Anselm. Hugh of Saint Victor gives voice to the desire to be loved as an individual, for oneself and unconditionally, not based on merit or on some universal love for all. This desire to be loved for and as oneself and the ecstatic features of mystical union are carried over into a transformation of heterosexual love in the tradition of courtly love or *fin'amours* in France in the eleventh and twelfth centuries, reconfiguring the positions of both men and women in romantic love and in the value of compassion for those who suffer.

If love of God is the ethical core, radiating out to love of others, contempt for or rejection of God is, contrarily, the core of sin. From this core the scope of sin expands to the violation of relationships with others. Augustine makes it clear that the problem with pagan virtue is that it is directed toward the glory of the self rather than the love of God and care of others. Augustine's inheritors in the Middle Ages struggle with the question of whether or how to reconcile Greek and Roman conceptions of virtue (and vice) with the religious notion of sin as offense against God. The result is a double movement, both toward and away from Greek/Roman philosophical conceptions. The reconciliation occurs in the account of moral obligation, attempting to show that what God requires is identical to what reason and nature know about good and evil, as we see in thinkers such as Thomas Aquinas and Albert the Great. The rationalization of sin takes different forms, both in the account of "natural law," the knowledge of God's law "written on our hearts" as the apostle Paul claimed, and in the attempts to catalog and rank sins by their gravity. But even these strategies are taken up in a context of the fundamental obligation to the transcendent God (e.g., the category of mortal sin as the rejection of God and loss of charity). Though scholastic authors such as Thomas Aquinas attempt to reorganize sin and the sins around the Aristotelian/Stoic list of cardinal virtues (and their vices)—courage, temperance, justice, prudence—the much more popular scheme, both for confessional manuals and preaching, was around "the seven deadly sins": pride, envy, anger, sloth, greed, gluttony, lust. These sins either do not appear at all in classical catalogs (e.g., pride, sloth or acedia) or do not receive the same kind of treatment (e.g., avarice and lust). All are given a decidedly relational interpretation in the Middle Ages and are mostly understood as matters of interior affect rather than outward action. Evident both in the speculative work of scholastic theologians and confessional interrogatories for everyone from church officials to merchants and peasants, is the inward turn to sin as a matter of conscience and will, a failure to feel correctly (charitably) toward others.

Further, as we shall see, the sins medieval writers focus on are the foibles of ordinary people, not Aristotle's aristocratic magnanimous man. Aristotle did not really care about what *most* people did or try to make them better because he did not really think they could change—instead dismissing the many who simply pursue pleasure. Christianity gives us ethics for everyone. That meant that medieval thinkers had to talk about the bad actions people do that Aristotle did not bother with (e.g., adultery, theft, etc.) and focus more on less than admirable but common feelings and desires (envy, sloth, greed), but it also means they believed people could change. In the confessional manuals and practice of confession we find concrete proof of those notions, as well as the evidence of a growing economic system in which standards of just exchange are being worked out.

LOVE AND RELATIONSHIPS: RECONFIGURING PASSION

Augustine and the redefinition of morality and ethical relations

Augustine makes the most important basic claims about the centrality of love in the Christian tradition. Augustine accepts the Stoic principle that one should not love what can be taken against one's will, even accepting that the category of what can be taken against one's will includes not only the material goods of wealth and one's own body, but also other human beings whom we might love.[1] This becomes the distinction between *uti* and *frui*, what is to be loved for its own sake versus being loved for its usefulness. The only thing that can be *frui*, loved for its own sake, is God, all else is merely *uti*, useful for the end of loving God.[2] Though the relationship that is defining is with God rather than other human beings, Augustine still leaves love and relationship at the center of human life and its ultimate foundation is affectivity, as opposed to rationality. The end or goal is ecstatic in the etymological sense, outside the self, the opposite of the self-contained, self-sufficient life of Stoic or even Aristotelian virtue.

Scholars have defended Augustine from the charge that he sees human relationships only as a means rather than an end in itself, citing especially his sermon on the Gospel of John in which Augustine comments on love, God as love, and the command to love one another. In the sermon, Augustine makes clear that love of neighbor means loving and acting for their benefit, not our advantage. This much is found in Aristotle, but it is clear that for Augustine, the language of love has in effect superseded the language of virtue. While pagan virtue is prideful and selfish, Christian love, whether for God or neighbor, is focused on the other. Augustine's principle is clear: "all these emotions are right in those whose love is rightly placed."[3] Of the passions, he writes, "they are evil if our love is evil; good if our love is good."[4]

Anselm and the twelfth century

The importance and emphasis on the affective life is found in a new way in Anselm's letters.[5] Unlike friendship in both Aristotle and Cassian, and to a much greater degree than Cicero, Anselm's letters are full of passionate longing and anguished grief at separation. Anselm's letters express fervent love for individuals, placing all his bliss in their presence and despair at their absence. As with later notions of romantic love, the very intensity of this love explains, at least partly, how it can last forever regardless of the parties' separation from one another.[6] It is not just that Anselm borrows his language of longing and fervor from physical and sexual love, but also that he uses the language of love of something *for its own sake* rather than as a means, treating those human relationships as *frui* rather than *uti*.[7] Like the evocation of the intimate love between mother and child, brother and brother, nursemaid and baby in his prayers, Anselm's letters acknowledge and affirm the human desire for these kinds of intense, physical, and exclusive attachments (Figures 3.1 and 3.2). The borrowing of the language of erotic love for a higher love has

FIGURE 3.1 Image of the Virgin and child, 1150–1200 CE, showing a formal rather than emotional connection between mother and child. © The Met Museum (public domain).

FIGURE 3.2 Image of the Virgin and child, 1260–1280 CE. This depiction of an intimate, loving relationship between mother and child, illustrates the changing view of the role of emotion in intimate human relationships. © The Met Museum (public domain).

precedents, of course, in Plato's ascent of the soul and, even closer to Anselm, in Christian mysticism, where longing for union and union itself with God is described in erotic terms. However, Anselm uses the kind of language mystics use for love of God for his love and longing for his fellow monks. He takes his language not just "up" from erotic love but also "down" from mystical union to human relationships. The reapplication of the language of mystical longing and union to human relationships, even the spiritual relationships of the monastery, places passionate human relationships at the center of human life; they are neither the optional ornament of virtuous life, nor characterized primarily by their careful management by reason.

Hugh of Saint Victor (d.1141) makes further important contributions on the nature and role of love in human life in the Western Christian tradition. Hugh's short work, *Soliloquoy on the Betrothal Gift of the Soul*, is an internal dialogue between the soul and the self, which explores the soul's desire to be loved uniquely and exclusively, for and as itself. Hugh does not try to redirect or sublimate the desire for particular love, only to show how it is fulfilled in God's love (Figure 3.3). The self's reply consists in a description of creation and salvation history in terms of the unique love of God for the individual soul. God's gifts to the individual come first in the form of existence and then

FIGURE 3.3 Master Heinrich von Konstanz, *Christ and Saint John*. Sculpture depicting the apostle John with his head on Jesus' shoulder in a very human depiction of Jesus' love directed specifically to John as "the disciple Jesus loved" (Jn 19:26). © Museum Mayer van den Bergh, MMB.0224. Image: Bart Huysmans.

the beauty of form. The actions and relationship to Jesus Christ are also explained in terms of particular love, as his choice and preference for the individual. "Your spouse, your lover, your redeemer, your God, chose and preferred you. He chose you among all and took you up from all and loved you in preference to all."[8] Only then is the soul satisfied, replying: "God does nothing else except provide for my salvation, and he seems to me so completely occupied with guarding me that he forgets all others and chooses to be occupied with me alone."[9]

Hugh also transforms the purely intellectual Neoplatonic ascent ending in union with divine into one completed in love rather than knowledge. According to Hugh, the final ecstasy of union with the beloved/God requires a shift from the active seeking of the intellect to one of *receiving* the beloved one cannot actively grasp.[10] This affirmation of passivity and receptivity stands over against the standard (if not universally held) view in ancient Western thought that denigrates passivity as feminine. In the Victorine account, all human beings are *receivers* of divine love, and even more surprisingly, union is cast in terms of *mutual* indwelling, as both partners are received into the other.

Both of these changes—the particularity of love not based on virtue or merit but simply for the individual with all their flaws, and an emphasis on being a passive receiver rather than an active master of one's own fate—leads to a valuing of the passions, including feeling for and with others in their suffering. In his account of the "four wills of Christ" Hugh of Saint Victor touts the importance of compassion as a moral virtue, exemplified in Christ's weeping for Jerusalem: "For this surely pertains to the goodness of mortal life, that one conform oneself to the conditions of others and be made a participant in another's passion through compassion [*per compassionem*], in order that, as that which is suffered is a necessity, so that which is co-suffered might be a work of goodness."[11] We see this ideal of compassion carried all the way forward into the Renaissance in Juan Luis Vives's account of the passions. Vives belittles the Stoic rejection of mercy and compassion, not only because we are more ready to help others when we feel for them in their suffering but also because "bending your soul to the affliction of others" *itself* alleviates others' pain and suffering.[12]

Courtly love

Though its origins and interpretations are controversial (even its existence as a new medieval creation has been disputed), texts that both portray and parody heterosexual love point to a model in which the knight/male lover is in a position analogous to the human being worshipping the divine—hoping to have love bestowed but unable and unworthy to claim it, languishing in the absence of the beloved, "wounded" by the excess of feeling in both the presence and absence of the beloved. William Reddy describes this transformation visible in the work of William IX,[13] the first troubadour, as "endowing the longing for association with a salvific spiritual force," "equat[ing] the adulterous sexual caressing of his beloved … not with lust but with a pledge of loyalty and with submission to her authority and protection, as well as with reverence before an apparition of great spiritual power."[14]

The interpretation of this secular love poetry originating in the south of France in the twelfth century as articulating a new kind of human love, "courtly love," has been described as having multiple origins—classical love poetry in Ovid, Cicero's account of friendship, Arabic love poetry, and of course, Neoplatonic and Christian mysticism. It has been described as being both an extension of mystical love and also as in opposition to it, even as a form of religious "dissent," and both as feminist and anti-feminist. But feminist or anti-feminist, Carin Franzén is surely right to point out that what we witness starting in the eleventh century is "a radical change regarding Plato's exclusion of the feminine."[15] A *public* set of practices and codes around love between men and women is what Louis-Georges Tin in his book entitled *L'invention de la culture hétérosexuelle* has described as the "supplant[ing of] traditional male friendship by a heterosexual culture."[16] In ancient Greek culture, there is no possibility of courtship of young women, since young women, unless they are prostitutes, do not appear in public, and while this changes to some degree in the Roman world, not much. Moreover, the world of the church is surely at least as unisex/male as Plato's Academy. Courtly love is a challenge to that all male world, one in which women come to *seen* in a more significant way, come to be able to function as subject and not just object. At the same time, there are countervailing forces reinscribing the traditional feminine role as passive object into the very codes that seemed designed to challenge that role.

Robertson's wry summary as he attempted to debunk the idea of courtly love (arguing that it is a sentimental invention of the eighteenth or nineteenth century) gives us the basics: "that the lady should be of a much higher station than the lover, that she should be located at a distance, that the lover should tremble in her presence, and that he should obey her slightest wish. He should, moreover, fall sick with love … preserve his chastity, and perform great exploits to attract the attention of the lady" (Figure 3.4).[17] Robertson finds this implausible and argues that the loves that are described in different forms in different texts are forms of "idolatrous passion."[18] C. S. Lewis acknowledges the existence of courtly love, but clearly sees it as a rival to Christianity.[19]

But courtly love is a rival to orthodox Christianity by mirroring it in significant ways. Robertson is quite right that it is, as he puts it, a "terrible nuisance," but that is exactly the point. It is constructed exactly as *passio* in the sense of both being the pursuit of both passivity and suffering for the male suitor. This model of secular love is an eros purified both in its idealized and unapproachable object and in the indefinite postponement of union with the beloved. As lovers of God, human beings are cast in the role of receiver, unable to actively control or master their fate, but dependent on the God who comes to them rather than reaching their goal themselves. I have already noted that this is in effect to "feminize" the position of all human beings. Anselm devoted an entire dialogue, *The Fall of the Devil*, to an explanation of Saint Paul's rhetorical question, "What do you have

FIGURE 3.4 In this depiction of courtly love, the knight kneels before his beloved, placing himself at her service. © University of Heidelberger, Cod. Pal. germ. 848 (public domain).

that you have not received?"[20] Being in the position of receiver means neither having nor being able to acquire what one wishes. This is for Anselm what it means to be creature and not creator, finite and not infinite.[21] It is these aspects of courtly love that brought the philosopher Emmanuel Levinas to find in it a model of his ethics of the Other: "There is in the erotic relationship a characteristic reversal of the subjectivity issued from position, a reversion of the virile and heroic I."[22] J. Alan Mitchell makes the argument that for both Chaucer and Levinas there is a notion of "ethics as radical passivity before fortune and future contingency: a passivity that resembles a kind of courtship, given its demanding waiting period and uncertain end, its privileging of heteronomy over the autonomy of the self, its disavowal of self-sufficiency and its subjection of self to the other."[23]

In his short work *De amore* (1185), Andreas Capellanus, a cleric, advises his friend Walter, at his request, on how to conduct a love affair, but as all readers have noted, the advice is mixed. He advises Walter to conduct himself according to the model of this elevated love, courting a woman of the nobility rather than the peasantry and advising him how to approach the unapproachable with words (rather than actual deeds) of love, with clear understanding of the paradox that the gratification of erotic desire that fuels it must be indefinitely postponed. The misery of the lover vainly seeking his impossible object, his being thrust in the mode of beseecher, passive receiver of her possible favors rather than active acquisition of them, is what we might call a feature rather than a bug. The normal and surely far more common model of sexual relations was (and, alas, in many quarters, still is), as a teacher of mine once remarked, one in which the virtue of a man consists in depriving a woman of hers. As many commentators have pointed out, there is an important sense in which the traditional gender relations are not even very convincingly hidden beneath the rhetoric of *fin'amours*, as the woman often becomes less the active bestower of love and favors and more the receiver of the exploits and attentions of her lover, able neither to honorably accept nor reject them, effectively removed from the field of agency altogether.

In the *De amore's* final section, Andreas advises Walter to eschew love altogether, winning divine pleasure by refraining from sin even though (having learned the art of love from Andreas) he could.[24] The rest of the text recounts the miseries of human love and the vices of the earthly woman who is its object. Andreas also points out that the lover in this earthly version is not really in selfless service to the other; rather his love is an "inborn suffering" deriving from "excessive meditation" on its object, and thus is more about his idealized object than the actual other.[25] This is essentially what the contemporary philosopher Slavoj Zizek claims when he writes that in courtly love "the elevation of woman to the sublime object of love equals her debasement into the passive stuff or screen for the narcissistic projection of the male ego-ideal."[26]

Like Andreas, but for different, non-misogynist reasons, Christine de Pisan also advises against engaging in love affairs. While in some of her earlier works, Christine seemed to describe a version of *fin'amours* capable of ennobling the lover, leading her to criticize vulgar and carnal accounts like those in Jean de Meun's *Roman de la Rose*, she seems to have become more skeptical over time.[27] In the literature of love debates about which bereft lover is the most unhappy, Christine sets up a cynical set of cases: a lady whose lover has left her allows another to woo her, a knight who cannot see his lady because of the jealous husband, a woman whose lover deserts her for someone more noble, but returns to her after failing to win the other. Christine leaves the judgment to her patron, but the work is already done by her choice of cases, as they are all cases in which loyalty and selflessness are absent. Christine seems close to abandoning the project of *fin'amours* for virtue almost in an Aristotelian sense. Nonetheless, Christine's rejection of misogyny and even creation of her *Cité des dames* (an allegorical city of virtuous women refuting misogynistic representations) is in a certain way made possible by the courtly legacy, both by reasserting its high virtues, which it fails to adhere to, and because courtly love has opened the door for women to be visible and to speak as a subject.[28]

SIN AND CONFESSION: ETHICS FOR THE COMMON MAN

Sin vs. Vice

Augustine launches the most powerful critique of "pagan virtue" in the *City of God*. The cardinal virtues are unable to do much more than forcibly restrain evil, in their very acts witnessing to their own defeat: temperance is nothing more than "internal warfare," fortitude "bears the most witness to human evils, because it is precisely these evils that it is compelled to endure with patience," while prudence teaches about evil but fails to remove it from life, and justice labors continually but does not achieve its end of giving each their due.[29] They do not just fail but become vices when not directed toward service of God but for oneself.[30] Augustine describes the Roman Empire as fueled by the desire for glory and honor, and criticizes Cicero for praising glory as a motive for virtue.[31] Moreover, Augustine argues that the desire for glory is the sin of pride; and pride quickly degrades to a lust for domination, since it rejects the notion of human beings as equal before God.[32]

While Plato and Aristotle locate moral obligation in the obligation to oneself, to one's own happiness and fulfillment, medieval thinkers must take account of the notion that wrongdoing is an act against God's written law. Ethical obligation is, first, unconditional and independent of the individual's own happiness or fulfillment, and, second, originates in the demand of the other. The recognition of that obligation is the realization that one's own standards do not constitute the whole of the world of value, that one's grasp of the good and the right is limited not only by one's ability to act ethically but even to imagine it. It is to experience oneself in relationships in which one always falls short in a fundamental, unavoidable, and unforeseen way.[33] In Corinthians Paul writes, "Whether you eat or drink, or whatever else you do; do all to the glory of God."[34] Medieval thinkers try come to terms with this as a total commitment to God—that all life's acts are a way of choosing, honoring, and loving God, or not; thus, all failures are the failure to choose God. This view is echoed by Anselm in *Cur Deus Homo*. No matter how slight an action might be in itself, Anselm argues, if it is contrary to the will of God, it cannot be preferred even to the preservation of all of creation.[35]

This issue is thematized most explicitly in the Latin tradition as the category of *sin* as distinct from *vice* as writers work to bring these two categories into some kind of relationship. Whereas sin is failure in relation to an obligation to God, vice is failure of self-mastery, a failure to fulfill one's nature as human. In his influential *Book of Sentences* Peter Lombard cites a number of definitions of sin, that it is "word, deed, or desire contrary to the law of God," that sin is the will refraining from or pursuing what justice forbids, that sin is "transgression of divine law and disobedience to heavenly precepts."[36] Albert the Great, Thomas Aquinas, and Bonaventure all prioritize the notion of sin as against God's law while maximizing the overlap and harmony between it and the Greek/Roman notion of vice, both in terms of the source of knowledge of the moral law—human reason or divine revelation—and in terms of the source of moral obligation—God's command or internal conscience. Natural law fits into this attempt to synthesize the different moral pictures because it is understood as human participation in the eternal law. At the same time, it makes it possible to distinguish between religious and secular ethics via the claim that all human beings have the natural law "written on their hearts" but that divine law, revealed in scripture, makes known what more is required to be united to God.

The seven deadly sins

The notion of moral failure as the rejection of God reconfigures the entire moral landscape, just as the redefinition of virtue in terms of love of God did. One way that becomes clear is in the medieval appropriation of the "seven deadly sins": pride, envy, anger, sloth, avarice,

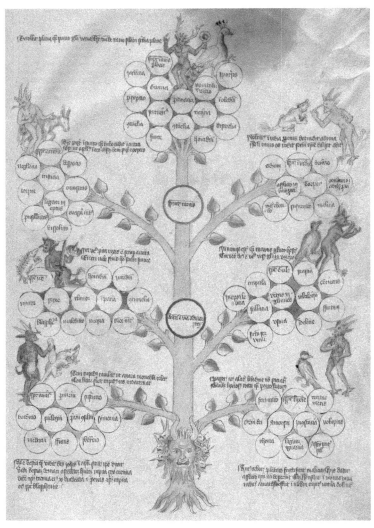

FIGURE 3.5 A depiction of the "seven deadly sins" Here each branch represents one of the seven sins (pride at the top, followed by sloth and envy, anger and gluttony, avarice and lust) and the leaves growing from each branch are the 'daughters' of each sin, i.e., the further sins to which each deadly sin gives rise, Wellcome Apocalypse, Ms. 49, c. 1420. © Wikimedia Commons (public domain).

lust, and gluttony (Figure 3.5). The seven sins were developed as part of early monastic practice utterly rejecting the pleasures of the world, and early figures such as Cassian and Gregory the Great represent the sins as the forces of evil attacking either the person or the virtues.[37] However, the ascetic and dualistic elements of the deadly sins, as well as their definition in terms appropriate to the monastic life, soften over time as explanations of their wrongness and their effects is given more in terms of their deleterious effects on human relationships. We can see this in the accounts of the "contrary virtues," those opposed to the seven deadly sins:

> The first form of praise is by a deep humility against the capital vice of pride; the second, by the warmth of brotherly love against the rancor of envy; the third is by patience against the plague of burning wrath; the fourth, by the copious largess of alms against the spirit of greed and avarice; the fifth, by a reasonable abstinence against the copious flow of gluttony; the sixth, by continence and chastity against the desirousness of lust; the seventh, in a good perseverance against the listlessness of sloth.[38]

Pride, envy, anger, and avarice are explicitly understood as relational and as countered by the correct kind of other-directed behavior—humility, brotherly love, patience; moreover, avarice and gluttony are not countered by monastic asceticism in the lack of all property and the extremes of self-denial but in sharing of one's goods in giving alms and in "reasonable abstinence."

When we look at the sins individually we see even more clearly the contrast to the classical view. Pride is absent from Platonic or Aristotelian catalogs of vice, but it has a central place in medieval accounts as both the first sin, that for which Adam and Eve were expelled from Eden, and the worst sin. Aquinas defines pride as an excessive desire for one's own excellence, which rejects subjection to God.[39] In Bernard of Clairvaux's *De gradibus humilitatus et superbiae tractatus*, the point of humility (and the problem with pride) is its effects not just vertically between the individual and God (or other superior) but its horizontal consequences across the community. Humility is a recognition of one's own failings, which then makes it possible to see others' failings with understanding and a willingness to help them. Pride is an impediment to seeing the truth about oneself and others, and, hence, to providing any aid to others, as the proud, focusing on the failings of others but not their own, will be moved to anger rather than pity and to judge rather than assist.[40] Bernard backs this view up with a long account of Jesus' life and suffering as the exemplar of humility, which leads to empathy for human sufferings and failings.

The question of the origin or root of all sin is a standard scholastic question, taken up by Peter Lombard and those who commented on his work, as was required by all masters as part of their studies.[41] The most common answers are pride or avarice/concupiscence (in these accounts avarice and concupiscence are often elided as desires for more material goods). Most seem to argue, as Peter does, that a case can be made for both; all types of sin can come from pride and from cupidity/avarice, and each can motivate the other.[42] John of Rupella opts for pride because pride desires preference, and the other goods— riches, delicacies, etc.—are ways of getting that preference for the self.[43] Aquinas makes a similar argument, that we desire the goods the other sins aim at so that through them we may acquire some perfection.[44] Thus pride is the "beginning of sin," yet avarice, as a special sin, the desire for money, is the root of sin since money can be the means to satisfying any sinful desire.[45]

These different answers on the root or origin of sin as pride or avarice or concupiscence are in a sense different perspectives on the same claim: the human failing is wanting more. Humans want to be more than they are, to be God rather than creature, and want more possessions, more excellence, more control over others. The core of human failure is in that desire for more, but the understanding of wrongness in that desire is not the failure to totally reject the world in ascetic dedication to God, but it is in the damage done to the community and human relationships. For Aristotle or Plato, virtue is moderation not asceticism, but more, virtue is for the individual, not for the other. Bloomfield speculates that the importance of pride as the source of all sins is a result of the "disciplined, corporate society" of the Middle Ages and its worries about "the dangers of independent thinking."[46] But this causal chain makes more sense reversed. For the location of pride as the first and worst sin, and of avarice as the path to feed the desire for more than one should have, which deprives others of enough, flows out of the definition of sin as a rejection of divine law, which is a rejection of one's status as creature (*equal to other creatures*) rather than creator. Such a notion of sin *yields* a less individualistic, more corporatist culture.

Envy exists on the list of vices in Aristotle as a version of emulation gone wrong. Someone else's possession of a good thing we desire can make us want to work to acquire it ourselves (emulation) or to want to deprive the other person of it (envy), according to Aristotle. The first is felt by good people, the second by bad.[47] But it is both a much more important vice in the medieval period and much further from anything virtuous. Envy is fundamentally the violation of Paul's command to "rejoice with those who rejoice, weep with those who weep."[48] When instead we rejoice at others' suffering and are saddened by their blessings, whether we are spurred to improve ourselves or not, it is a failure of charity and, thus, a mortal sin. As Aquinas says, using Aristotle as a support, "envy implies something opposed to charity from the very comparison of the act with its object: for it is of the nature of friendship to will good to our friends as we do to ourselves."[49] The fourteenth-century penitential treatise *Fasciculus Morum* maintains that the failure to share in others' joy and sadness is a contradiction of our very humanity; the devil's sin is envy, wanting perversely to deprive humankind of paradise without gaining anything himself.[50] Chaucer's "Parson's Tale" echoes many writings on the seven deadly sins pointing out that envy is unique among the sins since it gives no pleasure to the sinner.[51] According to Rosenfeld, Gower's *Confessio amantis* explores how envy is defeated by the insight "that all human beings are 'like' in a fundamental way," rooted in a "shared mortality, suggesting that compassion can cut through the apparent difference created by the distribution of temporal goods."[52] Thus, the path out of envy is in "grasping what it means to have things in 'common'" and to come to desire the common good. Envy, then, is what undermines the possibility of human fellowship, and compassion, its opposite, is what makes it possible.

Sloth or acedia is another sin not found in the classical canon of vices; in some lists of the sins, *tristitia*/sadness sometimes takes the place of acedia. Eventually the two notions are melded together, as the neglect of spiritual goods, but whether that neglect is one of outer (religious/moral) duties or a kind of spiritual barrenness shifts with different authors (Figure 3.6). In Peter Damian, for example, acedia is "the drowsiness or physical weariness which the monk must overcome in his ascetic practices of waking and praying."[53] James Williams has shown that monastic reformers in the Carolingian period (eighth to ninth century) countered acedia by focusing on reinvigorating the "culture of work" in monasteries that had grown more prosperous.[54] The Council of Aachen in 816 legislated requirements that monks work in the kitchen, mills, laundry, workshops, and fields. Thus, labor is no longer a prescription for spiritual dryness (*tristitia*) but what prevents falling

FIGURE 3.6 In this detail of acedia (or sloth), sloth is depicted both as spiritual, unable to accept the offer to join in prayer, and as inactivity, sitting with a pillow comfortably by the fire in contrast to those working outdoors. Hieronymus Bosch, The Seven Deadly Sins and the Four Last Things, *c.* 1500–1525. © Alamy Stock Photo.

into *acedia*—idleness, leisure, and gossip. According to Wenzel, in the twelfth century the focus of the analysis turns inward, where meanings range from "inner indolence which neglects to watch over disturbing and sinful thoughts; weariness and disgust (*taedium*); and tepidity or absence of fervor (*tepiditas*)."[55] Paradoxically, neglecting the central concern of divine things makes one "busy" in a myriad of other ways, searching endlessly for distractions. According to Wenzel's study of acedia between 700 and 1200 CE, the shift between acedia as a matter of neglectful *behavior* in one's duties to God and others as opposed to a *psychic state* "such as tedium, loathing, bitterness of mind" is not a matter of linear development from a more spiritual sense centered around the monastic life to an outward sense appropriate to civil life. Rather the notion of the core of acedia as interior or exterior shifts in different texts across different time periods depending upon the intended audience.[56]

After the integration of Aristotle in the schools in the thirteenth century, we see scholastic writers struggling with the way in which acedia as a sin seems to complicate the moral psychology found in Aristotle even more than envy. For envy the problem is that there seems to be no good or pleasure one gets by indulging it; acedia is the loathing of spiritual goods "as something contrary to [one]self," not the desire of some other earthly good instead (which would just simply be concupiscence).[57] Thus, acedia seems to break with the Aristotelian picture in two ways: first, insofar as it involves the rejection of a true good but not out of a mistaken preference for some apparent good instead; thus one declines to will the good one *knows* is good. Second, insofar as acedia as a sin is predicated on a life whose single direction is the transcendent good, it models a different kind of moral life than Aristotle's multivalent flourishing. The difference between *the* spiritual good, God, and spiritual practices of devotion, through which one is supposed to continue to direct oneself toward that end, is great, and keeping on that singular path, forsaking all others, is a struggle. Albert the Great seems to grasp that there can be a level of difficulty and weariness about this task because that good is so far from this world. Albert associates an extreme form of acedia with the more serious sin, despair, but also distinguishes acedia from another extreme, the sadness about the spiritual and physical trials experienced, for example, by Job and Jesus, both of whose anguish were not only not vicious but also "beyond" virtue (*supra virtutem*).[58] The task of holding on to the orientation to the transcendent good can be an act of super human virtue, one in the face of which even the very best experience anguish rather than natural inclination. This connection in Albert to what looks like acedia but is really extraordinary virtue in Job and Christ is echoed in Ockham's highest level of virtue: virtue that rises above every natural instinct, as we will see below. This notion of the good that is beyond nature, and of acedia as a different way of neglecting that good than mere immersion in lower goods, makes its way, on the one hand, into existentialist thinkers, such as Pascal in his notion of "diversion" and Kierkegaard in the notions of "anxiety" and "despair,"[59] and on the other, into notions of the virtuous character of work usually associated, of course, with Protestantism, but as we have seen, dating from the late eighth century.

Will/Conscience/Intention

The clear and consistent location of sin in *voluntas* in medieval thinkers is connected to the notion of sin as against divine law. If the full extent of virtue's appeal is that virtue is what is in our true interest, as it is for Aristotle and Plato, then it does not really make sense to think of willfully resisting its direction. There is no self-interest to hold against self-interest; moral failure can only be a lack of understanding or habituation, for which the cures are education and training. But because *sin* is the failure to meet an obligation *to another*, the rejection of an order transcending self-interest, sin is a problem of the will in a way vice cannot be.[60] In Socrates' argument against Callicles in the *Gorgias* or Thrasymachus in the *Republic*, there is no appeal to what they owe *another* but what leads to self-mastery.

Abelard sets up in an extremely clear way the link between the notion of sin and the location of moral worth in the will (what Abelard calls "consent"). Abelard defines consent to sin as "contempt for the creator ... not to do for his sake what we believe we ought to do for his sake, or not to renounce for his sake what we believe ought to be renounced."[61] Importantly it is about going against what we *believe* God requires of us. Hence, Abelard is able to defend those who do wrong but with the best intentions, for example, those who reject the Gospel, persecute martyrs, or even crucify Christ; if they act based on conscience, they do not do well, but would do worse if they acted against their conscience, even to do the right thing.[62] A consequence of the location of sin in the internal act of contempt for God is that only God can judge sin, while human law is left to judge the deed without access to guilt, falling back on principles of utility and deterrence.[63] Hence *sin* is what God judges and *crime* (*crimen*) what is judged by human courts.

In Ockham's *On the Connection of the Virtues* several of these strands come together: sin as against God, as in the will, and as what is contrary to natural inclination. In all five levels of virtuous action Ockham holds that the morality of action lies exclusively in the will and *not* in the passions. Ockham defines virtue in the higher levels by the degree to which the action is in opposition to natural inclinations (or passions). The first degree of virtue is when the will elicits an act in conformity with right reason. The second degree is when one wills according to right reason with the intention never to give up such works for any reason contrary to right reason, not even to avoid death. In the third degree, the will wills the performance of the work solely because it is dictated by right reason. A fourth level is when the will wills that act precisely on account of love of God. The last and fifth level is when the will wills to do or undergo something that naturally exceeds the common human state, contrary to the most basic inclination; this is heroic virtue.[64] The will's action is what defines an act as moral at all levels, and the intensification of the moral act at higher levels is effected solely by an intensification of the will's act in its increasing independence from "natural" inclinations, namely, passions in the sensitive appetite.

Confession

The dual aspects of virtue and, hence, sin as other directed and as a matter of the interior state of conscience and the will are both evident in the confessor's manuals. Not just confessors but also penitents had access to these manuals, and, according to Jacques Le Goff, the manuals contrived specially for lay use "devoted the greatest amount of space to the problems of professional conscience."[65] This was, Le Goff argues, a phenomenon of subjectivization and internalization of the spiritual life, from which introspection and hence the whole of modem Western psychology originated.[66] Michael Haren's edition and translation of the interrogatories for penitents from the *Memoriale presbiterorum* (mid-fourteenth-century England) shows the importance of the examination of conscience as well as of deeds. To those exercising ecclesiastical jurisdiction, the author asks, "Did you do anything in judgement or out of it through favour or through bribery, against your conscience and against justice, to the oppression of any party?"[67] Peasants are asked whether they have sworn and kept oaths of fealty to their lord, and it is noted that they are motivated by envy to speak ill of each other.[68] Thus from the highest social position to the lowest, not just outward but inward acts are inquired about.

Strikingly, the interrogatories are constructed not just for those of high status but also every step on the social ladder, including sailors, married women and widows, even children, along with knights, merchants, seneschals and bailiffs.[69] As Haren notes, the interrogatory he edited seems most concerned to protect those who fall under the authority of others and "whose denunciation is as severe of abuse in ecclesiastical structures as in secular."[70] The focus throughout is on the social dimension, the effects of wrongdoing on others. Of course, implied in that emphasis on social justice as well as by the separate list of questions for the different professions and roles within medieval society, is the underlying ethical principle that every role has its rights and duties, every role has a place in society and a place in the economy of salvation. Hugh of Saint Victor's *Didascalicon* enumerated the list of the liberal arts, along with the seven mechanical arts (weaving, architecture, hunting, medicine, metallurgy, navigation, theatrical arts) that serve to relieve our weakness, just as philosophy/the arts and theology serve to restore our nature.[71] Le Goff quotes Geroch of Reichersberg's notion of "the great factory of the universe," in which God is the first *Artifex*, and notes that in his book *Liber de aedificio Dei*, "Geroch goes on to assert that every human condition has a Christian value and that every profession is a valid means to salvation."[72] Out of a tradition with deep misgivings about money-making, in which the moral ideal is having no possessions in the monastic life and mendicant orders, emerge ethical standards for how to go about engaging in business and trade.[73] We see this reflected in records of confessional manuals in which notions of fair price and fair trading are introduced as grounds for examining the merchants who find their way into the confessional. Aristotle's elitist ethics, which asserts that only those free of the servitude of money-making can live a fully human life, is fully left behind by the High Middle Ages. What takes its place is the beginning of notions of both professional ethics and social justice.

CHAPTER FOUR

Politics and Economies

CARY J. NEDERMAN AND KAREN BOLLERMANN

Between the twelfth and fifteenth centuries, European economic life underwent a dramatic transformation. The historical threshold crossed after 1100 may be characterized by three key factors. First, market relations became a central feature of the social structures of the Latin Middle Ages, generating what Robert Lopez many years ago proclaimed to be a "commercial revolution."[1] Among the tokens of this revolution were the increased circulation of coinage, the expansion of long-distance trade, the formation of national markets, the emergence of systems of credit and banking, and the rising prominence of cities. Second, the period witnessed an expansion of technological development and improved productivity without precedent in Europe, running parallel to patterns of demographic growth and the extension of arable land. Agricultural management yielded levels of fertility (and wealth) that were previously unimaginable.[2] Finally, political and legal institutions capable of regulating and directing economic resources on a larger scale appeared rapidly after 1100. Government—whether in the form of kings and other territorial lords or of urban communes—received recognition as an important agent of economic administration and also as a beneficiary (through taxes, customs, and duties) of a vigorous economy.[3] Although the emergence of these phenomena was by no means uniform or unilateral, Europe in 1500 was a very different place economically—and also politically, legally, and socially—than it had been five hundred years earlier.

In general, those contemporary writers who addressed the sociopolitical implications of economic innovation tended to highlight the moral and religious dimensions of these practices. Thus, early canon lawyers expressed interest in regulating commerce so as to minimize its detrimental effects on both the souls of merchants and of those who associate with them. Was it proper for the Christian to sustain himself by buying cheap and selling dear? Do loans at interest or the acquisition of money necessarily entail avarice and thus jeopardize one's salvation? Must the possession and enjoyment of earthly comforts or luxuries lead to damnation? The main concerns of canon law, then, were with the spiritual consequences of economic enterprise. Wherever the pursuit of private profit endangered the human soul, canonists sought to legislate economic intercourse.[4]

Theologians and preachers reacting to the currents of economic change expressed similar concerns. Peter the Chanter (d. 1197) and his followers, who flourished in Paris around the turn of the thirteenth century, for example, devoted considerable attention to the control of usury and attendant impermissible practices on the grounds that these were sinful and wicked, constituting threats to the supernatural beatitude of those who engaged in them. Such teachings—supported by scriptural authority, canon law, and conciliar decree—enjoyed considerable currency among preachers, as revealed by a number of extant sermons that echo the prohibitions on precisely the same basis.[5]

Moreover, members of Peter's circle offered advice to princes concerning the fiscal management of their realms—including taxation and coinage—always with an eye to the impact of public conduct on personal salvation.[6] In sum, theological authors remained as deeply concerned as canonists about detrimental spiritual effects stemming from the new financial mechanisms. The work neither of canon lawyers nor of theologians, then, amounted to a systematic philosophical analysis of the temporal consequences of the emerging economic practices spreading throughout Europe.

Other important sources, however, testify to a less moralistic and more realistic medieval interest in economic questions. Many decades ago, historically minded economists such as Joseph A. Schumpeter and Raymond de Roover established the considerable debt owed by early modern economics to the medieval past.[7] This line of inquiry has been sustained by more recent investigations of the wide range of medieval contributions to economic thought.[8] The "commercial revolution" of the High Middle Ages stimulated authors, even before the rise of universities and scholastic discourse, to address the acquisition and use of wealth, especially in liquid form. This development was only fueled by the mid-thirteenth-century Latin translation and dissemination of Aristotle's *Nicomachean Ethics* and *Politics*, which contain extensive analyses of money, distributive justice, value, usury, and related matters. In the thirteenth and fourteenth centuries, moreover, the Franciscan-driven debate over evangelical perfection and Christ's ownership of property generated further heated discussion of basic economic issues.[9] Of course, much of the language used to express economic doctrines remained in embryonic form. Indeed, the term *oeconomicus* itself was understood throughout the Middle Ages to refer to the art of household management and domestic stewardship rather than to marketplace activities and relations.[10] Yet well before the transition from medieval to early modern Europe, it is certainly possible to speak of the presence of many ideas that were to become mainstays of later economic theory, including absolute private property, freedom of trade, natural rights, and the labor theory of value.[11]

More importantly, we identify the emergence of an approach to the study of economic questions distinct from those already addressed, which we might broadly term "political economy." By political economy, we mean, most generally, the investigation of the "wealth of nations" as a pursuit worthy in itself. Adam Smith (1723–1790) had defined political economy broadly in *The Wealth of Nations* as comprising "two distinct objects; first, to provide a plentiful revenue or subsistence for the people ... and secondly, to supply the state or commonwealth with a revenue sufficient for the publick services."[12] Political economy, thus understood, "is policy oriented and hence political, designed to make recommendations for governmental action in respect to economic matters. It is concerned with the functions of state and government, conceived of either positively or negatively, in contributing to the wealth of nations."[13] Political economy encompasses all issues raised by the relationship between the private accumulation of wealth and the public good, touching on topics ranging from taxation and government regulation of the economy to the promotion of economic opportunity within the marketplace. Its avowed purpose is to pinpoint policies most likely to encourage the greatest wealth among community members and to offer practical advice for its realization.

While the origins of political economy are conventionally associated with the late eighteenth-century work of the French physiocrats and with Adam Smith, scholars have increasingly traced the roots of the field backward into the seventeenth and even sixteenth centuries.[14] In this chapter, we propose that political economy was not the invention of the early modern period, but rather that the Middle Ages witnessed the emergence of economic theories of public life. We identify a discernible strain in late medieval thought that emphasized the worthiness of ensuring a satisfactory arrangement of economic goods primarily for the sake of meeting the physical, temporal needs of individuals of all classes and orders. On this terrain may be located the primordial wellspring of political economy and of an economic approach to politics. Such an assertion should not be entirely surprising. In conjunction with the commercial transformation of Europe, public systems of finance appeared and grew, which in turn generated a context for examining the key themes of political economy.

Medieval political economists, while they may have benefited from the writings of theologians and lawyers, were more oriented toward pragmatic issues related to how the public wealth within a community could be augmented or enhanced, and especially how governmental policies promoted or hampered this goal. They were mainly political reformers of economic life, not legal technicians or moral or religious critics. At times, however, the various attitudes to wealth could converge, making it potentially difficult to detect the political thrust standing behind the employment of theological or legal language. In support of these general claims, this chapter surveys the thought of an array of authors and texts (presented in chronological order), stretching from the middle of the twelfth century to the end of the fifteenth. Some of the thinkers examined are churchmen (John of Salisbury, William of Pagula), some are connected to government (Brunetto Latini, Christine de Pizan, John Fortescue), and some are scholastically trained academics (Marsiglio of Padua, Nicole Oresme). The discourses they employ are widely divergent and the conclusions they reach often discordant. Nevertheless, all of them may plausibly be counted among contributors to the development of political economy during the Middle Ages, inasmuch as they bring together elements of the interplay between economics and politics.

JOHN OF SALISBURY

John of Salisbury (1115/20–1180), an English churchman and philosopher, is best known for his *Policraticus* (completed in 1159), a philosophically pragmatic, wide-ranging meditation on the good life. Of importance here are the discussions contained therein of the body politic and of the government's role in promoting its economic well-being. While earlier classical and Christian authors had reviled the mechanical arts (i.e., the production of goods) as demeaning and incompatible with wisdom and civic virtue, the 1100s witnessed the appearance of a definite strand of philosophical thought that acknowledged the honorable and uplifting effects of human labor on both social order and individual character. In the *Policraticus*, John of Salisbury articulates this appreciation by integrating the mechanical arts into his famous metaphor of the body politic: He compares the ruler to the head, the senate (counselors) to the heart, the judges and proconsuls to the senses, the hands and arms to tax collectors and soldiers, the royal household servants to the flanks, the fiscal officers to the stomach and intestines, and notably, the peasants and artisans to the feet.[15] (Because John analogizes the clergy to the soul, their economic role is limited to encouraging the king to rule in accordance with Christian virtue.) John then details the duties associated with these functions, each of which is deemed necessary for a healthy political community. He explains how these tasks stand in a necessary relation to the whole, stressing the reciprocal character of the well-ordered body.

John grounds his inclusive deployment of the organic metaphor by reference to the natural order, wherein many parts constitute a whole. He thus embraces the participation of all social classes in the life of the community, including:

the feet who discharge the humbler offices ... the husbandmen, ... the many species of cloth-making and the mechanical arts, which work in wood, iron, bronze, and the different metals; also the menial occupations, and the manifold forms of making a livelihood ... all of which ... are yet in the highest degree useful and advantageous to the corporate whole of the community.[16]

For John, peasants and artisans must be accounted part of the political community because "it is they who raise, sustain, and move forward the weight of the entire body. Take away the support of the feet from the strongest body, and it cannot move forward by its own power."[17] Inasmuch as the practitioners of the mechanical arts confer dignity, not to mention material well-being, upon society, they deserve to be accorded a full place in it.

The naturalism that supports John's inclusive vision of community involves a profound normative dimension to the regulation of social order, including economic practice. Simply stated, nature has licensed the production and circulation of goods—the fruits of the mechanical arts—but only for the advantage of each and all of the members of the communal body. The pointed omission of the merchant class from John's ideal political body reflects his preference for a wholesale (direct) economy and his concomitant disdain for retail (indirect) enterprise (as well as for purely financial transactions).

At the same time, however, John accepts the realities of the monetized economy and of commerce that had taken root in Europe, particularly with regard to the role of government. He recognizes that the king's interests are best served when the property of subjects is protected and their wealth augmented. This conclusion derives from the communal and reciprocal structure of property holding posited in the *Policraticus*: neither king nor subjects are true owners of their goods in the modern sense, that is, as individual, private, and independent proprietors. The king is merely a steward who "will not therefore regard as his own the wealth of which he has custody for the account of others, nor will he treat as private the property of the fisc, which is acknowledged to be public."[18] Hence, the royal charge is to respect and defend the rights and liberties of his subjects, such that "each receives on the basis of his worth the resources of nature and the product of his own labor and industry."[19] When every person possesses what nature has determined that he deserves, according to his contribution to the whole, justice is done and the health and welfare of the body are preserved.

John also realizes that the king's position requires him to possess wealth adequate to his many vitally important tasks.[20] His income is to be cheerfully provided by his subjects to meet his needs, since the members of the body require the protection that he uniquely provides. In this regard, the principle of reciprocity ensures that the ruler who defends his realm will have the resources to hand to perform his proper functions. Just as the king is a fiscal steward, so too "the provincials are like tenants by *superfices*"—that is, their land is not their own, hence neither are the buildings and other improvements on it—"and when the advantage of the ruling power requires, they are not so much owners of their possessions as mere custodians. But if there is no such pressure of necessity, then the goods of the provincials are their own."[21] For the very reason, then, that the king must depend for his own income upon the economic health of his people, he must carefully guard against their maltreatment by magistrates. When the king fails to control his agents, he injures his own well-being by exhausting "the whole strength of the republic," as well as eventually succumbing to poverty and rendering himself hateful to his subjects.[22] Thus, in John's conception, the reciprocal nature of the political community entails a reciprocal economic duty of care and distribution.

BRUNETTO LATINI

Brunetto Latini's (1220–1294) *Li Livres dou Tresor* (*The Book of the Treasure*), probably completed *circa* 1265, is a long and eclectic work that was widely read and adapted throughout the Middle Ages. Knitted together out of a diverse array of source materials, the topics covered include speculative wisdom, religion, human history and the natural world, ethics, and, most important for present concerns, the art of government. Latini himself was a Florentine civil servant who was driven to exile in France amid the cutthroat conflicts of the era. Given his background, Latini's effusive praise for public affairs is perhaps not so surprising: "Politics ... without doubt is the highest wisdom and most noble profession that there is among men, for it teaches us to govern others ... according to reason and justice."[23] The "art of government" holds this special and vaunted place because, Latini contends, the main goal of politics must be to support and promote the peaceful flourishing of the disparate arts and trades that exist within a community. In Latini's view, the diversity of human arts constitutes a crucial foundation for communal life.[24] He observes that both the natural inclination of men toward association and the common weal of citizens in a community require the production and exchange of myriad goods that aid in the material well-being of all. "If a man needs something another person has, he receives it and gives him his reward and his payment according to the quality of the thing," Latini insists.[25]

Latini's paradigm of social order is consequently a fully functioning free and open market in which commercial activity facilitates the material benefit of all. Notice in this connection the extent to which he valorizes occupations that had customarily been reviled as demeaning, such as manual laborers ("mechanics") and merchants. The rights of citizenship accrue by virtue of the contributions made to the physical improvement of the community.[26] The universal desire for profit cements the communal order: "There is a common thing that is loved, through which they arrange and confirm their business, and that is gold and silver."[27] Seeking one's self-interest is neither inherently antithetical to citizenship for Latini, nor is it necessarily destructive of the public welfare. Indeed, he appears to define the communal advantage at least partially in terms of expanding personal gain.

Yet Latini is by no means unmindful of the potentially deleterious effects of the pursuit of private advantage. He asserts that "if to obtain gain we are willing to despoil and use force against another, it follows that the company of men, which is according to nature, is dissolved."[28] The greatest threat to communal order, somewhat ironically, stems from the very diversity of human capacities that makes civic life necessary and profitable. Since human beings possess divergent interests and pursue them in ways that may come into conflict, the great benefit that accrues to them when they share and cooperate always remains under threat. Latini accordingly stresses the need for a principle of justice to mediate between individuals who, left to their own devices, would injure one another. Without the mediating force of justice in economic intercourse, individuals who stand to profit from mutual service may nevertheless be tempted to cheat, steal, or otherwise take advantage of others and thus to destroy the bonds of social and political community.

Latini locates one source of justice, broadly speaking, in the self-regulatory functioning of the market itself, by means of the balancing that he claims is performed by the medium of money.[29] He acknowledges, however, that commercial intercourse must be supplemented by a statutory system enforced by an efficient executor.[30] The origin of government, as of money, stems primarily from abuse on the part of otherwise unregulated proprietors, those who, motivated by "evil desires," committed "evil deeds which went unpunished," as a consequence of which "a governor was chosen for the people with several duties."[31] Principal among a magistrate's duties is to "watch over the common good, ... maintain both outsiders and insiders, and ... respect the property and persons of all people in such a way that justice would not decrease in our city."[32] Thus, the justice of a magistrate's administration coordinates directly with the prosperity of the civic body.[33]

In addition to the government's law enforcement function, the *Tresor* enumerates various economic management duties of public officials that stem from the government's direct effects on the productive and commercial condition of the populace. Not only must the ruler exercise care that the public treasury is not squandered,[34] as chief financial officer, he is broadly charged with ensuring maintenance of "the rights of the commune, the taxes, jurisdictions, lordships, castles, cities, houses, courts, officials, public squares, highways, roads ... in such a way that the honor and profit of the city are not diminished, but rather they should increase and grow better in time."[35] This equation of just government with sound fiscal management runs throughout Latini's advice about the responsibilities of rulership. Toward this end, Latini offers numerous quite specific suggestions concerning communal facilities, infrastructure, and taxation.[36] The tools of public administration were beginning to emerge within the pages of medieval books advising rulers.

MARSIGLIO OF PADUA

Completed in 1324, the *Defensor pacis* (*Defender of Peace*) composed by Marsiglio (or Marsilius) of Padua (1275/80–1342/3) soon became one of the most incendiary and condemned texts of its age, primarily for its concerted attack on the powers claimed on behalf of the pope. Prefacing this controversial longer portion ("Dictio II") of the treatise is a much shorter discourse on the origins and nature of civil government. In some ways, Marsiglio's theory resembles that of Latini, though the former derived his position from a quite different premise. Marsiglio contends that human beings are invariably driven to realize their own good: "Everyone is prone to pursue one's own advantage and to avoid what is disadvantageous."[37] Marsiglio judges this to be a natural condition, rather than a vice, of temporal life, which follows directly from the principle of self-preservation. Since we are enjoined by nature to preserve our material existence, Marsiglio insists that "no one knowingly harms or wills injustice to oneself."[38] There is no moral content to the postulation of self-interest; men are not inherently vicious or evil, merely driven by the natural instinct to survive.

If humans lived in isolation and their activities were entirely self-directed, it would be unnecessary to set limits on behavior, since each person is best qualified to determine what is required for self-preservation. But Marsiglio recognizes that the self-interest of individuals is achieved most fully and "naturally" under conditions of human cooperation in the context of an ordered and organized community. Marsiglio holds that "human beings came together in the civil community in order to pursue advantage and a sufficient life and to avoid the opposite."[39] What he terms the "perfected community" emerges along with the differentiation of the functions (defined by the various arts created by humankind) necessary for a materially sufficient existence.[40] "Yet since these arts cannot be exercised except by a large number of people through their association with one another," he remarks, "it was necessary for human beings to assemble together to obtain advantage from them and to avoid disadvantage."[41] Social engagement thus arises naturally from the human imperative to assure one's own survival.

Marsiglio's perfected community, based on differentiation of function, is nothing short of a fully developed commercial society. Such a "perfected" civil association requires "the mutual association of citizens, their intercommunication of their functions with one another, their mutual aid and assistance and, in general, the power, unimpeded from without, of exercising their particular and common functions, and also the participation in common benefits and burdens according to the measure appropriate to each."[42] Marsiglio specifies these functions in terms of the occupations necessary to maintain the community's physical well-being: farmers, merchants, craftsmen, and warriors.[43] All of these occupations are necessary, and none are to be denigrated. Citizenship is consequently conferred on a strictly functional basis, judged according to the usefulness of various activities for meeting material needs. What is especially distinctive of such a civil society is that each person within it may profit individually, while all benefit together, except that "disputes and quarrels" unregulated by "a norm of justice" may arise.[44] Marsiglio fears that, without the existence of some authority to uphold the peace according to a fair standard of behavior, the community will crumble.

Marsiglio proposes an ingenious solution to bridge the potential conflict between individual and communal advantage. First, all whose interests are served or affected by a community must be conceded full membership in it and must consent to the conditions of association (i.e., law and rulership). Second, having so consented, all such citizens are absolutely bound to obey the law and the determinations made by rulers in accordance with it. The *Defensor pacis* holds that the legitimacy of both laws and rulers depends wholly upon their "voluntary" character, that is, the extent to which those citizens subject to their jurisdiction have publicly and overtly consented to their authority.[45] This involves for Marsiglio an extensive privilege on the part of each individual citizen to examine prospective laws and rulers. In the *Defensor pacis*, he details a method to express such approval or disapproval. "The common utility of all is better noticed by the whole community because no one knowingly harms himself," he observes. "Anyone can look to see whether a proposed law leans toward the advantage of one or a few citizens more than the rest of the community and can protest loudly in opposition."[46] By aggregating these individual determinations, Marsiglio provides a plausible solution to the problem of acknowledging a common interest that does not violate the fundamental principle of self-interest.[47] Thus, the government and legal system will necessarily always serve to bolster the commercially based system of exchange required for people to live a "sufficient life."

WILLIAM OF PAGULA

By the beginning of the fourteenth century, some theorists showed awareness of the socioeconomic importance of the peasant class and of the miserable conditions of these impoverished country dwellers. One such figure was William of Pagula (*c.* 1290–1332), an Oxford-trained parish vicar. In two closely related treatises, probably composed in 1331/2, William wrote a scathing first-person missive to English King Edward III. Known jointly by the title *Speculum regis Edwardi III* (*The Mirror of King Edward III*), these texts seek to demonstrate the ruinous consequences of royal policies for the most destitute of the king's subjects. The primary target of William's wrath is the practice of purveyance, the alleged royal prerogative to provide for his household and troops when touring the realm by confiscating local goods or by purchasing them at a fixed, non-negotiable price.

In the course of developing his critique of the crown's disregard for the economic depredations of the English peasantry, William demonstrates a refined appreciation of the relevance of economic policies to public administration. In particular, while upholding the primacy of the marketplace in determining price and value, William recurrently draws attention to the interdependence between royal fiscal policies and the economic well-being of private producers. To defend the proposition that the royal practice of purveyance constitutes robbery, William identifies volition as central to the sale of goods. He begins with the idea, largely uncontroversial at the time, that each person "is lord of his things, so that nothing [may be] seized from his goods against his will."[48] "Lordship" connotes an exclusive realm of power over one's property with which no other individual may rightfully interfere. "In this world," William declares, "men ought to be free to do for themselves and theirs, according to their will."[49] Robbery is an infringement of this basic liberty, since lordship entails the freedom to do as one wishes with what one legitimately possesses. For anyone (even the king) to violate this constitutes an injustice.[50] William then extends this doctrine to include compulsory exchanges of goods for money. Historically, the customary "privilege" of purveyance usually permitted the king's officials to buy whatever goods they required at a fixed rate. William argues that such mandatory or enforced sales constitute a form of extortion or theft, inasmuch as they violate the property owner's right either to set a price or to refrain from selling altogether. Because the consent entailed by one's lordship over an object is absolute and exclusive, William defines purveyance practices as robbery, pure and simple.[51]

William carefully documents the direct economic impact of royal purveyance upon the realm. One major effect of these exactions is interference with the laborers' cultivation of their own lands. This occurs in two ways. First, the confiscation of victuals cuts into supplies required for planting future harvests. As William explains, "Many poor people will not have what they need to sow their fields."[52] As a result, arable land goes fallow. Second, enforced labor contracts—for little or no payment—prevent peasants from working their own lands. Recounting his own observations, William reports the impact of the failure of royal officials to provide compensation: "On account of this diabolical deed, the lands of the poor were not cultivated, not planted, and the poor did not have any [surplus] goods by which they were able to sustain burdens of this sort."[53] Purveyance strains rural resources to the point at which agricultural production begins to decline. William recounts how royal exactions are directly to blame for subjects losing the land on which they depend for their very livelihood, resulting in their penury and eventual starvation.[54] When the king's indifference to the consequences of his servants' actions results in peasant deaths, Edward III stands accused of the "murder" of his people.[55] William describes the king's conduct as, in effect, "making war" on the inhabitants of his own realm.[56]

A ruler who demands goods and services with little or no payment from already impoverished subjects is, to William's mind, wholly self-defeating. The *Speculum regis Edwardi III* advises its addressee that, should he persist in his oppressive policies, "you will not be king in your land, nor will you find food and drink and other things necessary for you."[57] William warns of a twofold threat to the king: He will encounter political resistance to his authority as well as circumvention of his economic demands. Rural denizens achieve the latter mainly by stealth. When villagers hear of the approach of the royal entourage, "at once on account of fear they hide fowls, roosters and other goods, or they get rid of them, or they consume them by eating and drinking, lest they lose them upon your arrival."[58] The second danger, rural social unrest and insurrection, should concern the king to an even greater extent. William reminds Edward III that "the English people made you king" and that he should "be like one of them."[59] William's warning is overt and palpable: The continuation of purveyance presages "many evils [that] may happen to you and your kingdom," as a result of which the king and his officials "will perish."[60] The *Speculum regis Edwardi III* likens the position of the unloved king to that of a head which cannot lead its own body: "Your people ... are not of one mind with you, although they seem to be of one body with you; and indeed, if they had a leader, they would rise up against you, just as they did against your father [Edward II, who was deposed]."[61] By failing to recognize the interdependency of governor and governed, Edward III opens the door to the premature end of his own reign. He ignores the potential of the highly negative impact of political policies on economic conditions at his own peril.

NICOLE ORESME

Among the earliest medieval tracts to concentrate explicitly on a specific economic topic was a work titled *Tractatus de origine et natura, jure et mutationibus monetarum*, better known as *De moneta* (*On Money*), composed in the late 1350s by Nicole Oresme (1320/5–1382), a University of Paris-trained philosopher, theologian, and churchman who was closely associated with the French royal court. Oresme probably wrote this treatise in the context of an ongoing debate concerning the further debasement of the French coinage, a procedure from which the crown had profited for many years. *De moneta* made a powerful case in favor of the stabilization of the value of money over the royal temptation to raise revenue through reminting or coin clipping. Yet *De moneta* should not be read simply as a contribution to technical economics. Rather, Oresme expressly states that the work has two purposes: to identify the underlying political nature of the problem of currency manipulation, and to advise his countrymen in a pragmatic fashion about a matter of public policy. His specialized economic analysis is prefatory to his effort to bring economic concerns to bear on the duties of rulers and the needs of their subjects.

Central to this project is Oresme's contention that money "is well-suited for intercourse among a large number of human beings and the use of it is good in itself."[62] Economic enterprise makes key contributions to the public welfare, which is the intended purpose of exchange relations. Since, for Oresme, trade and commerce impact so markedly on the common good, he insists that the enabling medium of money must be the property of the community rather than of the ruler. Oresme stresses this principle throughout *De moneta*. Although the ruler is assigned responsibility for the actual minting and regulating of the money supply, he does so as an executive agent of the community, deputed to realize the public good of sound currency and equitable exchange. The dominant theme of Oresme's treatise is the communal ownership, and thus ultimate control, of money. From this precept follows the advice of *De moneta* about the debasement of coinage as a political phenomenon. Since the community requires money to engage in a full range of economic activities, and hence to promote the good of its individual members, the very idea that a ruler exerts private control over coinage is excluded from the start. As a result, the crown is strictly prohibited from manipulating the coinage to profit itself or its intimates.

Implicit in the ascription of money's ownership to the community is an economic conception of the common good itself. Oresme employs the traditional distinction between "true kingship" and "tyranny" in explicating the difference between well-ordered and evil government.[63] Unlike his predecessors, Oresme's examples of just and unjust rule are invariably couched in terms of the economic impact of a government's actions. In explaining why manipulation of the value of currency by a ruler is unjust, he draws an analogy to political interference in agricultural markets: "It would be like fixing a price for all the grain in his kingdom, buying it, and selling it again at a higher price. Everyone can clearly see that this would be an unjust exaction and indeed tyranny."[64] The value of the economic goods within a community can only be established in the first instance by voluntary exchanges among individuals. Tyranny thus occurs when legitimate economic choices are countermanded for the self-interest of those who hold political power. By contrast, good government or kingship has a decidedly economic overtone: the king reigns, one might say, not to make people "better" in a moral sense, but instead to make them "better off." Consequently, royal judgments about public policy ought to rest on determinations about the economic welfare of the community. The government that supports and enhances the material advantage of subjects is counted by Oresme as good.

Oresme highlights the fact that currency debasement is nonconsensual and therefore constitutes an act of force committed by the ruler upon the community. The volitional standard, one of the hallmarks of just economic exchange, disappears in the manipulation of currency, rendering the king-community relation an unequal and coercive one. The community becomes instead "enslaved" economically to the private interest of its government, as well as impoverished to the extent that "the amount of the ruler's profit is necessarily the same as the community's loss."[65] Debasement precipitates the economic decline of the republic in a number of ways, which Oresme describes in careful detail, based on his observations of events that "have lately been seen to occur in the kingdom of France."[66] First, an unstable currency is ruinous for all manner of trade. Imports cease, since "merchants *ceteris paribus* prefer to travel to those locales in which they may obtain good and certain money." In similar fashion, "the business of internal commerce in such a kingdom is disturbed and impeded by such changes" of currency, while fixed incomes are thrown into flux and "cannot be properly and justly valuated and taxed." Moreover, debased currency destroys the system of credit upon which commercial activity relies. In sum, inasmuch as "merchants and everything else mentioned are either necessary or extremely useful to human nature," alterations of coinage "are prejudicial and harmful to the whole civil community."[67] Monetary manipulation has a debilitating effect upon the good order of the community. Oresme even darkly hints that the ruler who introduces the many evils associated with monetary manipulation endangers his dynastic hold on the kingdom. Referring explicitly to the situation in his own nation, Oresme observes that the "free hearts of Frenchmen" will not stand to have economic slavery thrust upon them; and the French royal house, "bereft of its ancient virtue, will without doubt forfeit the kingdom."[68] Debasement is ultimately no less dangerous to the king than to his subjects.

CHRISTINE DE PIZAN

Christine de Pizan (1364–*c.* 1430), a French poet-author and Valois court intimate, should be counted among the most prolific political authors in medieval Europe. Of her nine such treatises, the best known are *Le Livre de la Cité des Dames* (*The Book of the City of Ladies*), *Le Livre des Trois Vertus* (*The Book of the Three Virtues*), and *Le Livre de Corps de Policie* (*The Book of the Body Politic*), all composed in the middle of the first decade of the fifteenth century. Writing from the self-identified perspective of a non-noble émigré widow who had become learned in French-language as well as (probably) Latin texts, she demonstrates considerable acquaintance with the intellectual traditions of her time.[69] Christine confidently critiques contemporary mores and practices and formulates pragmatic advice for a range of situations and persons. Her writings display, in particular, both sensitivity to the financial pressures facing Europe's monarchic governments and deep concern for the needs of the larger populace, including women, city dwellers, and the poor. The fulcrum on which she balanced these potentially competing interests is her insistence on an inescapably reciprocal relationship between the French people and the royal regime.

Christine approached the social complexity that characterized the late medieval landscape from the conventional model of the organic metaphor. As had some of her predecessors, Christine's body politic incorporated an inclusive, reciprocal, and interdependent conception of community:

> Just as the human body is not whole, but defective and deformed, when it lacks any of its members, so the body politic cannot be perfect, whole, or healthy if all the estates of which we speak are not well joined and united together. Thus, they can aid and help each other, each exercising its own office, which diverse offices ought to serve only for the conservation of the whole community, just as [with] the members of the body.[70]

For Christine, communal order ensues when the health of the entire public unit is preserved through the mutual coordination of the tasks necessary for its existence.[71] To despise any of the members, or to reduce any to a state of servitude, constitutes an attack on the well-being of the whole.

Christine extends medieval precedents by imputing to the body politic a noticeably secular orientation. Unlike her source, John of Salisbury's *Policraticus* (1159), the clergy in Christine's model are not the body's "soul," but simply one of the three branches of the common people.[72] Thus, for example, Christine expects the king, when necessary, to correct the errant "prelate, priest, or cleric."[73] Because Christine conceives of the king as ordainer and regulator of *all* estates within the realm, the church does not exercise supremacy over the temporal sphere. The overtly secular bearing of Christine's body politic informs her discussion of economic issues. Christine's insistence on the importance of all members' physical well-being and material improvement motivates her mandate that the ruler must orient his policies toward "increas[ing] and multiply[ing] the virtue, strength, power, and *wealth* of his country."[74] This explicit articulation of an economic goal as among government's central aims is unique. Accordingly, Christine promotes the general societal acquisition and accumulation of wealth—although not conspicuous consumption—as a worthy pursuit, and she recognizes government's crucial role in its achievement.

Christine's strikingly economic conception of community and governance is especially evident in the detailed attention she pays to the lives of merchants, artisans, and laborers, as well as to their relations with the king. Not only does Christine argue that men of commerce are not to be disdained but also she insists that without "the merchant class ... neither the estate of kings and princes nor even the polities of cities and countries could exist. ... By the[ir] industry ... all kinds of people are provided for without having to make everything themselves."[75] A nation can only reap the rewards of increased labor efficiencies when there is "trade and an abundance of merchants."[76] In an archetypical example of organic reciprocity, Christine holds that all classes benefit when commercial society is encouraged to flourish.

Christine likewise praises craftsmen and peasants, without whose labor "the republic ... could not sustain itself."[77] Because the goods produced and activities performed by such workers are necessary for meeting quotidian human needs, their contribution must be accorded value. While judgments may be made about how well individuals perform in their diverse offices, no office which contributes to the community's material welfare may be demeaned or disdained. The prince, therefore, must maintain and enhance the economic condition of the realm, oversee the efficient coordination of all necessary tasks, and protect against financial force and fraud. This central duty entails that the ruler first be familiar with the myriad activities necessary to the realm and "ought to hear sometimes about the common people, laborers, and merchants, how they make their profit."[78] Thus will the prince, fully appreciating the contributions of the lower orders, govern knowledgeably and competently.

Most importantly, the king must understand how his own policies impact the economic conditions of his realm. Poorly compensated soldiers, Christine explains, "pillage and despoil the country," exacerbating the economic hardships of the rural poor, whereas well-paid troops bolster the rural economy by purchasing "everything that they needed economically and plentifully."[79] Similarly, royal taxation policies ought to be "reasonable," to affect rich and poor equitably, and to not "gnaw ... poor commoners ... to the bone."[80] Christine's conclusion that wise "princes would rather be poor in a rich country, than to be rich and have plenty in a poor country" is less a moral principle and more an economic doctrine that naturally follows from an organic conception of communal interdependence.[81]

Another noteworthy element of Christine's thought is her inclusion of women in the realm's economic and sociopolitical life. Her distinctive adaptation of Cicero's account of social origination (found in his De inventione I.1–3) provides the justification for women's visibility in Christine's body politic. In her telling, Ceres and Isis "taught [the people] to build cities and towns,"[82] within which women developed most of the arts and civilized forms of labor, including weaving, olive oil extraction, cart construction, metal working, cultivation, tool-making, and gardening.[83] Without women's innovations and contributions, Christine asserts, humanity would have remained in a "bestial" state. Those who believe that mankind would be better off in this primitive condition blaspheme against the God-given skills and abilities that Ceres and Isis first discovered.

Moreover, women of all estates, Christine maintains, have the capabilities necessary (perhaps even uniquely) to contribute to the tasks associated with the maintenance of earthly well-being. While Christine surely knew Aristotle's argument, a mainstay of medieval political literature, for the exclusion of women from public life, she challenged this claim directly, envisioning, for example, the princess as a sort of ombudsperson.[84] Construed in organic terms, the princess furthers bodily intercommunication by serving as a mediating force between king and populace.[85] Toward this end, she must occasionally meet with burghers, merchants, and artisans to facilitate "love and good will," thereby strengthening public order and unity. Christine also recognizes that women of the commercial and laboring classes face special burdens. She warns merchants' wives, for example, to "avoid ostentation" in dress, as such conspicuous display "can cause new taxes for their husbands."[86] Christine's close attention to the complex intersections of gender and social class manifests in pragmatic counsel to women of various stations, aimed at sustaining a harmonious and cooperative body politic. Just as merchants, artisans, and the poor each have a legitimate and important role within Christine's organic system, so too are women integral at all levels.

SIR JOHN FORTESCUE

The fifteenth-century English jurist and legal theorist Sir John Fortescue (*c.* 1394–1479) is something of an enigma in the history of Western political thought: He has been viewed both as a culmination of medieval trends and as a forerunner of modern developments. In a series of legal-political treatises composed in the 1460s and 1470s, Fortescue used as his intellectual framework two categories of constitutional regime he appropriated from scholasticism: *dominium regale* (royal lordship, or the rule of a single man according to his own will) and *dominium politicum* (political lordship, namely, a mixed constitution based on consensual law and the sharing of power—in sum, a republic). Fortescue's innovation was a proposed synthesis of these systems into a single, superior, and all-embracing form of government, namely, *dominium regale et politicum*. This type of hybrid regime, in Fortescue's view, is no mere theoretical construct; rather, it is embodied by the rule of the English monarchy. In his two major works, *De laudibus legum Anglie* (*In Praise of the Laws of England*) (1468–1471) and *The Governance of England* (1471), Fortescue puts forth a detailed argument for the superiority of *dominium regale et politicum*. He emphasizes throughout that there are clear and tangible economic benefits for those who are governed by a mixed political and royal system.

Fortescue posits a direct connection between regime type and the physical welfare of the people. In *The Governance of England*, he demonstrates the failings of royal, as contrasted with royal and political, government by comparing the circumstances of France with those of England. Because the French royal regime taxes subjects arbitrarily and heavily, its populace lives "in the most extreme poverty and misery, and yet they dwell in one of the most fertile realms of the world."[87] After describing in great detail the abysmal diet, clothing, and working conditions of the French people, Fortescue lays the blame squarely on the royal system of rule through which France is governed.[88] Just as the purely royal king causes such poverty, so he must constantly be on his guard, lest his subjects muster the courage to rise up and oppose him, contributing to the general instability of the realm.[89]

The contrast Fortescue offers of England, with its "mixed" royal and political system, is striking:

> This land is ruled under a better law; and therefore the people are not in such penury, nor thereby hurt in their persons, but they are wealthy and have all things necessary to the sustenance of nature. Wherefore, they are mighty and able to resist the adversaries of this realm ... Lo, this is the fruit of "political and royal law," under which we live.[90]

The major reason for this, says Fortescue, is that the English king is restrained in his ability to lay claim to the goods of subjects, should he ever desire to do so. The royal and political ruler takes it as integral to his office not to drain income away from his subjects into his own coffers, but to enact policies that enhance the wealth of the entire nation. "It is the king's honor," Fortescue remarks, "and also his duty, to make his realm rich; and it is a dishonor when he has but a poor realm. Yet it would be a much greater dishonor, if he found his realm rich, and then made it poor."[91] In turn, the material satisfaction enjoyed by subjects that arises from royal and political rule acts as an assurance of public order. Inhabitants who enjoy physical well-being are, in Fortescue's estimation, more willing and able to fight for their realm; they are less likely to engage in rebellious and seditious activities; and they possess the resources, not to mention the goodwill, to subsidize the government in times of particular need. Fortescue's view, in short, seems to be that the public bearing of the governed is strictly determined by the measurable impact of government upon their private benefit: if they are content with their physical lot, they will gladly subject themselves to the king and will perform their roles; but, if their ruler adopts policies that impoverish them, they will express their displeasure directly and violently. "The greatest safety, truly, and also the most honor that may come to the king is that his realm should be rich in every estate," Fortescue observes.[92]

The material benefits accruing to those who submit to *dominium regale et politicum* are also underscored by Fortescue in *De laudibus legum Anglie*. Again, he stresses the economic misery that results from the royal regime of France. By contrast, the English king, who rules royally and politically, can in no way impose "tallages, subsides, or any other burdens whatsoever on his subjects, nor change their laws, nor make new ones, without the concession and assent of his whole realm expressed in his parliament."[93] Thus, the English people harvest the fruits of the earth in all their abundance, without fear of confiscation. Because it is by their own consent that subjects of a royal and political king are ruled, they cannot be involuntarily denied their goods and abused in their persons. On Fortescue's account, the immediate result of such government renders England a sort of earthly Garden of Paradise.[94] As in *The Governance of England*, the criteria employed by Fortescue to judge the impact of regime type on citizens are fundamentally economic and physical. Individuals are satisfied to leave the conduct of the daily affairs of government to the king and his ministers, so long as their material well-being is not imperiled. In turn, as private persons, they are encouraged (indeed, expected) to contribute to the public good by seeking their personal advantage in economic activity. Thus, a nation that possesses large numbers of merchants engaging in commerce is one, Fortescue insists, that has been truly blessed by God.[95]

CHAPTER FIVE

Nature

KELLIE ROBERTSON

When we think of nature today, we often imagine something outside of ourselves: the National Park on the map, the snowy peak in Ansel Adams's photograph, the sequoia, or the condor. Nature in the medieval Latin West, on the contrary, was imagined as something both inside and outside of the human being: our "nature" was an inherent inclination connecting us with all other earthly creatures and, ultimately, the entire spiritual world. Today, nature is the thing outside of us, a place that we venture out into. By contrast, medieval nature was both "out there" and "in here" simultaneously. If medieval people could somehow have encountered the phrase "human nature," they would have known immediately that the adjective was redundant.

Both then and now, nature is often defined by its opposite. In modern society, the opposite of nature can be many things, from nurture to culture to civilization. The Middle Ages also defined nature oppositionally. For Aristotle and his medieval commentators, the opposite of nature was "art," a category that included anything made by human hands. For the intellectual historian Hans Blumenberg, this distinction became fundamental in Western thought, one consequence being that the human was always seen to operate at a distance from the natural world and to engage with it only through imitation.[1]

Yet the medieval story of nature is more complicated than Blumenberg suggests. Medieval Latin writers inherited several classical views of nature, some of them in competition. To varying degrees, classical writers saw moral values reflected or contained within nature; the discovery of these values was one of the central goals of medieval theology as well as the physical and biological sciences, referred to collectively as "natural philosophy." Several prominent strands of thinking about nature can be traced across the period: the encyclopedic, the Platonic, and the Aristotelian. While these were interwoven to some extent, this chapter begins by identifying the primary features of each strand as a road map for the changes that would play out among competing ideas of nature and the principles that guided them. It then goes on to consider the cultural pressures that formed medieval views of nature and the controversies that resulted. How much power did nature possess? What was the relation between the natural and the divine? Why did medieval writers, both scientists and poets, so frequently personify nature's powers? The last section turns to the question that medieval writers frequently asked about nature's governance. To what extent was the human understood to be continuous with, or exempt from, the natural order?

NATURAL HISTORY AND THE ENCYCLOPEDIC LEGACY

The Latin encyclopedists Pliny and Isidore of Seville were known continuously and cited frequently by medieval popular and learned writers. For these writers, nature was both useful and exemplary insofar as it could benefit mankind and provide models for "natural" human behavior. Pliny's *Natural History* (*Historia naturalis*; *c.* 79) is a sprawling work that ennumerates the categories of earthly creatures (man, animals, plants, minerals, and metals) as well as the disciplines of astronomy, geography, medicine, and art. This encyclopedia argues that the nonhuman world is put here for human use: elephants are quickly tamed by barley juice and can serve for ferrying armed soldiers in war; plants such as monkshood, hellebore, and rue can be boiled to strengthen the heart; cinnabar can be mined for pigment. Pliny found in nature an affirmation of the cultural values prized in imperial Rome: simplicity, balance, and moderation as opposed to gluttony, greed, and vanity.[2] For Pliny, natural history was not just an objective enumeration of the contents of the visible world; it was a moral pageant meant to edify an audience that would learn from its figurative lessons (Figure 5.1).

FIGURE 5.1 Miniature showing Pliny in his study surveying a landscape with animals, rivers, the sea, sun and moon, *c.* 1457–1458, British Library, Harley MS 2677, fol. 1. © Courtesy of the British Library.

Isidore of Seville followed Pliny in believing that making lists and compiling facts were useful tools for revealing the secrets of nature. His encyclopedic works *On the Nature of Things* (*De natura rerum*; *c.* 612) and the *Etymologies* (*Etymologiarum libri XX*; *c.* 621) add another layer of Christian providentialism to Pliny's armature of cosmic description, a combination regularly reproduced in medieval writings. The *Etymologies* assume that, to know things fully, one must know the history of the words used to refer to them. Etymological knowledge connects our ideas about things to an external reality because words gloss the origin of things. According to Isidore, "Nature (*natura*) is so called because it causes something to be born, for it has the power of engendering and creating. Some people say that this is God, by whom all things have been created and exist."[3] Isidore's concept of generation equivocates on the distinction between divine and natural powers, declining to weigh in on whether these powers are different in kind or simply in extent. Given the scope and ambition of Isidore's encyclopedic works, it is unsurprising that they were immediately popular across Europe well into the Renaissance.

Pliny and Isidore imagined nature to be a source of wonder as well as a confirmation of the divine order at work. Isidore in particular continually draws his reader's attention to how the natural world can be understood in accordance with the Bible, and he intended that his *Etymologies* be used in pastoral and exegetical work.[4] Both writers freely passed along stories of *mirabilia*. Pliny tells of a woman who gave birth to four sets of quintuplets as well as another who gave birth to an elephant; alongside these obstetric wonders, he claims to have seen an Egyptian hippocentaur preserved in honey.[5] Wonder was the appropriate response when nature's mechanisms were not immediately apparent. Awe encourages the observer to meditate on the unknowability of the divine will, much as Augustine had done when he saw divine design written in the book of nature.[6] For encyclopedic writers, such stories attested to the inexhaustible diversity of divine creative power, even as they encouraged readers to investigate further the order behind the design in which such anomalies could exist.[7] In this way, natural histories stoked amazement and inspired debate over the limits of human comprehension.

The encyclopedic models of nature found in Pliny and Isidore were to remain popular throughout the Middle Ages, drawn upon for their vivid descriptions and for their trove of natural examples that lent themselves to moralization. This vision gets translated into the vernacular by later medieval writers, including the Florentine scholar and statesman Brunetto Latini (*c.* 1220–1294). Latini's encyclopedic project includes both a short Italian poem, the *Tesoretto* (or "Little Treasure"), and a much longer French prose work, *Li Livres dou Tresor* (*The Book of the Treasure*), both written in the 1260s and premised on the idea that true wealth consists in the possession of wisdom. Drawing on previous Latin natural histories, these works demonstrate how knowing nature provides a model for living in human society.[8] The *Tesoretto* opens with the author's exile from Florence due to civic factionalism; Lady Nature appears to console him and to show him the orders of creation. A fourteenth-century manuscript of the *Tesoretto* includes a drawing depicting the narrator on the left addressing a personified Lady Nature on the right, her head surrounded by stars and the sun and moon. Between them stands the entire order of creation, including flowers, fish, crabs, snakes, grasshoppers, snails, rabbits, lions, and even a unicorn.[9] Significantly, the animal kingdom also includes a pair of humans, implying that mankind falls under her governance and that knowledge of the natural order benefits the project of creating a harmonious civil society. Latini's vernacular works participated in an explosion of encyclopedic writing that marked the thirteenth century, a time when, as Mary Franklin-Brown observes, such works served as miniature libraries that became "'heterotopias' of knowledge—that is, spaces where many possible ways of knowing are juxtaposed."[10]

TRANSCENDENT NATURE: MEDIEVAL PLATONISM

If medieval writers looked to the encyclopedic nature of Pliny and Isidore as a source of utility and wonder, they turned to Plato and Aristotle to understand nature's relation to man and to the divine. Unlike Pliny and Isidore, these ancient Greek writers gained popularity in Western Europe only with the translation of the majority of their works into Latin over the course of the medieval period. The Platonic and Aristotelian models would have the most significant impact on medieval popular and learned writers, but their respective influences were neither synchronous nor geographically uniform. Instead, their influence appears in successive waves across Europe.

The historian M.-D. Chenu famously assigned the "birth of nature" to the twelfth century, a time when philosophers and theologians took a new interest in the material world and man's place in the cosmological order.[11] While critics debate the extent and character of this "discovery,"[12] it is clear that twelfth-century natural philosophy elaborated a new physics within the Platonic framework, focusing particularly on Plato's *Timaeus*.[13] In the *Timaeus*, physical nature is purposive and divinely ordained. Observing this orderly natural world, Plato asks: why is the cosmos so beautiful and how did it get that way? For Plato, this beautifully rational order has been created by an "artisan-god"—the Demiurge—who shapes all earthly and celestial creatures out of primal matter into the likenesses of eternal and unchanging forms. The matter of the cosmos is made up of the four elements—fire, air, water, and earth—elements that are harnessed together by the artisan-god to serve as the building blocks of all nature, from the stars to the human body. For Plato's artisan-god, the plan (form) exists prior to the creation of any specific entities (matter). The Platonic act of creation can therefore best be described as "mind imposing itself on reluctant matter."[14] On this account, the world is divided into two realms: the noumenal (the superior realm of immaterial forms and ideas that serve as patterns for the visible world below) and the phenomenal (the inferior realm of matter made up of the "copies" apparent to sensory perception). As in the famous example of Plato's cave, the phenomenal world that we see around us consists of the mere shadows of the ideal forms that reside in a noumenal dimension. The earthly things that surround us exist at a distinct distance from the immaterial models from which they are copied. Counterintuitively, the phenomenal world is therefore less "real" than the noumenal world, since truth is located in the noumenal forms above, while the phenomenal world below is a necessarily degraded imitation of that truth. This model of nature can be termed a "transcendent" one to the extent that the active engine for reality exists above rather than here below. This split is reproduced in the duality of human nature, divided as it is between a physical element (body/matter) and a spiritual one (soul/form). While humans combine the phenomenal and the noumenal, the mind is limited by its association with the material body. Plato and his medieval followers would go so far as to argue that the soul was trapped in the prison house of the body. The role of nature in this scheme is necessarily circumscribed, since ethical and moral authority do not inhere in nature per se. For this reason, Plato is most concerned with establishing the relation of man to cosmos (its mathematical, aesthetic, and spiritual consonances) rather than with the rest of the material world (the animals, plants, and rocks). The latter is not a primary or even secondary source of interest, since it occupies the status of a mere vestige of a higher truth located elsewhere.

While this Platonic view had been available to Western scholars through early Latin translations, its influence rose to particular prominence in the twelfth-century cathedral school at Chartres, where scholars such as William of Conches elaborated these doctrines in commentaries on the *Timaeus* as well as Neoplatonic works.[15] The representation of the cosmos that emerged from these commentaries was elaborated by twelfth-century allegorical writers such as Bernard Silvestris, who believed that divine truth could be read from the Book of Nature only with difficulty, since divine mysteries were revealed to the wise but concealed from the unworthy. This belief led Bernard to employ the *integumentum*, or covering, of allegory to convey physical and metaphysical truths.[16] Bernard's *Cosmographia* (c. 1147), for example, is a sprawling verse cosmogony that features a cast of Neoplatonic personifications, including Noys (god's providence) and her daughters Natura, Urania (the celestial goddess), and Physis (the sublunary goddess). The first half of this epic outlines the birth of the "macrocosm" or cosmic order, while the second focuses on the "microcosm" or humankind. To create a human, Natura summons Urania and Physis who respectively provide the soul and body of man, entities that are then united by Natura. The microcosmic human body is structurally similar to the macrocosm, not only because it is made of the same elemental matter but also because it is similar in form, the lesser patterned on the greater: "Physis knew that she would not go astray in creating the lesser universe of man if she took as her example the pattern of the greater universe."[17] Nature's role here is primarily that of ordering and regulation rather than generation. Blending pagan mythology and a Christianized physics, twelfth-century poets and natural philosophers understood nature to be a copy of the divine plan, a plan that assumed the formal creation of the visible world out of the undifferentiated chaos of matter.

IMMANENT NATURE: SCHOLASTIC ARISTOTELIANISM

The expressive power of Platonic nature remained influential, even as Aristotle's writings became predominant in the thirteenth century. If twelfth-century writers had shown that God worked through mythographic natural powers, thirteenth-century writers attempted to draw aside the integumental veil to reveal the mechanics of these processes. To do so, they returned to Aristotle's works on physical science such as the *Physics*, *De generatione et corruptione* (On Generation and Corruption), and *De caelo* (On the Heavens) as well as his biological works, including *De historia animalium* (History of Animals), *De partibus animalium* (On the Parts of Animals), and *De generatione animalium* (On the Generation of Animals). These Aristotelian works were only fully available in Latin from the end of the twelfth century; along with the philosopher's work on logic and ethics, these texts were to become the basis of the medieval university curriculum.

Aristotle's conception of nature differs significantly from that of Plato. Like Plato, Aristotle believes the natural world to be purposive and divinely created. He does not, however, believe that a chasm separates the visible world from the spiritual one. Aristotle's deity is not an artisan-god whose hands tug directly on the cosmic strings. Rather, God is a prime mover who directs the world through a chain of causes he sets in motion. These causes then inevitably work themselves out on earth through nature. In his *Physics*, Aristotle defines nature or *physis* as an inner principle of change that is expressed in a thing's being over time. Such changes are governed by design, but not the design of an intentional agent. Instead, nature, which is a vital force in all things, continually directs movement and rest. Even inanimate objects such as rocks contain this vital force that not only gives them existence but also directs their motion. Rocks fall downward, not on account of gravity, but because they seek to return to their proper place within the earth. Similarly, smoke rises to the sky because it is predominantly composed of the lighter elements of air and fire; it therefore floats upward to assume its rightful place in the firmament. If material things yearn after their true home, it is nature as the primary principle of motion that directs them there.[18] In this way, Aristotelian nature was seen as a constant and immediately active cause as opposed to a passive reflection of some transcendent pattern, as in Plato. Aristotle's forms were not separate from matter; instead, matter and form were inextricably related. A thing's form was already inside it, directing its growth and change toward ends determined by the form; such movement is described as teleological, or end-directed, since it follows from an intrinsic purpose. For these reasons, Aristotle's view of nature can be labeled "immanent," since nature directs from within toward a preestablished final form (Figure 5.2).

FIGURE 5.2 A philosopher looking at creatures in each of the four elements, from a collection of Aristotle's physical treatises, late thirteenth century, British Library, Royal MS 12 G. V, fol. 133. © Courtesy of the British Library.

For Aristotle, an acorn becomes an oak tree because the form of the oak—its nature—directs its natural transformation rather than reflecting some extra-worldly mathematical pattern. This teleological model has important implications for how Aristotelians viewed the human person. Since matter (body) and form (soul) were mutually predisposed to one another, the material body was not fissured by a basic underlying antagonism. This compatibilist view would later serve as the basis for understanding the moral resonance of the visible world, since that world can be understood to exist on a continuum with the spiritual one. Where Plato stressed the design of the artisan (its static perfection, its completion), Aristotle emphasized the continual process of growth and becoming that followed an inherent plan (its dynamism, its teleology). In this way, Aristotle's nature was more intimately and continuously connected to the metaphysical principles that determined it. Moreover, nature as an immanent principle of change had a clear moral authority as the principal actor directing earthly becoming toward the ends that its creator had ordained.

Following the full translation of Aristotle's scientific works, thirteenth-century scholastics sought to uncover these continuously active, but also hidden, causes at work in nature. They also tried to show the compatibility of this "new" Aristotelian nature with Christian doctrine. Unlike the Platonists of the twelfth century, the later Aristotelians emphasized nature as an autonomous, rule-governed entity that nevertheless worked according to God's plan. The wonders of nature—earthquakes, thunder, comets—could be explained through recourse not only to past authorities on natural history but also to reason and common experience where possible. Scholastics began to look at phenomena such as the rainbow with an eye toward explaining its colors and its shape, a project that assumes the causes of those things to be immanent to the phenomenon itself. For example, Robert Grosseteste (c. 1175–1253) explores the geometry of the rainbow as a part of his discussion of the science of perspective in his *De iride* (*On the Rainbow*). Grosseteste extends the account found in Aristotle's *Meteorology*, insisting on the role played by the refraction of light within the cloud's convex form.[19] Grosseteste's interest in light went beyond its phenomenal properties. His theory of *lux* joined the meteorological with the theological, combining an Aristotelian impulse to explain the behavior of light rays with an Augustinian search for inner spiritual illumination. This "metaphysics of light" characterized the theological and the scientific as complementary in the pursuit of truth, a view that would inform the work of later Oxford scholastics such as Grosseteste's student, Roger Bacon.[20] The thirteenth century delivered a new model of Aristotelian nature: instead of a degraded, material copy of a world of immaterial ideas, nature was now imagined to hold the divine design within itself, a design that could be accessed through human reason.

Importantly, the reception of Plato and Aristotle was also filtered through Jewish and Islamic interpreters. The translation of Aristotle's works in particular show the cultural diversity that marked the medieval study of nature. Aristotle's Greek works were transmitted to the Latin West primarily through an Arabic tradition of Aristotelianism, and several Mediterranean centers for translation arose during the twelfth and thirteenth centuries.[21] In France, Jewish scholars compiled knowledge of the natural world from Arabic and Latin sources. Gershom ben Solomon's Hebrew treatise *Sha'ar ha-Shamayim* (*The Gate of Heaven*, c. 1300) sought to unite the wisdom found in three separate spheres—physics, astronomy, and theology—by blending Aristotle's *Historia animalium* (*History of Animals*) and *De meteorologica* (*On Meteorology*), works newly translated into Latin, with Arabic commentary and the writings of the Torah scholar

Moses Maimonides.[22] Chief among the centers of Aristotelian translation was the Spanish city of Toledo, an intellectually active site of international exchange, where Greek and Arabic texts were translated into Latin, Hebrew, and vernacular languages by Christian, Jewish, and Arabic scholars.[23] Muslim Spain was a center of multilingual contact because it contained communities of Christians and Jews in addition to its vibrant Arabic culture; in Toledo, all of these communities contributed to the translation of Aristotle into Latin from Arabic, Greek, and Hebrew intermediaries. These translations were accompanied by those of Aristotle's great Islamic commentators, including Avicenna (Ibn Sīnā) and Averroes (Ibn Rushd), commentaries that were, according to Rega Wood, often viewed as equal in authority to Aristotle himself.[24] The history of medieval nature is therefore also the story of how cultural contact facilitated the circulation of knowledge through Northern Africa, the Mediterranean, and western Europe during this period.

Increased knowledge of ancient and Arabic philosophy would have a profound effect on how nature was imagined in the West, as these translated texts assumed a foundational role in the arts curriculum of the thirteenth-century university. The assimilation of this non-Christian knowledge was not always smooth. Scholastics such as Albertus and Aquinas promoted a synthesis between faith and reason, between biblical doctrine and Aristotelian science. This synthesis, however, was felt by some conservative theologians to threaten the sovereignty of ecclesiastical teachings. Beginning as early as 1210, the teaching of Aristotle's natural philosophy was the subject of repeated censures at the University of Paris, where masters and students were forbidden to discuss topics that touched too closely on theology, topics such as the eternity of the world and the necessity of fate. Those teaching Aristotelian philosophy came under increasing scrutiny as the thirteenth century progressed and, in 1277, the Bishop of Paris Étienne Tempier condemned over two hundred heretical propositions in a document that, among its propositions, censured the more radical implications of Aristotelian natural philosophy.[25] Why was this conception of nature seen to be dangerous? The intensifying search for natural causes was understood in some quarters to threaten God's omnipotence. If everything has a cause (as it does in the Aristotelian schema), what happens when God wants to intervene? Would such intervention constitute a violation of his own natural order? Searching for causal knowledge could also threaten the authority of biblical revelation. What happens when natural philosophers start to look for physical explanations for the burning bush or the Virgin Birth? If natural philosophers began applying the search for efficient causation too vigorously, such inquiries could imperil the value of miracles, since revealed doctrine could not be reduced to physical explanations. Moreover, the teaching of some arts masters threatened to blur the boundary between theology and natural philosophy. Some of the more radical masters even suggested that a knowledge of natural law could serve as the basis of ethical claims that could potentially have authority independent from ecclesiastical teachings.[26] Tempier's condemnations did not seek to undermine the Aristotelian view of nature but they did hedge its more radical implications by reaffirming the unknowability of some aspects of the natural world and its ultimate dependence on an omnipotent God.[27]

Modern historians of science continue to debate the effects of the 1277 Condemnation on scientific views of nature, though all agree that it was to have profound consequences for what could subsequently be said about the natural order.[28] If the condemnations had declared certain tenets of Aristotelian science erroneous, then Aristotle could be wrong about other things as well. This freedom to question basic assumptions about the natural order led to the modification (or even outright rejection) of certain Aristotelian principles in the fourteenth century. Following from the work of earlier theologians,

William of Ockham revived a fundamental division between spiritual and material worlds, refusing to use natural science to explain acts that seemed attributable to supernatural power, such as certain aspects of the Eucharist. Ockham distinguished between what God could do because he was omnipotent (through his absolute freedom) and what he had chosen to do when he created this particular world (the ordained order here on earth). This distinction asserted the contingency of all natural laws; God could change them at any moment. While medieval theologians denied that God would capriciously change the natural order, they likewise denied that Aristotelian necessity was always at work in nature.[29] This preoccupation with an unlimited divine power led to a flourishing speculative natural philosophy that modified long-held Aristotelian principles; for example, the late fourteenth-century philosopher and Aristotelian commentator Nicole Oresme speculated, contra Aristotle, that there could be many other worlds besides our own and that they might obey their own natural laws, even worlds located underneath us within the earth's crust or on the surface of the moon.[30] Debate over the so-called plurality of worlds became a place to conduct thought experiments about how nature operates without ever having to leave the comfort of the scholar's study.

Despite these caveats, the Aristotelian view of an immanent nature—one based on a synthesis of Greco-Arabic science and Christian natural philosophy—had become the standard model of nature by the fourteenth century. While there were limits on what could be said about how the laws of nature functioned with respect to divine power, one thing that all medieval writers could agree on was that nature was divinely ordered, purposive, and contained (to varying degrees) moral significance. The Aristotelian model assumed that this order did not come from outside of the earthly environment (following abstract patterns); rather, it was inherent in the material design itself, one that was divinely decreed and operated in a (usually) regular fashion. While this scientific consensus was to last for roughly another two centuries, nature's role as a source of ethical authority was debated continuously over the course of the later medieval period.

NATURE'S RULE

Aristotle had defined nature as the inherent principle of change and rest that all created things shared, from the inanimate rock to the sheep in the field to the rain that watered the crops. For medieval writers elaborating Aristotle's views, nature was the translator between the world we see and the invisible forces that shape it, whether imagined as the divine design or the planetary influences that regulated the sublunary world. To give an account of Nature's operative powers and guiding principles, Christian writers were forced to answer a set of related moral questions: what is the source of nature's authority? What is nature's relation to God? And, finally, could nature have too much authority?

One strategy for answering these difficult questions was to give nature its own voice, personifying an impersonal force by treating it as if it were a human, a technique we saw earlier in Brunetto Latini's *Tesoretto*. While the idea of a personified Natura had been in circulation since antiquity, it flourished in the later medieval period.[31] From the twelfth century onward, nature was regularly imagined as a queen or a teacher (or both). Alan of Lille's Neoplatonic allegorical poem *De planctu naturae* (*The Complaint of Nature*) dresses Lady Nature in allegorical clothing that signifies her role as cosmic lawgiver: her crown's gemstones represent the zodiac and the planetary influences, while her elaborately embroidered robe depicts every category of creation, including birds, mammals, fish, plants, and minerals. Throughout the poem, Nature offers ethical guidance to the narrator, who has failed to understand correctly the place of the human in the natural order. The source of Nature's "complaint" is that mankind in general had not recognized his primary obligation to her, an obligation readily acknowledged by the rest of creation. In Alan and elsewhere, speaking Nature was gendered feminine because the grammatical gender of the nominative Latin "natura" was feminine (like most other abstract nouns). This vision of a magisterial Lady Nature would influence the representation of nature in popular poetry and philosophy for the remainder of the medieval period.

A personified Nature could also explain, and in her own voice, the source of her ethical authority. That source was divine for almost all medieval writers, though they would struggle to resolve the exact nature of the relationship between God and Nature. Alan of Lille's *The Complaint of Nature* defines the goddess's role as one of generation, creating like from like and so allowing species to reproduce themselves in perpetuity:

> For this purpose [God] appointed me his agent-goddess, his vice-regent, coiner of the distinctive likenesses of the several kinds of creatures, to stamp out the images of things, each on its own anvil. I was never to allow what was formed to deviate from the form imposed at the forge, but through my diligent efforts the form of the copy would be derived directly from that of its exemplar, and it would be deprived of none of its natural attributes.[32]

Alan's image of nature is Platonic: God is the master artisan who lays out the designs, while Lady Nature hammers out earthly forms from the divine templates. Nature's role is secondary with respect to God's creative powers; divinity creates and Nature recreates. In this model, Nature's authority derives from the exactness of her copying. Just as natural philosophy was viewed as the handmaiden of theology within the medieval university curriculum, so too Nature was the divine handmaiden who carried out God's designs here below. Though her role was ostensibly that of deputy, Nature was also seen to be the most proximate sexual governor over humanity, since, as *generatrix*, she was responsible for ensuring the continuation of the species. She does so by threatening to exile those who commit homosexual acts or otherwise refuse to marry and to reproduce. For Alan, as for many medieval writers, Nature is the enforcer of the heteronormative order.[33]

Beyond the realm of sexual mores, Nature was also regularly portrayed as a teacher of social values more generally. The Middle English word "kynde" is often translated as "nature," but this does a disservice to its capacious medieval meaning. The term referred not only to the created world but also to the act of sex, to the inherent disposition of something that imparts its shape, to man's instinctive moral feeling, and to social class or to one's lineage. This broad semantic range blurs the line between culture and nature, bridging the human and nonhuman domains. So when the poet Geoffrey Chaucer defines God in his poem *Troilus and Criseyde* (*c.* 1380s) as the "auctor of kynde," this definition suggests that God is creator of not just the natural world but also the complex social structures responsible for human behaviors. We see this emphasis in a thirteenth-century Latin political treatise later translated and printed by William Caxton and known as *The Game and Play of Chesse* (*c.* 1470). This treatise sets out standards by which each professional class should fulfill its duties to the other classes, urging citizens to work in the best interest of all rather than in pursuit of their own singular desires:

> And here in ought we to folowe nature, for she sheweth to us that we shold do comyn proffyt, one to another. And the first fondement of justyce is that no man shold noye ne greve other, but that they ought do the comen proffyt.[34]

Just as all of the orders of the natural world complement one another to form a harmonious whole, so too mankind should work toward the "common profit" based on mutual cooperation rather than individual competition. Nature is here imagined as the regulator of the social order, telling us what "ought to be" rather than what is. Her voice takes on a monitory tone, and, in doing so, she serves as a warrant for the cultural norms that a society sought to enforce, a role that nature continues to play in modern society when we debate issues such as gender roles and the biological bases of human behavior.

While Nature's rule covered sexual mores and the mutual obligations that underpinned society more generally, that sovereignty raised concerns about how naturally occurring impulses in human beings might be understood within a Christian ethical framework. Understanding and resolving the tensions in that relationship required a nuanced account of nature's influence on human conduct. From within, nature functioned as an inherent inclination that directed creatures toward their final, mature form, the Aristotelian teleological impulse planted inside individuals. From without, nature was associated with a set of external (usually planetary) forces that acted upon creaturely bodies and actions. The movement of the heavens therefore governed humans, since the latter were generated by and living under the sway of constantly changing astronomical influences. But what happens, for instance, when the natural (and cyclical) urge to procreate, shared by humans and animals alike, conflicted with ecclesiastical proscriptions against sex? This conflict raised the problem of determinism: to what extent are human behaviors either disposed or determined by their natural inclinations and supervening planetary influences? Moreover, if these necessary forces acted on the human body in such a way that set it at odds with Christian teachings, how could those impediments to ethical behavior be overcome? This last question becomes a central philosophical problem in depictions of nature from the thirteenth century onward, animating one of the most popular (and controversial) of French love poems, *Le Roman de la Rose* (*The Romance of the Rose*, c. 1270s). Begun by Guillaume de Lorris and finished by Jean de Meun, the dream vision follows the narrator's pursuit of his lover, allegorized as a rosebud. Along the way, he encounters a variety of personified figures who either offer him help and guidance (Fair Welcoming, Courtesy, Reason) or repel his advances (Resistance, Shame, Chastity). Lady Nature takes a star turn among this cast, offering an extended monologue in which she lectures the narrator about larger philosophical issues. Like Alan of Lille's Lady Nature, whom she resembles, the *Rose*'s Nature is portrayed as working tirelessly in her cosmic forge to sustain the creaturely supply chain (Figure 5.3).

This is an encyclopedic vision of nature but one that represents the limits of the encyclopedic vision.[35] Nature laments that, while the rest of the created world follows her dictates, mankind alone does not. While mankind should acknowledge his place in the natural order, Nature adds a further caveat: the narrator should not imagine that natural forces wholly determine his fate however. Urging him to resist fatalism, she reminds him that his free will has the capacity to check influences that might otherwise be seen to determine human behavior. In arguing against determinism, Lady Nature gives voice to a medieval version of the "nature versus nurture" debate familiar from modern social science. While celestial powers can prompt people to certain actions, humans can resist those actions through virtuous education. In this way, the poem gives voice to a central medieval paradox around nature: humans are strongly predisposed to act in ways that may contravene cultural or religious norms, and it is only through an act of will that they can overcome these tendencies. In its fears of determinism, Nature's speech evokes concerns similar to those expressed in the 1277 Condemnation at the University

FIGURE 5.3 Lady Nature forging a baby from *Roman de la Rose*, *c.* 1490–1500, British Library, Harley MS 4425, fol. 140r. © Alamy Stock Photo.

of Paris, especially the idea that the external environment may exert too great a control over the human soul or that, by granting autonomy to natural processes, divine will may also be compromised.[36] Ironically, Nature both asserts her sovereignty and reminds her audience that humans are not solely Nature's creatures, since their distinguishing feature is the divinely implanted ability to choose a path that resists natural erotic longings. In effect, Nature says: follow my laws but do not follow them at all times, since humans most resemble their Creator with respect to their free will and their capacity for rational choice. As a personified character in this poem, Lady Nature makes available for discussion the limit of her powers, particularly the social and spiritual dangers associated with naturalism. While the *Romance of the Rose* does not offer easy solutions—indeed the dreamer seems to misuse his free will spectacularly at the end of the poem—the conflict over determinism and free will dramatized by a personified Nature was to remain a central preoccupation of both learned and popular late medieval writers.

THE HUMAN IN/OUT OF NATURE

Another pressing question raised by the debate over Nature's powers was the extent to which the human was understood to exist within or without nature. Medieval humanity was not imagined to be the opposite of nature but rather was seen to exist on a continuum with it. There was a range of perspectives on how best to articulate this relationship. At one end, there was the view that the two realms were largely coextensive and that the human was a subset of the larger natural whole. On the other end, one might hold that the human was utterly unique, an exception to the rules that governed the rest of nature. Today the unexceptionalist position would highlight the amount of genetic material shared by humans and other animals, while the exceptionalist position would cite various boundary phenomena thought to belong to the human alone, whether consciousness, complex memory, language, or tool use. The Middle Ages had its own continuum between human and nature, and then as now, there were significant arguments about where boundaries should be drawn.

We have already encountered a striking argument for the coextensivity of the natural and human worlds: the medieval habit of personifying nature to debate how tightly humans should be bound by her laws. The idea that the human was a subset of the natural was also expressed in medical, scientific, and philosophical texts that recognized the continuity of material substance between both human and nonhuman worlds. This model of shared embodiment is rooted in an accepted understanding of the elemental composition of human physiology. According to Greek physics, all bodies in the sublunary world were composed of the four elements—earth, water, air, and fire—that were in turn susceptible to celestial influence and therefore in flux. Each of these elements had a corresponding humoral fluid: blood (air), yellow bile (fire), phlegm (water), and black bile (earth). It was the balance of these fluids within the human body that established a person's "complexion," or what today we would call personality. It also determined medical care, since health was predicated on ensuring the proper accord among bodily humors. This theory linked the wider physical world to the individual in concrete ways that were cataloged at length in medieval encyclopedias that enumerated the qualities of the elements and humors as well as their effects on the human body. A vivid representation of the body's continuity with the elemental world is found in a diagram contained in a fifteenth-century manuscript containing medical and astrological treatises (Figure 5.4).

A male body stands with its arms raised in the middle of the world; lines connect the different parts of the body with the influences of the Zodiac and the heavens. The image represents the elemental and humoral makeup of the human body, suggesting that, at its most fundamental, the body is subject to the varying forces of nature. Beyond this, the image encourages the reader to imagine what it feels like to inhabit such a body, a precarious construction susceptible to the fluctuations of the elemental and humoral currents. If, as Aristotle asserts "nature is change," then the human body too was imagined to be in a constant state of environmentally induced flux.

This image is often referred to as "microcosmic man" because it demonstrates a shared sympathy between the human and the rest of creation that underlies the structural correspondence between the microcosm and the macrocosm. In this way, the image calls to mind the images of man and the cosmos that we encountered earlier in Bernard Silvestris's *Cosmographia*. His Neoplatonic allegory was composed of complementary halves: the megacosmos of the physical universe and the microcosmos of the individual human. These two halves were related physically (as we have seen) but also

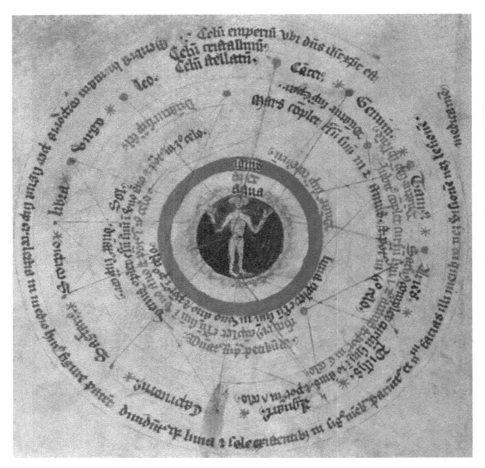

FIGURE 5.4 Diagram representing Microcosmic Man, early fifteenth century, British Library, Sloane MS 282, fol. 18. © Bridgeman Images.

metaphysically: Bernard's Physis (Nature) creates man as the "lesser universe" patterned after the "greater universe." The microcosmic trope of man as a "little world" (*minor mundus*) had a long history in classical writing, and it becomes ubiquitous in late medieval Christian exegesis.[37] For some writers, the doctrine functioned primarily to emphasize the elemental makeup of the microcosm, the fact that the human body shared its matter with the rest of the created world; for others, the figure served to emphasize the intimate correspondences between inner and outer, microcosm and macrocosm. This accord is memorably represented in an illumination included in a thirteenth-century manuscript of Hildegard of Bingen's *Liber Divinorum Operum* (*Book of Divine Works, c.* 1163–1170). A German abbess, theologian, and composer, Hildegard records her cosmology, an ecstatic vision joining physical causation to the larger providential plan. This image portrays the human body surrounded by concentric rings of physical and metaphysical powers: an inner circle depicting the sublunary influence of the wind on man's physiology (the twelve winds represented by animal heads), the astronomical forces of planets and stars, and enclosed by Christ and the Godhead in the outermost circle. The image is strafed by lines representing both the sublunary pneumatic currents that effect different parts of the body as well as superlunary influences (planetary and spiritual) that shape his fate. As such, it illustrates how the human, natural, and divine were intermingled with one another, since all of these influences were imagined to be at once internal and external to the body. As a microcosmic figure, this image represents the telescoping of individual into cosmos and back again. The individual body is less a container than a site of exchange, less a threshold or limen and more a constant negotiation between inner and outer.

The coextensivity of the human and the natural world was therefore modeled across many disciplines using a variety of tools: rhetorically through personification allegory; scientifically through elemental physiology, humoral medicine, and theories of biological kinship; and philosophically through a telescoping idea of microcosm and macrocosm. However, most medieval writers recognized a significant dividing line between the human and the rest of embodied creation: the rational soul. In medieval faculty psychology, the human mind was divided into three "faculties," each of which served a separate function with respect to nutrition, information processing, and volition. While this model developed over time and was much argued over, scholastics recognized that the mind was a combination of the vegetative soul (shared with both plants and animals, responsible for nutrition and growth), the sensitive soul (shared with animals, capable of responding to external stimuli), and the rational soul (belonging to humans alone, in which the higher powers of memory and imagination were located). This model implies an overlap with nature to the extent that the human mind houses within it the lower faculties common to other embodied creatures, much like a matroyshka doll. Having exclusive possession of a rational power is what allows humans to assess sensory data and compare it to past or future outcomes, to make rational choices, and most importantly, to exercise free will.

Medieval writers placed the human closer to or further away from the domain of nature by taking positions on the rational soul. Some writers stressed the commonalities between the rational soul and the other faculties. Thomas Aquinas, for instance, believed that the rational soul worked toward the same ends and through analogous means as the vegetative and sensitive souls. This perspective diminished the distance between the human and other living creatures, even if it remained a hierarchical relationship.[38] Other writers emphasized the uniqueness of the rational soul and, for many, this uniqueness served as the basis of an enthusiastic human exceptionalism. Returning once again to Bernard Silvestris's *Cosmographia*, we read that mankind is composed of the same elemental compounds as other animals, but in man alone do these elemental forces achieve balance. The harmonious makeup of the human humoral complexion differentiates it from the rest of creation, making only the human body a fitting receptacle for the rational soul. While donkeys have too much phlegm and lions too much choler, only the human can obtain the perfect humoral equilibrium: "For it would have been improper for the future abode of intellect and reason to suffer imbalance or disruption through any uncertainty in its design."[39] One consequence of this view was that the perfection of mankind's form licenses his use of the rest of the world for his own needs.

Such an instrumental view of nature continues to inform our contemporary relationship with it, a relationship that often assumes the environmental macrocosm to exist for the benefit of the human microcosm. To challenge this view, it is necessary to understand the historical, scientific, and theological pressures under which it took shape. Revisiting Nature's medieval forge shows us how such views were hammered out and, in turn, how such historical knowledge can help us to rethink those patterns and to imagine alternatives to them.

CHAPTER SIX

Religion and the Divine

CLAIRE M. WATERS

The story of Western (or Latin) Christianity from 500 to 1450 is that of a religion extending itself in the world—in terms of geographical reach, institutional power, and potential audiences—while keeping a wary eye on the temptations of that world. Beginning the period as the official religion of a defunct empire, whose former territories varied greatly in their adherence or resistance to its teachings, Christianity ended as the undisputed majority religion of all western European countries, with an estranged but powerful sibling in Eastern Orthodox Christianity. For the Western church, learning to exist in the world as an ongoing institution rather than one fighting for mere survival was the project of the first part of this period, roughly from the sixth to eleventh century. In the later period, its great undertaking, which arose out of the success of the first, was how to manage the contradictions of being a powerful institution with an immense earthly responsibility but an ultimate allegiance to the divine.

In turn, the denizens of the world—from powerful rulers to the least of the laity—had to consider the institutional church's claims on their exterior and interior lives, but also their individual duties to and understanding of God. In Christian society, "lay/clerical" is a foundational distinction, but over the course of this period the internal diversity of both categories and tensions between them became more evident. The mutually influential efforts of individuals, social groups, and institutions to navigate the competing claims of the worldly and the divine, and thus their relationships to one another, offer insight into a central problematic of Christian life: how to "live by God's standards in the pilgrimage of this present life," as Saint Augustine put it in his *City of God*.[1]

For Augustine, writing in a world where paganism was still a considerable force, the emphasis fell on maintaining a sense of apartness from the world. In the period 500–1450, the challenge became, rather, how to understand and manage the earthly pilgrimage. The appropriate balance, in a Christian life, between contemplation and action—which could also be formulated as love of God and love of neighbor, or as monastic *otium* (leisure for spiritual pursuits) as against worldly *negotium* (enmeshment in earthly activity)—was central to how both clerics and laypeople imagined and revised their place in a Christian world during this period. As Christian teaching and practices extended their geographical and social reach to ever wider audiences, they were reshaped through translation—between languages, but also between social roles and modes of life—that gradually transformed clergy and laity alike.

MONASTICS AND MISSIONARIES

Contemplation entails "attentive regard for God alone,"[2] but the foundational call to "go ... and teach all nations,"[3] offering them access to Christian life, entailed the church's responsibility to interact with the world as well as to keep faith with the divine. The need to consider the varieties and demands of earthly life while fostering an orientation toward God is evident in the works of two important sixth-century figures: Benedict of Nursia (c. 480–c. 547), creator of what came to be known as the Benedictine *Rule* (c. 545), the foundation of a great deal of monastic culture throughout the Middle Ages, and Gregory of Tours (c. 538–594), a Gallo-Roman bishop living in turbulent times whose lengthy *History of the Franks* sets Christianity firmly in its earthly political framework.

The entirety of Benedict's *Rule* centers on the worship of God and the keeping of the commandments, and considers how that worship can be best achieved and sustained in a community, the human context for the pursuit of the divine. Even as it insists that monks be set apart from the world, the *Rule* acknowledges that total isolation is impossible. Despite their enclosure, monasteries in Benedict's time and beyond were dependent on the lay world for new brethren, financial support, and protection.[4] Internally, meanwhile, alongside its central emphasis on the monks' obedience to the abbot as God's representative, the *Rule* shows an awareness that the abbot must "be of use to many diverse dispositions, humoring one brother, scolding another, entreating another, thus shaping and adapting himself to all according to the nature and intelligence of each individual" so as to encourage their salvation.[5] The role of religious institutions and authority figures in transmitting the heavenly toward the earthly and vice versa is already clear; even in a context organized around the contemplation of God, the need to interact with and help others requires action in the world.

If Benedict's *Rule* conveys how the world might enter into the realm of an enclosed monastery, Gregory of Tours' *History of the Franks* (594), from a little later in the century, attends to the role of the divine in worldly—particularly political—contexts. The enemies Benedict envisions are internal ones: sloth, disobedience, self-will. Gregory, writing as a metropolitan bishop in post-Roman Gaul under a succession of infighting Merovingian kings, saw the world from another angle. "The inhabitants of different countries keep quarrelling fiercely with each other and kings go on losing their temper in the most furious way. Our churches are attacked by heretics and then protected by Catholics; the faith of Christ burns bright in many men, but it remains lukewarm in others" he writes at the beginning of his preface.[6] His *History* gives an account of "the wars waged by kings and the holy deeds of the martyrs" as these play out in the contexts of national or local sovereignty, doctrinal purity, and righteous individual devotion.[7]

The latter, it is clear, has an uphill battle in a world where even a life of religious enclosure is under constant threat from without and within, from political machinations and failures of will. In a letter to neighboring bishops, Radegund—Frankish queen, founder of the Abbey of the Holy Cross at Poitiers, and later a saint herself—catalogs the dangers that might afflict her monastery after her own death: outside interference, internal revolt, claims on the community's property, nuns leaving their vows.[8] Above all, she is concerned that the abbess never "sanction a decline in holy living, never permitting her own will or that of any other individual to run counter to it."[9] If the contemplative life could become a political force, by shaping the powerful institutions that were royally founded and funded monasteries, that very influence pointed to its inextricability from earthly concerns and desires.

Benedict and Gregory of Tours begin to sketch two poles of the church's relationship to the world; a third and enormously influential figure in a sense combines the two. Pope Gregory I (c. 540–604), known as Gregory the Great, was an almost exact contemporary of Gregory of Tours, and was abbot of Saint Andrew's monastery in Rome when he was called to become bishop of Rome—or, as we would now say, pope—in 590, a role he was outspokenly averse to taking on. His voluminous writings make it clear that while for him, as for most medieval thinkers, the *vita contemplativa* was superior to the *vita activa*, the two were "related modalities of the Christian life" rather than alternatives to one another (Figure 6.1).[10] Their conjunction is especially evident in his enthusiasm and skill as a teacher; these emerge in his *Dialogues,* which, cast as a conversation with his disciple Peter, recounts in a lively format the deeds of holy men of the preceding century, including Saint Benedict himself. Like Gregory of Tours' promotion of the cult of Saint Martin of Tours—who became one of the most widely known of the "universal" saints of the church, featuring in comic literature as well as sermons and hagiography—Gregory I's account of Benedict both highlights the saint's monastic virtues and emphasizes his accessibility to everyday Christians, the role he can play in earthly matters.

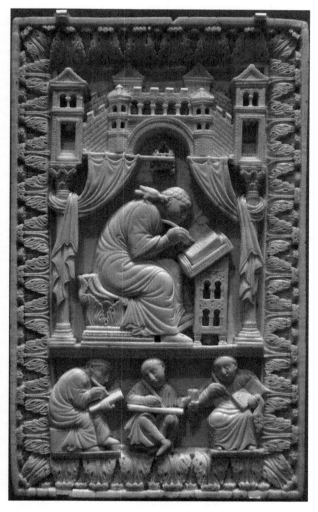

FIGURE 6.1 On a late tenth-century ivory book cover, possibly from Lorraine, Saint Gregory the Great, inspired by the Holy Spirit, composes his works; below him, three scribes make copies, Kunsthistorisches Museum, Vienna. © Wikimedia Commons (public domain).

The delicate balance between devout contemplation of God and active service to others shapes Gregory's thoughtful, almost anxious attention to the role of the pastor in both the *Dialogues* and his *Pastoral Rule* (also known as *Pastoral Care*). The *Rule* treats questions of how one should approach and behave in a pastoral role, how one should teach others, and what weaknesses the pastor needs to watch for in himself. The book's first two sections emphasize the balance between humility and duty that should condition acceptance of a pastoral office, as well as the need for the pastor to lead an exemplary life. "His voice," Gregory writes, "penetrates the hearts of his hearers the more readily, if his way of life commends what he says"[11]—a principle embraced by more or less every work on Christian preaching throughout the Middle Ages. Gregory I's anxiety about the balance between inner and outer duties remained a concern for those who took on pastoral responsibilities. Centuries later, Bernard of Clairvaux (1090–1153), another theorist of the active and contemplative lives, wrote to his former student, now Pope Eugenius III, about the need to manage the inner focus of "thought searching for truth" and the outer demands of his office, attending to, as Bernard put it, "yourself, what is below you, around you, and above you"[12] and how to navigate among his duties to himself, his "stewardship over the world,"[13] the demands of Rome and the Curia, and contemplation of the divine.

While the demands on and role of the pope concerned both Gregory and Bernard, Gregory especially concerns himself with the bishop's role as preacher. Recalling Benedict's advice that the abbot take account of each monk's individual nature, Part 3 of the *Pastoral Rule*, which constitutes roughly two-thirds of its total length, considers how one should address different types of audiences, imagined by way of social status (the poor and the rich; subjects and superiors; the married and the celibate) but also, and primarily, by temperament (the impudent and the timid; the kindly and the envious; the slothful and the hasty) or behavior—"those who do not even begin to do good, and those who begin to do good but do not finish it," for example.[14] In thinking about the pastor himself, Gregory suggests that he must be "in sympathy a near neighbour to everyone, in contemplation exalted above all others … He must not be remiss in his care for the inner life by preoccupation with the eternal; nor must he in his solicitude for what is internal, fail to give attention to the external."[15] The idea that the Christian leader must show both similarity to and distinction from those he leads, and in doing so balance action and contemplation, is one of Gregory's most characteristic and influential teachings.

Gregory's concern with the connection between preacher and audience, with sharing spiritual experience and extending its reach, had its most visible manifestation in a mission he sent to England, whose Christianization under Roman rule had given way to a primarily pagan culture under the Anglo-Saxon kings. While Christianity had spread across the Roman Empire after the conversion of the emperor Constantine in the early fourth century, incursions by pagan "barbarians"—Visigoths, Franks, Angles, Saxons, and so forth—on Roman or post-Roman territories meant that over time the "apparatus of organized Christianity" fell apart, even if the religion itself did not die out.[16] The result was a wave of missionary efforts from two directions: surviving Christian communities in far-flung areas, such as Ireland, and Rome itself.

Gregory's own alleged desire to undertake a mission to the English—which led the Northumbrian monk Bede (672/3–735) to call him England's "own apostle"[17]—was not approved, but led him, on becoming Pope, to send a delegation of monks to the distant island of Britain. Augustine of Canterbury (?–604), the leader of the group, and his companions, according to Bede, embraced principles espoused by Gregory. Having settled in England, "they practiced what they preached" so that "before long a number of heathen, admiring the simplicity of their holy lives and the comfort of their heavenly message, believed and were baptized"—a number that eventually included the king himself, Ethelbert or Æthelberht of Kent (c. 560–616).[18] The king's conversion encouraged that of his people, a reminder that the church's efforts to spread Christian belief could be complemented, as well as hindered, by the structures and ties of lay society.

We see a further instance of this in the Old English translation of Gregory I's *Pastoral Rule*, made in the 890s by King Alfred the Great. In his preface to the work, Alfred says that he translated it in an effort to ensure that, despite a decline in Latin learning, all people have the knowledge they need to ensure both worldly well-being and salvation. "Consider what torments we have suffered, on this world's account," he writes, "when we ourselves have neither loved wisdom nor permitted other men to acquire it; all we loved was to be known as Christians; not many of us were concerned with putting Christian virtues into practice."[19] The king's determination to translate the *Pastoral Rule* and have it copied and disseminated to every bishopric in his realm was itself a form of mission, recapitulating Gregory's commitment to reaching the widest possible range of audiences while anticipating the much larger wave of vernacularization of Christian teaching that arose in the twelfth century and beyond.

The continuing use of Latin for ecclesiastical purposes, even as it became less intelligible to the European population as a whole, worked to create a transnational church culture but also required translation to convey that culture to the church's various local populations. The church councils of the ninth century, for example, increasingly emphasized the need for priests, not just bishops, to engage in regular preaching, and to do so in a language and style comprehensible to their audiences. The Council of Tours in 813, in addition to decreeing that priests should preach when the bishop could not, urges that bishops "should take care to translate [their] homilies clearly into the rustic Roman language [i.e., early French], or German, so that everyone may more easily understand the things that are said."[20] Like Alfred's dissemination of the *Pastoral Rule*, the decree highlights the importance of teaching and learning at every level of Christian society, from sermons to convert doubters to exhortations to deepen the faith of believers to the kinds of education designed to create new teachers and preachers.[21]

Such efforts could be very effective, encouraging a deeply spiritual life among laypeople (particularly, in this period, the nobility) as well as clergy. Dhuoda, the wife of Bernard, duke of Septimania (in what is now southeast France, on the Mediterranean and bordering Spain), composed for her son William the *Liber manualis* (c. 843), a handbook to teach virtuous living to young noblemen. The book urges William to strive to please "not only the world but him who formed you from clay," and stresses the urgency of reading and prayer for grounding a secular life: "Surely, it is a good thing for the mind to cleanse itself as much as possible of daily affairs and cling to divine, celestial, spiritual things, so that the celestial can be revealed to it. Nothing in this mortal life can make us cling more closely to God than the divine praises of psalmody."[22] The sense that contemplative practice is available even to those actively engaged in the world is consonant with the "blending of instruction for clergy and laity" that we see in the scholar Alcuin's treatise for the nobleman Wido[23] and reflects the general sense of shared culture that characterizes Carolingian religious and secular education.

REFORM AND SOCIAL BOUNDARIES: THE EVOLUTION OF LAY AND CLERICAL ROLES

The church's extension of its spatial claims through missions from the sixth to tenth century, and its growing sway over secular powers, through approval of military campaigns and the blessing of kings and emperors, strengthened its worldly foothold. The cost of such externally focused efforts, however, could be a relative neglect of the interior aspects of Christian belief. The fear Gregory I had expressed, that the pastor might become "remiss in his care for the inner life by preoccupation with the external,"[24] here appears on an institutional scale. Concessions to secular power, in the form of permitting royal and aristocratic influence on ecclesiastical appointments, and to human frailty, in the form of turning a blind eye to clerical concubines, became, in the eleventh century, a new focus of attention as the church shifted its efforts toward internal reform rather than external expansion.

The pursuit of reform, from the beginning, highlighted complexities in the relationship between clergy and laity. On the one hand, the clergy's status was enhanced by the insistence that they set themselves apart from the laity through celibacy, a bodily sign of their adherence to God alone that substantiated their right to guide others. On the other hand, the implied right of the laity to expect a high standard from their pastors acknowledged that they had an institutional stake in the matter too. As Humbert, a cardinal in the reforming papacy of Gregory VII (c. 1015–1085), wrote, "Just as secular matters are forbidden to the clergy, ecclesiastical matters are forbidden to the laity"—but, he went on to add, "the masses ... although they are subject to the ecclesiastical and secular powers, ... are at the same time indispensable to them."[25] The distinction between clerical and lay realms thus cut both ways, and meant that, in addition to the need for celibacy (which had long been an unenforced canonical requirement), receiving clerical office from a secular ruler—a common occurrence by the year 1000—was unacceptable: it was, in fact, simony, the sin of buying or selling religious offices or privileges. The term derives from the biblical account of Simon Magus, who offered the apostles money in exchange for the power to impart the Holy Spirit. Saint Peter's reply, "May your money perish with you, because you thought you could buy the gift of God with money! You have no part or share in this ministry, because your heart is not right before God,"[26] insists on the need for interior connection to the divine as the grounds for a pastoral role, and on the separation of spiritual authority from worldly *negotium*, that made lay influence on spiritual office anathema to the church.

If reformist efforts within the ecclesiastical hierarchy acknowledged the laity's stake in religious institutions even as they tried to sustain a distinction between clergy and laity, some of the earliest lay reform movements began to test that boundary. An early and well-documented instance of laypeople claiming access to biblical authority is the Patarene sect that arose in Milan in the eleventh century. In 1045, Emperor Henry III installed a new Archbishop of Milan without regard to the candidates that the church and people had put forward—a clear instance of lay investiture and thus a form of simony. The response from the people was a movement that sought "to impose its own legal authority ... based on a literal reading of the Bible,"[27] a reading the Patarenes disseminated through public teaching—or, in effect, preaching. While the aim of such a movement might have seemed in line with the growing papal emphasis on reform, many clerics reacted with considerable alarm to the prospect of their monopoly on biblical interpretation, and the dissemination of that interpretation, being infringed upon by non-clerics; they regarded the Patarenes not as reformers, but as heretics.

As the Patarene example shows, while the reformist insistence on the distinction between clergy and laity aimed to "divide the world ... into two distinct and autonomous realms,"[28] countervailing forces made this project a complicated one. In addition to the critique of clerical failings—whether of chastity, knowledge, or integrity—that reform encouraged, two particular tendencies worked against a neat lay/clerical division: the growing, and increasingly visible, diversity of religious roles among the clergy and laity, and an ever closer focus on the establishment and maintenance of each individual's relationship with the divine.

The medieval world had no shortage of ways to categorize people. Clergy and laity; those who pray, those who fight, and those who work (*oratores, bellatores, laboratores*); virgins, widows, and married people: these were all ways to imagine the structures of society, and in all of them those considered least involved in secular *negotium* were at the top. But these categories could be subdivided, whether in recognition of their internal diversity or as a way to assert the value of one subgroup. Abbo of Fleury, for example, the abbot of the powerful monastery of Saint-Benoît-sur-Loire (988–1004), claimed that the hierarchical arrangement was not simply laity and clergy, but laity, clergy, and monks, of which "the first is good, the second better, the third excellent."[29] This threefold scheme reflects the long-standing distinction between monks and secular clergy (the latter so called because they worked in the world, the *saeculum*)—a distinction that, of course, individuals could cross, as Gregory I had, but that nevertheless reflected the divide between a contemplative and an active focus. If monks had a more immediate claim on the kinds of purity prized by the Gregorian Reform, they were at the same time held to a very high standard, one that the increasingly wealthy monastic foundations of the turn of the millennium did not always reach. Moreover, their ability to act in and on the world was, of necessity, limited by their enclosed life. If the secular clergy had the right to pastoral care of the laity and greater influence in the world, they were also more entangled in its temptations, and (in the view of monks) further from heaven.

Even as monks and secular clergy struggled over their respective rights and spheres, the laity—who had had a relatively modest role in the Christian imagination from the sixth to eleventh century—began to see their earthly activities recast in terms of their connection to the divine. One example is the status of "those who fight." While churches relied on the support and defense of secular patrons, the ideal of the *miles Christi*, the "knight of Christ," had been understood largely as an allegorical one, deriving from Saint Paul's epistle to the Ephesians: "Stand firm then, with the belt of truth buckled around your waist, with the breastplate of righteousness in place."[30] Moreover, earthly knights were certainly known, at times, to fail to live up to their duties to the church, to use violence for personal gain. By the late eleventh century, however, a new way to direct that violence arose, in the form of the First Crusade, preached by Pope Urban in 1095. The idea of a specifically knightly Christianity emerged and eventually was formalized in such orders as the Knights Templar, the Knights Hospitaller, and the Teutonic Knights.[31]

The language of Urban's call to crusade (as recounted by various chroniclers) reinforced the aims of the Gregorian Reform, urging, "establish ecclesiastical affairs firm in their own right, so that no simoniac heresy will take root among you" and "uphold the Church in its own ranks altogether free from all secular power."[32] But it also pointed to a new, spiritual role for those who fought and encouraged them to turn away from the pride and rage of earthly knighthood, to "lay down the girdle of such knighthood ... [and] advance boldly, as knights of Christ."[33] Crusade was imagined as an armed pilgrimage, a religious journey in which the crusader would "make a vow to God and ... offer himself as a living sacrifice, holy, acceptable to God," wearing the sign of the Cross as the emblem of the "soldiery of God."[34] With Christ as their "standard-bearer and inseparable forerunner," the crusaders would gain proximity to him, both earthly and eternal.[35]

In practice, the violence of the Crusaders, particularly in later Crusades, proved impossible to contain. They fought against internal as well as external "enemies," from Jews to heretics to political rivals or, indeed, whoever was unfortunate enough to get in their way. But the potential for crossover between religious and chivalric culture took root, giving rise to, among others, the story of the quest for the Holy Grail—first imagined as an Arthurian romance by the French poet Chrétien de Troyes (?–1191) in his *Perceval, ou le conte del graal*, and later recast in a more fully religious mode by an anonymous Cistercian monk in the early thirteenth-century *Queste del saint Graal*, where the successful Grail knights become full-fledged contemplatives. From another angle, the English *Ancrene Wisse* (Guide for Anchoresses), also from the early thirteenth century, imagines Christ as a chivalric beloved coming to rescue the soul: "He entered the lists, and for love of his love had his shield pierced on every side in the fight, like a brave knight."[36] Aristocratic lay readers of romance, monks, and enclosed women religious, it seems, could all find something to value in the conjunction of knighthood and divinity.

Beginning in the twelfth century, the group lowest in the traditional hierarchy, that of "those who work," likewise began to gain increased spiritual attention. Such varied groups as merchants, sailors, lawyers, horse-traders, minstrels, and scholars, to name but a few, became the subjects of instructive stories and the addressees of sermons. We see this in *sermones ad status* (sermons to various social statuses or professions), which hark back to Gregory I's *Pastoral Rule* in their attention to the specifics of audience. While Gregory's distinctions among people had mainly to do with their moral state, late medieval *ad status* sermons give detailed attention to particular professions as well as to moral categories. Often, as with the encouragement to crusaders to see themselves as soldiers of Christ, such sermons translate the typical behavior of a group into a holier mode. Thus Honorius Augustodunensis (1080–1154), a prolific author and one of the first to write estates sermons, observes of a merchant who left his profession to become a hermit, "O how fortunately he bargained, who purchased for himself such heavenly things."[37] Here, worldly business is explicitly transformed into spiritual reward, the active life into the contemplative.

Another group that had historically ranked low in terms of spiritual merit was married people. While this did not cease to be the case, ways of counteracting the spiritual deficit created by concession to fleshly desires became increasingly part of the cultural imagination. Chaste marriage, for example, could offer a high-quality excuse for childlessness on the part of a king or queen, but also a means of expressing sanctity for those lower on the social scale.[38] The choice of chaste marriage leveraged the immense power of reversal inherent in Christianity: in a religion whose God had embraced the ultimate weakness and humiliation and turned it into strength, beginning from a lowly position was by no means entirely a disadvantage. The point is demonstrated by the story of a saintly abbot who, growing a little too pleased with his own virtue, was advised by God that there were two married women in a nearby town who excelled him in holiness. Upon inquiring, he learned that they had, in deference to their husbands, given up their pursuit of a monastic life, and that they never quarreled. He willingly conceded their greater spiritual merit.[39] The story suggests that the full and willing embrace of a seemingly lowly role could miraculously transmute one into the spiritual peer of an eminent cleric.

In various ways, then, social categories were reimagined to allow behaviors and roles previously the domain of the clergy to become somewhat available to laypeople. This shift mirrors, in a sense, the clergy's adaptation to the world over the course of the early medieval period, with the growth of the papacy into an earthly empire and the increasing wealth and political influence of the monasteries. In the eleventh century and beyond, though, clerical roles, like those of the laity, diversified. An early manifestation of this shift was the appearance of new and reformed versions of monastic life that sought to reengage contemplative ideals in response to the increased demands, and potential contamination, of earthly allegiances. In some cases, such as that of the influential monastery of Cluny, this could mean increasing the amount of time devoted to prayer, in what was portrayed as a return to the glory of the Benedictine way of life. The Cistercians, named for their mother-house of Cîteaux (founded in 1098), took another tack and aimed to go the Cluniacs one better in their embrace of a strict form of the Benedictine *Rule*, taking on the manual labor that had in many Benedictine monasteries become the work of lay brothers rather than vowed monks. The Carthusians, founded in 1084, created a new rule for themselves blending eremitic and monastic lives. They put their energies into copying books so that they could spread the word of God without breaking their strict physical enclosure. All of these groups sought to ensure that intense devotion to daily prayer and contemplation remained at the center of monastic life, while reaffirming the need for distance from earthly concerns. As the Carthusian example particularly shows, however, they retained a sense of duty toward the world beyond their walls, reflecting the continuing difficulty of negotiating the boundary between contemplative and active life.

Two other new orders approached the balance between monastic life and the demands of the world in a different way. While preaching against the dualist Cathar (or Albigensian) heretics of southern France in the early thirteenth century, Bishop Diego of Osma realized that he had a public relations problem: the people whose doctrine he critiqued lived conspicuously—though, in his view, deceptively—holy lives. Only by outshining them in holiness did he and his fellow missionaries, who included a Spanish canon and priest called Dominic (1170–1221), stand a chance. Accordingly, on Diego's advice, "they abandoned all their splendid horses and clothes and accoutrements, and adopted evangelical poverty, so that their deeds would demonstrate the faith of Christ as well as their words" and draw the heretics back to the true church.[40] This commitment to purity of life and effective preaching became the basis for the new order Dominic founded in 1216, known as the Dominicans. Around the same time, in Italy, a silk merchant's son called Francis (c. 1181–1226) similarly confronted the challenge of living an effective Christian life in the world. Becoming (according to hagiographic accounts of his life) gradually more disillusioned with earthly wealth and enamored of poverty, he eventually gathered followers and began to preach to the people—an activity forbidden to a layman, and one for which earlier groups, from the Patarenes in the eleventh century to the Waldenses and Humiliati in the twelfth and thirteenth, had been regarded as heretics.

Dominic and Francis were fortunate to have undertaken their entry into religious life during the papacy of Innocent III (c. 1160–1216), who was willing to be flexible and innovative in his efforts to improve the church's pastoral care. He saw the new groups' commitment to preaching as a valuable contribution to these efforts, provided they were obedient to the pope.[41] Despite a ban on new monastic rules, he permitted both Dominic and Francis to establish their orders and to undertake a version of the *vita apostolica*, the apostolic life lived by Christ's closest followers, embracing humility, poverty, chastity, and a commitment to spread the word of God. The latter meant that they could not live enclosed as earlier monastic orders had; instead, Dominican and Franciscan friars (so called from *fratres*, "brothers") traveled to wherever there was a need for preaching. In doing so, they managed to offend both monks, who regarded them as a throwback to the despised "gyrovagues" (wanderers) execrated by Benedict in his *Rule*,[42] and the secular clergy, who regarded them as a considerable threat to their control over their own parishes. But their ability to cross the divide between the divine and the earthly, expressed in their lively and effective preaching, made them popular with a range of audiences, especially in towns and cities, while the consistent contemplative strain in their spiritual practice emphasized a connection to the divine, bringing it into a kind of proximity with the earthly realm.

INDIVIDUALS AND THE DIVINE

The combination of contemplative and active lives practiced by the Dominicans and Franciscans echoed the intensification of contemplative practices in the lives of the laity, as means of closer individual access to the divine proliferated. One immensely significant form of such access was attention and devotion to the human life and death of Jesus. The coming of the millennium gave focus to fears of the end of the *saeculum* that had always been part of Christian belief, and the anniversary of Christ's Passion, in 1033, took place amid a ferment of religious activity, from extensive rebuilding of churches to the first stirrings of what became the Gregorian Reform. Those energies, as noted above, took various forms, but one of the most influential was what is sometimes called affective devotion, a sense of interior, emotional connection to the suffering Christ, reflected by the emergence around this time of crucifixes showing Christ "not as the living conqueror of death but rather as the dead or dying man" (Figures 6.2 and 6.3).[43] Such images could be understood—going back to a famous statement of Gregory I on the value of images for those who could not read—as offering a kind of universal teaching. As Bishop Gerard of Arras proclaimed in an eleventh-century sermon, those "who cannot look upon these things through the Scriptures … may contemplate them through the lineaments of a certain picture, that is, Christ in that humility according to which he willed to suffer and die for us," and in doing so "the mind of the inner man is to be aroused through that visible image."[44]

Several elements of Gerard's formulation—the attention to access to scripture (or lack thereof), the focus on Christ's humility, the inner receptivity sparked by the image of Christ—recur over the next centuries and shaped both individual experience and the discourse around Christian belief. The desire for affinity with Christ, particularly when it emphasized his humanness and fragility, for instance, encouraged and to some degree legitimated a desire for access to scripture. If humility, voluntary self-lowering, was the linchpin of salvation, it became harder to argue against the ability of those supposedly lower on the spiritual scale to make efforts toward their own salvation. Increasingly, in the later Middle Ages, lay access to the Bible could ignite fears of heterodox belief, the blind leading the blind, but there were also many paths by which laypeople gained knowledge of the Word of God, both mediated and unmediated, whether through preaching or the increasing efforts to translate religious instruction into the vernacular. Even in the thirteenth century, when there had already been condemnation of groups such as the Waldensians, who pursued lay Bible study and preaching, it was possible for Innocent III to take a nuanced approach to vernacular translations of scripture, and for a French Bible, as well as many partial versions, to be produced without inciting hysteria.[45] Both the effort to translate scripture for lay readers and the increasing emphasis on the historical

FIGURE 6.2 An eighth-century Irish Crucifixion scene shows a powerful Christ attended by angels, National Museum of Ireland. © Getty Images.

meaning of the Bible that characterized the twelfth-century Victorine monks and spread to preachers and teachers helped to emphasize the human life of Jesus.[46] The "medieval popular Bible," retellings and expansions of scriptural material (often with apocryphal additions), similarly served to make the divine more vividly available to the imagination.[47]

The imaginative availability of Christ, the emotive power of his life and his person, encouraged attention to the inner responsiveness that Bishop Gerard had urged. This was evident in the increasing pressure to ensure that the laity had sufficient spiritual knowledge to make a good confession. *Summae* for confessors gave them careful instruction in what kinds of questions to ask (and avoid), how to elicit the circumstances of sin so as to impose appropriate penance, how to inspire their parishioners to the true contrition that would

FIGURE 6.3 A thirteenth-century depiction from Romania emphasizes Christ's human suffering, Prejmer Fortified Church, Romania. © Getty Images.

enable their sins to be fully absolved.[48] The preacher Jacques de Vitry (*c.* 1180–1240) recounts the tale of a cleric so overcome with remorse that he could not speak for weeping. The priest urged him to write his sins down rather than speaking them. He did so, and gave them to the priest—but when the paper was opened before the bishop, it was blank. The penitent's inward contrition had literally erased his sins from the record.[49] Repeated private penance was by no means a novelty. But like the Gregorian Reform, which insisted on the fuller observance of existing rules about celibacy and simony, the penitential renewal of the high and late Middle Ages reflected an organized institutional attention to Christian practice that aimed to bring the intensely inward focus of penance to a wider, lay audience. One of the most famous canons of the Fourth Lateran Council of 1215, presided over by Innocent III, decreed that "Everyone of either sex" (*Omnis utriusque sexus*) must make at least yearly confession,[50] while other canons aimed to strengthen the teaching abilities of the clergy so that those confessions would be thoughtful ones.

Another manifestation of a more widespread sense of access to the divine was the "flowering" of Christian mysticism, "the direct consciousness of the presence of God," in the period after 1200.[51] Some mystics—notably the great German abbess Hildegard of Bingen (1098–1179)—spoke with God the Father, but mystical connection with Christ is the more characteristic mode of this period. The sermons of Bernard of Clairvaux on the biblical Song of Songs, exploring the ecstatic union of Christ the bridegroom with the human soul, the *anima* (a feminine noun, putting the human participant in the role of bride), offered a rich vocabulary for thinking of Christ in affective and intimate terms, and mystics and contemplatives of the later Middle Ages embrace this mode. At times the emotive aspects of such devotion are at the fore: the early thirteenth-century

Wooing of Our Lord, composed for women living an anchoritic life, has as its refrain, "Ah, Jesus, sweet Jesus, grant that love of you be all my pleasure," and meditates on the beauty, humility, and suffering of the human Jesus.[52] In other works, the experience of close, personal intimacy with Christ becomes the basis for theological investigation. The anchoress Julian of Norwich (1342–c. 1416) had a series of visions, beginning with one of Christ "who for love wished to become a mortal man," crowned with thorns. The experience was so powerful and complex that she spent the next twenty years of her life exploring the implications of what she had seen.[53]

While mystical experiences were an immediate, interior phenomenon, their effects were only truly felt once they were made public. In the thirteenth and fourteenth centuries, saintly women of the Low Countries, France, and Germany—nuns, beguines (women who chose to live together in communities without taking vows or following a monastic rule), and laywomen—inspired others with their untrammeled access to conversation with Christ, conveyed through texts written down by their sisters in religion or by their male confessors.[54] Mystics, and those who made them known, thus reflect the move between inner and outer, the balance of contemplative and active lives, that characterizes the whole period under consideration here but became ever more urgent as Christianity expanded its audiences and its earthly reach.

In some cases, the immense power of inner mystical experience grounded and authorized activity in the world. Figures such as the Dominican lay sister Catherine of Siena (1347–1380) and Birgitta of Sweden (1303–1373), an aristocratic wife and mother who later entered religious life and founded an order, counseled princes and popes in ways usually denied to women but admissible—indeed, with appropriate clerical sanction, welcomed—since they were messengers of God. Both Catherine, who according to her biographer Raymond of Capua sometimes walked up and down reciting the Psalms with Jesus, as though he were a fellow monk, and Birgitta, who spoke with Jesus and Mary on topics of major spiritual import as well as domestic details of their human lives (Mary tells Birgitta, for instance, that Christ never suffered from lice or tangled hair), drew on such intimate conversations to ground their pronouncements on earthly powers and problems.[55]

Direct experience of the divine, as Birgitta's example shows, could take the form of interaction not just with God but with Mary or other saints. The rise of affective devotion to Jesus was inextricably intertwined with the explosion of interest in his mother Mary—a figure of immense importance in Christian theology, since she guaranteed the humanity of Christ, and one whose imaginative significance greatly increased as that humanity became a more central focus (Figure 6.4).[56]

Devotion to the Virgin was a universal phenomenon, engaging the theological and lyrical energies of monks, bishops, and popes but also the resources of monarchs and aristocrats and the daily commitment of the laity. Key figures in the Gregorian Reform movement and its aftermath, from Peter Damian (1007–1072) to Anselm of Canterbury (1033–1109) to Honorius Augustodunensis, meditated on Mary's spiritual meaning. The twelfth century saw an outpouring of Latin and vernacular works about her, from lyrics that drew on Marian liturgical hymns and antiphons to massive miracle collections designed to show her commitment to every possible social group. Thirteenth-century works such as the *Cantigas de Santa Maria*, composed at the behest of King Alfonso X of Castile and León (1221–1284), or the *Miracles de Nostre Dame* of the Benedictine monk Gautier de Coinci (1177–1236), bring these traditions together in sumptuous manuscripts that convey their message through image, narrative, lyric, and music (Figure 6.5). The tales they tell involve anything from Mary acting as laundress for a clumsy cleric who

FIGURE 6.4 Mary and Jesus with the so-called Holy Kinship—Mary's mother and sisters and their children, as well as other female saints—emphasizing their role in an earthly as well as a heavenly family, Ortenberg Altarpiece, *c*. 1410–1420, Hessische Landesmuseum, Darmstadt, German. © Getty Images.

FIGURE 6.5 Musicians and dancers perform for Mary and Jesus, at the encouragement of King Alfonso X, *Cantigas de Santa Maria*, *c*. 1280, Biblioteca de El Escorial, MS B.I.2. © Getty Images.

spills wine on his vestments, to her taking the place of a nun who elopes from her abbey until the nun can come to her senses. Without ceding her place as Queen of Heaven and Empress of Hell, Mary shows herself willing, in these narratives, to participate in the full range of earthly concerns, and to provide an ever-welcoming and protective link to the divine.

LAY SPIRITUALITY AND MIXED LIVES

The growing sense of access to the divine and the diversification of both lay and clerical roles reflect both the laity's increasing engagement with the contemplative life and the church's ever-growing earthly work. Such efforts could, and often did, involve cooperation between different groups or institutions—male confessors and women mystics, pastoral clergy and secular patrons, reformist monks and the papacy. But the very blurring of boundaries that such cooperation reflected could also lead to conflict. The English theologian John Wyclif (1330–1384), for example, and his Wycliffite (or Lollard) followers regarded the institutional church as hopelessly corrupted by its earthly wealth and power. Wyclif argued for the church's divestment of its worldly holdings and the need for each individual to have direct access to scripture and thus to God, without what he saw as the unnecessary mediation of the sacraments, the cult of saints, or religious imagery. Not for nothing has this movement been called a "premature reformation";[57] many of Wyclif's objections, like those of his admirer Jan Hus (c. 1365–1415) in Bohemia, anticipate Protestant critiques of the sixteenth century. The English monarchy and aristocracy, who would have been the great beneficiaries of clerical disinvestment, were enthusiastic about Wyclif's program. The church, after his death, condemned him and his writings, and in 1428 dug up his bones to burn them. Hus, less fortunate, was burned alive in 1415.

But if Wyclif and Hus point to the contradictions of the church as an earthly institution with a spiritual mandate, we might conclude by considering the vexed but not unnavigable path created by those who aimed to espouse the highest spiritual ideals without abandoning the *saeculum*. An example is the Beguines of the thirteenth and fourteenth centuries, whose hybrid lay-religious life created suspicion, but also received support from the Dominicans and, at times, the papacy, and flourished into the fourteenth century.[58] Also in the Low Countries and Germany, the Sisters and Brothers of the Common Life, part of the *Devotio Moderna* movement founded by the learned deacon Geert Groote (c. 1340–1384), similarly aspired to a communal life of purity and religious commitment that did not involve formal vows.[59] Such groups posed "one more threat to the already battered ideal of a papally controlled and systematically organized Christian society,"[60] and it is not surprising that they drew the ire of conservatives; at the same time, they show the ongoing thirst among the laity for what the English writer Walter Hilton influentially called the "mixed" life, one that combined active support of others and contemplative engagement with God.[61]

From the very end of the period comes a figure who exemplifies the difficulty of maintaining deep spiritual commitments as a layperson. The Englishwoman Margery Kempe (c. 1373–after 1438), the mother of fourteen children, experienced a religious conversion through a vision of Christ and undertook to change her way of living. This involved many of the resources for religious life discussed above: as detailed in the book she later dictated about her experiences, Kempe persuaded her husband to make their marriage a chaste one, with such success that Christ declared to her that she was dearer

FIGURE 6.6 Fifteenth-century German tapestry showing fashionably dressed laywomen engaged in spiritual activity, taking Communion from a priest on the left and visiting with nuns on the right, Victoria and Albert Museum, London, ref. 4025–1856. © Getty Images.

to him than any virgin. She sought the spiritual counsel of Julian of Norwich and was devoted to Saint Birgitta of Sweden. She went on pilgrimages to Rome and Jerusalem, and energetically attended sermons and made confession (Figure 6.6).

As this list suggests, Kempe was thoroughly orthodox and had no desire to challenge the church's power or rights. At the same time, as a visionary and an outspoken woman who lacked the institutional protection of an enclosed religious life, aristocratic status, or a powerful clerical sponsor, Kempe roused considerable antipathy both in some of her fellow Christians (who found her religious fervor suspiciously demonstrative) and in members of the clergy. She was accused of preaching due to her willingness to offer moral rebuke or comment on scripture in public, but she rejected the charge, with its heretical associations, saying, "I preach not ... I come into no pulpit," neatly delineating the clerical sphere and setting herself outside it in a way that allowed her to continue to express her religious experiences.[62] Although put on trial for heresy at one point, she managed to walk the fine line between lay devotion and usurpation of clerical privilege. She was acquitted and even praised by some of those present.

In a sense, Margery Kempe shows both the unintended consequences of the clerical reform and outreach movement of the eleventh to fifteenth centuries and the unresolved tensions at its heart. By her time, the expansion of both contemplative and active modes of religious experience that had been gradually or fitfully emerging over centuries had created a landscape in which lay access to monastic, theological, and instructional forms was imaginable—and to a considerable degree already available—on a much broader scale than a sixth-century observer could possibly have anticipated.

CHAPTER SEVEN

Language, Poetry, Rhetoric

WESLEY CHIHYUNG YU

I sleep nevere on the Mount of Pernaso,
Ne lerned Marcus Tullius Scithero.
Colours ne know I none, withouten drede,
But swiche colours as growen in the mede.[1]

The medieval art of rhetoric owes its existence to antiquity. But medieval rhetoric also evinces a rich, complex history that cannot be fully understood without studying its place in relation to medieval theories of language. There is a thought-provoking example of this complexity offered by the Franklin of *The Canterbury Tales*, written by Geoffrey Chaucer (*c.* 1340–1400). In his prolegomena, the Franklin addresses unadorned speech, contrasting the rhetorical tricks or "colours" of Ciceronian rhetoric to the colors of the meadow. The Franklin's statement may seem to sideline rhetoric, but in fact, it employs rhetoric to highlight the ways that knowledge depends upon the varied and changing contexts in which words are used. Learned medieval readers of rhetorical, grammatical, and logical works would have recognized in the Franklin's meadow a commonplace that had generated commentary by thinkers such as Abelard, Thierry of Chartres, William of Conches, and Thomas Aquinas, who were especially concerned about words that drift from their proper meanings.[2] Given the Franklin's own rhetorically effective tale, his remark suggests something deeper to be considered about rhetoric. His statement points to a role for rhetoric to investigate the relationship that can be said to exist between figurative language and the entities or things in the world that language names.

Rhetoric occupies an extraordinary place in this examination of language because it considers how we must fit our language to the world or states of affairs that confront us. Medieval thinkers were deeply indebted to ancient authorities who understood human knowledge to be a function of metaphysics.[3] Like the ancients, medieval thinkers held to idealized depictions of human cognition that often placed the axioms of high philosophy over the evidence of the world in front of them. Not that theologians and arts masters ignored actual experiences of the world. Increasing emphasis is placed on observable reality by the late Middle Ages, as suggested for instance by the work of the Scholastic theologian and philosopher William of Ockham (*c.* 1287–1349). But while the overarching narrative about medieval intellectual development emphasizes this metaphysical heritage, there remain indications of a continuous parallel attention in linguistic theory to earthly conditions not neatly explicated by textual authority. That attention becomes evident when we consider rhetoric's subtle filtration into other discursive arts and practices, such as grammar, philosophy, and logic.

This attentiveness to the material, circumstantial, and contingent conditions of the physical world was rooted in what Emmanuelle Danblon has called the "practical" nature of early rhetoric. This practical nature inheres in "a humanistic conception of rationality" based in rhetorical theory.[4] While Danblon accords this practical nature to the Renaissance, its outlines are visible much earlier. The medieval milieu reveals intellectual attitudes furnished by rhetorical and poetic uses of language that encompass the wider purview of practical reasoning. Not just an intellectual matter for later Scholastic philosophers and theologians, this wider sense of reasoning has its background in rhetoric. Medieval rhetoric draws together conventional aspects of linguistic craft or *technê* with a type of cognition "grounded in shared sensations and emotions," exercised by common sense, the ultimate aim of which is collective concord built upon principles of communal ethics.[5] For example, rhetorical pedagogy "encouraged the analysis of character," which focused on psychological factors derived from Roman courts of law.[6] It aimed to "produce a representation of the world" through which individuals would "deliberate in public life" to achieve communal judgment.[7] Rhetoric thus teaches people how to comport themselves in relation to the world and each other. In this way, language craft, human feeling, common sense, and ethical action together form the practical foundation for rhetorical reasoning.

In this chapter, rhetorical practice encompasses linguistic analysis, *technê*, practical wisdom, and argumentation. We will explore these practices in the tradition of commentary, civil life, and logic through which rhetoric conveys an ever-present engagement with experiential conditions that is mapped out in theory and literary practice. To examine rhetoric in this way reveals that medieval literature does not only reflect the changing intellectual dispositions of its era from a distance. This literature also actively participates in intellectual transformation through poetry's historical ties to rhetoric. Medieval rhetoric and poetics, through the auspices of their communicative *technai*, draw close to the known and observable world; they take from the conditions of life, reconsider established theories of knowledge, and serve as linguistic instruments for medieval epistemological insight.

DEFINING RHETORICAL DISCIPLINE IN THE MIDDLE AGES

Any student in the Middle Ages would have known that rhetoric was one of the three language arts of the *trivium*, situated after grammar and alongside dialectic (a form of early logic). Rhetorical craft was recognized as an art of persuasion divided into judicial, deliberative, and epideictic branches; and it was known to consist of the catalog of tropes and figures, put to the service of Cicero's five canons (106–43 BCE)—invention, arrangement, style, memory, and delivery. Yet, while classical rhetoric shaped much of its medieval successor, a concrete or systematic medieval program of rhetoric is hard to define. Scholars have long understood the Middle Ages to be an age of Aristotelian dialectic, grounded upon principles of grammar.[8] Rhetoric, meanwhile, lost its status as a separate discipline,[9] due to its historical distribution into other arts such as commentary and poetry. This distribution and its effects are easily overlooked if rhetoric is regarded solely as the study of tropes and figures or the rules for persuasion.

The rhetorical sources themselves fall under three general categories: the study of rhetoric *as rhetoric*, as applied to theology, and in the field of early logic.[10] Several different rhetorical traditions are present within these categories: Aristotelian, Ciceronian, grammatical, and sophistic.[11] Medieval students of rhetoric did not often have access to whole original texts. In the early Middle Ages, knowledge of rhetoric appeared in "slight and original increments of erudition" within larger compendia of knowledge.[12] The earliest sources for rhetoric known to medieval students up to the ninth century came from late antiquity through Saint Augustine (354–430), Martianus Capella (fl. 410–39), Cassiodorus (*c.* 490–583), and Boethius (*c.* 475–526) (Figure 7.1), all of whom provide a general understanding of a rhetoric based to varying degrees on Cicero's *De inventione* and the pseudo-Ciceronian *Rhetorica ad Herennium*, which appeared in numerous glosses and commentaries through the fifteenth century.[13] Quintilian's *Institutio oratoria* (*Institutes of Oratory*) was also known through later rhetorical commentaries on Cicero's *De Oratore* and *Topica*. From the seventh century, relevant texts include those written by Isidore of Seville (*c.* 560–636), Bede (*c.* 673–735), Alcuin (*c.* 735–804), and Rabanus Maurus (778–856), who were influenced by earlier poets and grammarians, including Horace (65–8 BCE), Victorinus (d.365), and Donatus (fl. 350).

Some new circumstances in the Middle Ages tell us about how rhetoric survived in medieval theories of language. Medieval rhetoric reached a high point in the twelfth

FIGURE 7.1 Scholastic miscellany containing Boethius' *De topicis differentiis*, 1309–1316, British Library, MS Burney 275, fol. 256v. © Courtesy of the British Library.

century, and with the growth of commentaries and glosses on Cicero's *Rhetorica* toward the end of the Middle Ages.[14] At least three major factors led to the blossoming of medieval rhetorical practices from the twelfth century to the later Middle Ages. First, the recovery of Aristotle's corpus of logic provided western Europe with the full text of Aristotle's foundational rhetoric. Boethius had been the primary authority on Aristotelian thought before this. Second, the taste for handbooks of rhetorical composition in the twelfth and thirteenth centuries generated a spate of manuals that drew upon the conventional association of the rhetorical arts with *technê*: the *ars praedicandi* for preaching, the *ars dictaminis* for letter-writing, and the *ars poetriae* for poetic composition. Prior to the twelfth century, medieval students relied on the handbooks of the late antique Minor Latin Rhetoricians, which in their simplicity and brevity, "limited rhetoric to a more restricted field than Cicero and Quintilian."[15] The new rhetorical manuals for preaching, letter-writing, and poetry were similarly focused on the practical craft of writing. They translated the oratorical aims of rhetoric into written action by aiding in the composition of simple homilies and administrative correspondence as first seen in Monte Cassino and Bologna.[16] They also "updated" Horace's *Ars poetica*[17] providing poetic theory for a new generation. These developments not only paved the way for systematic rhetorical instruction in Bologna as early as the twelfth century and Oxford by the fifteenth century,[18] but inspired the search for the original sources. Notwithstanding the work of George of Trebizond (*c.* 1395–1472), who composed his own treatise, *Rhetoricum libri V* (*Five Books of Rhetoric*), Humanist rhetoricians largely concentrated on the recovery of texts from classical antiquity. These included Quintilian's complete *Institutio*, Cicero's *De oratore*, and other previously unknown orations of Cicero discovered by Poggio Bracciolini (1380–1459).[19]

The broad sequence above shows that rhetorical instruction had concerned practicalities of craft; but the emphasis on craft alone obscures other surviving dimensions of rhetorical "practicality" that permeated medieval linguistic education. Indeed, rhetoric's historical practicality reaches beyond the formal techniques and classifications found in rhetorical manuals. Rhetorical *technê* also informs aspects of discourse that Aristotle had treated as a part of argumentation, and together they present a notable feature of medieval intellectual history that takes the form of rhetorical reasoning.

One of the more intriguing features of rhetorical practicality is the sense of the immediate world it raises. According to Brian Stock, unlike philosophical notions of language according to which "the ideas represented by signs were eternal," rhetoric took the "raw material" of experience as language's ultimate referent.[20] Whereas philosophy considered the relation between ideas and signs in "purely logical" terms, rhetoric's orientation toward worldly conditions and descriptive observation gave it a practical heft that filtered into other communicative arts.[21] For instance, since rhetoric was almost always associated with medieval poetry,[22] poetry's relevance for ethics was evident to a certain anonymous medieval commentator of Horace "because it [poetry] is about behaviour"; for others, poetry "pertains to logic, because it is about language."[23] According to this understanding, poetry relates to a living world beyond the mere prescriptions of rhetorical handbooks. Poetry and, by extension, rhetoric make an impact that is therefore not unimpressive despite rhetoric's absorption into other arts. Advancing John O. Ward's estimation that medieval adaptations of classical rhetoric serve as a "yardstick for intellectual history,"[24] we can say that what lay beneath rhetoric's transmission history is its ability to help medieval authors produce discourse about the condition of human situatedness in the world. This situatedness draws from "language, literature, and logical statements in the cognition of being" to reveal the whole range of intellectual tools used by medieval epistemologists to explore their world.[25]

MEDIEVAL COMMENTARY AND THE STRUCTURE OF INTERPRETATION

Commentary is a major instrument of medieval intellectual vitality and it consists of scriptural exegetics as well as texts of general learning (*summae*) on theology, philosophy, logic, and poetics. As studied by scholars such as Judson B. Allen, Rita Copeland, Alastair Minnis, and Eileen Sweeney, the commentary tradition is not just about the content that passes from source to interpretation but also about how rhetorical principles furnish an apparatus for intellectual engagement. Externally, the form of this engagement may seem standardized by technical rules of craft to collate, explicate, and transmit learning from earlier sources. However, commentary also reflects the deeper work of inferential investigation of sources to organize and reconcile opposing, sometimes inconsistent, authorities. While translation of sources is often the main objective, translation also generates interpretive work that differs from the source enough to become new compositions in themselves.[26]

More importantly, as Copeland has argued, medieval commentary augments its grammatical emphasis with rhetorical principles. Prior to the Middle Ages, students learned to engage in the practice of linguistic analysis through their studies of grammar, a practice known as commentary on the classical poets. The early Middle Ages are typically noted for their "confusion" of grammar with rhetoric.[27] Copeland, however, redefines this confusion as an intellectual necessity symptomatic of new preoccupations in medieval culture, and shows that the structure of commentary draws upon principles of rhetorical argumentation to be adapted to grammatical analysis. The inventional scope of rhetoric, which pertains to its status as an eristic or argumentative art, combines with the analytical processes of grammar to address a rising need in translation and commentary. Indeed, in medieval commentary, grammar's analytical exercises assume "the double function of historical recuperation [of sources] and rhetorical interpretation of texts, and the grammarians provide the paradigm for the art of textual exposition in all intellectual fields."[28] An example of this combination might be seen in ovum in Bede's theory of allegory in the seventh century. Though Bede notably downplays rhetorical invention in *De schematibus et tropis* (*Concerning Figures and Tropes*), he recognizes dual operations in allegory when he discusses the trope's two types: "historical" (or biblical) and "verbal" (or poetic). Bede's two allegories, in other words, suggest an intertwining relationship between linguistic analysis and rhetoric's argumentative capabilities in invention.

At the same time that commentary recuperates the classical *auctores* through the bookish subtleties of translation and interpretation, rhetoric's service to "sacred commentary" concerns the practical action of medieval preaching.[29] Theology was the summit of rhetorical activity, hence the sermon, being anchored to sacred commentary, comes to take the place of oratory.[30] No preaching manuals exist for the Anglo-Saxon era, so it is significant that the prose sermons of Ælfric (*c.* 955–1010) and Wulfstan (d.1023) drew some of their homiletic eloquence from poetic technique.[31] With the adaptation of pagan learning to preaching, the "justification of eloquence probably gains its firmest hold in the Carolingian period, when Rabanus Maurus resurrects the preaching program in book 4 of Augustine's *De doctrina christiana* (*On Christian Doctrine*) as a practical guide for clerics."[32] The application of rhetoric to sermon-writing spurred the production of the *ars praedicandi* and its emphasis on rhetorical *technê*; but by the thirteenth century, theologians would advance models of interpretation shaped by the Aristotelian leanings of Thomas Aquinas (*c*. 1225–1274) and the Augustinian program of Bonaventure (*c*. 1217–1274).[33] During this time, Aristotelian-influenced preachers adopt a logical emphasis in their new "thematic" sermons, more systematic and structured than the simple homily.[34]

Understood in this way, rhetoric involves a form of linguistic theory beyond prescriptions for homiletic design. Rhetoric remains true to its ability to communicate through preaching, but also structures acts of reasoning through linguistic analysis and argumentation. Whether addressing clerical or lay audiences, medieval theological discourse applies rhetorical styles of reasoning that depend in large part upon the author's ability to write or speak persuasively, and to gather consensus around a common base of moral understanding. Auditors and readers can then be edified in their social worlds, affected by acts of rhetorical admonition. The meeting of analytical (grammatical) and inventional (rhetorical) objectives in rhetoric's adaptation to commentary thus discloses a practice of indirect reasoning that hinges on communication, translation, and the presentation of a common morality.

RHETORIC, PRACTICAL WISDOM, AND ETHICS

The communal impact of rhetorical reasoning can hardly be separated from its political potential. Rhetoric demonstrates its investment in the world of human experiences by means of a practical outlook that appears especially in the fits and starts of medieval civic engagement. In Roman times, rhetoric possessed platforms for the exercise of "practical wisdom," Greek *phronesis*, in arenas of public address; differing from "idealistic philosophy,"[35] *phronesis* supersedes philosophy for its "application to civic affairs."[36] The original definition of rhetoric as a civil science, that is, "a discipline dealing with civic questions,"[37] continued to be important in the Middle Ages. Though rhetoric lost its special applications to civic affairs in public arenas for argumentative and deliberative oratory, which no longer existed by the Middle Ages,[38] civic questions evolved into the study of ethics and law. Additionally, the civic registers of rhetoric permeated communal life, sharing with sermons a focus on the well-being of a community based on a common morality and ethics. Medieval rhetoric thus renews its communicative function in a political realm as "practical wisdom" through its concern with secular virtues and ethics.

Rhetoric's broad ties to the communal lives of people were manifest in its original role as an instrument to allow rhetoricians throughout the Middle Ages to explore and preserve social and moral functions. Looking to the vestiges of the Roman Empire, for instance, we find that secular operations shaped rhetorical practice to differing degrees in two distinct parts of the medieval globe. The eastern part of the empire boasted enduring civic traditions that defined rhetoric in terms of its familiar guise of public address and legal discourse.[39] Whereas the eastern empire maintained the tradition of public rhetoric, this proved impossible in the western territories of the empire, which suffered the destabilizing effects of invasion, war, and crusade. Those original civic environments in which rhetoric flourished were largely gone by the fifth-century fall of the western empire. Nevertheless, rhetoric combined public discourse and shared values, if differently in the West than in the East.

Only a handful of fourth-century rhetorical sources survived in the Western Mediterranean. With rhetoric's "discernible relevance to external, public affairs" having diminished in the West, commentaries tended to suppress the system of rhetorical *inventio*, or the discovery of argumentative starting points.[40] Instead, these sources appear to concentrate on individual uprightness, introducing the examination of morality and virtue before the end of the tenth century.[41] Sources such as Martianus Capella's *De Nuptiis Philologiae et Mercurii* (*On the Marriage of Philology and Mercury*) and Cassiodorus' *Institutiones divinarum et saecularum litterarum* (*Institutions of Divine and Human Reading*) emphasize the relation of style and eloquence to virtue. The Carolingian Renaissance in the eighth century was a good moment for the nascent reclamation of rhetoric's original civic scheme as it emerges in medieval ethics.

When it came to ethics, medieval thinkers imagined a "broad moral vision" overseen by religious systems of penance and monasticism.[42] Beyond scriptural interpretation and sermons, however, rhetoric conveys the memory of its civic past by intertwining concerns about virtue with secular rulership in the early Middle Ages. This impulse remains subordinate to rhetoric's primary application to commentary during this era, yet rhetorical application could find secular pathways that kept it close to its civic roots. These civic applications of rhetoric show up in Alcuin's rhetorical treatise, *Disputatio de rhetorica et de virtutibus* (*Dialogue Concerning Rhetoric and the Virtues*), an eighth-century dialogue with Charlemagne that follows a Ciceronian tradition.[43] For Alcuin, as for his source Victorinus, virtue integrates itself into "the moral structure of rhetoric," harking back to Roman views of rhetorical eloquence as an instrument of political wisdom.[44] Alcuin further signals his interest in rhetorical *technê* by treating *inventio* as an exercise for students to develop a foundation for "legal and civic dispute."[45] Medieval ethics "was increasingly shaped by Aristotle" by the twelfth century, awakened by the availability of the *Nicomachean Ethics* in Latin, also known as the "New Ethics," the first complete translation of which was produced in about 1247 by Robert Grosseteste (*c.* 1175–1253).[46] For Aquinas, this text facilitated the recovery of rhetoric's old relation to "civil questions," which Aristotle distinguished from the practical art of politics.[47]

By contrast, rhetoric in the eastern empire maintained its links to oratory and the intensive study of law. Here were preserved many of the Greek sources that remained lost to the medieval West, recovered in the fifteenth and sixteenth centuries by Renaissance humanists who traveled to the Mediterranean in search of complete manuscripts.[48] This political thread runs consistently through the history of Italian rhetoric, owing to Italy's proximity to the Byzantine Empire.

As early as the eighth century, "glimmerings of new civic life" are discernible in Italy that laid a foundation for rhetoric's apparent renewal.[49] The "appreciation of antiquity" would bolster "the study of Roman law in the eleventh century,"[50] leading to the revival of law and rhetoric in Bologna.[51] Indeed, the University of Bologna devised the first curriculum in these areas.[52] Town or city leaders composed of Italian citizens, known as *communes*, "discovered their link with the Roman past," and remained receptive to political ideas and institutions of the ancient polis.[53] The Italian *communes* consequently reestablished "what might be called a popular oratory" descended from Cicero.[54] The intellectual life of the *communes*, who were "citizens with academic training in law, rhetoric and *ars notaria*,"[55] relied upon a practical wisdom tied to the exercise of rhetoric.[56] Rhetorical practices in the eleventh and twelfth centuries tuned in to the "legal issues of the day,"[57] during which the political scope of rhetorical theory found growing support. This period witnesses the emergence of handbooks to teach the art of administrative correspondence (*ars dictaminis*), first in Monte Cassino in the later twelfth century and becoming widespread in the West by the thirteenth.

Separately from the handbook genre of the *ars dictaminis*, Brunetto Latini (*c.* 1220–1294) helped "to lay the foundations of civic culture" in Florence.[58] In the late thirteenth century, Brunetto's *Li livres dou trésor* (*The Books of the Treasure*) advances rhetoric's place in the political sphere of medieval Italy.[59] Brunetto presents Cicero in his "civic context" in vernacular French[60] and treats rhetoric within the framework of ethics and politics throughout books 2 and 3, determining politics to be one of the three nodes of knowledge, distinct from theoretical and practical knowledge.[61] Brunetto's student, Dante Alighieri (1265–1321), further considered the ethical, political, and religious valences of rhetorical practice; and in his treatise on the illustrious vernacular, *De vulgari eloquentia* (*On vernacular eloquence*), he imagined Italian poetry as capable of the functions of reforming and teaching. Dante's vernacular poetry demonstrates the ways that linguistic theory, hermeneutic acts, and communal ends converge in rhetorical reasoning, and becomes a "domain of ethically responsible discourse that Christian rhetoric had reclaimed from the decadent remains of ancient civic oratory."[62] Dante drew forth these deeper Ciceronian elements; he aligned rhetoric with moral philosophy to produce discourse that might transform an audience.[63]

In this light, rhetorical practicality geared toward law and the *ars dictaminis* is not "harmful to classical studies."[64] This "humanist" reasoning based in rhetoric actually reveals a lineage that draws back before Humanism's proper coinage in the Renaissance. Brunetto's reach extends through Dante to Petrarch (1304–1374) and "links up with the ideas of the fifteenth century humanists."[65] Through medieval rhetoric, the "ground was fertile with the seeds for a *cultura Latina* which continued the old and prepared the new humanism."[66] In essence, the humanist inquiry inspired by the critical mass of Cicero commentaries and glosses generated in the fourteenth and fifteenth centuries[67] arose from the tradition of medieval rhetoric that housed practical rationality. This influence on discourse concerning ethics and morality contributes to the advisory "mirror for princes" genre of literature in England up through the fifteenth century. Italian rhetoric, for its part, is well on its way to becoming the philological enterprise that defined the humanist spirit. Yet, those humanists who "travelled in search of manuscripts, collected libraries, sifted and compared texts, identified authors and, finally, wrote Latin poetry and prose on classical models" receive their start at least a generation before Petrarch and Boccaccio.[68] These later humanists not only extend a program of textual recovery that began with the Latin translations of Aristotle since the thirteenth century[69] but also illuminate the long-standing intellectual vitality of medieval rhetorical reasoning and its practical outlook.

RHETORIC AND LOGIC

The pragmatic dimension of rhetoric has been exemplified thus far in the hermeneutics of commentary, in the exercise of social or political consensus, and in acts of linguistic analysis. This rhetorical practicality also finds expression through one of the most reputed currents of medieval intellectual history: logic. It is worth considering the extent to which rhetoric played a role in the legacy of Scholastic argumentation, which intriguingly reveals how rhetorically inflected reasoning impacts the study of medieval logic. Though Aristotle had written the earliest treatment of rhetoric, his text was little known until the late twelfth century, and it was "used very rarely in the middle ages as a rhetorical text" even after its recovery.[70] Instead, Aristotle's rhetorical influence was felt most immediately in the arena of medieval logic, which was not distinct from dialectic before the late twelfth century.[71]

Between the tenth and twelfth centuries, Aristotelian rhetoric was known through Boethius's treatise on argumentation in the fourth book of *De topicis differentiis* (*On the Differentiation of the Topics*); by the twelfth and thirteenth centuries, Book 4 was considered to be a textbook of rhetoric.[72] Boethius envisioned a rhetoric that partnered with early logic in this treatment of invention. It is unsurprising, given Boethius's Aristotelian proclivities, that his understanding of rhetoric aligns with the opening of Aristotle's *Rhetoric* in which the Greek philosopher announced rhetoric to be dialectic's *antistrophos* or counterpart.[73] Boethius organizes his work under a theory of probable arguments (arguments that deal with reasonable opinion rather than that which can be demonstrated with certitude) and shows that the two disciplines governed different areas of emphasis: dialectic concentrates on generalities that support the formalities of syllogistic argumentation, while rhetoric takes on a far more narrative and hypothetical approach to arguments with its capacity to focus on particulars of circumstance. At the same time that Boethius's discussion adapts the works of Cicero and Themistius, it also draws from the rhetoric of Hermagoras of Temnos whose seven *circumstantiae* or circumstances (who, what, when, where, why, in what manner, and by what means) became "a cornerstone" for Boethian rhetorical method.[74] This argumentative or judicial aspect of rhetoric is underscored by the interrogative impulses of the *circumstantiae* (and so integral to literary description), which shape the analytical work of argumentation that pairs rhetoric with dialectic.

Well into the later Middle Ages, this argumentative or "philosophical rhetoric"[75] introduced by Boethius was bolstered by the logical dominance of the "scholastic method."[76] Yet the scholastic tendency to place rhetoric within a logical program was preceded by the very tradition from which Western logicians originally received their corpus of Aristotelian logic. Aristotle's *Organon*, meaning "instrument," arrived in the West through Arabic commentators[77] whose works were translated into Latin by Dominicus Gundissalinus (*c.* 1110–1190) and Hermannus Alemannus (d.1272).[78] The curious global network of the Middle Ages emerges fully here, which reshapes the curriculum of Western logic after the thirteenth century. As intimated by Boethius's treatment of dialectical and rhetorical invention, the Arabic commentators had packaged Aristotelian rhetoric and poetics along with the logical texts, their *compilatio* suggesting a continuity with and coherency within the Aristotelian logical program (Figure 7.2).

In Islamic philosophy, Aristotle's *Rhetoric* and *Poetics* were considered the seventh and eighth (and therefore lowest) parts of logic.[79] The philosopher Al-Fārābī (*c.* 870–950) wrote the earliest Arabic commentary on Aristotle's *Rhetoric*, followed by Avicenna (*c.* 980–1037) and Averroes (1126–1198), who were "fully credited" by Western thinkers.[80] Gundissalinus and Hermannus worked from this precedent to pass on this logical scheme to medieval scholastics, shaping the Western advancement of Aristotelian thought.[81] This compilation does more than simply present a range of Aristotle's texts; it illustrates the coherence of rhetoric and poetics within the Arabic system of logic.[82] The inclusion of rhetoric and poetics did not compromise the strength and rigor of logic, attesting to the intricacy by which these philosophers situated rhetorical and poetic objectives within a whole idea of reasoning. In the Arabic understanding of the art, rhetoric's practical manifestation was the ethical example. Rhetoric and poetics are logically effective because they give examples and formulate analogies that remain consistent with the rigor of higher forms of logical reasoning. Thus, the example- and analogy-forming work of rhetoric and poetics is viewed as a diminished version of the demonstrative (*apodeictic*)

FIGURE 7.2 Man in Eastern dress holding a book of Aristotle in a manuscript, 1260–1299. Brunetto Latini's *Li livres dou trésor*, British Library, MS Add 30024, fol. 91r. © Courtesy of the British Library.

objective of logic,[83] falling instead under a species of argumentation that is probable in nature and therefore governed by dialectic and rhetoric.

While some scholars see under this overarching logical design an idea of rhetoric that is "severely rationalistic" in its "approach to the art of argumentative discourse,"[84] rhetoric's partnership with logic communicates a great deal about an aspect of medieval reasoning that holds to the vitality of life and its conditions as discussed above. With their use of "tropes, figures, operational definitions, and ad hoc interpretations," rhetoricians accepted the intricate relationship between texts and "the universe of sense experience by which nature was ultimately known."[85] This philosophical rhetoric affirms its intrinsic attunement to the practical outlook of the Middle Ages in the absence of a systematically empirical consciousness.

Studying this strain of medieval philosophical rhetoric reveals a great deal about developments in medieval intellectual culture that contributed to a "general transformation in theories of knowledge" by the late thirteenth century.[86] Argumentation, common sense, and immediate observation of the world combine to form perceptually nuanced challenges to philosophical tradition in the Middle Ages. For instance, the immediacy of direct observation wields the power to disturb ancient philosophies of perception. Epistemological insight into the workings of worldly phenomena, Dallas Denery explains, emerges through the medieval study of perceptual errors and distortions in the natural world through acts of direct observation. Such perceptual errors indicate a distinction for some philosophers, such as John Duns Scotus (c. 1266–1308), between cognitions that directly grasp the "presence and existence" of a singular object in the world, and cognitions that abstract an object's presumed, unseen essence.[87] An epistemology such as this, "in which primacy was … given to the individual objects known,"[88] takes from the cognition of material objects and forms an important groundwork for the observational astuteness of the medieval thinker that would impact medieval linguistics as well. These acts of direct observation find their linguistic counterpart in the ways words semantically fluctuate in meaning. Indeed, late medieval logic acknowledges and studies the many ways words can signify depending upon the semantic contexts in which they appear.[89] These insights are, however, native to the practical interests of rhetoric. In its argumentative capacity, rhetoric focuses on the articulation of factors that are encountered in lived reality, appeals to a commonsense rationality, and asserts the plainness of direct perceptual experiences to rethink epistemological presumptions.

While logic was central to the medieval world, its relationship to rhetoric in the Middle Ages importantly anticipates the objectives of Humanism. Humanist rhetoricians of the fifteenth and sixteenth centuries concentrate on the "social and political effects of language" rather than on "propositional consistency";[90] and as the work of Rudolph Agricola (c. 1444–1485) demonstrates, Humanists continue to explore the relationship shared between rhetoric and logic.[91] The Humanist critique of medieval logic results in logic's serving a more "modest role" in a student's education.[92] These Humanists sought to offer a simpler, purer Aristotle than the scholastics had recourse to;[93] revising the curriculum of dialectic, this Humanist program "reflected a desire for a flexible *organon* reorientated to include the kinds of ad hoc and occasional arguments appropriate to oratory and the law-courts."[94] Redefining dialectic's relation to rhetoric as ancillary,[95] some Humanist rhetoricians such as Lorenzo Valla (c. 1407–1457) position rhetoric as the most important art of the trivium, while others such as Agricola uphold dialectic's operations with a renewed understanding of rhetoric's role in dialectic.[96] Regardless of differences, Humanist rhetoricians overall appear to reclaim the core basis of reasoning in rhetoric's practical registers that more clearly spells out the idea that "*oratio* may be persuasive, even compelling" without needing to be "amenable to analysis within traditional formal logic."[97] Put simply, Humanist rhetoric makes explicit the idea that arguments in a practical register may hold valid in ways that are not always expressible under formal, syllogistic procedures of argumentation.

Medieval rhetoricians indeed share a connection with Renaissance Humanists insofar as the Latin tradition was concerned.[98] More specifically, while it is possible to call rhetorical reasoning a "humanist" phenomenon, its history exhibits an integral continuity with the world of medieval scholastics that draws back to the practical matter of medieval argumentation. Medieval argumentation forms a complex scheme by which to consider the implications for a rhetoric and poetics taken as the humbler disciplines of logic. This broadened logical scope necessitates "a greater recognition of the implicit cognitive aims of rhetoric and poetics themselves,"[99] crucially expanding our idea of medieval epistemology.

What this reveals about rhetoric is its power as an argumentative instrument that wields a circumstantial and particularizing acuity to participate in a system of whole reasoning.

POETRY, RHETORICAL OBSERVATION, AND REASON

Transmitted through Hermannus's translation of Averroes's commentary on the *Poetics*, rhetorical and poetic doctrine in the West had for several centuries existed within the study of logic. Scholastic philosophers understood, then, that "poetry was a part of logic."[100] Late medieval literary commentary moreover draws upon Aristotelian paradigms furnished by Aristotle's *Physics* and *Metaphysics* more than from his *Poetics*.[101] For instance, authorial prologues (*accessus ad auctores*) often explained an author's intention for a literary work using the model of the Aristotelian causes.[102] Poetics too could present conditions of the material world bequeathed it by the practical outlook that comprises medieval rhetorical theory. But while medieval poetics could describe those conditions of the observable world, this poetics was far from being a theory of mimesis, which had "long fallen by the wayside."[103] The "function of poetry," as Minnis explains, "is not simply to image nature passively but to heighten or exaggerate certain natural qualities relating to what is fair and what is foul, in order to condition an audience's response to whatever is thus represented."[104] The poet uses the representational offices of poetic art, "firmly rooted in nature," to hold the "poet's affective imaginations" close to the probable.[105] In this way, rhetorical thinking combines representation, descriptive observation, and social or moral consensus based in the experiential access to an audience with close attention to conditions of probability.

Rhetoric's exercise of probable reasoning displayed in poetic style, then, depends upon its ability to describe. Its descriptive work is aligned with practical wisdom, social and political action, and linguistic mastery as discussed above. Rhetorical reasoning, Danblon notes, "is itself built on the political function of the spectator and his counterpart, the poet."[106] The poet, as a "citizen who observes ('*theôrêsai*') the best ways to persuade in a given situation," is very much like a rhetorician attuned to the space and time of oration.[107] Such a poet considers a variety of changing circumstances to understand the best ways to persuade an audience at hand. Medieval poetic style, likewise, is not simply something to be prescribed by handbooks and mechanically replicated, but rather represents an author's witness to the best means of persuasion guided by rhetorical reasoning. Reasoning rhetorically, poets can deploy scenarios that represent points of view based in experience and feeling, indirectly asserting alternative possibilities for thought and knowledge-making that might compete with the abstractive requirements of medieval metaphysics. In this way, the intellectual work performed by rhetoric, language, and poetry magnifies experiential factors that generate moments of pause, self-consciousness, or wonder as if the practical mindset of the medieval poet anticipates a systematic analytics for the experiences he or she describes that contrasts with the focus on ontology.

Medieval poems are a fascinating capstone for a cultural history enlivened by rhetoric's presence in discursive cognition, a history that harbors the cumulative strengths of practicality, craft, perceptual plainness, and worldly experience. Indebted to the philosophical capacities of rhetoric, sometimes this poetry explores medieval questions about how words mean. We can think of the Old English riddles of the Exeter Book. For instance, Riddle 95, itself a poem, asks its auditors to guess the solution, which might be "a poem."[108] As Patricia Dailey has shown, the genre of the riddle at times "makes its own decoding part of its narrative,"[109] and Riddle 95 indeed explains the degree of linguistic self-awareness it performs: the riddle's speaker proclaims, "ic swaþe hwilum / mine bemiþe" ("I often conceal / my tracks," line 10), describing the circumlocution that yields to persistent listeners the poem's "beorhtne god" ("bright reward," line 4). The pure ratiocinative work that the riddle performs is embedded in the mystery of signification, whose wisdom it reveals "where the word is not spoken" ("no þær word sprecað," line 8). These unspoken words can mean the figures it uses, but also the solution whose name it conceals. When situated next to riddles whose answers range from weapons to food and to body parts, these poetic lines show how they are rhetorically situated to explore an object's placement and utility in the world, its impact on readers, its manner of manifestation. As the riddle's description narrows down to an elemental noun, it illuminates the web of circumstances in which the word is suspended, through which the question of semantic meaning takes shape. The Anglo-Norman *lais* of Marie de France (fl. 1160–1215) display a similar onomastic playfulness in dramatic predicaments through which words and names unveil their etiologies in actual narrative time. The meta-poetic voice of the Old English riddles finds a match, for instance, in Marie's self-aware "Bisclavret," where the name of the werewolf indefinitely stands for the name and acts of the good knight. At heart is a semantic slippage as the *lai* recounts the hypothetical circumstances under which nobility signifies relatively: nobles can be beastly, and beasts can be noble. Like the riddles, the name expedites its slippage in signification, between an ideal definition and worldly circumstance, made ponderable by the descriptive turns of a story.

Poetic style facilitates reasoning sometimes by performing logic from a distance. In romances, dialectical patterns structure experimental and performative acts of poetic cognition. Noting the active use of dialectical patterns of argumentation deployed in the composition of romance,[110] Sarah Kay shows that the combination of Aristotelian and Augustinian patterns of contradiction evidenced in lyric and hagiography also informs courtly literature.[111] Elsewhere, women and cultural "others" in literature provide curious opportunities to explore what seem to be the dangerous plausibilities of the practical mindset. The thirteenth-century German romance *Tristan and Isolde*, for example, maneuvers the strategic intelligence of practical women thinkers. Gottfried von Strassburg (d.1210) presents Isolde and her daughter of the same name as practitioners of empirical reasoning. Working together to reveal at times the falsity of knights, their association with medical science relegates them to being occult figures.[112] In their tireless efforts, they are capable of testing the validity of knightly claims to heroism by resorting to strictly material evidence. These inferring women are considered knowledgeable healers who also possess powers of language, as much as the trickster, Tristan, who momentarily disguises himself under the name of Tantris. Later, the daughter-Isolde is able to use two parts of Tantris's broken sword to solve the riddle of this knight's true identity. Not only does Isolde rationally infer from the material sign but also her perspective highlights the similar thinking work of other women, such as the Wife of Bath, for whom experience forms her *auctoritee*. Upholding plain observation or common sense, such forms of literal reading are dangerous also for their religious implications as in *The Travels of Sir John Mandeville* or the Croxton *Play of the Sacrament*. Both works affirm the general perception of Jewish readers as dangerous for their literal manner of reading, whether of scripture or sacramental rituals. While Christian hegemony might posit a moral code by which literal reading is discouraged, such texts insistently explore the probable soundness of empirical inquiry. These literary moments elucidate the ways in which medieval culture over time consciously constructs challenging scenarios that call upon tradition and orthodox belief to thoughtfully engage with the common sense engendered by physical experience.

Rhetorically inflected reasoning can impact the very shapes that poetry takes. For instance, a civic scheme furnishes the backdrop for the Italian adaptation of the intricate *dolce stil nuovo* (sweet new style) to courtly romance.[113] More dynamically than this, structural experiments arise from rhetorical stylistics. Exegetical hermeneutics, for instance, prompt Dante to supplement his own poetry with self-authored commentary. The influential *Roman de la rose*, too, reveals a preoccupation with the history of its formal self-awareness, as Daniel Heller-Roazen argues. Started by Guillaume de Lorris (*c.* 1210–1237) and finished after Guillaume's death by Jean de Meun (*c.* 1240–1305), the *Roman* turns the experiment of its completion into a platform for contemplating the nature of contingency itself.[114] Poetry in this way becomes the groundwork for the possibility of perspectival change or multiplicity, so far from the unifying idealisms of a metaphysical orientation. Chaucer, too, considers how contingencies and multiple perspectives shape the narrative structure of poems through his use of the frame-tale genre. The frame tale is fascinating for its capacity to display various points of view based upon the well-drawn psychologies of multiple characters. While Chaucer had apparently borrowed the story-within-stories genre from Giovanni Boccaccio (1313–1375), Katharine Gittes reminds us that the genre is an "Arabic invention that originally reflected an Eastern or Arabic outlook,"[115] recalling the impact of Arabic philosophy on Western poetic theory. Chaucer's perspectival playfulness appears appropriately at a time when logicians such as Walter Burley (*c.* 1275–1344), Ockham, and John Buridan (*c.* 1300–1361) contemplate the ways that the truth conditions of an argument might depend upon the time or circumstances under which a proposition was made.[116] In practice, reasoning modulated by rhetoric allows an author to stage such contingencies and multiple perspectives as are reflected in the "rhizomatic" structure of *Piers Plowman*[117] or the narrative wandering of *The Book of Margery Kempe*. Both works conduct narrative experiments that alter form to give expression to the conditions of the world, its circumstances, and its multiple points of experiential access.

We could say that these instances of rhetorical and poetic reasoning hold close to the world as it is experienced. This proximity makes increasing sense considering the continuous growth of the mirror-for-princes genre across the Middle Ages through to the fifteenth century, a form of "advisory writing" that combines medieval political theory with courtly literature.[118] Literary production thus countenances experiential factors and integrates itself into the world of possible social action. If we recognize this argumentative practicality as the very nature of rhetorically inflected reasoning, lending itself to handbooks of craft as much as to the appeal to the common rationality of auditors, we more readily understand why the analogy- and example-forming activities of rhetoric and poetics had always been incorporated into ethics. Commentarial evidence for "literary" theory or a medieval "poetics" indeed presumes ethics.[119]

This form of rhetorical reasoning in its practical, human-centered register surprisingly bridges the Middle Ages with the world of Petrarch and the humanists who follow. For it seems less clear that a shift has taken place between the fragmented transmission history that stands behind medieval rhetoric and the cognitive activities of rhetorical reasoning ascribed to early modernity. While medieval poetic reasoning is informed by the subtleties of a metaphysical outlook, it pays special attention to experiential points of view. The examples above show some of the ways rhetoric's particularizing outlook is expressed through literary practice, whether through the signification of things, or the playful use of logical patterns, or the late medieval emphasis on contingency and perceptual multiplicity. These examples make evident the intellectual possibilities of rhetoric in the Middle Ages, showing how experiential knowledge shapes the medieval study of language to provide a special field of epistemological wonder in poems.

CONCLUSION

By considering commentary, civic wisdom, logic, and poetry together, we find that medieval rhetoric survives in large part within a cultural history of reasoning that accentuates the collective force of common sense, linguistic craft, and practical knowledge. These are the unexpected pathways through which medieval intellectual history attends to the special contingencies of the world as that very world is experienced. Rhetoric's principles reveal a practical outlook capable of intensifying worldly perspectives. Medieval intellection thus conveys a developed experiential orientation that draws from the practical nature of rhetorical argumentation, enabling medieval thinkers to wield a language for perceptual variance and empirical witness through which to refine their acts of reasoning.

CHAPTER EIGHT

The Arts: Medieval Art in Western Europe

HEIDI C. GEARHART

The art of the Middle Ages challenges modern viewers to reconsider what "art" can be. A reliquary from the early Middle Ages, made to encase fragments of holy sites, may not be considered beautiful, but it was a highly precious object, accessible only to a privileged few. Its images are coarse, but they authenticate the relics within, thus heightening the effect of divine presence. By the later Middle Ages ideas about art had changed significantly, as had its audience. A chapel built to glorify a king, for example, or a book filled with illuminations to help private families perform religious rituals and remember the past, show how art might be used to evoke wonder and create an aesthetic experience. This chapter will look at some key works from across the Middle Ages and use them to consider how ideas about art changed over the centuries. It will examine issues of patronage, craftsmanship, functionality, and materiality and question the assumption that medieval art was static, dogmatic, or homogeneous. Works have been selected to demonstrate the diversity of media from the period, from illuminated manuscripts to metalwork to architecture, and while the focus is on western Europe, which was predominantly Christian, the objects reveal that this world was diverse, multicultural, and globally aware.

ART OF THE EARLY MIDDLE AGES

Books and relics: The encounter with the divine

From Christianity's first centuries, worshippers sought out contact with the physical remains of the holy dead. Tombs have been found clustered around the burial site of Saint Peter in Rome, showing that Christians wished to be buried in closest proximity to the disciple. In the second century, the bones of Polycarp, martyred in 156 CE, were described as "more valuable to us than precious stones, and finer than refined gold," and they were thus kept as objects of veneration.[1] The tendency to venerate the holy dead extended beyond the tomb, and relics too—remains of saints or objects and material that had contact with saints, holy persons, or events—became objects of veneration and focal points for Christian communities.[2]

A reliquary now in the Vatican demonstrates the importance of tangible remnants of a sacred past. Made around 600 in the area of Palestine, it comprises a wooden box that opens to reveal stones from sacred sites of the Holy Land (Figure 8.1). The exterior of the lid is painted with a cross and mandorla, while the interior of the lid is decorated with five scenes from the life and Passion of Christ: the Nativity, Christ's baptism, the

FIGURE 8.1 Reliquary with stones from the Holy Land, *c.* 600, Vatican Museum, Cat. 61883.2.1-2. © Alamy Stock Photo.

Crucifixion, the Resurrection, represented by the holy women at the empty tomb, and the Ascension. Inside, stones and pieces of wood are inscribed in Greek with the names of places whence they came, and correspond to the scenes above: a piece of wood "from Bethlehem," three stones "from Zion," "from [the place of] the life-giving Resurrection," and "from the Mount of Olives."[3]

While the inscriptions claim authenticity for the wood and stones, the images fill in the story. Through the wood and stones, the viewer encounters the tactile, physical remains of sacred ground of the very sites where Christ walked, lived, died, and was resurrected. The images, meanwhile, carefully depict details of place, but they are not documentary. The empty tomb of Christ, for example, resembles more the *Anastasis* that would have been visible to contemporary pilgrims than the stone tomb described in the Gospels. In this way the images conflate the pilgrim's experience of the sixth century with the sacred history of the life of Christ.[4] Moreover, the images, stones, and fragments of wood could invite a viewer who had *not* been on pilgrimage to imagine these sacred sites and to embark on a "pilgrimage of the mind."[5]

The scholar Bruno Reudenbach has noted that while the sanctity of the stones and wood depend on their geographical origins, the reliquary disengages them from that original context. Instead, the cross on the exterior of the reliquary box brings the fragments of earth, stone, and wood together into a new Christological and eschatological whole.[6] Few would have seen the box, and even fewer the images and the stones within. The box and the images are mediators, authenticating and protecting the contents, limiting their access. The stones and pieces of wood, meanwhile, are *not* particularly visually appealing, but their power derives from their physicality. The sacred presence of the relics brings the viewer closer to the physical sites of the Holy Land, to the life of Christ, and to the Christian promise of salvation.

While physical remnants of Christian history were kept as relics, the Christian story was remembered via scripture. The written texts of the Gospels and the Bible testified to the historical and trans-historical presence of Christ, and justified Christian belief in Jesus as the Messiah. These texts were also fundamental for the performance of the liturgy, and thus they were necessary tools for missionaries seeking to spread Christianity. According to the Venerable Bede, Pope Gregory the Great sent a group of men to England to assist the missionary Saint Augustine of Canterbury in the year 601, and with them, "all things in general that were necessary for the worship and service of the Church, to wit, sacred vessels and altar-cloths, also church-furniture, and vestments for the bishops and clerks, as likewise relics of the holy Apostles and martyrs; besides many manuscripts."[7] That Gregory would send not just one book from Rome but "many" shows how important and precious these books were.

A book now at Corpus Christi College, Cambridge, may be one of these books brought by Saint Augustine of Canterbury. Copied in Italy in the late sixth century, the volume seems to have been in England soon after, for it contains corrections and markings by an English hand of the late seventh century. The book has lost many leaves, and just two illustrations survive: a full page of miniatures, telling the story of the Passion of Christ, and a portrait of the Evangelist Luke. In the portrait Luke sits on a large chair, wearing Roman robes, with his book on his lap. He is framed by an elaborate arch, and images between the columns refer to stories of the Gospels told within the text. Above him hovers a winged ox. The ox was one of the four beasts described in the Book of Ezekiel and in the Book of Revelation, and Jerome interpreted each of these beasts as an evangelist: Matthew was the man, Mark the Lion, Luke the Ox, and John the Eagle.[8]

The portrait of Luke hearkens back to antique prototypes, when authors' portraits were typically included as the preface to books, as an early fifth-century copy of Virgil attests.[9] Such portraits were a testament of authenticity and authority, and here the image of Luke performs the same function, proving the authenticity of the text. The symbol of the ox and the images in the columns bring Revelation and Gospel stories to the surface of the page, adding new Christian layers of meaning to this antique tradition.

Images were vital for early Christian missionaries. Paulinus of Nola, writing in fifth-century southern Italy, wrote that "people, for long accustomed to profane cults, in which their belly was their God, are at last converted into proselytes for Christ while they admire the works of the saints in Christ open to everybody's gaze."[10] Three centuries later, Bede described the arrival of missionaries in England and their success when the local king realized that they had come "endued with Divine, not with magic power, bearing a silver cross for their banner, and the image of our Lord and Saviour painted on a board; and chanting litanies, they offered up their prayers to the Lord for the eternal salvation both of themselves and of those to whom and for whom they had come."[11] Important in these descriptions is the function images serve: in the first the converts admire the works of God through the saints, in the second, the image and cross are signs that the missionaries were endued with sacred authority. The divine is not *in* the image, nor do images move viewers by their imitative forms; rather, the images are signs and testaments of divine power.

Accordingly, sacred books were to be decorated splendidly. In about 735, the Anglo-Saxon missionary to Germany, Saint Boniface wrote to the Abbess Eadburga of the abbey of Minster-in-Thanet, Kent, to request that she complete a copy of the book of the epistles of Peter for him, written in gold:

> And so I beg you to continue the good work you have begun by copying out for me in letters of gold the epistles of my lord, St. Peter, that a reverence and love of the Holy Scriptures may be impressed on the minds of the heathens to whom I preach, and that I may ever have before my gaze the words of him who guided me along this path.[12]

It is clear Boniface had already received books from Eadburga, but this one seems to be special, for as Boniface explains, he desires it for use in conversion and for his own inspiration. While it is hard to know to what extent these books would have actually been read by converts, and how many people would actually have seen the pages, it is clear that the visual display of the text and its splendor is important.

The books made for Boniface by Eadburga confirm that the ornamentation of books was valued as a testament to sanctity and an inspiration to devotion. They also are evidence that multiple books were being copied in monasteries in Britain only a hundred years after Augustine's missionaries had arrived. Moreover, Boniface's letter shows that even the most elaborate and fine books were being copied by women. Indeed, because of the need for books for liturgy and for study, most of the earliest manuscripts were made by and for monasteries. For these readers, the display and ornamentation of text became even more important.

A manuscript known as the Lindisfarne Gospels, made at the abbey of Lindisfarne in Northumbria in the late seventh or early eighth century, is one of the most splendid examples of early manuscript illumination. Written in a fine script by a single hand, the manuscript begins each Gospel with a portrait of the Evangelist. The one of Matthew in the Lindisfarne Gospels is an "author portrait," but of a rather different style than the portrait of Luke from the Gospels of Augustine. Instead of the author's hefty form and classical architectural frame, this page is rather more abstract, a careful arrangement of form and color (Figure 8.2). Matthew sits on a bench or stool, with his book resting in his lap. His sandaled feet rest on a mat of some kind, which emerges somewhat illogically from the crossbar of the stool.

There is little sense of pictorial depth in the image: the frame of Matthew's stool recedes at varying angles, the pillow on which he sits is painted in a single, flat color of red, and the man who peeks out from the behind the curtain has no body; only his head and cloth-covered hand are visible. No architecture frames the space. The use of text further flattens the page. Above the winged man the words *imago hominis* are written in uncial script, a Roman script; to the right, near Matthew's halo, a larger text is written in Greek: *O Agios Mattheus* (Saint Matthew) in a style that mimics Anglo-Saxon runic

FIGURE 8.2 Lindisfarne Gospels, Matthew Portrait, British Library, Cotton MS Nero D>iv, fol. 25v. © Wikimedia Commons (public domain).

scripts. Just as the figure of Matthew seems to borrow from ancient prototypes of authors and modifies it, so too the blending of scripts here mixes classical and local elements.[13] Both text and image have been consciously manipulated, and create a new hybridized, pictorial mode. The style of this image has been interpreted in many ways, but important for purposes here is the way in which this new mode takes precedent over the naturalism seen in the Gospels of Augustine. The image presents the reader or viewer with a highly complex viewing experience that might evoke the intricacies and richness of divine mystery.

The Vatican reliquary, and the Gospels of Augustine and Lindisfarne show that in these early centuries of Christianity, art mediated sacred presence. Manuscripts, reliquaries, and intricately decorated bookcovers evoked the divine, even as, at the same time, they served to protect it, to conceal it. Viewers and patrons were of the elite. For these audiences, art could make the divine present through signs, as in the images of the Evangelists and their beasts, or through memory, as in the relics of the holy land. In the Carolingian era, the sacred presence of art took on additional meanings, particularly political ones. This was also combined with an increasing interest in human actions and human offices, creating new functions for art and architecture.

CAROLINGIAN AND OTTONIAN ART

Architecture, manuscripts, and reliquaries: Sanctifying power

One of the supporters of Boniface and his missionary activities was Pepin the Short, who became King of the Franks in 751. Pepin's rule brought to an end the Merovingian dynasty, which over the prior two centuries, had consolidated rule over the former region of Roman Gaul, transforming it into the Christian Kingdom of Francia. The rule of Pepin marks the beginning of the Carolingian dynasty, and it was Pepin's son Charlemagne who brought under his rule the former kingdom of the Lombards, in Italy, as well as territories of Saxony, Bavaria, and upper Thuringia, unifying vast territories of Europe. Charlemagne was crowned emperor by Pope Leo III in Rome, on Christmas Day, 800.

In 790, Charlemagne's court architect Odo of Metz began work on a palace complex for him at Aachen, in northern Germany. Consecrated in 805 by Leo III, the complex comprised of an audience hall and chapel linked by a long, covered gallery. The chapel, which still survives, is an octagonal building, with two layers of eight arches; the apse is located opposite the entrance, and a throne for Charlemagne was placed in the upper gallery, above the entrance, directly across from the altar (Figure 8.3). The building's octagonal shape is symbolic, for like an octave in music, the number eight was a sign of regeneration and new life. The form is also a nod to the Church of San Vitale, in Ravenna, a church built for the Byzantine emperor Justinian in a city that had once been the capital of the Western Roman Empire. Yet Odo of Metz clarified and simplified this Byzantine form; at Aachen flat piers and arches with alternating black and white voussoirs define the eight sides of the space, and a gallery opens the space behind them. Charlemagne was astutely aware of the power of using the ancient Roman Empire as a model, and his biographer and courtier Einhard writes that he intentionally brought columns and marble from Rome and Ravenna to decorate the chapel.[14] These columns are still visible today in the galleries: distinctive for their reddish-purple color, they are made of porphyry, a stone associated with the Roman emperors and revered in the Christian era because their hue was likened to the blood of Christ.

Through its layout and decorative features, Charlemagne's chapel at Aachen linked him to ancient Rome and demonstrated his piety and devotion to the church. Yet his military might was not forgotten. A fortress with two towers, or *castellum*, was built over the entrance, framing the throne area. Later known as a westwork, this addition created balance with the altar. As a result, the chapel not only brought into the present a Roman imperial heritage but also symbolically embodied the two sides of the emperor's power: on one side was the altar, a sign of the sanctified nature of his rule; on the other, the worldly seat, with its implications of military might.

One of the ways Charlemagne solidified his empire was by strengthening the church hierarchy and standardizing the liturgy. A Sacramentary in Metz, in eastern France, made for the Archbishop Drogo around 850 is a result of this trend (Figure 8.4), for it contains the prayers to be said during the Mass as revised and regularized by Alcuin of York, an advisor in Charlemagne's court. Drogo was an illegitimate son of Charlemagne and the book was most certainly made for his own use, and perhaps under his direction.[15]

FIGURE 8.3 Palatine Chapel, Aachen, 792–805. © Getty Images.

One of the most impressive illuminations in the manuscript marks the first words of the canon of the Mass: "Te igitur, clementissime Pater" (to you, therefore, most merciful Father). The eight letters of the first two words fill the entire page, with the first initial letter "T" the biggest and placed in the center. The other letters are arranged on either side of the post of the "T," diminishing in size. Within the letter "T" itself are four scenes. In the crossing of the T is the figure of Melchisedek, beside him, in the arms of the cross, are Abel with a lamb and Abraham with a ram, while below, two oxen occupy the base of the "T." The images show correlations between the Old and New Testaments: Melchisedek was seen as the precursor for the Christian celebrant, while Abel with his lamb and Abraham with the ram are both examples of sacrifice, and the oxen are a reference to the Old Covenant.[16]

This imagery of sacrifice, along with the size and placement of the letter "T" and the hand of God, which reaches down from the heavens, makes the "T" resemble a large cross. It is, moreover, drenched in a reddish purple, a color that would have evoked for medieval viewers the blood and royalty of Christ, while the vines that wrap around the letter suggest the new life brought by the crucifixion of Christ and harken back to classical ornamentation.

FIGURE 8.4 Sacramentary for Drogo, *Te Igitur*, Bibliothèque Nationale de France, MS lat. 9428, *c.* 850. © Alamy Stock Photo.

More than simply letters to be read then, the arrangement of the *Te Igitur* text and the images placed within it are analogies for the crucifixion of Christ and the remembrance of that event as celebrated in the Eucharist. Thus in this manuscript the form and ornamentation of letters is taken farther than in the Lindisfarne Gospels, for the images comment upon and enrich the meaning of the words and the function of the book. The letter is a frame for the images within and an image in itself. It also might be seen to sanctify the actions of Drogo, whose performance of Communion—as he reads these pages and raises his hands, mirroring the image of Melchisedek—brings the memory of the Last Supper back to life.

Drogo's manuscript is an example of a practice of arranging images together to evoke richer understandings and present analogous ideas; this became a primary mode of art making from the Carolingian period onward. Saint Augustine, writing in the fourth century, was apprehensive about images in the church, but his ideas about how ideas of faith could be understood by man paved the way for a new way of thinking about the function of images and signs. As Augustine put it:

We have wandered far from God; and if we wish to return to our Father's home, this world must be used, not enjoyed, so that the invisible things of God may be clearly seen, being understood by the things that are made—that is, that by means of what is material and temporary we may lay hold upon that which is spiritual and eternal.[17]

For Augustine, humankind can only understand the world through what they know; and thus one must use these earthly things as signs to become closer to God. Moreover, as archbishop as well as confessor and half-brother to Louis the Pious, Drogo is an example of the close link between courtly and episcopal powers in the Carolingian era.

By the time of the Ottonian dynasty in the eleventh century, bishops had become even more powerful, and art displayed that authority. Around 980, the archbishop Egbert of Trier, a city in northwestern Germany not far from Metz, had a golden staff made, covered in gold foil, and topped with an orb covered in gems and enamels (Figure 8.5). A long inscription claims that this is the staff of Saint Peter, handed down and used to

FIGURE 8.5 Staff of Saint Peter made for Egbert of Trier, *c.* 988, Limburg Cathedral. © Bridgeman Images.

miraculous effect by the early bishop Eucharius.[18] The enamels reinforce the theme: at the very top of the orb are the four beasts of the Apocalypse, while below them are Peter, Eucharius, and his companions Maternus and Valerius. Below these are the twelve apostles, and below these, portraits of popes and bishops of Trier, all leading to Egbert himself. By placing himself in a lineage of Peter, Egbert makes a claim for the apostolic primacy of Trier.

The role of the reliquary as container here differs from earlier relics such as the Vatican box with stones from the Holy Land. There, the sacred presence of the stones was clarified and verified through images and text. Here, the shape of the reliquary expands upon the relic itself, mimicking the original shape of the staff, but in golden, glittering form. The materiality of the relic is proved venerable by its encasement, and inscriptions and enamels nevertheless assert sanctity and display episcopal authority, sanctifying his actions and office.[19]

These works—the chapel of Charlemagne, the Sacramentary of Drogo, and the staff reliquary of Egbert—all employ signs of the divine, from the form of the chapel to the images of the cross and Egbert's golden staff. In each case, they function to evoke not only the sacred in the space at hand but also the sanctity of the actions of the patron: the Palatine Chapel shows Charlemagne to be the embodiment of political, military, and sacred power; the Sacramentary of Drogo underscores the sacred function of the priest's performance of Communion, while Egbert's Staff of Saint Peter connects the bishop of Trier to a prestigious line of bishops, saints, and apostles, and his work in his church—his use of that staff—to theirs. Here Augustine's emphasis on signs and symbolism is at work, but the function of the object and its use remain paramount. In the Romanesque era, these signs and symbolism become a path to the divine in themselves.

ROMANESQUE ART

A world of signs and the path to God

While the art seen thus far has focused on Christian Europe, the medieval world was far more diverse than a claim of lineage like Egbert's might suggest. By the twelfth century, imports from the Islamic world were increasing; meanwhile, monastic art in Europe became ever more learned, geared toward an audience trained in skills of exegesis and interpretation. The close examination of objects was, for these audiences, akin to the study of scripture—a difficult but necessary task that leads one further on a path toward God.

A small silver box now in Liège, Belgium and decorated with inscriptions belies a rich history (Figure 8.6). The inscriptions are made in niello, a complex inlay technique in which a silver, copper, lead, and sulfur alloy is fused onto an incised surface, and are written in an Arabic script known as Kufic. Around the sides of the object, the text reads "Perfect blessing, complete bounty, well-being and glory," while the top panel, which slides back to reveal an inner chamber, reads "Blessing to its owner."

The box likely came from Al-Andalus. In the eleventh century, many Christians embarked on a pilgrimage, traveling across the northern region of Spain to visit the shrine of Saint James at Santiago de Compostela. A monk from the Benedictine abbey of Saint

FIGURE 8.6 Reliquary casket, before 1056. © Museum for Religious and Mosan Art in Liège.

Jean in Liège is known to have led such a pilgrimage at this time, and this silver box was probably brought back from that journey. Kept at the Church of Saint-Jean in Liège, the box was used as a reliquary. Such a transformation is not unusual, for many objects made in the Islamic world were imported into Europe, and many survive today as reliquaries.[20] While it is possible that the newly Christianized box could have signified the triumph of Christianity over Islam, travel to Spain and trade with the East may mean that such items were more common than is acknowledged. The Arabic inscriptions and a foreign origin may have imparted to the object an exotic, special quality for northern European viewers, links to a higher court culture that the Europeans sought to emulate.[21] Unlike the reliquary box from the Vatican or the reliquary staff of Egbert, whose forms authenticate their contents, this box derives its value from its fine materials, workmanship, and foreign origin. Its sanctity is based on function.

Not all interactions between Christians and the Muslim world were peaceful. In 1095, Pope Urban II traveled to Clermont France, and famously called for a crusade by Christians to aid the Byzantines in Constantinople, and to "free" the city of Jerusalem from the Muslims. Thus began a series of crusades that would continue through the twelfth and thirteenth centuries.

In 1147, the abbot Bernard of Clairvaux called for a crusade from the city of Vezelay, France and its abbey church, setting off the Second Crusade. Bernard of Clairvaux was a Cistercian monk, and though he espoused a far more ascetic lifestyle than his Benedictine counterparts, he recognized the power of art to capture the imagination. In a letter to William of Saint-Thierry, Bernard explained his point of view, writing of the distractions and corruptions caused by imagery in the monastery:

> in the cloister, under the eyes of the Brethren who read there, what profit is there in those
> ridiculous monsters, in that marvelous and deformed comeliness, that comely deformity?
> ... In short, so many and so marvelous are the varieties of divers shapes on every hand,

that we are more tempted to read in the marble than in our books, and to spend the whole day wondering at these things rather than meditating the law of God. For God's sake, if men are not ashamed of these follies, why at least do they not shrink from the expense?[22]

As many scholars have noted, however, the specificity and emotion latent in Bernard's complaints about art show him to have been a careful, and engaged, viewer.[23] Indeed, his comments suggest that images are powerful because they lead the mind somewhere beyond the image itself; Bernard's fear is that in a monastery, this somewhere else might not lead to God.

Yet for Bernard, Vezelay was different. The choice of Vezelay as a site for a call to crusade confirms Bernard's claim that images could communicate an idea, but it seems that in this context—the public entryway to the church—such a use of images was not so problematic. Indeed, at Vezelay the crowd that gathered to hear the call would have seen images set upon the main portal of the church that reinforced the intent of the crusade. Built between 1104 and 1132, and set within a narthex, the portal is ornamented by what is known as a tympanum—a semicircular shape set above the double doors filled with sculpted figures (Figure 8.7). At the center presides Christ, enclosed in a mandorla, or almond-shaped frame. His knees bend to one side and his hands extend out, with rays emanating from his palms. Below are the apostles arranged in a variety of poses. Half sitting, half standing, they point and gesture, their robes are carved with curving, swooping folds that give their bodies a sense of vitality and movement.

FIGURE 8.7 Tympanum, Vezelay, *c.* 1125. © Getty Images.

The image depicts the Pentecost, an event described in the acts of the Apostles: "And there appeared to them parted tongues as it were of fire, and it sat upon every one of them: And they were all filled with the Holy Ghost, and they began to speak with diverse tongues, according as the Holy Ghost gave them to speak."[24] The miracle of Pentecost was understood by medieval Christians to signify the founding of the church and the beginning of its missionary activity. The apostles receive the tongues of fire and are sent out into the world—to the ends of the earth, in fact—to baptize the many. Accordingly, more figures occupy the archivolt, which runs around the outer edge of the tympanum, and the lintel, which runs across the bottom. Depicted here are not only Gentiles and Jews, but the peoples thought to inhabit the ends of the earth, such as the dog-headed Cynocephali, on the upper left, and large-eared Panotii, on the lower right. Beyond them, in the outermost archivolt, are a series of medallions that alternate with images of the zodiac signs and labors of the months.

From this perspective the tympanum makes a fitting backdrop for Bernard of Clairvaux's call to action in the Second Crusade. The representation of the various peoples and the references to labor and astrology in the outer medallions underscore the long history of the church and its steady missionary activity as it proceeds through time and space, coming ever closer to the end of time and the triumphant return of Christ. It encourages viewers to act, to further the mission of the apostles in spreading the word of Christ to the ends of the earth.

This period of the late eleventh and twelfth centuries is sometimes referred to as the Romanesque period because of its distinct style of art, as evidenced in these twisting, expressive figures. The figures are not naturalistic, but the exaggerations bring attention to the meaning of the image: here, for example, Christ's large hands call attention to the tongues of fire that emanate from his fingers, and his swirling drapery is echoed in the drapery of the apostles sent to fulfill his mission, the visual movement broken only by the solid mandorla that reminds viewers of Christ's heavenly realm. Thus the images serve as signs, communicating to viewers the theological idea of the spread of Christianity in time and space through a complex arrangement of figures and exaggerations of form.

As Bernard of Clairvaux's comments suggest, much art was being produced for monasteries in this period, and much of it was intended to serve spiritual goals. Indeed, in the twelfth century many monasteries were large and wealthy, and they were the patrons of luxurious objects of *ars sacra*—or liturgical arts—which expressed complex ideas of theology for a sophisticated, learned audience. One example of such an object is a crucifix foot made for the Abbey of Saint Bertin at Saint Omer in northern France (Figure 8.8). Covered in gold, with champlevé enamel and cast bronze figures, the object consists of a small pier and ornamented capital into which the crucifix would be set, which in turn rests upon a hemispherical base.

The visual program of the object is rich. Figures cast in bronze and gilded emerge from the capital at the top of the object, two of which are inscribed as Sea and Earth (*mare* and *terra*). The other two are not identifiable, but were probably air and fire, the remaining two elements.[25] Four scenes from the Old Testament decorate the pillar and four more encircle the hemispherical base. Made in champlevé enamel, these are allegories and prototypes for the sacrifice of Christ: the writing of sign of the Tau on Jewish houses at the Passover, for example, or the offering of Isaac. Four cast bronze beasts—the signs of the Evangelists—lean out from between the pillar and the base. Like the images in enamel, these beasts, first mentioned in Ezekiel, also encapsulate the role of the Old

FIGURE 8.8 Crucifix foot, Abbey of Saint Bertin at Saint Omer, France, *c*. 1180.
© Musee-Hotel Sandelin.

Testament as a justification of the New. The Evangelists themselves lean over their books
below, holding up the entire object.

Like the tympanum at Vezelay, the crucifix foot reveals something about Christian time.
Engrossed in their work, the Evangelists write the scriptures that will spread the Christian
message through the world. The figures of the earth and sea at the top of the crucifix foot,
meanwhile, underscore the cosmic importance of this scheme. The program of the crucifix
foot draws on a deep understanding of scripture, and as a small object it would have been
visible only to a small few, likely the highly educated members of the monastic community.
Its juxtaposition of biblical references visualizes the monastic practice of scriptural exegesis,
as if it were a puzzle of images, each bringing to mind a religious idea or story, arranged
to communicate to an educated viewer the unending meanings and lessons inherent in
spiritual texts, to help him (or her) become closer to God.

Manuscripts, too, were illuminated with images that conveyed learned and spiritual
themes. One of these is the *Hortus Deliciarum*, or *Garden of Delights*, composed
between 1176 and 1195 by the abbess Herrad of Landsberg for her nuns at the abbey of

Hohenberg, in Alsace. The manuscript is a kind of encyclopedia and guide; as she writes at the beginning of the text:

> Like a bee guided by the inspiring God I drew from diverse flowers of sacred and philosophical writing this book called "Garden of Delights." And I have put it together for the praise of Christ and the Church, and for your enjoyment, as though into a sweet honeycomb. And therefore you must diligently seek your pleasing nourishment in this book and refresh your weary spirit with its sweet honey drops, so that ... you may safely hurry over what is transitory, and possess lasting happiness through delight.[26]

Herrad's book draws on the most sophisticated and prominent thinkers of her day, including Rupert of Deutz, Honorius of Autun, Peter Comestor, and Peter Lombard, and she draws on the antique tradition as well, using Aristotle, Plato, and Cicero in her text.[27] The manuscript was destroyed in Prussian bombings of Strasbourg in 1870, but copies made for the Comte Auguste de Bastard in the nineteenth century survive.

One image demonstrates the blending of learning and spirituality embraced by Herrad particularly well. Here, the personification of philosophy, *Philosophia*, is surrounded by the seven liberal arts, the standard categories of medieval education: the so-called trivium, of Grammar, Rhetoric, Dialectic, and the quadrivium, of Music Arithmetic, Geometry, and Astronomy. With each art placed in an arch, and philosophy at the center, the image shows the relationship of wisdom and the liberal arts, ideas established by Martianus Capella, Boethius, and Hugh of Saint Victor. In a testament to the continuation of classical learning, the figures of Socrates and Plato sit just below the figure of *Philosophia*, as if exemplars of the ideal. Below, four more writers compose, with birds to their ear, their actions also demonstrating the link between education, careful study, and the pursuit of God and wisdom.

Herrad's book and the crucifix foot from Saint Bertin show the high level of sophistication and learning that drove much of monastic life in the twelfth century, and the ways in which art directly served the spiritual goals of the community. Images carry meaning, and their lessons—and the process of deciphering them—are complex. In the case of Vezelay and the reliquary box in Liège, images, decoration, and artistic skill could communicate sanctity and the ideas and goals of the church. All of these objects operate according to Augustine's injunction to understand the world so that one might better understand the signs of scripture, but they go far beyond it, for they also show learning and the exploration of the world as an endeavor of spiritual import that leads to God.

THE GOTHIC ERA

Visions of the divine

The later twelfth and thirteenth centuries saw great economic growth, and the beginnings of what might be called a market economy. Courts needed literate clerks, and as the Papacy expanded its power it needed literate administrators. As a result, the fields of learning that were driven by monastic spirituality in the twelfth century became ever more a part of the secular world. Artistic production changed accordingly: books and art objects were increasingly made by professional artisans, for a secular clientele. In the last quarter of the twelfth century, Peter of Blois, archdeacon of Bath, recounted an ill-fated encounter with a bookseller in Paris, in which he saw some books he desired, agreed on a price with the bookseller, but then returned to find they had been sold at a higher price to someone else.[28] By the thirteenth century, the need for books for university students was great enough that professional stationers worked on a *pecia* system, in which chapters of books were sent out for copying, thereby speeding up the process of reproducing the entire text.[29] Prayer books written in the vernacular and made for lay patrons were some of the most popular and sought-out objects, and they speak to a change in how images functioned: the puzzles, juxtapositions, symbolism, and abstraction seen so much in the Romanesque gives way to images that are meant to be read and understood clearly by a literate, lay audience.

The Bible moralisée, a moralized bible made for King Louis IX of France, and commissioned by his mother, Blanche of Castile, is certainly not an ordinary case, but it is a telling one. The frontispiece of the book shows Blanche, sitting on the upper left, gesturing to her son, Louis, on the upper right (Figure 8.9). Below, a monk on the left echoes the gesture of Blanche, pointing his hand toward the figure on the right, who by his dress and cap appears to be a layman. This figure, likely the artist, bends over the

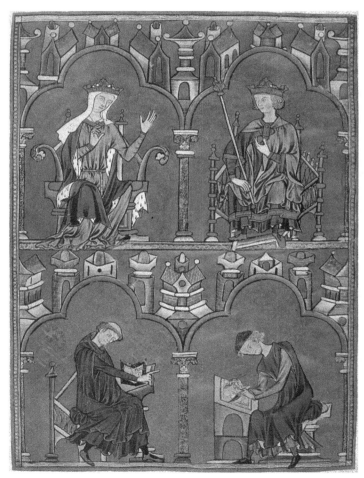

FIGURE 8.9 Blanche and Louis, Bible moralisée fragment, *c.* 1227–1234. The Morgan Library & Museums, MS M.240, fol. 8. © Getty Images.

page in front of him, which displays a series of circles within a rectangular border. The frontispiece thus makes clear a hierarchy of artistic production: Blanche orders the book to be made for Louis; while the monk explains the content to the artist—a layman—who is responsible for painting the images.

Moralized bibles were made in Paris, primarily for royal lay patrons, and their extensive image program made them very expensive. The Morgan frontispiece attests that such manuscripts were not made by one person, but by a number of persons, each with a portion of labor. Yet even more, the manuscript is a teaching tool, presenting complex material in a way that laymen can remember, and from which they can learn. A portion of one now in Oxford's Bodleian Library shows the images following the format of circular medallions seen on the artisan's drawing in Saint Louis's copy (Figure 8.10). Here, eight medallions fill each page, with a column of text on the sides. The images are paired, so that the top row and the third row refer to the biblical text, while the second row and fourth row comment on the medallions above. In one, showing the creation of Eve from the Book of Genesis, God holds the rib of Adam in his right hand and the arm of Eve in his left. Only the top half of her body shows, as she is being formed from the body of the resting Adam, below. Beneath this image, another medallion visually explains the Eve image in Christian terms: here Christ is shown on the cross, and from his side—his

FIGURE 8.10 Genesis, with the creation of Eve, mid-13th cent. Oxford/London/Paris Bible moralisée. © The Bodlein Libraries, University of Oxford, MS. Bodley 270b fol. 6r.

wound—God pulls a small figure of a crowned woman, holding a chalice. The woman is Ecclesia, the personification of the church, who, as the side text explains, was born from the blood of the crucifixion. Just as God made Eve from Adam, the interpretation goes, so too God pulled Ecclesia from the side of Christ. Through the sacrifice of Christ the church makes salvation from the sin (of Eve) possible.

The Bible moralisée is thus quite a different book from the early Gospels of Lindisfarne. Written in the vernacular (here, French), embellished in gold leaf, and entirely illustrated, the book is not concerned with the mystery of incarnation or contemplation of scripture, but seeks to clearly teach lessons of Christianity to a lay but literate patron through its comparative images and textual explanations. Text and image occupy a discreet space, while meaning is certain.

One of the most spectacular monuments of the thirteenth century was also made under King Louis, the Sainte-Chapelle in Paris (Figure 8.11). This chapel was built between 1239 and 1248 to house a relic of Christ's crown of thorns purchased by King Louis from his cousin, Emperor Baldwin II of Constantinople.[30] From the exterior the building reveals only engaged buttressing, pinnacles, and a steep roof. Inside, however, the walls are almost entirely made of stained glass, so that the space is saturated by colored light. The sense of weightlessness is achieved by clustered columns that extend into pointed Gothic "ribs" in the ceiling, springing from one side to the other, channeling the weight to the ground.

Since the first of the Capetians, the Kings of France had sought to associate themselves with biblical ancestors, creating a cult of divine kingship.[31] Accordingly, the windows in the chapel promote the cult of the relics of the crown of thorns and the king himself. A "Relic Window" depicts King Louis carrying the crown of thorns into the city of Paris.

FIGURE 8.11 Sainte-Chapelle. © Getty Images.

Cleverly, it is placed directly following windows with scenes from the Old Testament Book of Kings, as if King Louis is the inheritor of that sacred line, connected to Christ and the ancient kings David and Solomon. Christian history and contemporary, Parisian, history merge. This blending of sacrality and kingship in a palace chapel goes back to the Chapel of Aachen, which was designed to convey the sanctity of the office of the emperor. Yet there, Charlemagne himself was elusive. At Sainte-Chapelle, however, the program, the architecture, and above all, the relic glorify and sanctify King Louis.[32]

The splendor of the chapel and its glass, with the colors changing with the light of day, was not lost on contemporary viewers. Built to house relics, the chapel is, as Robert Branner has described it, a "super-shrine turned outside in."[33] Indeed, in 1323 the scholastic Jean de Jandun described the chapel as a place so beautiful one might think it to be heaven:

> But also that most beautiful of chapels, the chapel of the king, most fittingly situated within the walls of the king's house, enjoys a complete and indissoluble structure of most solid stone. The most select colors of the pictures, the precious gilding of the images, the beautiful transparency of the gleaming windows on all sides, the most beautiful cloths of the altars, the wondrous merits of the sanctuaries, the figured work on the reliquaries externally adorned with dazzling gems, bestow such a hyperbolic beauty on the house of prayer that, in going into it from below, one understandably believes oneself, as if rapt to heaven, to be entering one of the best chambers of Paradise.[34]

Jandun's concern here is for the overarching effect of the chapel and viewer's experience of the space as an analogy for the realms of heaven.[35] This reaction shows a characteristic of the Gothic era that sets it apart from earlier periods. While Herrad of Landsberg's book had spoken of learning as a ladder, or ascendant, difficult path, that reaches toward God, and while the crucifix foot at Saint Bertin invited viewers to contemplate the meanings of stories and ideas set in relation to each other, here the experience of vision is of utmost importance. Sainte-Chapelle was a visual analogy for heaven itself, and through its beauty viewers are as if transported, given a glimpse of the divine.

The idea that vision could be a vehicle for devotion to God is also evident in splendid carved altarpieces from the period. A high altar retable made around 1350 for the Cistercian monastery of Marienstatt, Germany is still in situ and displays an impressive array of figures (Figure 8.12). On the top row are the twelve apostles, each in his own niche; in the center of the row is a larger niche, with a group of the Christ and the Virgin. The background of the figures shows a starry sky, as if to evoke a heavenly, higher realm. The apostles sway delicately in their spacious niches, while the central group shows Christ blessing the Virgin. Below are twelve busts of the martyred virgins of Saint Ursula of Cologne. At the bottommost level, the wooden tracery of the frame forms a grille, through which is even now visible a set of wrapped skulls. Niches in the Virgin's busts were probably once relic containers, covered with rock crystal—valued in the Middle Ages for its pure clarity and solid state—so that like the skulls, the viewer can see the relics.[36]

The altar of Marienstatt might be understood as a type of reliquary; yet relics from earlier periods were enclosed and protected in a box, as seen in the reliquary box of stones at the Vatican, or covered in a sheath of gold, as in Egbert's staff. Here the relics are on display for all to see. The busts of the virgins even outsize the image of Christ and the Virgin in the central niche, as if the vision of the relics provides the link to these

FIGURE 8.12 Ursula Altar, Marienstatt, 1350. © Wikimedia Commons (public domain).

distant figures. Moreover, doors on the altar could be opened or closed: the former for feast days and the latter for periods of atonement, as during Lent. The vision of the relics would thus be at one moment an occasion, at others a memory or a desire. Unlike the reliquary of Trier or Liège, where the divinity of the contents was implied in its form or exotic decoration, here the link to the divine occurs directly through the sense of sight.

These ideas about vision were not limited to art made for Christian patrons and rulers. An illuminated Haggadah, made in the region of Aragon in the first third of the fourteenth century, contains a cycle of illuminations based on the Hebrew Bible, and the texts required for a Passover seder. The Sarajevo Haggadah, as it is known, contains selections from the Creation and Genesis, Exodus, and Deuteronomy, three scenes depicting contemporary Jewish life and the celebration of Passover, and an image of a rebuilt Temple of Jerusalem (Figure 8.13).

By combining scenes of Genesis, Exodus, and Deuteronomy with contemporary Passover ritual and the rebuilt temple, the Haggadah cycle situates the reader's celebration of Passover within a larger narrative of sacred history. As a line from the text reads: "In every generation one is required to see oneself as if he or she had gone out of Egypt … for it was not our ancestors alone whom God redeemed but even us with them."[37]

To this end, the cycle does not end with the crossing of the Red Sea, but instead with Miriam, leading the Israelite women in a song of praise, as if an invocation and reminder to viewers to do the same.[38] In the upper half of the page, the Israelites move through the narrow space of the parted red sea; debris floats beside them in the water, while the Pharoah stands on the side of the picture plane. Below, Miriam stands with five women, who hold their hands as if in dance, while Miriam plays the tambourine. As Adam Cohen

FIGURE 8.13 Sarajevo Haggadah. © National Museum of Bosnia and Herzogovina.

has argued, the images in this manuscript emphasize lived, sensual experience—the figures crossing the sea crowd into one another, the dancing women touch one another's hands, and the tambourine is a reminder of the music that played—and thus help the viewer to imagine all aspects of the experience, to place him- or herself there.[39] Even the procession moves from right to left, following the direction of the Hebrew text, and into the space of the left hand of the reader as he or she turns the page. Like the images of Sainte-Chapelle, these images invite the viewer to raise his or her mind toward something beyond the world at hand.

It is not known for whom this book was made, but it has been argued that books like these were made for women, as gifts for betrothal or wedding, and kept as family heirlooms.[40] This Haggadah seems to have been preserved among family belongings for generations, even under the most difficult circumstances, for it contains an inscription written by a Venetian inquisitor in 1609 saving it from destruction. By 1894 it was in

Sarajevo, when it was given to the National Museum of Bosnia and Herzegovina by Josef Cohen, and it remained there through the Nazi occupation of Bosnia in 1941 thanks to the efforts of the museum's curator, who kept it hidden and safe. Like the stories it contains, the book is a powerful reminder of survival and adversity, and the importance of art objects as witnesses to history and bearers of culture.

CONCLUSION

The Sarajevo Haggadah is a fitting end for this survey, for it is a reminder that the world of medieval Europe was far more diverse, international, and culturally rich than is often believed. Made in Aragon, its artists seem to be masters of the painterly styles newly current in artistic centers such as Paris. Perhaps made for a woman, as a gift and sign of her wedding union and new life. As this chapter has shown, medieval art was made not only for kings and bishops, but for monks, for women, for lay patrons. As the world of the later Middle Ages became ever more urban, and its laity more literate, the numbers of books and manuscripts being made grew exponentially. So too did the variety of art objects made for lay and religious use.

The objects in this chapter cross boundaries between sacred and secular, classical and Christian, Christian, Jewish, and Muslim. These categories were fluid, as is evident in the image from the *Hortus Deliciarum*, the box in Liège, or the Sarajevo Haggadah. The role of the artist was also more complex and changing than might be assumed: patrons such as Blanche of Castile or the archbishop Drogo might well have played a significant role in conceiving the objects that they had made, artists of the Haggadah were likely working for different contexts and clients, adapting their imagery and style for each.

The Haggadah also shows the importance of vision in the later period, and the role of art in creating such "visions." This chapter has shown how images and objects might provide an encounter with the divine, or be vehicles for the contemplation of it. In the early period the relics of the Holy Land enabled a very special viewer to behold fragments of sacred sites; by the time of Bishop Egbert the relics were sheathed in gold, made into a staff for performance of the liturgy; by the Gothic era, relics were made visible to large audiences, incorporated into altars and put on display, as the busts in the altar from Marienstatt attest. As a book made for the celebration of the Seder, the Haggadah manuscript invites the viewer to consider the experience of the Exodus at the time of Passover, going beyond words and images to consider the sounds, touch, and feel of the event. Through a vision of sacred history, it blends the biblical past with the rituals of the present and the hope for the future.

CHAPTER NINE

History

MATTHEW KEMPSHALL

It is a long-standing criticism of Western Latin historiography in the Middle Ages that it either was not interested or deliberately ignored the analysis of historical causation. And yet causation had been made central to history-writing by notable classical authorities: Tacitus intended to describe "not just the occurrence and outcome of events but their reason and causes" (*non modo casus eventusque rerum ... sed ratio etiam causaeque*);[1] Vergil declared "happy ... the person who has been able to understand the causes of things."[2] This focus carried consequences for classification into genre. For Aulus Gellius, history is an exposition or demonstration of "deeds done;" it is superior to annals because, whereas annals simply compile *res gestae*, following the order of each year, history expounds the reason (*ratio*) and the prudential deliberation (*consilium*) behind them.[3] If historiography from the period 750–1350 was dominated by annals, therefore, then this is as revealing as it is damning of the sophistication of the ideas that informed it.

For every problem, of course, there is a solution that is neat and simple and wrong. The alleged distinctiveness of this "medieval" sense of history offers a prime example. "It is history," Augustine writes, "when deeds done, whether by God or by humans, are commemorated; ... it is aetiology when the causes of what is said or done are set out."[4] This is the conceptual demarcation that underpins Augustine's otherwise blunt statement that he will not be providing a narrative of the calamities of the Second Punic War because, were he to set these out, he would become nothing other than a writer of history.[5] For Augustine, at least, investigating the cause of a particular historical event went beyond the remit of what should be classified as history. If the meaning of history, the significance of past events, lay in identifying causes, the reasons *why* something happened, then this task belonged, strictly speaking, not to the historian, but to preachers or to prophets—individuals who explain what God wills in the future, but also in the present and the past. This did not imply, for Augustine, that historiography was otiose. Commemorating an individual's *res gestae* could still serve a moral-didactic function: history is useful because it teaches through examples (*utilis historia quae nutrit exemplis*) and thereby constitutes the first of seven steps of spiritual understanding.[6] Nonetheless, as far as Augustine was concerned, the writing of history should otherwise be restricted to the divinely instituted *ordo temporum*:

> what has already gone into the past and cannot be undone must be considered part of the order of time, whose creator and controller is God. There is a difference between narrating what has been done and teaching what should be done. History narrates past events in a faithful and useful way, whereas the books of haruspices and similar literature set out to teach things to be done, or observed, with the boldness of admonition rather than with the trustworthiness (*fides*) of a witness.[7]

One consequence of Augustine's strictures in the Middle Ages was for writers of history to concentrate primarily on chronography, on recording the sequence of events in time. In formal terms, this might mean annotating events to Easter tables, but the practice carried an interpretative significance too. According to Augustine, time is experienced by humans as a distension of the soul and, as such, is an expression and consequence of sin. Past, present, and future, by contrast, exist simultaneously in God as a single point of "now" (*simul nunc*). This differentiation of human from divine perception applies to the temporal succession of individual events, but also to the entirety of world history. As a result, it is only when the created universe is seen in its totality that the significance of the *ordo temporum* becomes clear. As Bonaventure put it, "no reader can appreciate the beauty of a song unless they look at all the verses. In the same way, no human can appreciate the beauty of universal order and governance unless they see it as a whole. No-one lives long enough to witness all history with their own eyes; nor can they foresee the future for themselves."[8] This is why prophets—human beings who shared, at least in part, God's atemporal perspective—used the past tense to speak of events in the future. This is also why chroniclers left the providential significance of events open to interpretation by their continuators—they saw their work as a process, a record inherited from their predecessors to be passed on to their successors. Such modesty appeared in disclaimers. "I leave the allegorical readings and interpretations appropriate to human conduct to be expanded by the learned," wrote Orderic Vitalis, "setting myself the task of relating ... straightforward history (*simplex historia*)." His own aim was simply to record events whose significance would be revealed only in the future, or by those blessed with greater understanding and ability than his own.[9] Such restraint was doubly important for contemporary events. This approach was indebted, once again, to Augustine, in this case his division of the history of the world into Six Ages.[10] On this reckoning, "sacred history" was complete at the end of the Fifth Age, with the death, Resurrection, and Ascension of Jesus Christ. Thereafter, the world had entered into an old age (*senectus mundi*) characterized by exterior decay and interior spiritual renewal. Events in this Sixth Age still fall under the governance of God, but they will not necessarily have the significance to the economy of salvation that could be traced for the events recorded in scripture in ages one through to five. God can, and will, continue to intervene directly in human history, but such active providence will be even harder to unveil—"God's ways are inscrutable and his judgments are past searching out."[11] More prevalent in the Sixth Age is permissive providence—God will allow events, and Nature, to take their course.[12]

Augustine focused the attention of medieval writers on the constraints under which they were writing. History was formally distinct from aetiology, chronography from prophecy, permissive providence from active providence. While humans could still learn from individual moral *exempla* and chart the natural order of events in time, the exact providential order of those same events might be unknown and, in the Sixth Age, unknowable. Medieval writers were given room for maneuver, however, by the discussion of divine and human causation which they found in Boethius and, in particular, his distillation of Cicero's analysis of intrinsic arguments drawn from circumstance—what happens before, during, and after a particular event. This type of argumentation concentrated on dissecting efficient causes and what they bring about. Knowledge of causes produces knowledge of effects, but also vice versa—just as the cause shows what has been effected, so the effect demonstrates the nature of the cause. This extends to secondary causes—what the Stoics termed "fate"—namely, those things (place, time, material, means) that do not, in themselves, produce an effect, but without which that effect cannot be produced. Some of these secondary causes are the result of Nature, some of human will; some are clear, some lie hidden. Causes which are clear pertain to human will; causes which are hidden are subject to "fortune"—a shorthand for causes that are unknown: "since nothing happens without a cause, fortune is simply what is effected by an obscure and hidden cause."[13]

Boethius's commentary on Cicero had a profound impact on how subsequent writers thought about, and used, the notions of cause and effect. In discussing "fate," for example, Boethius defined it as "a certain intricate interweaving and chain-like connection of antecedent causes and consequent events."[14] Like Cicero, Boethius sought to preserve human free will against the necessity of events, and he did so by distinguishing between different types of antecedent cause. When discussing "fortuitous occurrences" (*fortuitis casibus*), therefore, he proffered a formulation based on Aristotle's definition of "chance" (*casus*): "whenever something is done for the sake of some given end, and another thing occurs, for some reason or other, different from what was intended, it is called chance ... Now this is indeed believed to have happened by chance but it does not come from nothing; for it has its proper causes, and their unforeseen and unexpected coming together appears to have produced a chance event."[15] For Boethius, both "fortune" and "chance" denoted the unintended consequence of a particular action or the unforeseen result of a conjunction of separate causes. Chance events were thus the product of a chain of causes, not a random force.

Belief in an underlying principle of cosmic order placed Boethius's definitions of fate, fortune, and chance within a broader understanding of the overarching operation of divine providence and thereby provided medieval writers with a wide theological and philosophical field in which to place their language of causality.[16] Reference to the "fluctuations" of fortune and chance might reflect no more than a comparison of the world to the unpredictable character of the sea. However, fortune and chance could also indicate a recognition that unexpected events arise from the combination of several different causes. Boethius's commentary on Cicero presupposed a clear sense of where such terminology fitted into a series of different types of cause—intended or unintended, known or unknown. These were categories of argument with a precise explanatory role in uncovering antecedent, secondary, and efficient causes, and for a universe whose intrinsic order was, at least in principle, open to identification by the microcosm of the rational human soul. Reasons could be given, accounts could be rendered (*reddere rationes*). Crucially, Boethius's approach also squared with a medieval understanding of Plato's *Timaeus* based on Calcidius's discussion of the way in which a divinely ordained universe operates under providence, fate, fortune, and chance. Given that some things are necessary, some are possible and some are contingent (*dubium*), Calcidius had argued that there is no intrinsic contradiction in distinguishing between a primary (or principal) cause and secondary (or incidental) causes. Human deliberation over contingent subjects expresses their moral freedom to perform acts of virtue and vice, but the consequences of these actions may themselves interact and produce unintended and uncontrollable results. Fortune is therefore defined as "the concurrence of two simultaneously occurring causes that draw their origin from an intention, from which concurrence something happens that occasions surprise independently of what was hoped for."[17] This aetiology accommodated, rather than rejected, the epistemological uncertainty that might otherwise be acknowledged to characterize a particular course of events. An appeal to the terms "providence" and "fortune," in other words, was not an admission of historiographical defeat; instead, it represented the interweaving of causes and the temporal ordering of what happens in a world that is ultimately governed by God.

Narrating individual events in the Sixth Age posed definite epistemological and interpretative challenges. Augustine's distinction between history and aetiology, between what is humanly and divinely instituted, could clearly dovetail with Boethius's and Calcidius's discussion of causes that human understanding may, or may not, be able to grasp. Chronography was an acknowledgment of the limits on human understanding, but this did not stem from any lack of interest in causation, be it primary providence or secondary *gesta*. Compiling the *ordo rerum* within the divinely instituted sequence of time was one task; commenting on and understanding the providential order of those same events was quite another; using those individual events as particular *exempla* to instruct an audience in more general truths of ethical conduct, the human institution of history, was different again. The influence of such a deliberate and theoretically informed approach was far-reaching. Reluctance to claim prophetic insight into the divine meaning of events was balanced by a well-developed language of causality and by awareness of the level of causation that *was* more clearly discernible by human understanding, namely, individual human actions, *res gestae*. Recording this last type of secondary cause, moreover, was given scriptural sanction by the Book of Life at the Last Judgment—the moment at which not only would individuals have to render an account of their own lives but also where a narrative of their deeds would be read out in front of them.[18] However, this form of writing presented problems too, as Augustine, again, had recognized.

Books 10 and 11 of the *Confessions* contained Augustine's meditation on the nature of memory and the way in which it is necessarily bound to the experience and understanding of time. Time is a part of creation. While it might conveniently and conventionally be used as a measure provided by motion of the celestial bodies, the movement of the sun and the moon, there are also as many experienced times as there are physically moving objects. Time, in other words, is also relative to subjective human experience.[19] For Augustine, this principle had important consequences for the operation of human memory. Indeed, in this regard, *De Trinitate* was just as significant for Augustine's ideas on historiography as the *Confessions*, because of its examination of the interdependent relationship between three faculties of the human soul—memory, understanding, and will. Sense memories have to be actively ordered and reordered by the mind for them to be retrieved, so that their significance can be understood by individual human beings.[20]

If memory is not a passive process, then the act of reminiscence is not without its dangers, since remembrance of past deeds—the precondition for both confession in this life and the final reckoning at the Last Judgment—necessarily involves the re-presentation, the reenactment in the mind, of what has happened in the past. The goal may be compunction and repentance, but the attendant risk is that the original temptation will return. This also applies to remembrance on the Day of Judgment. According to Hugh of Saint Victor, reading from the Book of Deeds involves a very specific type of memory—one that is free from emotion. For the blessed, the memory of the past will prompt, not pain, but joy. In so far as it pertains to rational knowledge, souls will be mindful of their past evils, but in so far as it pertains to the sensation of experience, they will be utterly forgetful. There are, Hugh explains, two types of knowledge of evil: one by which evil does not escape the power of the mind, the other by which it clings to the senses of the person who experiences it.[21] When deeds are remembered, in other words, this has to be done carefully. For Gregory the Great, it was a major challenge for those who needed to remember their own history, good deeds as well as bad, because the memory of virtue can always serve as a pitfall to pride.[22] The fates of Orpheus and Lot made the same point. "Do *not* look back" might, in these circumstances, be the counsel of prudence: "No man putting his hand to the plough and looking back is fit for the kingdom of God."[23] Forgetting one's past, in other words, was as active a process as remembering; amnesia could be as important as commemoration. This applied to individual humans but also to communities—"amnesty," not just memory, was central to the construction of collective identity.

Recording the past in writing was a deliberate decision for medieval historians. It was also difficult, and it could be both a presumptuous and a dangerous thing to do. There were other ways of remembering the past than writing down a narrative of deeds or compiling the sequence of events in time. Jewish historiography provided a case in point: from the first century CE through to the sixteenth, ritual and liturgy provided a more significant means of commemorating and interpreting past events. Written history, by comparison, was not the primary vehicle for memory.[24] For Christian writers in the Sixth Age, the line of least resistance may likewise have been not to attempt historiography at all, or to restrict themselves to commemorating "sacred history" but only up to the destruction of the Second Temple or up to the life, death, and Resurrection of Christ. Anything beyond that necessarily involved taking a position along a very broad spectrum, from annotated chronography all the way to prophecy. It was a delicate balance to strike. Not everyone agreed where to draw the line. Augustine may have cautioned restraint, but other models were available. Since Augustine himself had composed neither history nor chronography, medieval writers turned to Eusebius of Caesarea (who paired "ecclesiastical history" with synchronised tables of events) and Orosius (who integrated history and chronology into a single work). Indeed, for all his protestations of fidelity to Augustine, Orosius provided a strikingly different model of historiography to the one counseled by his "teacher." While Orosius acknowledged the inscrutability of God's judgments ("all of which we cannot know, nor can we explain those which we do know"), he remained sufficiently confident in his own insight to detect and expound a well-defined pattern of cause and effect in the "hidden order" of events.[25] Orosius found the paradigm for this narrative in the retributive justice of the Old Testament.

Orosius's typological interpretation of the ten scourges (*plagae*) of Egypt as a key to the ten persecutions of the Church—an interpretation whose validity was immediately questioned by Augustine[26]—opened up the possibility of reading historical events in the Bible as a programmatic template for historical events in the Sixth Age, in the period between the New Testament and the Second Coming. Correlating the construction, destruction, and restoration of the Temple at Jerusalem with the planting, scourging, and reformation of the Christian Church, or the rise and fall of the kingdoms of Israel and Judah with the rise and fall of kingdoms within Christendom, could provide an appealingly clear explanation for the vicissitudes of contemporary events. Twelfth-century writers such as Rupert of Deutz, Honorius Augustodunensis, Gerhoh of Reichersberg, and Anselm of Havelberg all pushed this pattern hard, identifying a *specific* providential order to the sequence of events in the Sixth Age and finding it in the seven gifts of the Holy Spirit from Isaiah (11:2) or the seven seals and the seven-headed dragon from Revelation. This was the tradition that culminated in Joachim of Fiore's elaborate concordance of individual events in the Old Testament with individual events in Christian history since the New—a pairing that revealed the imminence of the opening of the sixth seal in the third *status* of the Holy Spirit and a corresponding age of spiritual renewal.[27]

Augustine and Orosius pulled medieval readers in different directions. The strain often showed. Otto of Freising, for example, was deeply committed to Orosius's identification.

of the order of divine judgment in history, but also stressed its inscrutability. As it had done for Augustine, Romans 11 prompted Otto to reflect that humans cannot comprehend the secret counsels of God. Writing his world history in the 1140s, Otto therefore claims that his intention was simply to write down what was done (*res gestas scribere*), not to justify or render an account of the reason *why* it was done (*rerum gestarum rationem reddere*). And yet, Otto remarks, humans are frequently obliged to try to give an account of the reasons behind events. "Are we, then, to attempt an explanation of things we are unable to understand?," he asks. "We can certainly provide human reasons (*rationes humanae*)," he concludes, "even though we may still be unable to comprehend divine reasons (*rationes divinae*)."[28] Having warned against relying on human reasoning to uncover the causes of things, Otto underlines Augustine's paradigm of the inability of the human judge to perceive the inner workings of the human heart[29] and concludes by reiterating the same epistemological uncertainty:[30] "for, as I have said above of Augustine, some matters are set down in his writings, not as assertion, but only on the basis of opinion and investigation, and the scrutiny of a definitive judgment has been left to those who are wiser."[31] Like Augustine, Otto accordingly falls back on chronography. The most straightforward function served by his *Chronicle* is to set out what he terms "the sequence of history" (*series historiae*), epitomized by a numerical listing of emperors, kings, and popes, and the synchronization of alternative systems of dating. Establishing this ordered sequence of deeds (*series rerum gestarum*), Otto explains, reflects a commitment to truth—just as grammar and logic select only what is useful, so the function of chronographers (*facultas chronographorum*) is to choose the truth and to avoid lies.[32] Earlier in the twelfth century, Hugh of Fleury had cautioned that those *res gestae* which are presented without the certitude provided by chronology should not be accepted as history.[33] Otto follows suit, and appeals directly to "the diligent student [who] will find the sequence of past events set out in a manner which is free from confusion."[34] In the same sentence, however, Otto also moves beyond such annotated chronography to appeal equally to "the devout listener [who] will observe what is to be avoided by reason of the countless miseries which are wrought by the unstable character of worldly affairs." In doing so, Otto drew attention to the underlying moral purpose of his work. Recording the ups and downs of the Sixth Age, the *mutabilitas rerum*, could—and should—serve as consolation for the sufferings of the present.

Boethius's *Consolation of Philosophy* had drawn out the value of contemplating the mutability of Fortune and the transitoriness of worldly goods as a meditation on examples of how temporal power and happiness can be so swiftly overthrown.[35] Viewed in these terms, the writing of history retained its classical connection with tragedy, a literary form whose sorrowful subject matter, in Isidore of Seville's formulation, comprised *antiqua gesta*, the misfortunes of kings and of great men and the *res publica*.[36] This Stoic notion ("the greatest solace exists in the thought that what has happened to you has been suffered by everyone before you and will be suffered by everyone who comes after"[37]) resonated strongly with late antique and early Christian historiography. Rufinus stated that he had been asked to translate Eusebius into Latin for the sake of consolation as well as edification;[38] Macrobius presented history as an antidote to sorrow.[39] Orosius, meanwhile, took his cue from Vergil's *Aeneid*,[40] where Aeneas sought to bring solace to those of his companions who had survived dangers and shipwreck by saying "perhaps it will help one day to remember even these things."[41] This *sententia*, Orosius comments, may have been made up to suit one occasion, but, in his view, it carried a more general significance still. Only a comparison of events across time will produce correct judgment on the relative degree of present suffering. His own contemporaries should therefore be consoled by the remembrance of the wars, plagues, and famines of the past—they provided consolation for the sufferings of the present.[42]

Otto of Freising's hesitation in offering definitive judgments, be they on the providential significance of events or the justification for individual actions, is a marked feature of his *Chronicle*. He was certainly not unaware of the didactic purpose that his writing could still serve—history commemorates deeds that are worthy of record and of being handed down to posterity, or which can serve as a warning and reproof.[43] However, he was adamant that his work was not intended to provide *exempla* that would inspire exploits in war—it was not the Book of Maccabees. Nor was it a vehicle for maxims and moral reflections. Instead, Otto wanted to set out the calamities, suffering, and changeability of events in this world, woven together "in the manner of a tragedy."[44] Some ten years later, when Otto came to compose the *Deeds* of Frederick Barbarossa, the difference in his approach was striking. The theme of mutability remains, but Otto now stated that he was writing, not tragedy, but *iocunda historia*, "pleasurable history."[45] Its didactic purpose is made immediately clear: "the intention of all those who have written down *res gestae* before us has been to extol the shining deeds of brave men in order to move the minds of humans to virtue and either suppress with silence the dark deeds of the wicked or, if they are brought into the light, to set them down as a source of terror."[46] Otto adjusts his own language accordingly—the simple diction of history (*plana historica dictio*) will be interspersed with a more amplified and loftier style when dealing with more philosophical subjects. Inspirational and enjoyable *gesta* clearly required a different approach to consolatory chronicle, just as exemplary deeds expressed a different approach to time from chronography.[47]

Otto of Freising's recognition of a methodological range to the writing of history was, in part, a reflection of the different traditions that he was interweaving, and his attempt to reconcile Orosian and Augustinian historiography could not conceal their underlying tensions. However, it also reflected the different purposes and audiences that his *Chronicle* and *Gesta* were addressing. In both instances, causation required careful handling, but it is only in recording the *deeds* of Frederick that he expresses the explicit aim of describing, not *casus*, but *causae*.[48] The difference in approach, in other words, was also a question of rhetoric.

One good reason why there is no clearly defined genre of history-writing in the Middle Ages is that writers could already find enough in the way of guidelines and principles within handbooks of classical rhetoric.[49] Cicero himself had wondered why no one had tried to assemble precepts of history-writing into a single set of rules and, *faute de mieux*, had put one together himself.[50] In the first instance, this meant that subsequent historiography was understood to be governed by the three basic functions of classical rhetoric—to teach, to move, and to please or entertain (*docere, movere, delectare*)—each of which, not least the pleasure principle, carried consequences for the way in which history should be written. In the second instance, it meant that the writing of history also followed rhetoric in its three basic divisions—demonstrative, judicial, and deliberative oratory—each of which required the construction of a narrative of deeds done, *narratio rei gestae*.

The first category of rhetoric—demonstrative rhetoric—concerned the praise and commemoration of distinguished individuals, or indeed with the castigation and denunciation of the wicked. In both cases, it was marked by an attention to reputation (*fama*) and remembrance by posterity (*memoria posteritatis*). Praising the deeds of individuals was also intended as an incentive to imitation since, as the twelfth-century proverb put it, an *exemplum* is a better means of instruction than a precept.[51] Such historical material was accordingly taught in the Middle Ages, alongside poetry, as part of an initial training in grammar and as a form of moral philosophy tailored to the instruction of an audience of young, simple, or ignorant minds. This was the historiographical legacy embodied by Valerius Maximus' *Memorable Deeds and Sayings*.[52] It also established a close relationship with the genre of "mirror-for-princes" (*speculum principis*). The deeds of predecessors were written down to be instructive, so that they could be imitated and emulated by sons and successors. As Wipo's *Gesta Chuonradi* put it, the emperor Henry III should look at his father as in a mirror, but with the sharp admonition that he should take care that the reflection matched: "It often comes to pass that shamefacedness and perturbation of the mind on the part of descendants is born easily from praise of their ancestors if, although they have praised their deeds with repute as their teacher, they have not at least equalled them."[53]

The second category of rhetoric—judicial rhetoric—concentrated on setting out who, what, where, when, why, how, by what means, and in what circumstances an event took place, all with a view to accusing or defending an individual on a charge of having done that particular deed. This extended to the character of the individual or individuals performing that action and thereby to combining a depiction of character with a narrative of deeds, as a means of accusation but also as a means of defense. Describing what sort of person an individual is (*qualis est*) accordingly became central to whether or not they had performed the action in question. Again, the influence of this strand of rhetoric on medieval historiography is marked, not least in the number of medieval "lives" that were written to defend an individual against certain accusations— in the ninth century, for example, when Paschasius Radbertus defended Wala in the *Epitaphium Arsenii*,[54] or in the eleventh century, with the deliberately anonymous "life" of the emperor Henry IV. Judicial rhetoric also considered anything that was subject to differing views, literally "controversy" (*controversia*), including the interpretation of disputed documents such as a dead person's will. Again, judicial rhetoric used narrative to harmonize character with action and word: was this the sort of person who would have written such a text and, if so, what was their intention? For medieval writers, it was a natural corollary to develop historiography from cartularies, that is, from collections of charters which described the circumstances of particular bequests of rights and lands. Judicial rhetoric, lastly, covered the language and testimony of human witnesses, either as individuals or in the form of popular opinion. Gildas, in the fifth century, composed his *Ruin of Britain* by constructing a case for the prosecution of its kings and clergy. Galbert of Bruges, in the twelfth century, established who exactly did what, where, when, and why, in the events surrounding the murder of the count of Flanders—his "history" was a personal response to the failures of human justice and of the sworn inquest (*inquisitio*) that had been set up ostensibly to answer precisely those questions.

The third category of rhetoric, deliberative rhetoric, comprised speeches or texts composed for or against a particular course of political action. This approach underpinned a historiography that was concerned, first and foremost, with delivering counsel and advice. Describing the events of the past constituted an appeal to precedent or to experience, but it also evoked specific criteria for whether or not an action should be taken: is the course of action morally worthy (*honestum*), is it expedient or advantageous (*utile*), is it necessary or even possible (*possibile*)? The deliberation that resulted, often as a set-piece debate, became a marked feature of historical writing. Establishing the cause of an action involved uncovering not only *rationes* but also *consilia*.

One consequence of the close association between rhetoric and the writing of history in the Middle Ages was for historiography to be considered a secondary subject. It was not autonomous, either as a branch of knowledge or as a capitalized abstract noun.[55] Definitions of *historia* generally appear, instead, under the much broader guise of *narratio rei gestae*, "narrative of events,"[56] where narrative is understood as "the exposition of deeds done," *narratio est rerum gestarum expositio.*[57] Considered in these terms, the writing of history was understood to follow a further tripartite distinction from classical rhetoric, this time between the qualities that define *all* narrative—brevity, clarity, and what was termed plausibility or verisimilitude. Brevity and clarity do what they say; plausibility or verisimilitude, meanwhile, is effected through invention, that is, by finding the right argument for the point being made, be it specific to the case in question or one which is typical or commonplace to the situation under discussion. The goal of such probable argumentation is not truth, but faith (*fides*), a quality of trustworthiness that derives from the narrator (hence the credibility established in the prologue) and from the narrative which is then produced. Such argumentation "produces conviction (*fides*) in something that is otherwise in doubt (*dubium*)."[58]

According to manuals of rhetoric, narratives secure plausibility and trustworthiness through a number of different techniques, classified under external and internal testimony. External testimony comprises individual witnesses and popular opinion; internal testimony is intrinsic to the argument itself and includes circumstances, antecedent events, causes, and consequences. Plausibility is accordingly governed by the subject matter of what is narrated, by what generally happens or conforms to Nature, and by what corresponds to the opinion of one's audience. One of the most effective techniques is *enargeia*, the vividness that is given to a narrative so that it seems as if events are happening before the audience's very eyes.[59] This strategy moves the audience by appealing to their emotions, but, as with Isidore's etymology for the word "history" itself, it also makes a narrative convincing as the product of eyewitness testimony or autopsy.[60] Given that *enargeia* was translated into Latin as *evidentia*, this is what "evidence" meant, strictly speaking, when historiography was defined as "narrative of deeds done."

This much, then, might be regarded as common ground for all medieval writers who were taught grammar and rhetoric, schooled in Cicero's *De Inventione* or the *Rhetorica ad Herennium* or one of the numerous digests through which their contents were transmitted. It provides a consistent and fundamental underpinning to the writing of history throughout the Middle Ages.[61] Where problems arise is with the category of rhetorical verisimilitude. Whether history is written to teach moral lessons, to defend individual reputations, or to deliver political advice, the plausible reconstruction of what might have happened becomes just as important as what actually did. From here it was only a short step to expand the definition of history to "narrative of what was done *or might have been done*" (*narratio rei gestae aut ut rei gestae*).[62] Medieval historians, as a result, could not avoid the issues that were raised by the fact that parts of their narrative comprised material which had been made up.

Verisimilitude was not a new problem for writers of history in the Middle Ages; it was there from the start. It also did not go away. There are four moments when the lines of controversy become particularly clear—in the fifth, twelfth, late thirteenth, and fourteenth centuries—where writers were drawn into spelling out exactly what the writing of history could, and should, involve. The first of these triggers was the sharp exchange between Augustine and Jerome over Paul's letter to the Galatians.

Augustine's interest in how humans store and understand the past experience of events extended to how the memory actually recalls "past sensibles." The problem here lay with the fact that these *sensibilia* are, strictly speaking, false—what is recalled is only the generated image of experience, not the experience itself. When Augustine analyzes the epistemological status of these *sensibilia*, he therefore refers to them as opinion (*opinio*) rather than knowledge (*scientia*). As a result, Augustine took a keen interest in verisimilitude as a rhetorical strategy *and* an epistemological category. And yet the term is striking by its absence from *De doctrina Christiana*, the text that says most about the utility of rhetoric in the service of Christian truth. The context in which the notion is discussed, therefore, becomes all the more revealing. Those who try to make falsehood persuasive, Augustine writes, produce a narrative that is brief, clear, and plausible.[63] There are lots of made-up fables and falsehoods, he observes; these are human creations, lies that serve to give people pleasure; they are false and mendacious.[64] We call something false, he explains, when the signification of something is not what it is said to be. It comes in two forms: those things that cannot exist as such and those things that do not exist even though it is possible that they could.[65]

Rhetorical verisimilitude clearly troubled Augustine. In a specifically historiographical context, it was central to his disagreement with Jerome over Paul's correction of Peter in Galatians 2:11–21. According to Augustine, Jerome had argued that Paul made up the episode in order to make an instructive point—the event itself had not actually happened, as it was described in scripture but was staged to illustrate a spiritual truth. As a question of exegesis, Augustine believed this interpretation went to the heart of how Christians should use classical rhetoric to elucidate the Bible since, if verisimilitude was invoked to explain Paul's action on this one occasion, then the truth of the entire New Testament would be called into question. As a result, the need to clarify the nature of narrative verisimilitude prompted Augustine to write, not one, but two treatises on the subject of lying—*De mendacio* and *Contra mendacium*. A made-up narrative, Augustine concludes, which nonetheless has a true meaning or signification is, strictly speaking, not a lie, since a lie depends on the intention to deceive. The deployment of such *ficta narratio*, however, at least beyond the use of parables, was, in his view, *not* applicable to the historical account of the apostles' actions in the New Testament.

Augustine himself acknowledged that he did not explain himself as clearly as he might have done on the subject of lying.[66] What his analysis left open was the question of historical narrative *outside* of the New Testament, a question that already had a long pedigree in Neoplatonism in discussion of the role of fictive material in philosophy. According to Macrobius, fables come in two forms: those that serve no other function than pleasure (this is the category of which Augustine was so dismissive in *De doctrina Christiana*) and those that inspire their audience to perform virtuous deeds. Within this second category, Macrobius draws a further distinction between fables that are entirely made up (which have no place in philosophy) and those that have a foundation of truth and which present morally worthy subject matter beneath a covering or veil of allegory. It is this second category of fabulous narrative, Macrobius concludes, that *can* be deployed in the service of moral truth.[67]

Familiarity with both Augustine and Macrobius ensured that medieval writers who narrated extra-scriptural events had to consider a series of conceptually distinct terms through which their text could be approached: truth, opinion, verisimilitude, fable, falsehood, and lies. Add to this complexity the various categories of causation, providence, fortune, consolation, and moral *exemplum* with which they were familiar from Boethius, and it should not be surprising to find medieval writers responding to this challenge in a variety of different ways.

The second focal point for debate over verisimilitude was provided by the distinction between three basic types of narrative—history, argument, and fable.[68] According to this classification, *historia* is a narrative of what actually happened; *argumentum* a narrative of events that have been shaped or made up but that nevertheless could have happened (in other words, what is plausible and possible); and *fabula*, finally, is a narrative of events that neither happened nor could have happened (in other words, what is implausible and impossible). What this threefold categorization precipitated in the twelfth century was, in many respects, a turf-war between the two disciplines that otherwise laid claim to the narrative forms at either end of this scale, namely, historiography and poetry.[69]

Given that grammar and rhetoric were taught through the study of both classical historians and classical poets, it was perhaps only natural that the precise status of verisimilitude should become such a bone of contention. This was, in part, a reflection of the overlap in subject matter and language, when rhetoric and poetry were regarded as prose and verse types of the same principles of writing and when verse historical narrative comprised tragedy and heroic deeds. Both history and poetry could appeal to conformity with what usually happens; both of them used material that was appropriate primarily for less well-educated groups of people. It was the latter consideration, for example, that exercised Guibert of Nogent when he invoked a mixed audience for his account of the First Crusade (boldly entitled the *Deeds of God through the Franks*)—the learned would look for the spiritual meaning of what he was narrating, the simple would be moved by the literal account of deeds but would also need to be entertained by digressions and, in some cases, by fable. This overlap between rhetoric and poetry had important consequences for a language of "fiction" (*fictio, fingere*) that could be commensurable with constructing a plausible and convincing narrative of events but which could also be correlated with falsehood (*falsa*) and lies (*mendacia*). Indeed, it had the quite practical result of making some writers attempt to shift the concept of verisimilitude from an ontological to an aesthetic category of narrative. According to John of Garland, fabulous narrative (*fabula*) can be defined as lying with probability.[70] "We ought to lie with probability," explains Geoffrey of Vinsauf, "so that false narration is presented as if it were true."[71]

Aesthetic verisimilitude has frequently been linked to the so-called "rise of literary fiction" with which the twelfth century is often credited. However, it also posed a real challenge to writers of history for whom verisimilitude had hitherto played such a central role in the construction of a plausible narrative of events. This is best illustrated by John of Salisbury, in the 1150s, when he used Boethius's *De Topicis Differentiis* to classify three types of approach to knowledge: demonstrative logic, probable logic, and sophistry. Demonstrative logic, John states, is concerned with necessity, with that which cannot be otherwise, a truth which is determined irrespective of what any particular audience might think or assent to. Probable logic, meanwhile, is concerned with propositions that seem to be true, either to everyone or to many people or to the wise; such opinion is the field of dialectic and rhetoric. Sophistry, finally, is concerned merely with the appearance of probability and not at all with the truth; although it may, on occasion, use true and probable arguments, it otherwise deals in deceit.[72] Of the three categories, John of Salisbury is interested, first and foremost, in the probable opinion utilized by dialectic and rhetoric. The degree of epistemological certainty in any discipline, he explains, is conditioned by the nature of its subject matter. As a result, whereas demonstrative logic will be applicable to mathematics, and sophistry to poetry, probable logic is better suited to the changeable substance of Nature.[73] This does not mean that probable opinion cannot be turned into belief or conviction, and even approach certitude, at least as far as human judgment is concerned. For this principle, John quotes definitions of *fides* put forward by Aristotle—"very strong opinion"[74]—and Hugh of Saint Victor—"voluntary certitude concerning something which is not present, greater than opinion but falling short of knowledge."[75] Nonetheless, John concludes, probability and verisimilitude are the closest humans will get to a knowledge of Nature and, by extension, to the subject matter of historical narrative.

What needs underlining here is the challenge that twelfth-century moves toward a poetic understanding of verisimilitude presented for the writing of history. Once verisimilitude could be construed as a purely aesthetic category, as John of Garland and Geoffrey of Vinsauf suggested, rather than a claim about reality, as John of Salisbury maintained, the idea of a plausible reconstruction of events made writers of history much more nervous of using this rhetorical strategy for fear of being branded, not only as fabulists but also as liars. This was the charge that William of Newburgh leveled against the "fabrications" (*figmenta*) and "lies" (*mendacia*) of Geoffrey of Monmouth.[76] Such anxiety was reflected in increasing concern over the narrative re-presentation of historical truth and even to have precipitated the methodological retreat that is often identified as a defining feature of twelfth-century historical writing—away from the sort of ambitiously rhetorical narratives that characterized the first half of the century toward the more limited annalistic chronicles of the second. Writing in the 1190s, Gervase of Canterbury distinguishes the annalistic form of his *Chronicle* from the writing of history on the basis that "history" makes greater use of the techniques of rhetoric. Chronicles and histories may share intention and subject matter (both of them aim at the truth and set out didactic *exempla* for living well) but each has a different way of handling their material. Gervase then concedes that such a clear-cut distinction is difficult to sustain when chronicles so frequently transgress this boundary.[77]

The problems posed by historiographical verisimilitude were not resolved in the twelfth century. In many respects, they deepened and complicated over the course of the thirteenth century with the recovery of Aristotle's natural philosophy. The idea that an empirical narrative of individual events could never form the basis of "scientific" knowledge was aired in the *Nicomachean Ethics*, when Aristotle crisply dismissed the claims of Sophists to teach political science. This sort of rhetorician, he argued, is completely ignorant of the knowledge that underpins the act of legislation; they assume that politics is the same as, or subordinate to, rhetoric, and that legislation is therefore simply a matter of collecting examples of good laws. Instead, they should realize that both the acquisition of political knowledge and the capacity to discern which laws are good require systematic reflection on underlying principles and assumptions.[78] For a commentator such as Albertus Magnus, the conclusion was clear: without an understanding of the principles of politics (the goal of the political community, say, or the different forms of government), a true knowledge of politics is impossible.[79] As far as Albertus Magnus was concerned, the target for the charge of sophistry was law and lawyers, but it was not long before the same critique was being leveled at history and historians.

Aristotle's *Poetics* had famously compared history to poetry and very much to the advantage of the latter: "the poet's function is to say, not what was done (*gesta*), but the sort of thing that would happen; as a consequence, poetry is more philosophical and worthwhile than history, for poetry deals more with universal statements, history with particulars. A universal statement sets out what sort of person would, probably or necessarily, say or do what sort of thing, and this is what poetry aims at, although it attaches proper names; a particular statement tells us what Alcibiades did or what happened to him."[80] More directly influential on medieval writers was Aristotle's analysis of the nature of scientific knowledge in the *Physics*[81] and *Metaphysics*:[82] we know something only when we know its causes and principles; "scientific" knowledge therefore presupposes a knowledge of causes. Both science and art, Aristotle states, derive from experience (*experimentum*), where experience is the accumulation in the memory of a plurality of individual things. Whereas experience retains knowledge only of those singular particulars, art makes a universal judgment about the similarities it finds in the many things that memory has derived from experience. Experience may therefore have knowledge that something is (*quia, quod*), but art has a knowledge of the cause and the reason why (*causa, propter quid*). If art has a knowledge of causes, then, unlike experience, it can be taught, since teaching requires a knowledge of causes. This is not to say that Aristotle thought that there was no value in the experience of particulars—this, after all, is the point of the *Historia Animalium*, as an accumulation of raw material preparatory to more analytical and explanatory study. This more positive evaluation, however, depends both on the level of knowledge being aimed at and the nature of the audience being addressed. Aristotle's *Problemata* accordingly asked why it is that people in general derive more pleasure from *exempla* than from enthymemes?[83] The answer is that most people learn more readily by induction, from the particulars that are accessible to their senses, than by deducing from what is universal.

For late thirteenth-century writers there were clear implications to reading Aristotle's emphasis on causality as the proper object of knowledge, in both science and art, alongside Augustine's distinction between history and aetiology. This conjunction was present right at the start of Aquinas' *Summa Theologiae*[84] and the consequences were spelled out by Vincent of Beauvais. In a painstaking chronological account of *res gestae* from the beginning of the world to the present day, arranged according to the sequence of time (*series temporum*), Vincent suggests that this history will be a source of wonder (*admiratio*), refreshment (*recreatio*), and utility (*utilitas*) to his readers. However, he also points out that such material does not pertain to philosophy because it narrates only singular deeds and, according to Aristotle, art cannot result from particulars.[85] The impact of this reservation can be seen soon afterwards in Giles of Rome's *De Regimine Principum*, a mirror-for-princes that starts with the explicit disclaimer that it will *not* proceed in a narrative manner.[86] Giles does not deny the utility of an exemplary didactic method—a ruler ought to read about praiseworthy deeds and should frequently contemplate the history of his kingdom in order to learn how to rule correctly himself.[87] Nonetheless, Giles is careful to echo Albertus's warning to philosophers who might be tempted to follow suit—to descend from general principles to such particulars is to practise the same sort of unreflective political expertise as sophistry.[88]

Giles of Rome's caution posed a methodological challenge for writers of history in the later Middle Ages. While historiography might still serve as a narrative vehicle for the moral instruction of less well-educated audiences, its own status as either a science or an art was open to question. Indeed, on this reckoning, a combination of aesthetic verisimilitude and Aristotelian empiricism might be thought sufficient to have broken off the relationship between rhetoric and the writing of history—that is, as soon as poetry laid exclusive claim to plausibility and the fictive, and philosophy and poetry to the universal. The difficulty here, of course, is that one of the more striking features of fourteenth-century historiography is its vigorous *re*statement of the connection between history and rhetoric, especially for the role of moral didactic *exempla*. Petrarch emphasized this in the 1350s when he stressed the value of *exempla* as inspirations to virtue, but also the combination of utility and pleasure that makes history such a superior vehicle for communicating the truths of moral philosophy to a general audience.[89] This line is reiterated by Coluccio Salutati in the 1390s when he runs through the three branches of rhetoric—demonstrative, judicial, and deliberative—and shows how each of them revolves around a narrative of what has, or has not, been done.[90] In the early fifteenth century, it is the same moral–didactic rhetorical tradition that drives the demonstrative and deliberative historiography of Leonardo Bruni, and which accounts for the subsequent popularity of the works of Sallust, Livy, and Plutarch. This was an approach to the writing of history that would not have been out of place three hundred years earlier.

Where, then, does this leave "medieval" historical writing as a discrete category of Western Latin historiography? Because it was an auxiliary subject of study, not an autonomous branch of knowledge, "history" could encompass a wide range of different types of writing, covering—and often combining—world chronicles, annals, histories of communities, deeds of individuals, hagiographies, biographies, autobiographies, and epic poems.[91] In part, this diversity was due to the plurality of traditions—classical, biblical, and patristic—within which medieval writers were working and which they were deliberately adapting and connecting. In part, it was due to a reluctance to claim the authority of prophecy for their interpretation of the significance of past and present events, particularly in the Sixth, and final, Age. The intersection of historiography with the remembrance of past events, moreover, was explicitly acknowledged to make the very act of commemoration far from straightforward. The consequence was a very broad spectrum of understanding, ranging all the way from "history" as a form of poetic or fictive narrative to "history" as a chronological record of individual deeds and events. Exactly where a medieval writer positioned their historical work along this line was bound up with the particular purpose and the particular audience that their text was intended to serve. A common thread may have been provided by an understanding of history-writing as a narrative of what was done, or may have been done, in the past, but the re-presentation of these events posed challenges all of its own, particularly in the form of verisimilitude.

By tracing the writing of history to its patristic roots, especially in Augustine, and by taking rhetoric seriously as a discipline that is concerned with more than just style, with the strategic use of language rather than with trope-spotting, any idea of a distinctively "medieval" conceptualization of historiography might start by flattening out the conventional notions of a twelfth-century "renaissance," the thirteenth-century "rediscovery" of Aristotle, or fourteenth-century "humanism" providing definitive period breaks. This is not necessarily the traditional picture. Viewed in terms of post-Enlightenment paradigms, these are still centuries in which modern commentators have detected a process of historiographical "de-rhetoricisation."[92] That picture can afford to be refined. In the twelfth century, any trend toward de-rhetoricization is primarily a reaction to what poetry is doing to verisimilitude. *This* is what makes historians rather more wary of this category of rhetorical presentation, not a desire to be free from rhetoric per se. In the fourteenth and early fifteenth centuries, humanist philology does not mark a break from a "medieval" approach to the past—instead, it is a matter of degree; indeed, the emphasis on moral-didacticism constituted a vigorous restatement of its continuing utility. Twelfth-, thirteenth-, and fourteenth-century historiography, in sum, was responding to very similar theoretical questions: where to draw a line of demarcation between history and poetry and, by extension, how much argument and verisimilitude to accommodate within a narrative whose truthfulness was always acknowledged to rest on credibility and trust rather than on certainty and knowledge, on *fides* rather than *scientia*.

History-writing in the Middle Ages was neither crude nor confused nor conceptually unsophisticated. It tackled many of the same issues of form and content, narrative and truth, that are supposed to have dawned in historiographical consciousness only in the late twentieth century and after the Linguistic Turn.[93] "Medieval" historiography emerges from this account as less discrete or distinctive when compared to what immediately preceded and succeeded it, but also, in its own terms, as a form of writing that was more intellectually complex and self-aware than it is often given credit. It certainly deserves better than to be treated with such apparent condescension by modernity. At the very least, it might be accepted that the polarization of truth and fiction, the opposition of veracity to lies and falsehood, fails to do justice to a "medieval" understanding and a "medieval" vocabulary for the problematic bit in the middle—*argumentum*, verisimilitude, *fides*— territory that it has taken only the last generation of "modern" historians to begin to acknowledge once more.[94]

NOTES

Introduction

1 M.L. McLaughlin, "Humanist Concepts of the Renaissance and Middle Ages in the Tre- and Quattrocentro," *Renaissance Studies* 2, no. 2 (1988): 131–42.

2 Jacob Burckhardt, *The Civilization of the Renaissance in Italy*, translated by S.G.C. Middlemore (Vienna: The Phaidon Press, 1937), 70; emphasis added.

3 Reinhart Koselleck, *Futures Past: On the Semantics of Historical Time*, translated by Keith Tribe (Cambridge, MA: MIT Press, 1985), 16–17; Kathleen Davis and Michael Puett, "Periodization and 'The Medieval Globe': A Conversation," *The Medieval Globe* 2, no. 1 (2015): 4; cf. Helga Jordheim, "Against Periodization: Kosseleck's Theory of Multiple Temporalities," *History and Theory* 51, no. 2 (2012): 151–71.

4 Matt Drwenski and David Eaton, "Class Warfare: Changes to the AP World History Course," *Perspectives on History*, June 15, 2018.

5 Thomas Carlyle, *Thomas Carlyle: Historical Essays*, edited by Chris R. Vanden Bossche (Berkeley: University of California Press, 2002), 54.

6 Kathleen Davis, *Periodization and Sovereignty: How Ideas of Feudalism and Secularization Govern the Politics of Time* (Philadelphia: University of Pennsylvania Press, 2008); Andrew Cole and D. Vance Smith, eds., *The Legitimacy of the Middle Ages* (Durham, NC: Duke University Press, 2010).

7 Charles Homer Haskins, *The Renaissance of the Twelfth Century* (Cambridge, MA: Harvard University Press, 1955), 4.

8 Richard Sullivan, "Changing Perspectives on the Middle Ages," *The Centennial Review* 28, no. 2 (1984): 82.

9 Patrick Geary, *Before France and Germany: The Creation and Transformation of the Merovingian World* (New York: Oxford University Press, 1988), 226–31.

10 Cary Nederman, "Empire and the Historiography of European Political Thought: Marsiglio of Padua, Nicolas of Cusa, and the Medieval/Modern Divide," *Journal of the History of Ideas* 66, no. 1 (2005): 1–2.

11 Eric Metaxas, *Martin Luther: The Man Who Rediscovered God and Changed the World* (New York: Viking, 2017).

12 Hans Blumenberg, *The Legitimacy of the Modern Age* (Cambridge, MA: MIT Press, 1983), 181–203.

13 Nancy Bradley Warren, "In Praise of Messiness, or What is Gained by Losing Strong Periodization," *Journal for Early Modern Cultural Studies* 13, no. 3 (2018): 138–43.

14 Richard C. Trexler, *Public Life in Renaissance Florence* (New York: Academic Press, 1980).

15 Peter of Blois, "Epistola XCII," *Patrologia Latina*, 2nd series, vol. 207, edited by J.-P. Migne (Paris: 1904), 290.

16 Niccolò Machiavelli, *The Prince: Second Edition*, translated by Harvey Mansfield (Chicago: University of Chicago Press, 1998), 109–10.

17 Lynn Thorndike, "Newness and Craving for Novelty in Seventeenth-Century Science and Medicine," *Journal of the History of Ideas* 12, no. 4 (1951): 584–98.

18 Louis Dupré, *Passage to Modernity: An Essay in the Hermeneutics of Nature and Culture* (New Haven, CT: Yale University Press, 1993); Michael Allen Gillespie, *The Theological Origins of Modernity* (Chicago: University of Chicago Press, 2008).

19 Thomas Aquinas, *Summa Theologica*, Prima Pars, Q.25, a.6, translated by Fathers of the English Dominican Province (New York: Benziger Brothers, 1946), 141.

20 Aquinas, *Summa Theologica*, Prima Pars, Q.3, aa.1–8: 14–20.

21 Aquinas, *Summa Theologica*, Prima Pars, Q.2, a. 2: 12.

22 Bonaventure, *Breviloquium*, in *The Works of St. Bonaventure*, translated by José de Vinck, vol. 2 (Patterson, NJ: St. Anthony Guild Press, 1963), 101.

23 Edward Grant, *God and Reason in the Middle Ages* (Cambridge: Cambridge University Press, 2001), 148–206.

24 Heiko Oberman, *The Harvest of Medieval Theology: Gabriel Biel and Late Medieval Nominalism* (Cambridge, MA: Harvard University Press, 1963), 255.

25 Amos Funkenstein, *Theology and the Scientific Imagination* (Princeton, NJ: Princeton University Press, 1986), 131–2.

26 Robert Holkot, *Seeing the Future Clearly: Questions on Future Contingents*, edited by Katherine H. Tachau and Paul A. Streveler (Toronto: Pontifical Institute of Mediaeval Studies, 1995).

27 Hester Gelber, *It Could Have Been Otherwise: Contingency and Necessity in Dominican Theology at Oxford, 1300–1350* (Leiden: Brill, 2004), 191–222, 309–50.

28 Johan Huizinga, *The Waning of the Middle Ages: A Study of the Forms of Life, Thought, and Art in France and the Netherlands in the XIVth and XVth Centuries* (London: E. Arnold, 1924); Oberman, *The Harvest of Medieval Theology*.

29 Funkenstein, *Theology and the Scientific Imagination*; Katherine Tachau, "Logic's God and the Natural Order in Late Medieval Oxford: The Teaching of Robert Holcot," *Annals of Science* 53 (1996): 235–67; Edward Grant, *The Foundations of Modern Science in the Middle Ages: Their Religious, Institutional, and Intellectual Contexts* (Cambridge: Cambridge University Press, 1996).

30 Karl Löwith, *Meaning in History: The Theological Implications of the Philosophy of History* (Chicago: University of Chicago Press, 1949), 33–51.

31 Charles Taylor, *A Secular Age* (Cambridge: The Bellknap Press of Harvard University Press, 2007).

32 Alasdair MacIntyre, *After Virtue: A Study in Moral Theory* (Notre Dame: University of Notre Dame Press, 1981); Alasdair MacIntyre, *Whose Justice? Which Rationality?* (Notre Dame, IN: University of Notre Dame Press, 1988).

33 Rod Dreher, *The Benedict Option: A Strategy for Christians in a Post-Christian Nation* (New York: Sentinel, 2017), 26–9.

34 Brad S. Gregory, *The Unintended Reformation: How a Religious Revolution Secularized Society* (Cambridge, MA: Harvard University Press, 2012), 371.

35 J.M.M.H. Thijssen, *Censure and Heresy at the University of Paris, 1200–1400* (Philadelphia: University of Pennsylvania Press, 1998).

36 Marshall McLuhen, *Understanding Media: The Extensions of Man* (New York: McGraw-Hill, 1964).

37 Jean Leclerq, *The Love of Learning and the Desire for God: A Study of Monastic Culture*, translated by Catharine Mishrahi (New York City: Fordham University Press, 1982).

38 Anselm of Canterbury, *Prosologion*, translated by Jasper Hopkins and Herbert Richardson (Minneapolis, MN: Arthur J. Banning Press, 2000), 112.

39 Marcia Colish, "Systematic Theology and Theological Renewal in the Twelfth Century," *Journal of Medieval and Renaissance Studies* 18, no. 2 (1988): 154–5; Alex Novikoff, *The Medieval Culture of Disputation: Pedagogy, Practice, and Performance* (Philadelphia: University of Pennsylvania Press, 2013), 133–71.

Chapter 1

1 Miles Hollingworth, *Saint Augustine of Hippo: An Intellectual Biography* (Oxford: Oxford University Press, 2013), 142–70; Augustine, *Confessions*, translated by Carolyn J.-B. Hammond (Cambridge, MA: Harvard University Press, 2014–2016), 4.2, 6.14–15, 9.12.

2 Peter Brown, *Augustine of Hippo: A Biography* (Berkeley: University of California Press, 1967), 27–8, 50–2, 79–81, etc.

3 Augustine, *Confessions*, 8.12–14.1.

4 Augustine, *Confessions*, 391.

5 Karla Pollman and Willemien Otten, eds., *The Oxford Guide to the Historical Reception of Augustine* (Oxford: Oxford University Press, 2013).

6 Éric Rebillard, *Christians and their Many Identities in Late Antiquity, North Africa, 200–450 CE* (Ithaca, NY: Cornell University Press, 2012).

7 Jason König and Tim Whitmarsh, eds., *Ordering Knowledge in the Roman Empire* (Cambridge: Cambridge University Press, 2007), 5.

8 Peter Brown, *Power and Persuasion in Late Antiquity: Towards a Christian Empire* (Madison: University of Wisconsin Press, 1992); Arthur Urbano Jr., "'Read It Also to the Gentiles': The Displacement and Recasting of the Philosopher in the *Vita Antonii*," *Church History* 77, no. 4 (2008): 877–914.

9 Augustine, *Letters*, translated by Wilfrid Parsons (Washington, DC: Catholic University of America Press, 1951–1989), 75; cf. John Marenbon, *Pagans and Philosophers: The Problem of Paganism from Augustine to Leibniz* (Princeton, NJ: Princeton University Press, 2015).

10 Jerome, letter 70; cf. Deut. 21.10–13.

11 Jürgen Renn, ed., *The Globalization of Knowledge in History: Based on the 97th Dahlem Workshop* (Berlin: Edition Open Access, 2007), ch. 9; Peter Fibiger Bang and Dariusz Kołodziejczyk, *Universal Empire: A Comparative Approach to Imperial Culture and Representation in Eurasian History* (Cambridge: Cambridge University Press, 2012).

12 Trevor M. Murphy, *Pliny the Elder's Natural History: The Empire in the Encyclopedia* (Oxford: Oxford University Press, 2004).

13 Isidore of Seville, *The Etymologies of Isidore of Seville*, ed. and trans. Stephen A. Barney, W. J. Lewis, J. A. Beach, and Oliver Berghof (Cambridge: Cambridge University Press, 2006), 34.

14 Isidore, *Etymologies*, 366–70.

15 Hrotswitha, *The Plays of Hrotswitha of Gandersheim*, translated by Lanissa Bonfante and edited by Robert Chipok (Mundelein, IL: Bolchazy-Carducci Publishers, 2014), 3.

16 John J. Contreni, "Learning for God: Education in the Carolingian Age," *Journal of Medieval Latin* 24 (2014): 92–3, 98; Owen M. Phelan, "New Insights, Old Texts: Clerical Formation and the Carolingian Renewal in Hrabanus Maurus," *Traditio* 71 (2017): 63–89; Matthew Innes, "The Classical Tradition in the Carolingian Renaissance: Ninth-Century Encounters with Suetonius," *International Journal of the Classical Tradition* 3, no. 3 (1997): 265–82.

17 Mas'ūdī, *From the Meadows of Gold*, translated by Paul Lunde and Caroline Stone (London: Penguin, 2007), 3.

18 Dimitri Gutas, *Greek Thought, Arabic Culture: The Graeco-Arabic Translation Movement in Baghdad and Early 'Abbāsid Society (2nd–4th/8th–10th Centuries)* (London: Routledge, 1998), 1.

19 Uwe Vagelpohl, "The User-Friendly Galen: Ḥunayn ibn Isḥāq and the Adaptation of Greek Medicine for a New Audience," in *Greek Medical Literature and its Readers From Hippocrates to Islam and Byzantium*, edited by Petros Bouras-Vallianatos and Sophia Xenophontos, 113–30 (London: Routledge, 2017), 116.

20 Nicola Di Cosmo, *Empires and Exchanges in Eurasian Late Antiquity: Rome, China, Iran, and the Steppe, ca. 250–750* (Cambridge: Cambridge University Press, 2018); Christopher I. Beckwith, *Warriors of the Cloisters: The Central Asian Origins of Science in the Medieval World* (Princeton, NJ: Princeton University Press, 2012).

21 Charles Burnett, *Arabic into Latin in the Middle Ages: The Translators and their Intellectual and Social Context* (Farnham, UK: Ashgate, 2009); Jarbel Rodriguez, ed., *Muslim and Christian Contact in the Middle Ages: A Reader* (Toronto: University of Toronto Press, 2005), 370–401.

22 Grant, *God and Reason in the Middle Ages*; Ian Wei, *Intellectual Culture in Medieval Paris: Theologians and the University, c. 1100–1330* (Cambridge: Cambridge University Press, 2012).

23 Richard Kieckhefer, *Magic in the Middle Ages* (Cambridge: Cambridge University Press, 1989); Agostino Paravicini Bagliani, *The Pope's Body*, trans. David S. Peterson (Chicago: University of Chicago Press, 2000).

24 Steven J. Williams, *The Secret of Secrets: The Scholarly Career of a Pseudo-Aristotelian Text in the Latin Middle Ages* (Ann Arbor: University of Michigan Press, 2003), 109–41.

25 Dennis M. Kratz, *The Romances of Alexander* (New York: Garland Publishing, 1991), 75–6.

26 Amanda Power, *Roger Bacon and the Defence of Christendom* (Cambridge: Cambridge University Press, 2012).

27 Cf. Caroline Dodds Pennock and Amanda Power, "Globalising Cosmologies," *Past and Present* 238 (2018): 88–115.

28 Renn, *The Globalization of Knowledge in History*.

29 Adam of Bremen, *History of the Archbishops of Hamburg-Bremen*, trans. Francis Joseph Tschan (New York: Columbia University Press, 1959), 67, 211.

30 James C. Scott, *The Art of Not Being Governed: An Anarchist History of Upland Southeast Asia* (New Haven, CT: Yale University Press, 2009).

31 For example, Gerald of Wales, *The History and Topography of Ireland*, trans. J. O'Meara (London: Penguin Classics, 1982), 101–2; James C. Scott, *Against the Grain: A Deep History of the Earliest States* (New Haven, CT: Yale University Press, 2017) esp. 1–35.

32 Sylvain Piron, *L'Occupation du monde* (Brussels: Zones Sensibiles, 2018); Donna Haraway, *Staying with the trouble: making kin in the Chthulucene* (Durham: Duke University Press, 2016).

33 Bryan Ward-Perkins, *The fall of Rome and the end of civilization* (Oxford: Oxford University Press, 2005), 167.

34 Chris Wickham, *Framing the Early Middle Ages: Europe and the Mediterranean 400–800* (Oxford: Oxford University Press, 2005), 12, 517–70.

35 Michael Mann, *The Sources of Social Power, Volume 1: A History of Power from the Beginning to AD 1760*, 2nd edition (Cambridge: Cambridge University Press, 2012).

36 Scott, *The Art of Not Being Governed*.

37 Peter Thonemann, "Phrygia: an Anarchist History, 950 BC–AD 100," in *Roman Phrygia: Culture and Society*, edited by Peter Thonemann, 1–40 (Cambridge: Cambridge University Press, 2013).

38 For example, Ibn Fadlān, *Ibn Fadlān and the Land of Darkness: Arab Travellers in the Far North*, translated by Paul Lunde and Caroline Stone (London: Penguin Classics, 2012).

39 James Palmer, "Defining Paganism in the Carolingian World," *Early Medieval Europe* 15, no. 4 (2007): 402–25.

40 Adam of Bremen, *History of the Archbishops of Hamburg-Bremen*, 199.

41 Don C. Skemer, *Binding Words: Textual Amulets in the Middle Ages* (University Park: Pennsylvania State Press, 2006).

42 Richard Firth Green, *Elf Queens and Holy Friars: Fairy Beliefs and the Medieval Church* (Philadelphia: University of Pennsylvania Press, 2016).

43 Kyle Harper, *The Fate of Rome: Climate, Disease, and the End of an Empire* (Princeton, NJ: Princeton University Press, 2017), 198–287; Adam Izdebski and Mulryan, Michael (eds), *Environment and society in the long late antiquity* (Leiden: Brill, 2019); Ulf Büntgen *et al*, 'Cooling and societal change during the Late Antique Little Ice Age from 536 to around 660 AD', *Nature Geoscience*, 9 (2016), 231–236.

44 John L. Brooke, *Climate Change and the Course of Global History: A Rough Journey* (Cambridge: Cambridge University Press, 2016), 361–2.

45 Brooke, *Climate Change and the Course of Global History*, 358–60.

46 Richard Hoffman, *An Environmental History of Medieval Europe* (Cambridge: Cambridge University Press, 2014), 71–8, 135–8.

47 Gerald, *The History and Topography of Ireland*, 102–4.

48 Hoffman, *An Environmental History*, 148.

49 Bonaventure, *The Journey of the Mind to God*, translated by Philotheus O. F. M. Boehner and Stephen F. Brown (Indianapolis, IN: Hackett, 1993), 5, 38–9; emphasis added.

50 Richard Barber, *Bestiary: Being an English Version of the Bodleian Library, Oxford M.S. Bodley 764* (London: Folio Society, 1992), 110–11; cf. Isidore, *Etymologies*, 254.

51 Kenneth Baxter Wolf, *The Life and Afterlife of St. Elizabeth of Hungary: Testimony from her Canonization Hearings* (Oxford: Oxford University Press, 2010), 205.

52 H. E. J. Cowdrey, *The Cluniacs and the Gregorian Reform* (Oxford: Clarendon Press, 1970).

53 Peter Damian, *Letters 91–120*, trans. Owen J. Blum (Washington, DC: Catholic University of America Press, 1998), 282.

54 Mary Martin McLaughlin and Bonnie Wheeler, ed. and trans., *The Letters of Heloise and Abelard: A Translation of Their Collected Correspondence and Related Writings* (Basingstoke, UK: Palgrave Macmillan, 2009), 54, 26–8.

55 Dallas G. Denery II, *Seeing and Being Seen in the Later Medieval World: Optics, Theology, and Religious Life* (New York: Cambridge University Press, 2005), 76–82, 100–15.

56 John H. Van Engen, ed., *Learning Institutionalized: Teaching in the Medieval University* (Notre Dame, IN: University of Notre Dame Press, 2000).

57 Wei, *Intellectual Culture in Medieval Paris*; Rita Copeland and Ineke Sluiter, *Medieval Grammar and Rhetoric: Language Arts and Literary Theory, AD 300–1475* (Oxford: Oxford University Press, 2009); Novikoff, *The Medieval Culture of Disputation*.

58 Dyan Elliott, *Proving Woman: Female Spirituality and Inquisitional Culture in the Later Middle Ages* (Princeton, NJ: Princeton University Press, 2004).

59 Peter Lombard, *The Sentences, Book 1: The Mystery of the Trinity.*, trans., Giulio Silano (Toronto: Pontifical Institute of Medieval Studies, 2007), 4.

60 Fiona J. Griffiths, *The Garden of Delights: Reform and Renaissance for Women in the Twelfth Century* (Philadelphia: University of Pennsylvania Press, 2006).

61 Power, *Roger Bacon and the Defence of Christendom*, 50–1, 115–20.

62 Max Horkheimer and Theodor W. Adorno, *Dialectic of Enlightenment: Philosophical Fragments* (Stanford, CA: Stanford University Press, 2002).

63 Brown, *Augustine of Hippo*, 229–39.

64 Augustine, *Letters*, 2:56–106, quotation at p. 75.

65 Anna S. Abulafia, *Christians and Jews in the Twelfth-Century Renaissance* (London: Routledge, 1995).

66 *De sac.* I.10.3; *Sent.* IV.2.

67 Norman P. Tanner, ed., *Decrees of the Ecumenical Councils*, 2 vols. (London: Sheed & Ward; Washington, DC: Georgetown University Press, 1990).

68 John H. Arnold, *Belief and Unbelief in Medieval Europe* (London: Hodder Arnold, 2005); Fatemeh Chehregosha Azinfar, *Atheism in the Medieval Islamic and European World: The Influence of Persian and Arabic Ideas of Doubt and Skepticism on Medieval European Literary Thought* (Bethesda, MD: Ibex Publishers, 2008).

Chapter 2

1 Guibert of Nogent, *Autobiographie*, edited and translated Edmond-René Labande (Paris: Belles lettres, 1981), 1.3, pp. 9–10.

2 Guibert, *Autobiographie*, 19.

3 Guibert, *Autobiographie*, 19–21.

4 Michel de Montaigne, *The Complete Essays*, translated by M. A. Screech (London: Penguin, 1987), 1.28, p. 206.

5 Jean-Luc Nancy, *Ego sum: Corpus, Anima, Fabula*, translated by Marie-Eve Morin (1979, New York: Fordham University Press, 2016).

6 Jean-Jacques Rousseau, *Confessions*, translated by J. M. Cohen (London: Penguin, 1953), 17.

7 Montaigne, *The Complete Essays*, 1.

8 Wallace K. Ferguson, *The Renaissance in Historical Thought: Five Centuries of Interpretation* (Boston: Houghton Mifflin, 1948); Walter Kudrycz, *The Historical Present: Medievalism and Modernity* (London: Bloomsbury, 2011).

9 Jacob Burckhardt, *The Civilization of the Renaissance in Italy*, translated by S. G. C. Middlemore (New York: Harper & Brothers, 1958).

10 Burckhardt, *The Civilization of the Renaissance in Italy*, 26–7, 144–5.

11 Burckhardt, *The Civilization of the Renaissance in Italy*, 303.

12 Burckhardt, *The Civilization of the Renaissance in Italy*, 307.

13 Haskins, *The Renaissance of the Twelfth Century* (Cambridge, MA: Harvard University Press, 1955).

14 Ferguson, *The Renaissance in Historical Thought*, 190–1.

15 Ferguson, *The Renaissance in Historical Thought*, 324–33.

16 Ferguson, *The Renaissance in Historical Thought*, 338–40.

17 Peter Dronke, *Poetic Individuality in the Middle Ages: New Departures in Poetry, 1000–1150* (Oxford: Clarendon, 1970).

18 Colin Morris, *The Discovery of the Individual, 1050–1200* (Toronto: University of Toronto Press, 1987), 3.

19 Guibert of Nogent, *Monodies and On the Relics of Saints: The Autobiography and a Manifesto of a French Monk from the Time of the Crusades*, translated by Joseph McAlhany and Jay Rubenstein (New York: Penguin, 2011), 1.5, pp. 14–16.

20 Guibert, *Monodies*, 1.14, p. 41.

21 Jay Rubenstein, *Guibert of Nogent: Portrait of a Medieval Mind* (New York: Routledge, 2002), 73–5, 61–2.

22 John F. Benton, "The Personality of Guibert of Nogent," *Psychoanalytic Review* 57 (1970/1): 563–86.

23 Guibert, *Monodies,* 1.17, p. 56.

24 Rubenstein, *Guibert of Nogent,* 44–71.

25 Rubenstein, *Guibert of Nogent,* 64.

26 Mary Carruthers, *The Book of Memory: A Study of Memory in Medieval Culture* (Cambridge: Cambridge University Press, 1990).

27 Rubenstein, *Guibert of Nogent,* 64.

28 Brian Stock, "The Self and Literary Experience in Late Antiquity and the Middle Ages," *New Literary History* 25 (1994): 839–52.

29 Gerald A. Bond, *The Loving Subject: Desire, Eloquence, and Power in Romanesque France* (Philadelphia: University of Pennsylvania Press, 1995).

30 Bond, *The Loving Subject,* 5–10.

31 Cicero, *De officiis,* edited by Michael Winterbottom (Oxford: Oxford University Press, 1994), 1.30–31, 37–9.

32 Bond, *The Loving Subject,* 10.

33 Louis Althusser, "Ideology and Ideological State Apparatuses (Notes Toward an Investigation)," in *Lenin and Philosophy and Other Essays,* translated by Ben Brewster, 123–73 (London: New Left Books, 1971).

34 Sarah Kay, *Subjectivity in Troubadour Poetry* (Cambridge: Cambridge University Press, 1990).

35 Peter Haidu, *The Subject Medieval/Modern: Text and Governance in the Middle Ages* (Stanford, CA: Stanford University Press, 2004).

36 For an overview of this kind of interpretation, see Jean-Pierre Thuillat, *Bertran de Born: histoire et légende* (Périgueux: Fanlac, 2009).

37 Gérard Gouiran, "Bertran de Born: troubadour de la violence?," in *La violence dans le monde médiéval,* 235–51 (Aix-en-Provence: Publications du CUERMA, 1994).

38 Bertran de Born, *The Poems of Bertran de Born,* edited and translated by William D. Paden, Jr., Tilde Sankovitch, and Patricia H. Stäblein (Berkeley: University of California Press, 1986), lines 1–5, p. 296.

39 Bertran, *The Poems of Bertran de Born,* lines 9–16, p. 296.

40 Bertran, *The Poems of Bertran de Born,* lines 17–22, p. 296.

41 Bertran, *The Poems of Bertran de Born,* lines 1–10, p. 338.

42 Bertran, *The Poems of Bertran de Born,* lines 41–4, p. 298.

43 Bertran, *The Poems of Bertran de Born,* lines 1–4, p. 192.

44 Abelard and Heloise, *The Letter Collection of Peter Abelard and Heloise,* edited by David Luscombe, translated by Betty Radice (Oxford: Oxford University Press, 2013), Letter 1 ¶ 16.

45 Abelard and Heloise, *The Letter Collection,* Letter 1 ¶ 18.

46 Abelard and Heloise, *The Letter Collection,* Letter 2 ¶ 8.

47 Abelard and Heloise, *The Letter Collection,* Letter 2.

48 Abelard and Heloise, *The Letter Collection,* Letter 3.

49 Abelard and Heloise, *The Letter Collection,* Letter 4 ¶ 12–13.

50 Michel Foucault, *The History of Sexuality, Volume 1: An Introduction,* translated by Robert Hurley (New York: Vintage Books, 1990), 70.

51 For a review and rebuttal of the various arguments for forgery, see John Marenbon, *The Philosophy of Peter Abelard* (Cambridge: Cambridge University Press, 1997), 82–93.

52 Susan Crane, *The Performance of Self: Ritual, Clothing, and Identity during the Hundred Years War* (Philadelphia: University of Pennsylvania Press, 2002), 4, 178.

53 Crane, *The Performance of Self,* 10.

54 Crane, *The Performance of Self*, 176.

55 Dyan Elliott, "Review of Susan Crane, *The Performance of Self*," *Journal of English and Germanic Philology* 103 (2004): 402.

56 Guillaume de Berneville, *La Vie de siant Gilles*, edited and translated by Françoise Luarent (Paris: Champion, 2003), lines 3056–8.

57 Andrew Martindale, *Heroes, Ancestors, Relatives and the Birth of the Portrait* (Maarssen, the Netherlands: SDU Publishers, 1988), 20–3.

58 C. Stephen Jaeger, *The Envy of Angels: Cathedral Schools and Social Ideals in Medieval Europe, 950–1200* (Philadelphia: University of Pennsylvania Press, 1994), 331–48.

59 Georgia Sommers Wright, "The Reinvention of the Portrait Likeness in the Fourteenth Century," *Gesta* 39, no. 2 (2000): 117.

60 Martindale, *Heroes, Ancestors, Relatives*; Wright, "The Reinvention of the Portrait Likeness."

61 Martindale, *Heroes, Ancestors, Relatives*, 31–3.

62 Wright, "The Reinvention of the Portrait Likeness," 132.

63 Kathleen Nolan, *Queens in Stone and Silver: The Creation of a Visual Imagery of Queenship in Capetian France* (New York: Palgrave Macmillan, 2009).

64 Nolan, *Queens in Stone and Silver*, xvii.

65 Nolan, *Queens in Stone and Silver*, 27–8.

66 Theodore Evergates, *Marie of France: Countess of Champagne, 1145–1198* (Philadelphia: University of Pennsylvania Press, 2019).

67 Brigitte Miriam Bedos-Rezak, "Medieval Identity: A Sign and a Concept," *American Historical Review* 105 (2000): 1527.

68 Bedos-Rezak, "Medieval Identity," 1531.

69 Bedos-Rezak, "Medieval Identity," 1532.

70 Thomas E. A. Dale, "The Portrait as Imprinted Image and the Concept of the Individual in the Romanesque Period," in *Le Portrait: la représentation de l'individu*, edited by Agostino Paravicini Bagliani, Jean-Michel Spieser, and Jean Wirth (Florence: SISMEL, Edizioni del Galluzzo, 2007), 109.

Chapter 3

1 Augustine, *On the Free Choice of the Will*, in *On the Free Choice of the Will, On Grace and Free Choice and Other Writings*, edited and translated by Peter King, 3–126 (Cambridge: Cambridge University Press, 2010), 1, 12.24–16.35.

2 Augustine, *On the Free Choice of the Will*, 1, 3, 3.

3 Augustine, *The City of God*, translated by William Babcock (Hyde Park, NY: New City Press, 2013), 14, 9.

4 Augustine, *The City of God*, 14, 7.

5 Eileen C. Sweeney, *Anselm of Canterbury and the Desire for the Word* (Washington, DC: Catholic University of America Press, 2012).

6 Anselm, *Epistolae*, in *S. Anselmi Cantuariensis archiepiscopi Opera Omnia*, edited by F. S. Schmitt, 5 vols. (Stuttgart: Friedrich Fromann Verlag, 1984) *Ep.* 75, v. 3, 197, 7–10.

7 Augustine, *Teaching Christianity*, trans. Edmund Hill (Hyde Park, NY: New City Press, 1996), 1, 3, 3.

8 Hugh of Saint Victor, *Soliloquoy on the Betrothal Gift of the Beloved*, in *On Love: A Selection of Works of Hugh, Adam, Achard, Richard and Godfrey of St. Victor*, translated by Hugh Feiss (Hyde Park, NY: New City Press, 2012), sec. 50, 219.

9 Hugh, *Soliloquoy on the Betrothal Gift of the Beloved*, sec. 65, 226.

10 Boyd Taylor Coolman, "The Medieval Affective Dionysian Tradition," *Modern Theology* 24, no. 4 (2008): 623.

11 Luke 19:41–4; Boyd Taylor Coolman, "Hugh of St. Victor on 'Jesus Wept': Compassion as Ideal *Humanitas*," *Theological Studies* 69 (2008): 542.

12 Juan Luis Vives, *The Passions of the Soul: The Third Book of De Anima et Vita*, translated by Carlos G. Noreña (Lewiston: Edwin Mellen Press, 1990), 46.

13 William IX is William, ninth duke of Aquitaine and seventh count of Poitou (1071–1126). He is credited with being the earliest-known troubadour.

14 William Reddy, *The Making of Romantic Love: Longing and Sexuality in Europe, South Asia, and Japan 900–1200 CE* (Chicago: University of Chicago Press, 2012), 99.

15 Carin Franzén, "The Legacy of Courtly Love and Feminine Position," in *(Re-)Contextualizing Literary and Cultural History: The Representation of the Past in Literary and Material Culture*, edited by Elisabeth Wåghäll Nivre, Beate Schirrmacher, and Claudia Egere, 93–114 (Stockholm: Acta Universitatis Stockholmiensis, 2013), 96.

16 Louis-Georges Tin, *L'invention de la culture hétérosexuelle* (Paris: Autrement, 2008), 29.

17 Durant Robertson Jr., "The Concept of Courtly Love as an Impediment to the Understanding of Medieval Texts," in *Essays in Medieval Culture*, 257–72 (Princeton, NJ: Princeton University Press, 1980), 259.

18 Robertson, "The Concept of Courtly Love," 260.

19 C. S. Lewis, *The Allegory of Love* (New York: Oxford University Press, 1956), 1–43.

20 1 Corinthians 4: 7.

21 Sweeney, *Anselm of Canterbury and the Desire for the Word*.

22 J. Allan Mitchell, "Romancing Ethics in Boethius, Chaucer, and Levinas: Fortune, Moral Luck, and Erotic Adventure," *Comparative Literature* 57, no. 2 (2005): 111.

23 Mitchell, "Romancing Ethics," 102.

24 Andreas Cappellanus, *The Art of Courtly Love*, translated by John Jay Parry (New York: Norton, 1969), 3, 187.

25 Cappellanus, *The Art of Courtly Love*, 1, 28.

26 Slavoj Zizek, *The Metastases of Enjoyment: Six Essays on Woman and Causality* (London: Verso, 1994), 108.

27 Douglas Kelly, "Love, Reason, and Debatable Opinion," in *Christine De Pizan's Changing Opinion: A Quest for Certainty in the Midst of Chaos*, 107–41 (Woodbridge, UK: Boydell and Brewer, 2007).

28 Franzén, "The Legacy of Courtly Love," 110.

29 Augustine, *The City of God*, 19, 4.

30 Augustine, *The City of God*, 19, 25.

31 Augustine, *The City of God*, 5, 12–13.

32 Augustine, *The City of God*, 19, 12.

33 Eileen C. Sweeney, "Aquinas on Vice and Sin," in *The Ethics of Aquinas*, edited by Stephen J. Pope, 151–68 (Washington, DC: Georgetown University Press, 2002).

34 1 Corinthians 10:31.

35 Anselm, *Cur Deus homo*, in *S. Anselmi Cantuariensis archiepiscopi Opera Omnia*, 1:21.

36 Peter Lombard, *Sentences*, translated by Giulio Silano (Toronto: Pontifical Institute of Mediaeval Studies, 2008), bk. 2, dist. 35.

37 Morton Bloomfield, *The Seven Deadly Sins: An Introduction to the History of a Religious Concept, with Special Reference to Medieval English Literature* (East Lansing: Michigan State College Press, 1952), 3–41; Carole Straw, "Gregory, Cassian and the Cardinal Vices," in *In*

the Garden of Evil: The Vices and Culture in the Middle Ages, edited by Richard Newhauser, 59–73 (Toronto: Pontifical Institute of Mediaeval Studies, 2005), 42; Cassian, The Monastic Institutes consisting of On the Training of a Monk and The Eight Deadly Sins, translated by Jerome Gertram (London: The Saint Austin Press, 1999), 73–4.

38 Richard Newhauser, "Preaching the 'Contrary Virtues,'" Mediaeval Studies 70 (2008): 135.

39 For example, Thomas Aquinas, Summa theologiae, edited by Leonine Edition (Rome, 1888). Available online: http://www.corpusthomisticum.org/sth0000.html (accessed January 31, 2022), Part 2-2, 162, 1, 5.

40 Bernard of Clairvaux, De gradibus humilitatis et superbiae tractatus (Paris: J.-P Migne, 1859), PL 182, cols. 939–972 c., 3–4.

41 Eileen C. Sweeney, "Sin and Grace," in Cambridge Companion to Medieval Ethics, edited by Thomas Williams, 348–72 (New York: Cambridge University Press, 2018), 360–2.

42 Lombard, Sentences, bk. 2, dist. 42, c. 8.

43 Silvana Vecchio, "The Seven Deadly Sins Between Pastoral Care and Scholastic Theology: The Summa de viciis of John of Rupella," in In the Garden of Evil: The Vices and Culture in the Middle Ages, translated by Helen Took, edited by Richard Newhauser, 104–27 (Toronto: Pontifical Institute of Mediaeval Studies, 2005), 122.

44 Aquinas, Summa theologiae, 1–2, 84, 2; cf. Summa Theologiae 2, 132, 4.

45 Aquinas, Summa theologiae, 1–2, 84, 1; cf. Albert the Great, Super II sententiarum, vol. 27 (Paris: Ludovicum Vivès,1884), II, dist. 42, a. 7.

46 Bloomfield, The Seven Deadly Sins, 75.

47 Aristotle, Rhetoric, in The Basic Works of Aristotle, edited by Richard McKeon, translated by W. Rhys Roberts (New York: The Modern Library, 2001), 2, 11, 1388a1–b1.

48 Romans 12:15.

49 Thomas Aquinas, On Evil, translated by Jean Oesterle, in The Collected Works of St. Thomas Aquinas, Electronic Edition, vol. 5 (Charlottesville, VA: InteLex Corp, 1993), Past Masters, Q.10, a.2.

50 Jessica Rosenfeld, "Compassionate Conversions: Gower's Confessio Amantis and the Problem of Envy," Journal of Medieval and Early Modern Studies 42, no. 1 (2012): 84–5.

51 Rosenfeld, "Compassionate Conversions," 85.

52 Rosenfeld, "Compassionate Conversions," 92, 94.

53 Siegfried Wenzel, "'Acedia' 700–1200*," Traditio 22 (1966): 83.

54 James B. Williams, "Working for Reform: Acedia, Benedict of Aniane and the Transformation of Working Culture in Carolingian Monasticism," in Sin in Medieval and Early Modern Culture, edited by Richard G. Newhauser and Susan J. Ridyard, 19–42 (York: York Medieval Press, 2012), 19–37.

55 Siegfried Wenzel, ed., Fasciculus Morum: A Fourteenth-Century Preacher's Handbook (University Park: Pennsylvania State University Press, 1989), 89.

56 Wenzel, "'Acedia' 700–1200*," 102.

57 Aquinas, Disputed Questions on Evil, 11, 2.

58 Albert the Great, Summa theologiae, vol. 33 (Paris: Ludovicum Vivès, 1885), pt. 2, tr. 18, q. 118, m. 1; a. 2.

59 Rainer Jehl, "Acedia and Burnout Syndrome: From an Occupational Vice of Early Monks to a Psychological Concept in Secularized Professional Life," in In the Garden of Evil: The Vices and Culture in the Middle Ages, edited by Richard Newhauser, 455–76 (Toronto: Pontifical Institute of Mediaeval Studies, 2005), associates this strain of acedia with notions of grief, boredom, and versions of despair in many more thinkers: Schopenhauer, Nietzsche,

Heidegger, and Sartre to name only a few, and further argues it shares much in common with the contemporary notion of "burnout."

60 Sweeney, "Sin and Grace."

61 Abelard, *Ethics sive Scito teipsum*, in *Peter Abelard's "Ethics*," edited by D. E. Luscombe (Oxford: Clarendon Press, 1971), 1:7.

62 Abelard, *Ethics sive Scito teipsum*, 1:110–12, 126.

63 Abelard, *Ethics sive Scito teipsum*, 1:77–83.

64 William of Ockham, *De connexione virtutum*, in *Ockham on the Virtues*, edited and translated by Rega Wood (West Lafayette, IN: Purdue University Press, 1997), a. 2, lines 116–67.

65 Jacques Le Goff, "Trades and Professions as Represented in Medieval Confessors' Manuals," in *Time, Work and Culture in the Middle Ages*, translated by Arthur Goldhammer, 107–21 (Chicago: University of Chicago Press, 1990), 112.

66 Le Goff, "Trades and Professions," 114.

67 Michael Haren, "The Interrogatories for Officials, Lawyers, and Secular Estates of the *Memoriale Presbiterorum*," in *Handling Sin: Confession in the Middle Ages*, edited by Peter Biller and A. J. Minnis, 123–64 (York: York Medieval Press, 1998), 126–7.

68 Haren, "The Interrogatories for Officials, Lawyers, and Secular Estates," 154–7.

69 Haren, "The Interrogatories for Officials, Lawyers, and Secular Estates," 154–7.

70 Michael Haren, "Confession, Social Ethics and Social Discipline in the *Memoriale Presbiterorum*," in *Handling Sin: Confession in the Middle Ages*, edited by Peter Biller and A. J. Minnis, 109–22 (York: York Medieval Press, 1998), 111.

71 Hugh of Saint Victor, *Hugonis de Sancto Victore Didascalicon de studio legendi: A Critical Text*, edited by Charles Henry Buttimer (Washington, DC: Catholic University Press, 1939), bk. 1, 4–5.

72 Le Goff, "Trades and Professions," 116.

73 Roberto Lambertini, "Wealth and Money according to Giles of Rome," in *Reichtum im späten Mittelalter: politische Theorie, ethische Norm, soziale Akzeptanz*, edited by Peter Hesse and Petra Schulte, 39–53 (Stuttgart: Franz Steiner Verlag, 2015); Odd Langholm, *Economics in the Medieval Schools: Wealth, Exchange, Value, Money and Usury according to the Paris Theological Tradition, 1200–1350* (Leiden: E. J. Brill, 1992).

Chapter 4

1 Robert S. Lopez, *The Commercial Revolution of the Middle Ages 950–1350* (Cambridge: Cambridge University Press, 1976); see John Day, *The Medieval Market Economy* (Oxford: Oxford University Press, 1987).

2 Georges Duby, *The Early Growth of the European Economy*, translated by Howard B. Clarke (Ithaca, NY: Cornell University Press, 1974); H. E. Hallam, *Rural England (1066–1348)* (Hassocks, UK: Harvester Press, 1981); George Ovitt Jr., *The Restoration of Perfection: Labor and Technology in Medieval Culture* (New Brunswick, NJ: Rutgers University Press, 1987).

3 Richard S. Bonney, ed., *State and Fiscal Administration in Europe* (Cambridge: Cambridge University Press, 1995), 1–160; Susan Reynolds, *Kingdoms and Communities in Western Europe, 900–1300*, 2nd edn. (Oxford: Oxford University Press, 1997), 39–66, 155–339.

4 John W. Baldwin, *Medieval Theories of the Just Price: Romanists, Canonists, and Theologians in the Twelfth and Thirteenth Centuries*, Transactions of the American Philosophical Society 49, pt. 4 (Philadelphia: American Philosophical Society, 1959).

5 John W. Baldwin, *Masters, Princes and Merchants: The Social Views of Peter the Chanter and His Circle*, 2 vols. (Princeton, NJ: Princeton University Press, 1970), 1:261–311.

6 Baldwin, *Masters, Princes and Merchants*, 1:228–51.

7 Joseph A. Schumpeter, *History of Economic Analysis* (New York: Oxford University Press, 1954); Raymond de Roover, *Business, Banking, and Economic Thought in Late Medieval and Early Modern Europe*, edited by Julius Kirshner (Chicago: University of Chicago Press, 1974).

8 Odd Langholm, *The Legacy of Scholasticism in Economic Thought: Antecedents of Choice and Power* (Cambridge: Cambridge University Press, 1998).

9 Lester K. Little, *Religious Poverty and the Property Economy in Medieval Europe* (Ithaca, NY: Cornell University Press, 1978).

10 Cary J. Nederman, "Aristotelianism and the Origins of 'Political Science' in the Twelfth Century," *Journal of the History of Ideas* 52 (1991): 184–9.

11 Diana Wood, *Medieval Economic Thought* (Cambridge: Cambridge University Press, 2002); James Davis, *Medieval Market Morality* (Cambridge: Cambridge University Press, 2012).

12 Adam Smith, *An Inquiry into the Nature and Causes of the Wealth of Nations*, edited by R. H. Campbell and A. S. Skinner (Oxford: Clarendon Press, 1976), IV, Intro.1.

13 Neal Wood, *The Foundations of Political Economy* (Berkeley: University of California Press, 1994), 252–3, n. 1.

14 Joyce Oldham Appleby, *Economic Thought and Ideology in Seventeenth-Century England* (Princeton, NJ: Princeton University Press, 1978); David McNally, *Political Economy and the Rise of Capitalism* (Berkeley: University of California Press, 1988); Terence Hutchison, *Before Adam Smith: The Emergence of Political Economy, 1662–1776* (Oxford: Blackwell, 1988); Bonney, *State and Fiscal Administration in Europe*, 21–52.

15 John of Salisbury, *Policraticus: Of the Frivolities of Courtiers and the Footprints of Philosophers*, edited by Cary J. Nederman (Cambridge: Cambridge University Press, 1990), 5.2.

16 John of Salisbury, *Policraticus*, 6.2.

17 John of Salisbury, *Policraticus*, 5.2.

18 John of Salisbury, *Policraticus*, 4.5.

19 John of Salisbury, *Policraticus*, 1.3.

20 John of Salisbury, *Policraticus*, 4.5.

21 John of Salisbury, *Policraticus*, 6.1.

22 John of Salisbury, *Policraticus*, 6.1.

23 Brunetto Latini, *The Book of the Treasure (Li Livres dou Tresor)*, translated by Paul Barrette and Spurgeon Baldwin (New York: Garland Publishing, 1993), 1.4.5.

24 Latini, *The Book of the Treasure*, 2.50.1.

25 Latini, *The Book of the Treasure*, 2.29.2.

26 Latini, *The Book of the Treasure*, 2.5.2.

27 Latini, *The Book of the Treasure*, 2.44.18.

28 Latini, *The Book of the Treasure*, 2.122.4.

29 Latini, *The Book of the Treasure*, 2.38.6.

30 Latini, *The Book of the Treasure*, 3.75.1.

31 Latini, *The Book of the Treasure*, 3.77.1.

32 Latini, *The Book of the Treasure*, 3.77.1.

33 Latini, *The Book of the Treasure*, 2.29.3.

34 Latini, *The Book of the Treasure*, 3.93.1–2.

35 Latini, *The Book of the Treasure*, 3.93.3.

36 Latini, *The Book of the Treasure*, 3.97–3.99.

37 Marsiglio of Padua, *Defender of Peace*, translated by Alan Gewirth, 2nd edn. (New York: Columbia University Press, 2000), II.8.9.

38 Marsiglio of Padua, *Defender of Peace*, I.12.8.

39 Marsiglio of Padua, *Defender of Peace*, I.12.7.

40 Marsiglio of Padua, *Defender of Peace*, I.3.2–5.

41 Marsiglio of Padua, *Defender of Peace*, I.4.3.

42 Marsiglio of Padua, *Defender of Peace*, I.19.2.

43 Marsiglio of Padua, *Defender of Peace*, I.5.6–9.

44 Marsiglio of Padua, *Defender of Peace*, I.4.4.

45 Marsiglio of Padua, *Defender of Peace*, I.9.5, I.12.3.

46 Marsiglio of Padua, *Defender of Peace*, I.12.5.

47 Marsiglio of Padua, *Defender of Peace*, I.12.5.

48 William of Pagula, *The Mirror of King Edward III*, in *Political Thought in Early Fourteenth-Century England*, edited by Cary J. Nederman (Tempe: Arizona Center for Medieval and Renaissance Studies, 2002), B, 16.

49 William of Pagula, *The Mirror of King Edward III*, A, 5.

50 William of Pagula, *The Mirror of King Edward III*, A, 1; B, 44.

51 William of Pagula, *The Mirror of King Edward III*, see A, 12.

52 William of Pagula, *The Mirror of King Edward III*, A, 9.

53 William of Pagula, *The Mirror of King Edward III*, A, 15.

54 William of Pagula, *The Mirror of King Edward III*, A, 3; A, 37; B, 43.

55 William of Pagula, *The Mirror of King Edward III*, A, 16.

56 William of Pagula, *The Mirror of King Edward III*, B, 37.

57 William of Pagula, *The Mirror of King Edward III*, B, 9.

58 William of Pagula, *The Mirror of King Edward III*, B, 6.

59 William of Pagula, *The Mirror of King Edward III*, B, 16; cf. B, 1.

60 William of Pagula, *The Mirror of King Edward III*, A, 10.

61 William of Pagula, *The Mirror of King Edward III*, A, 11.

62 Nicole Oresme, *De moneta*, edited by Charles Johnson (Edinburgh: Thomas Nelson, 1956), 5.

63 Oresme, *De moneta*, 42.

64 Oresme, *De moneta*, 16.

65 Oresme, *De moneta*, 24, 30.

66 Oresme, *De moneta*, 30.

67 Oresme, *De moneta*, 33.

68 Oresme, *De moneta*, 46–7.

69 Charity Cannon Willard, *Christine de Pizan: Her Life and Her Works* (New York: Persea, 1984).

70 Christine de Pizan, *The Book of the Body Politic*, edited by Kate Langdon Forhan (Cambridge: Cambridge University Press, 1994), 90.

71 Christine de Pizan, *The Book of the Body Politic*, 91.

72 Christine de Pizan, *The Book of the Body Politic*, 19, 95–9.

73 Christine de Pizan, *The Book of the Body Politic*, 14.

74 Christine de Pizan, *The Book of the Body Politic*, 39; our emphasis.

75 Christine de Pizan, *The Book of the Body Politic*, 103, 104; also Christine de Pizan, *The Treasury of the City of Ladies*, translated by Charity Cannon Willard (New York: Bard Hall/Persea, 1989), 196.

76 Christine de Pizan, *The Book of the Body Politic*, 104.

77 Christine de Pizan, *The Book of the Body Politic*, 105.

78 Christine de Pizan, *The Book of the Body Politic*, 10.

79 Christine de Pizan, *The Book of the Body Politic*, 17.

80 Christine de Pizan, *The Book of the Body Politic*, 19.

81 Christine de Pizan, *The Book of the Body Politic*, 22.

82 Christine de Pizan, *The Book of the City of Ladies*, translated by E. J. Richards (New York: Persea, 1982), 76.

83 Christine de Pizan, *The Book of the City of Ladies*, 73–7.

84 Christine de Pizan, *The Book of the City of Ladies*, 84–7.

85 Christine de Pizan, *The Book of the City of Ladies*, 85.

86 Christine de Pizan, *The Book of the City of Ladies*, 6.

87 Sir John Fortescue, *On the Laws and Governance of England*, edited by Shelley Lockwood (Cambridge: Cambridge University Press, 1997), 88, 89.

88 Fortescue, *On the Laws and Governance of England*, 89–92.

89 Fortescue, *On the Laws and Governance of England*, 88, 110–11.

90 Fortescue, *On the Laws and Governance of England*, 90.

91 Fortescue, *On the Laws and Governance of England*, 109.

92 Fortescue, *On the Laws and Governance of England*, 109.

93 Fortescue, *On the Laws and Governance of England*, 52.

94 Fortescue, *On the Laws and Governance of England*, 52–3.

95 Fortescue, *On the Laws and Governance of England*, 75.

Chapter 5

1 Hans Blumenberg, "'Imitation of Nature': Toward a Prehistory of the Idea of Creative Being" [Nachahmung der Natur': Zur Vorgeschichte der Idee des schöpferischen Menschen], first published in 1957, translated by Anna Wertz, *Qui Parle* 12, no. 1 (2000): 17–54.

2 Mary Beagon, *Roman Nature: The Thought of Pliny the Elder* (Oxford: Clarendon Press, 1992); Beagon, "Variations on a Theme: Isidore and Pliny on Human and Human-Instigated Anomaly," in *Isidore of Seville and his Reception in the Early Middle Ages: Transmitting and Transforming Knowledge*, edited by Andy Fear and Jamie Wood, 57–74, Late Antique and Early Medieval Iberia 2 (Amsterdam: Amsterdam University Press, 2016); Aude Doody, *Pliny's Encyclopedia: The Reception of the Natural History* (Cambridge: Cambridge University Press, 2010), 69–71; Andrew Wallace-Hadrill, "Pliny the Elder and Man's Unnatural History," *Greece & Rome* 37, no. 1 (1990): 85–96.

3 Isidore of Seville, *Etymologies*, 11.1, p. 231.

4 Isidore of Seville, *Etymologies*, 17–24; Andrew Fear, "Putting the Pieces Back Together: Isidore's De natura rerum," in *Isidore of Seville and his Reception in the Early Middle Ages: Transmitting and Transforming Knowledge*, edited by Andrew Fear and Jamie Wood, 75–92, Late Antique and Early Medieval Iberia 2 (Amsterdam: Amsterdam University Press, 2016).

5 Pliny the Elder, *Natural History: A Selection*, translated by John F. Healy (New York: Penguin, 2004), 80.

6 Olaf Pedersen, *The Book of Nature* (Notre Dame, IN: University of Notre Dame Press, 1992).

7 Mary Beagon, "Situating Nature's Wonders in Pliny's Natural History," in *Vita Vigilia Est: Essays in Honour of Barbara Levick*, edited by E. Bispham and G. Rowe, 19–40, Bulletin of the Institute of Classical Studies Supplement 100 (London: Institute of Classical Studies, 2007).

8 Brunetto Latini, *Li Livres dou Tresor*, edited by Spurgeon Baldwin and Paul Barrette (Tempe: Arizona Center for Medieval and Renaissance Studies, 2003), xi–xxi; Latini, *The Book of the Treasure*; Francis J. Carmody, "Brunetto Latini's *Tresor*: Latin Sources on Natural Science,"

Speculum 12, no. 3 (1937): 359–66; Brunetto Latini, *Il Tesoretto* (*The Little Treasure*), edited and translated by Julia Bolton Holloway (New York: Grand Publishing, 1981), xix–xxvi.

9 Jean C. Campbell, *The Commonwealth of Nature: Art and Poetic Community in the Age of Dante* (University Park: Pennsylvania State University Press, 2008), 39–47.

10 Mary Franklin-Brown, *Reading the World: Encyclopedic Writing in the Scholastic Age* (Chicago: University of Chicago Press, 2012), 6–8.

11 M-D. Chenu, *Nature, Man, and Society in the Twelfth Century; Essays on New Theological Perspectives in the Latin West*, translated by Jerome Taylor and Lester K. Little (Chicago: University of Chicago Press, 1968), 1–48.

12 Andreas Speer, "The Discovery of Nature: The Contribution of the Chartrians to Twelfth-Century Attempts to Found a Scientia Naturalis," *Traditio* 52 (1997): 135–51; Anna Somfai, "The Eleventh-Century Shift in the Reception of Plato's 'Timaeus' and Calcidius's 'Commentary,'" *Journal of the Warburg and Courtauld Institutes* 65 (2002): 1–21; Sara Ritchey, "Rethinking the Twelfth-Century Discovery of Nature," *Journal of Medieval and Early Modern Studies* 39, no. 2 (2009): 225–55.

13 David C. Lindberg, *The Beginnings of Western Science: The European Scientific Tradition in Philosophical, Religious, and Institutional Context, 600 B.C. to A.D. 1450* (Chicago: University of Chicago Press, 2008), 209–15.

14 Clarence J. Glacken, *Traces on the Rhodian Shore: Nature and Culture in Western Thought from Ancient Times to the End of the Eighteenth Century* (Berkeley: University of California Press, 1967), 45.

15 William J. Courtenay, "Nature and the Natural in Twelfth-Century Thought," in *Covenant and Causality in Medieval Thought: Studies in Philosophy, Theology, and Economic Practice*, ch. 3 (London: Variorum Reprints, 1984); Paul Edward Dutton, *The Glosae super Platonem of Bernard of Chartres*, Studies and Texts 107 (Toronto: Pontifical Institute of Mediaeval Studies, 1991); William of Conches, *A Dialogue on Natural Philosophy (Dragmaticon Philosophiae)*, translated by Italo Ronca and Matthew Curr (Notre Dame, IN: University of Notre Dame Press, 1997).

16 Peter Dronke, "Bernard Silvestris, Natura, and Personification," *Journal of the Warburg and Courtauld Institutes* 43 (1980): 16–31; Brian Stock, *Myth and Science in the Twelfth Century: A Study of Bernard Silvester* (Princeton, NJ: Princeton University Press, 1972), 31–62.

17 Bernard Silvestris, *Cosmographia*, translated by Winthrop Wetherbee (New York: Columbia University Press, 1973), 121.

18 Monte Ransome Johnson, *Aristotle on Teleology*, Oxford Aristotle Studies (Oxford: Clarendon Press, 2005); Helen Lang, *Aristotle's "Physics" and Its Medieval Varieties* (Albany: State University of New York Press, 1992).

19 Translated in Edward Grant, ed., *A Source Book in Medieval Science* (Cambridge, MA: Harvard University Press, 1974), 388–91; David C. Lindberg, "Roger Bacon's Theory of the Rainbow," *Isis* 57, no. 2 (1966): 238–41.

20 James McEvoy, *Robert Grosseteste*, Great Medieval Thinkers (New York: Oxford University Press, 2000), 87–95.

21 Charles Burnett, "The Institutional Context of Arabic-Latin Translations of the Middle Ages: A Reassessment of the 'School of Toledo,'" in *Vocabulary of Teaching and Research Between Middle Ages and Renaissance*, edited by Olga Weijers, 214–35, Proceedings of the Colloquium London, Warburg Institute, March 11–12, 1994 (Turnhout: Brepols, 1995).

22 Gershom ben Solomon, *The Gate of Heaven (Shaar ha- Shamayim)*, edited and translated by F. S. Bodenheimer (Jerusalem: Kiryath Sepher, 1953); Gad Freudenthal, "The Aim and Structure of Gershom ben Solomon's Sha'ar ha-shamayim," *Zutot* 14, no. 1 (2017): 49–63.

23 Bernard G. Dod, "Aristoteles Latinus," in *The Cambridge History of Later Medieval Philosophy*, edited by Norman Kretzmann, Anthony Kenny, Jan Pinborg, and Eleonore Stump, 45–79 (Cambridge: Cambridge University Press, 1982); David C. Lindberg, "The Transmission of Greek and Arabic Learning to the West," in *Science in the Middle Ages*, edited by David C. Lindberg, 52–90 (Chicago: University of Chicago Press, 1978).

24 Rega Wood, "The Influence of Arabic Aristotelianism on Scholastic Natural Philosophy," in *The Cambridge History of Medieval Philosophy*, edited by R. Pasnau and C. Van Dyke, 247–66 (Cambridge: Cambridge University Press, 2009).

25 Roland Hissette, *Enquête sur les 219 articles condamnés à Paris le 7 mars 1277* (Louvain: Publications Universitaires, 1977); Thijssen, *Censure and Heresy at the University of Paris*.

26 Luca Bianchi, *Censure et liberté intellectuelle à l'Université de Paris: XIIIe–XIVe siècles* (Paris: Les Belles Lettres, 1999).

27 Lindberg, *The Beginnings of Western Science*, 248.

28 Jan A. Aertsen, Kent Emery Jr., and Andreas Speer, eds., *Nach der Verurteilung von 1277. Philosophie und Theologie an der Universität von Paris im letzen Viertel des 13. Jahrhunderts. Studien und Texte* (Berlin: Walter de Gruyter, 2001), 1–19.

29 William J. Courtenay, *Capacity and Volition: A History of the Distinction of Absolute and Ordained Power* (Bergamo: P. Lubrina, 1990); Funkenstein, *Theology and the Scientific Imagination*, 117–74.

30 Nicole Oresme, *Le Livre du Ciel et du Monde*, edited by Albert J. Menut and Alexander J. Denomy, translated by Albert D. Menut (Madison University of Wisconsin Press, 1968), 166–71.

31 George Economou, *The Goddess Natura in Medieval Literature* (Cambridge, MA: Harvard University Press, 1972); Barbara Newman, *God and the Goddesses: Vision, Poetry, and Belief in the Middle Ages* (Philadelphia: University of Pennsylvania Press, 2002).

32 Alan of Lille, *De planctu naturae*, in *Literary Works*, edited and translated by Winthrop Wetherbee, 219–517, Dumbarton Oaks Medieval Library 22 (Cambridge, MA: Harvard University Press, 2013), 109–10.

33 Newman, *God and the Goddesses*, 66–73.

34 William Caxton, *The Game and Playe of the Chesse*, edited by Jenny Adams, TEAMS (Kalamazoo, MI: Medieval Institute Publications, 2009) 3.2, lines 219–21, p. 60.

35 Franklin-Brown, *Reading the World*, 183–214.

36 Kellie Robertson, *Nature Speaks: Medieval Literature and Aristotelian Philosophy* (Philadelphia: University of Pennsylvania, 2017), 128–76.

37 George Boas, "The Microcosm," in *The History of Ideas: An Introduction*, 212–38 (New York: Scribners, 1969); George Perrigo Conger, *Theories of Macrocosms and Microcosms in the History of Philosophy* (New York: Russell and Russell, 1967); Stock, *Myth and Science in the Twelfth Century*, 204–19.

38 Robert Pasnau, *Thomas Aquinas on Human Nature: A Philosophical Study of Summa Theologiae 1a 75–89* (Cambridge: Cambridge University Press, 2002).

39 Silvestris, *Cosmographia*, 120–1.

Chapter 6

1 Augustine, *Concerning the City of God against the Pagans*, translated by Henry Bettenson, 2nd edn. (Harmondsworth, UK: Penguin, 1984), 561.

2 Bernard McGinn, *The Growth of Mysticism* (New York: Crossroad Publishing Company, 1994), 55.

3 Matthew 28:19.

4 Peter Brown, *The Rise of Western Christendom: Triumph and Adversity, A.D. 200–1000*, 2nd edn. (Malden, MA: Blackwell Publishing, 2003), 224.

5 Benedict of Nursia, *The Rule of St. Benedict*, edited and translated by Bruce L. Venarde (Cambridge, MA: Harvard University Press, 2011), 25.

6 Gregory of Tours, *History of the Franks*, translated by Lewis Thorpe (Harmondsworth, UK: Penguin, 1978), 63.

7 Gregory of Tours, *History of the Franks*, 103.

8 Gregory of Tours, *History of the Franks*, 536.

9 Gregory of Tours, *History of the Franks*, 537.

10 McGinn, *The Growth of Mysticism*, 75; Giles Constable, *Three Studies in Medieval Religious and Social Thought: The Interpretation of Mary and Martha, The Ideal of the Imitation of Christ, The Orders of Society* (Cambridge: Cambridge University Press, 1995), 3–43.

11 Gregory I, *Pastoral Care [Regula Pastoralis]*, translated by Henry Davis, SJ (New York: Newman Press, 1978), 48.

12 Bernard of Clairvaux, *Five Books on Consideration: Advice to a Pope*, translated by John D. Anderson and Elizabeth T. Kennan (Kalamazoo, MI: Cistercian Publications, 1976), 52.

13 Bernard of Clairvaux, *Five Books on Consideration*, 80.

14 Gregory I, *Pastoral Care*, 92.

15 Gregory I, *Pastoral Care*, 45.

16 Richard Fletcher, *The Conversion of Europe: From Paganism to Christianity 371–1386 AD* (London: Fontana Press, 1998), 132.

17 Bede, *A History of the English Church and People*, translated by Leo Sherley-Price, revised by R. E. Latham (Harmondsworth, UK: Penguin, 1968), 94.

18 Bede, *A History of the English Church and People*, 70.

19 Alexandra H. Olsen and Burton Raffel, *Poems and Prose from the Old English* (New Haven, CT: Yale University Press, 1998), 198.

20 Michel Zink, *La prédication en langue romane avant 1300* (Paris: Honoré Champion, 1982), 89.

21 Pierre Riché, *Écoles et enseignement dans le Haut Moyen Âge: Fin du Vᵉ siècle–milieu du XIᵉ siècle* (Paris: Picard, 1989), 285–334.

22 Dhuoda, *Handbook for Her Warrior Son: Liber manualis*, edited by and translated by Marcelle Thiébaux (Cambridge: Cambridge University Press, 1998), 49, 233.

23 J. M. Wallace-Hadrill, *The Frankish Church* (Oxford: Clarendon Press, 1983), 208.

24 Gregory I, *Pastoral Care*, 45.

25 Quoted in André Vauchez, *The Laity in the Middle Ages: Religious Beliefs and Devotional Practices*, edited by Daniel E. Bornstein, translated by Margery J. Schneider (Notre Dame, IN: University of Notre Dame Press, 1993), 42.

26 Acts 8:20–1.

27 Brian Stock, *The Implications of Literacy: Written Language and Models of Interpretation in the Eleventh and Twelfth Centuries* (Princeton, NJ: Princeton University Press, 1983), 66.

28 Robert I. Moore, *The First European Revolution, c. 970–1215* (Oxford: Blackwell, 2000), 11.

29 Vauchez, *The Laity in the Middle Ages*, 41.

30 Ephesians 6:14.

31 Wojciech Iwanczak, "Miles Christi: the Medieval Ideal of Knighthood," *Journal of the Australian Early Medieval Association* 8 (2012): 77–92; Martin Aurell and Catalina Girbea,

Chevalerie et christianisme aux XIIe et XIIIe siècles (Rennes: Presses Universitaires de Rennes, 2011).

32 Edward Peters, ed., *The Chronicle of Fulcher of Chartres and Other Source Materials*, 2nd edn. (Philadelphia: University of Pennsylvania Press, 1998), 51.

33 S. J. Allen and Emilie Amt, eds., *The Crusades: A Reader* (Toronto: University of Toronto Press, 2010), 44.

34 Allen and Amt, *The Crusades: A Reader*, 46.

35 Allen and Amt, *The Crusades: A Reader*, 46.

36 Anne Savage and Nicholas Watson, eds., *Anchoritic Spirituality: Ancrene Wisse and Associated Works* (Mahwah, NJ: Paulist Press, 1991), 191.

37 Claire M. Waters, *Translating* Clergie: *Status, Education, and Salvation in Thirteenth-Century Vernacular Texts* (Philadelphia: University of Pennsylvania Press, 2016), 76.

38 Dyan Elliott, *Spiritual Marriage: Sexual Abstinence in Medieval Wedlock* (Princeton, NJ: Princeton University Press, 1993); Vauchez, *The Laity in the Middle Ages*, ch. 6.

39 Waters, *Translating* Clergie, 232, n. 37.

40 Simon Tugwell, ed., *Early Dominicans: Selected Writings* (Mahwah, NJ: Paulist Press, 1982), 54.

41 Jane Sayers, *Innocent III: Leader of Europe, 1198–1216* (New York: Longman, 1994), 150–3.

42 Benedict of Nursia, *The Rule of St. Benedict*, 19.

43 Rachel Fulton, *From Judgment to Passion: Devotion to Christ and the Virgin Mary, 800–1200* (New York: Columbia University Press, 2002), 80.

44 Fulton, *From Judgment to Passion*, 86.

45 Leonard Boyle, "Innocent III and Vernacular Versions of Scripture," in *The Bible in the Medieval World: Essays in Memory of Beryl Smalley*, edited by Katherine Walsh and Diana Wood, 97–107 (Oxford: Basil Blackwell for the Ecclesiastical History Society, 1985); Susan Boynton, and Diane J. Reilly, eds., *The Practice of the Bible in the Middle Ages: Production, Reception, and Performance in Western Christianity* (New York: Columbia University Press, 2011), chs. 11 and 14.

46 Franklin T. Harkins, *Reading and the Work of Restoration: History and Scripture in the Work of Hugh of St. Victor* (Toronto: Pontifical Institute of Mediaeval Studies, 2009).

47 James H. Morey, "Peter Comestor, Biblical Paraphrase, and the Medieval Popular Bible," *Speculum* 68, no. 1 (1993): 6–35.

48 Peter Biller, "Confession in the Middle Ages: Introduction," in *Handling Sin: Confession in the Middle Ages*, edited by Peter Biller and A. J. Minnis, 3–33 (York: York Medieval Press, 1998), 7–18.

49 Thomas Frederick Crane, ed., *The Exempla or Illustrative Stories from the* Sermones vulgares *of Jacques de Vitry* (New York: Burt Franklin, 1940), 126.

50 Tanner, *Decrees of the Ecumenical Councils*, 1:245.

51 Bernard McGinn, *The Flowering of Mysticism: Men and Women in the New Mysticism (1200–1350)* (New York: Crossroad Publishing Company, 1998), 12.

52 Savage and Watson, *Anchoritic Spirituality*, 247–54.

53 Nicholas Watson and Jacqueline Jenkins, eds., *The Writings of Julian of Norwich: A Vision Showed to a Devout Woman and A Revelation of Love* (University Park: Pennsylvania State University Press, 2006), 40.

54 McGinn, *The Flowering of Mysticism*, 31–69, 153–98.

55 Conleth Kearns, trans., *The Life of Catherine of Siena* (Dublin: Dominican Publications, 1980), 104; Denis Searby and Bridget Morris, trans., *The Revelations of St. Birgitta of*

Sweden: Liber caelestis, Volume 3, Books VI–VII (Oxford: Oxford University Press, 2012), 19.

56 Miri Rubin, *Emotion and Devotion: The Meaning of Mary in Medieval Religious Cultures* (Budapest: Central European University Press, 2009).

57 Anne Hudson, *The Premature Reformation: Wycliffite Texts and Lollard History* (Oxford: Clarendon Press, 1988).

58 Walter Simons, *Cities of Ladies: Beguine Communities in the Medieval Low Countries, 1200–1565* (Philadelphia: University of Pennsylvania Press, 2003).

59 John Van Engen, *Sisters and Brothers of the Common Life: The Devotio Moderna and the World of the Later Middle Ages* (Philadelphia: University of Pennsylvania Press, 2014).

60 R. W. Southern, *Western Society and the Church in the Middle Ages* (London: Penguin, 1970), 342.

61 Walter Hilton, *Walter Hilton's* Mixed Life *Edited from Lambeth Palace MS 472*, edited by S. J. Ogilvie-Thomson (Salzburg: Institut für Anglistik und Amerikanistik Universität Salzburg, 1986), 14–16.

62 Margery Kempe, *The Book of Margery Kempe*, edited by Sanford Brown Meech and Hope Emily Allen, EETS o.s. 212 (London: Oxford University Press for the Early English Text Society, 1997), 126.

Chapter 7

1 Geoffrey Chaucer, "The Franklin's Tale," in *The Riverside Chaucer*, edited by Larry D. Benson (Boston: Houghton Mifflin Co., 1987), 721–4.

2 Irène Rosier-Catach, "Prata rident," in *Langages et philosophie: hommage à Jean Jolivet*, edited by Alain de Libera, Abdelali Elamrani-Jamal, and Alain Galonnier, 156–76 (Paris: Vrin, 1997), 155, 171.

3 Marcia Colish, *Mirror of Language: A Study in the Medieval Theory of Knowledge* (Lincoln: University of Nebraska Press, 1983), 1.

4 Emmanuelle Danblon, "The Reason of Rhetoric," *Philosophy and Rhetoric* 46, no. 4 (2013): 493.

5 Danblon, "The Reason of Rhetoric," 505.

6 Marjorie Curry Woods, "Chaucer the Rhetorician: Criseyde and Her Family," *The Chaucer Review* 20, no. 1 (1985): 29.

7 Danblon, "The Reason of Rhetoric," 501.

8 M. Irvine, *The Making of Textual Culture: "Grammatica" and Literary Theory, 350–1100* (Cambridge: Cambridge University Press, 1994), 8; John Marenbon, *Early Medieval Philosophy (480–1150): An Introduction*, 2nd edn. (New York: Routledge Press, 1988), 128.

9 M. C. Leff, "Boethius' *De differentiis topicis*, Book IV," in *Medieval Eloquence: Studies in the Theory and Practice of Medieval Rhetoric*, edited by James J. Murphy, 3–24 (Berkeley: University of California Press, 1978), 20; Richard McKeon, "Rhetoric in the Middle Ages," in *Critics and Criticism*, edited by R. S. Crane, 260–96 (Chicago: University of Chicago Press, 1952), 262.

10 McKeon, "Rhetoric in the Middle Ages," 263.

11 James J. Murphy, *Three Medieval Rhetorical Arts* (Tempe: Arizona Center for Medieval and Renaissance Studies, 2001), viii–xii.

12 McKeon, "Rhetoric in the Middle Ages," 260.

13 Murphy, *Three Medieval Rhetorical Arts*, xiv; John O. Ward, "From Antiquity to the Renaissance: Glosses and Commentaries on Cicero's Rhetorica," in *Medieval*

Eloquence: Studies in the Theory and Practice of Medieval Rhetoric, edited by James J. Murphy (Berkeley: University of California Press, 1978), 31.

14 Ward, "From Antiquity to the Renaissance," 46.

15 George A. Kennedy, *Classical Rhetoric and its Christian and Secular Tradition* (Chapel Hill: University of North Carolina Press, 1999), 124.

16 Murphy, *Three Medieval Rhetorical Arts*, xvi.

17 Martin Camargo, "Tria Sunt: The Long and the Short of Geoffrey of Vinsauf's *Documentum de modo et arte dictandi et versificandi*," *Speculum* 74, no. 4 (1999): 950.

18 Kennedy *Classical Rhetoric and its Christian and Secular Tradition*, 212; James J. Murphy, "Rhetoric in Fourteenth-Century Oxford," *Medium Aevum* 34 (1965): 13.

19 Peter Mack, "Humanist Rhetoric and Dialectic," in *Cambridge Companion to Renaissance Humanism*, edited by Jill Kraye (Cambridge: Cambridge University Press, 1996), 82–5.

20 Brian Stock, *Listening for the Text: On the Uses of the Past* (Baltimore: Johns Hopkins University Press, 1990), 50.

21 Stock, *Listening for the Text*, 50.

22 Paul E. Prill, "Rhetoric and Poetics in the Early Middle Ages," *Rhetorica* 5, no. 2 (1987): 135; Woods, "Chaucer the Rhetorician," 28.

23 A. J. Minnis, A. B. Scott, and David Wallace, eds., *Medieval Literary Theory and Criticism, c.1100–c.1375* (Oxford: Clarendon Press, 1988), 33, 279.

24 Ward, "From Antiquity to the Renaissance," 65.

25 Colish, *Mirror of Language*, 3.

26 Rita Copeland, *Rhetoric, Hermeneutics, and Translation in the Middle Ages: Academic Traditions and Vernacular Texts* (Cambridge: Cambridge University Press, 1991), 103.

27 James J. Murphy, *Rhetoric in the Middle Ages: A History of Rhetorical Theory from Saint Augustine to the Renaissance* (Berkeley: University of California Press, 1974), 42.

28 Copeland, *Rhetoric, Hermeneutics, and Translation in the Middle Ages*, 58.

29 Copeland, *Rhetoric, Hermeneutics, and Translation in the Middle Ages*, 62.

30 Copeland, *Rhetoric, Hermeneutics, and Translation in the Middle Ages*, 59.

31 Jackson J. Campbell, "Adaptation of Classical Rhetoric in Old English Literature," in *Medieval Eloquence: Studies in the Theory and Practice of Medieval Rhetoric*, edited by James J. Murphy (Berkeley: University of California Press, 1978), 178; Derek Pearsall, *Old English and Middle English Poetry* (London: Routledge & Kegan Paul, 1977), 66–70.

32 Copeland, *Rhetoric, Hermeneutics, and Translation in the Middle Ages*, 59.

33 McKeon, "Rhetoric in the Middle Ages," 286.

34 Kennedy, *Classical Rhetoric and its Christian and Secular Tradition*, 223.

35 Danblon, "The Reason of Rhetoric," 497.

36 Copeland, *Rhetoric, Hermeneutics, and Translation in the Middle Ages*, 153.

37 McKeon, "Rhetoric in the Middle Ages," 271.

38 Murphy, *Three Medieval Rhetorical Arts*, xxiii; Copeland, *Rhetoric, Hermeneutics, and Translation in the Middle Ages*, 153.

39 Kennedy, *Classical Rhetoric and its Christian and Secular Tradition*, 183.

40 Copeland, *Rhetoric, Hermeneutics, and Translation in the Middle Ages*, 39.

41 McKeon, "Rhetoric in the Middle Ages," 274.

42 Scott MacDonald, "Late Medieval Ethics," in *A History of Western Ethics*, edited by Lawrence C. Becker and Charlotte B. Becker, 52–9 (New York: Garland Publishing, 1992), 46.

43 Murphy, *Three Medieval Rhetorical Arts*, xiv.

44 Copeland, *Rhetoric, Hermeneutics, and Translation in the Middle Ages*, 78.

45 Copeland, *Rhetoric, Hermeneutics, and Translation in the Middle Ages*, 59.

46 MacDonald, "Late Medieval Ethics," 54.

47 McKeon, "Rhetoric in the Middle Ages," 285.

48 Kennedy, *Classical Rhetoric and its Christian and Secular Tradition*, 230.

49 Kennedy, *Classical Rhetoric and its Christian and Secular Tradition*, 196–7.

50 J. K. Hyde, *Society and Politics in Medieval Italy: The Evolution of Civil Life, 1000–1350* (New York: St. Martin's Press, 1973), 63.

51 Hyde, *Society and Politics in Medieval Italy*, 65.

52 Kennedy, *Classical Rhetoric and its Christian and Secular Tradition*, 197, 212.

53 Helene Wieruszowski, *Politics and Culture in Medieval Spain and Italy* (Rome: Edizioni di storia e letteratura, 1971), 611.

54 Murphy, *Three Medieval Rhetorical Arts*, xxiii.

55 Wieruszowski, *Politics and Culture in Medieval Spain and Italy*, 612.

56 Wieruszowski, *Politics and Culture in Medieval Spain and Italy*, 606.

57 Ward, "From Antiquity to the Renaissance," 46–7.

58 Hyde, *Society and Politics in Medieval Italy*, 91.

59 Ward, "From Antiquity to the Renaissance," 36.

60 Hyde, *Society and Politics in Medieval Italy*, 92.

61 Copeland, *Rhetoric, Hermeneutics, and Translation in the Middle Ages*, 209.

62 Copeland, *Rhetoric, Hermeneutics, and Translation in the Middle Ages*, 181.

63 Copeland, *Rhetoric, Hermeneutics, and Translation in the Middle Ages*, 181.

64 Wieruszowski, *Politics and Culture in Medieval Spain and Italy*, 606.

65 Hyde, *Society and Politics in Medieval Italy*, 92.

66 Wieruszowski, *Politics and Culture in Medieval Spain and Italy*, 606.

67 Ward, "From Antiquity to the Renaissance," 39.

68 Wieruszowski, *Politics and Culture in Medieval Spain and Italy*, 620; Nicholas Mann, "The Origins of Humanism," in *Cambridge Companion to Renaissance Humanism*, edited by Jill Kraye, 1–19 (Cambridge: Cambridge University Press, 1996), 13.

69 Kennedy, *Classical Rhetoric and its Christian and Secular Tradition*, 229.

70 Murphy, *Three Medieval Rhetorical Arts*, xv.

71 McKeon, "Rhetoric in the Middle Ages," 269.

72 McKeon, "Rhetoric in the Middle Ages," 271.

73 Aristotle, *Rhetoric* 1.1.

74 Copeland, *Rhetoric, Hermeneutics, and Translation in the Middle Ages*, 69.

75 Kennedy, *Classical Rhetoric and its Christian and Secular Tradition*, 225.

76 Murphy, *Three Medieval Rhetorical Arts*, xv.

77 Murphy, *Rhetoric in the Middle Ages*, 90; Lahcen Elyazghi Ezzaher, ed., *Three Arabic Treatises on Aristotle's* Rhetoric: *The Commentaries of al-Farabi, Avicenna, and Averroes* (Carbondale: Southern Illinois University Press, 2015), 6.

78 Minnis, Scott, and Wallace, *Medieval Literary Theory and Criticism*, 3, 280.

79 McKeon, "Rhetoric in the Middle Ages," 279; Minnis, Scott, and Wallace, *Medieval Literary Theory and Criticism*, 279–80.

80 Ezzaher, *Three Arabic Treatises on Aristotle's* Rhetoric, 5–7.

81 Minnis, Scott, and Wallace, *Medieval Literary Theory and Criticism*, 277, 279–80.

82 Deborah L. Black, *Logic and Aristotle's Rhetoric and Poetics in Medieval Arabic Philosophy* (Leiden: Brill, 1990), 2.

83 Black, *Logic and Aristotle's Rhetoric and Poetics in Medieval Arabic Philosophy*, 304.

84 Leff, "Boethius' *De differentiis topicis*, Book IV," 24.

85 Stock, *Listening for the Text*, 50–1.

86 Dallas G. Denery II, "The Appearance of Reality: Peter Aureol and the Experience of Perceptual Error," *Franciscan Studies* 55 (1998): 28.

87 Denery, *Seeing and Being Seen in the Later Medieval World: Optics, Theology, and Religious Life*, 125.

88 K. L. Lynch, *Chaucer's Philosophical Visions* (Rochester, NY: D. S. Brewer, 2000), 38.

89 Colish, *Mirror of Language*, 112–13.

90 Leff, "Boethius' *De differentiis topicis*, Book IV," 17.

91 E. J. Ashworth, *Language and Logic in the Post-Medieval Period* (Boston: D. Reidel Publishing Company, 1974), 11.

92 Lisa Jardine, "Humanstic Logic," in *Cambridge History of Renaissance Philosophy*, edited by Charles B. Schmitt, Quentin Skinner, Eckhard Kessler, and Jill Kraye, 173–98 (Cambridge: Cambridge University Press, 1988), 177.

93 Ashworth, *Language and Logic in the Post-Medieval Period*, 8.

94 Jardine, "Humanstic Logic," 197.

95 Leff, "Boethius' *De differentiis topicis*, Book IV," 17.

96 Mack, "Humanist Rhetoric and Dialectic," 86–7.

97 Jardine, "Humanstic Logic," 175.

98 Paul Oskar Kristeller, *Renaissance Thought: The Classic, Scholastic, and Humanistic Strains* (New York: Harper & Brothers, 1961), 13–15; Concetta C. Greenfield, *Humanist and Scholastic Poetics* (Lewisberg, PA: Bucknell University Press, 1981), 17.

99 Black, *Logic and Aristotle's Rhetoric and Poetics in Medieval Arabic Philosophy*, 14.

100 Minnis, Scott, and Wallace, *Medieval Literary Theory and Criticism*, 280.

101 Minnis, Scott, and Wallace, *Medieval Literary Theory and Criticism*, 3.

102 The rhetorical underpinnings of the *acccessus* tradition predating Scholasticism is evident with the Carolingians and the practices of Remigius of Auxerre in the late ninth century (Copeland, *Rhetoric, Hermeneutics, and Translation in the Middle Ages*, 66).

103 Karla Mallette, "Beyond Mimesis: Aristotle's 'Poetics' in the Medieval Mediterranean," *PMLA* 124, no. 2 (2009): 585.

104 Minnis, Scott, and Wallace, *Medieval Literary Theory and Criticism*, 284.

105 Minnis, Scott, and Wallace, *Medieval Literary Theory and Criticism*, 284.

106 Danblon, "The Reason of Rhetoric," 500.

107 Danblon, "The Reason of Rhetoric," 499.

108 G. P. Krapp and E. K. Dobbie, eds., *The Exeter Book* (New York: Columbia University Press, 1936), 243. The solution is variously given by Krapp and Dobbie as "wandering singer," spirit/mind or, more controversially, "riddle" (381).

109 Patricia Dailey, "Riddles, Wonder and Responsiveness in Anglo-Saxon Literature," in *The Cambridge History of Early Medieval English Literature*, edited by Clare A. Lees, 451–74 (Cambridge: Cambridge University Press, 2013), 455.

110 Eugene Vance, *From Topic to Tale: Logic and Narrativity in the Middle Ages* (Minneapolis: University of Minnesota Press, 1987), 43, 45.

111 Sarah Kay, *Courtly Contradictions: The Emergence of the Literary Object in the Twelfth Century* (Stanford, CA: Stanford University Press, 2001), 52.

112 See Ann Marie Rasmussen, "The Female Figures in Gottfried's *Tristan and Isolde*," in *A Companion to Gottfried von Strassburg's* Tristan, edited by Will Hasty, 137–58 (Rochester, NY: Camden House, 2003), 144.

113 Hyde, *Society and Politics in Medieval Italy*, 175.

114 Daniel Heller-Roazen, *Fortune's Faces: The* Roman de la Rose *and the Poetics of Contingency* (Baltimore: Johns Hopkins University Press, 2003), 7.

115   K. S. Gittes, *Framing the* Canterbury Tales: *Chaucer and the Medieval Frame Narrative Tradition* (New York: Greenwood Press, 1991), 2.

116   Calvin Normore, "Some Aspects of Ockham's Logic," in *The Cambridge Companion to Ockham*, edited by Paul Vincent Spade, 31–52 (Cambridge: Cambridge University Press, 1999), 44.

117   D. Vance Smith, *The Book of the Incipit: Beginnings in the Fourteenth Century* (Minneapolis: University of Minnesota Press, 2001), 84.

118   Seth Lerer, "Humanism, Philology, and the Medievalist," *Postmedieval* 5 (2014): 514.

119   Judson Boyce Allen, *The Ethical Poetic of the Later Middle Ages: A Decorum of Convenient Distinction* (Toronto: University of Toronto Press, 1982), 217.

Chapter 8

1   Martina Bagnoli, Holger A. Klein, C. Griffith Mann, and James Robinson, *Treasures of Heaven: Saints, Relics and Devotion in Medieval Europe* (New Haven, CT: Yale University Press, 2010), 19, n. 10.

2   Peter Brown, *The Cult of the Saints: Its Rise and Function in Latin Christianity* (Chicago: University of Chicago Press, 1982).

3   Bagnoli et al., *Treasures of Heaven*, 36 cat. no. 13; Bruno Reudenbach, "Reliquien von Orten: ein frühchristliches Reliquiar als Gedächtnisort," in *Reliquiare im Mittelalter*, edited by Bruno Reudenbach and Gia Toussaint, Hamburger Forschungen Zur Kunstgeschichte 5, 21–41 (Berlin: Akademie Verlag, 2005); Derek Krueger, *Liturgical Subjects: Christian Ritual, Biblical Narrative, and the Formation of the Self in Byzantium* (Philadelphia: University of Pennsylvania Press, 2014), 69–70 and 234, n. 4.

4   Krueger, *Liturgical Subjects*, 69; see also Harold R. Willoughby, "The Distinctive Sources of Palestinian Pilgrimage Iconography," *Journal of Biblical Literature* 74, no. 2 (1955): 61–8.

5   Jean Leclercq, "Monachisme et peregrination du IXe au XIIe siècle," *Studia Monastica* 3 (1961): 33–52; Giles Constable, "Opposition to Pilgrimage in the Middle Ages," *Studia Gratiana* 19 (1976): 125–46; and Daniel K. Connolly, "Imagined Pilgrimage in the Itinerary Maps of Matthew Paris," *Art Bulletin* 81, no. 4 (1999): 598–622.

6   Reudenbach, "Reliquien von Orten," 21–41; see also Cynthia Hahn, "The Meaning of Early Medieval Treasuries," in *Reliquiare im Mittelalter*, edited by Bruno Reudenbach and Gia Toussaint, Hamburger Forschungen Zur Kunstgeschichte 5, 1–20 (Berlin: Akademie Verlag, 2005).

7   *Bede's Ecclesiastical History of England, Revised translation, with Introduction, Life, and Notes by A. M. Sellar* (London: George Bell and Sons, 1907). Available online: http://www.gutenberg.org/files/38326/38326-h/38326-h.html (accessed January 31, 2022), bk. 1, ch. 29.

8   Ezekiel 1:10; Revelation 4:7; Saint Jerome, Preface to the *Commentary on Matthew*, Fathers of the Church 117 (Washington, DC: Catholic University of America Press, 2008), 55.

9   Virgil, *Opera*, Rome, Vatican, Biblioteca Apostolica, Ms. cod. lat. 3867, fol. 3v.

10 Paulinus of Nola, *Carmina XXVII*, pp. 512–95, in Caecilia Davis-Weyer, ed., *Early Medieval Art 300–1150, Sources and Documents* (Toronto: University of Toronto Press, 1986), 19.

11 Bede, *Ecclesiastical History*, bk. 1, ch. 25.

12 Boniface, letter to the Abbess Eadburga, letter 21, in C. H. Talbot, ed. and trans., *The Anglo-Saxon Missionaries in Germany, Being the Lives of SS. Willibrord, Boniface, Leoba and Lebuin together with the Hodoepericon of St. Willibald and a selection from the correspondence of St. Boniface* (London: Sheed and Ward, 1954), 91–2.

13 Catherine E. Karkov, *The Art of Anglo-Saxon England* (Woodbridge, UK: Boydell, 2011), 33–40; see also Eva Frojmovic and Catherine E. Karkov, eds., *Postcolonising the Medieval Image* (New York: Routledge, 2017).

14 Einhard, *The Life of Charlemagne*, translated by Samuel Epes Turner (New York: Harper & Brothers, 1880); reprint in *Internet History Sourcebook* (New York: Fordham University, 1999), ch. 26.

15 Charles R. Dodwell, *The Pictorial Arts of the West, 800-1200* (New Haven, CT: Yale University Press, 1993), 60.

16 Elizabeth Saxon, "Carolingian, Ottonian and Romanesque Art and the Eucharist," in *A Companion to the Eucharist in the Middle Ages*, edited by Ian Levy, Gary Macy, and Kristen Van Ausdall, 251–324 (Leiden: Brill, 2012), 255–7.

17 Augustine, *On Christian Teaching [De Doctrina Christiana]*, edited and translated by R. P. H. Green (Oxfordr: Clarendon Press, 1995), I.4.

18 Cynthia Hahn, *Strange Beauty: Issues in the Making and Meaning of Reliquaries, 400–circa 1204* (University Park: Pennsylvania State University Press, 2012), 4–5; Hiltrud Westermann-Angerhausen, *Goldschmiedearbeiten der Trierer Egbertwerkstatt* (Trier: Spee-Verlag, 1973), 36.

19 Thomas Head, "Art and Artifice in Ottonian Trier," *Gesta* 36, no. 1 (1997): 72.

20 Avinoam Shalem, *Islam Christianized: Islamic Portable Objects in the Medieval Churches of the Latin West*, Ars Faciendi, Beiträge und Studien zur Kunstgeschichte, 7 (Frankfurt: Peter Lang, 1996).

21 Eva Hoffman, "Pathways of Portability: Islamic and Christian Interchange from the Tenth to the Twelfth Century," *Art History* 24, no. 1 (2001): 17–50.

22 Bernard of Clairvaux, *Letter to William of St. Thierry*, translated by G. G. Coulton, in *Early Medieval Art, 300–1150, Sources and Documents*, edited by Caecilia Davis-Weyer (Toronto: University of Toronto Press, 1986), 170.

23 Meyer Schapiro, "On the Aesthetic Attitude in Romanesque Art," in *Romanesque Art, Selected Papers*, edited by Meyer Schapiro, 1–27 (London: Chatto & Windus, 1993), 8–9.

24 Acts 2:1–4.

25 Sophie Balace, et al., *Une Renaissance, L'art entre Flandre et Champagne* (Saint-Omer: Musée de l'hôtel Sandelin, 2013), cat. no. 47, pp. 114–15.

26 Carolyn Muessig, "Learning and Mentoring in the Twelfth Century: Hildegard of Bingen and Herrad of Landsberg," in *Medieval Monastic Education*, edited by George Ferzoco and Carolyn Muessig, 87–104 (London: Leicester University Press, 2001), 97; transcribed in Rosalie Green, T. Julian Brown, and Kenneth Levy, *Herrad of Hohenberg Hortus Deliciarum* (London: The Warburg Institute, 1979), II, 4.

27 Muessig, "Learning and Mentoring in the Twelfth Century," 96.

28 Christopher De Hamel, *A History of Illuminated Manuscripts*, 2nd edn. (London: Phaidon, 2006), 113–17.

29 John Graham Pollard, "The *pecia* System in the Medieval Universities," in *Medieval Scribes, Manuscripts & Libraries: Essays Presented to N.R. Ker*, edited by Malcolm B. Parkes and Andrew G. Watson, 145–61 (London: Scolar Press, 1978), 147–8.

30 Daniel Weiss, "Architectural Symbolism and the Decoration of the Ste.-Chapelle," *Art Bulletin* 77, no. 2 (1995): 308.

31 Weiss, "Architectural Symbolism and the Decoration of the Ste.-Chapelle," 317; Meredith Cohen, "An Indulgence for the Visitor: The Public at the Sainte-Chapelle of Paris," *Speculum* 83, no. 4 (2008): 840–83.

32 Alyce Jordan, *Visualizing Kingship in the Windows of the Sainte-Chapelle* (Turnhout: Brepols, 2002).

33 Robert Branner, "The Painted Medallions in the Sainte-Chapelle, in Paris," *Transactions of the American Philosophical Society* 58, no. 2 (1968): 8.

34 Jean de Jandun, *Tractatus de laudibus Parisus*, in Erik Inglis, "Gothic Architecture and a Scholastic: Jean de Jandun's 'Tractatus de laudibus Parisius' (1323)," *Gesta* 42, no. 1 (2003): 67.

35 Inglis, "Gothic Architecture and a Scholastic," 71–2.

36 Rainer Kahsnitz, *Carved Splendor: Late Gothic Altarpieces in Southern Germany, Austria and South Tyrol* (Los Angeles: J. Paul Getty Museum, 2006), 13–24; Christof L. Diedrichs, *Vom Glauben zum Sehen: Die Sichtbarkeit der Reliquie im Reliquiar; Ein Beitrag zur Geschichte des Sehens* (Berlin: Weissensee Verlag, 2001).

37 Adam S. Cohen, "The Multisensory Haggadah," in *Les Cinq Sens au Moyen Âge*, edited by Éric Palazzo, 305–31 (Paris: Éditions Cerf, 2016), 308.

38 Exodus 15:20–1; Cohen, "The Multisensory Haggadah," 305–31.

39 Cohen, "The Multisensory Haggadah," 305–31.

40 Julie Ann Harris, "Love in the Land of Goshen: Haggadah, History, and the Making of British Library MS Oriental 2737," *Gesta* 52, no. 2 (2013): 179–80.

Chapter 9

1 Tacitus, *Histories*, translated by C. H. Moore, Loeb Classical Library (Cambridge, MA: Harvard University Press, 1925), 1.4, p. 8.

2 Vergil, *Georgics*, translated by H. Rushton Fairclough, revised by G. P. Goold, Loeb Classical Library (Cambridge, MA: Harvard University Press, 2000), 2.490, p. 150.

3 Aulus Gellius, *Noctes Atticae*, translated by J. C. Rolfe, Loeb Classical Library (Cambridge, MA: Harvard University Press, 1927), 5.18, pp. 433–5.

4 Augustine, *The Literal Meaning of Genesis [De Genesi ad Litteram]*, trans. J. H. Taylor, Ancient Christian Writers, 41–2 (New York: Newman Press, 1982), 147; Augustine, *The Advantage of Believing [De utilitate credendi]*, translated by Ray Kearney, in *On Christian Belief*, edited by Boniface Ramsey (New York: New City Press, 2005), 3, 119–23.

5 Augustine, *De civitate dei*, 3.18, p. 116.

6 Augustine, *True Religion [De vera religione]*, translated by Edmund Hill, in *On Christian Belief*, edited by Boniface Ramsey (New York: New City Press, 2005), 26.49, p. 61.

7 Augustine, *De doctrina christiana*, 2.28.109, p. 107.

8 Bonaventure, *Breviloquium*, trans. E. E. Nemmers (London: B. Herder, 1946), prol.2.4, p. 10.

9 Orderic Vitalis, *The Ecclesiastical History of Orderic Vitalis [Historia Ecclesiastica]*, edited and translated by M. Chibnall, Oxford Medieval Texts (Oxford: Clarendon Press, 1980), 1.prol., p. 133; 8.16, p. 229.

10 Augustine, *De civitate dei*, 10.14, p. 392; 16.24, p. 683; 16.43, p. 710; 22.30, p. 1091.

11 Romans 11:33.

12 R. A. Markus, *Saeculum – History and Society in the Theology of Augustine* (Cambridge: Cambridge University Press, 1970).

13 Cicero, *Topica*, edited and translated by Tobias Reinhardt (Oxford: Oxford University Press, 2006), 15.58–17.63, pp. 425–31.

14 Boethius, *In Ciceronis Topica*, translated by E. Stump (Ithaca, NY: Cornell University Press, 1988), 5, p. 155.

15 Boethius, *Consolation of Philosophy*, trans. S. J. Tester, Loeb Classical Library (Cambridge, MA: Harvard University Press, 1973), 5.1, pp. 387–9; Aristotle, *Physics*, translated by R. Waterfield (Oxford: Oxford University Press, 1996), 2.4–6, pp. 42–8.

16 Lodi Nauta, "The *Consolation*: The Latin Commentary Tradition, 800–1700," in *The Cambridge Companion to Boethius*, edited by John Marenbon, 255–78 (Cambridge: Cambridge University Press, 2009).

17 Calcidius, *On Plato's Timaeus*, edited and translated by John Magee, Dumbarton Oaks Medieval Library 41 (Cambridge, MA: Harvard University Press, 2016), 159, p. 377.

18 Revelation 20:12; Athanasius, *Life of Antony [Vita Antonii]*, trans. Carolinne White, *Early Christian Lives*, 1–70 (Harmondsworth, UK: Penguin, 1998), 55, pp. 43–4; 65, p. 49; Henry of Huntingdon, *History of the English [Historia Anglorum]*, edited and translated by Diana Greenway, Oxford Medieval Texts (Oxford: Oxford University Press, 1996), 9.47, p. 683.

19 Cf. Aristotle, *Physics* 4.10–12, pp. 102–12; Robert Kilwardby, *On Time and Imagination [De Tempore]*, edited and translated by A. Broadie (Oxford: Oxford University Press, 1993), 1–2, pp. 25–8.

20 Janet Coleman, *Ancient and Medieval Memories – Studies in the Reconstruction of the Past* (Cambridge: Cambridge University Press, 1992).

21 Hugh of Saint Victor, *On the Sacraments of the Christian Faith [De Sacramentis Christianae Fidei]*, translated by R. J. Deferrari (Cambridge, MA: Mediaeval Academy of America, 1951), 2.18.22, pp. 475–6.

22 Gregory I, *Pastoral Care*, 4.1, pp. 234–5.

23 Luke 9:62.

24 Yosef Hayim Yerushalmi, *Zakhor—Jewish History and Jewish Memory* (Seattle: University of Washington Press, 1982).

25 Orosius, *The Seven Books of History against the Pagans*, translated by R. J. Deferrari, The Fathers of the Church 50 (Washington, DC: Catholic University of America Press, 1964), 7.41, p. 359; 7.9, pp. 302–3.

26 Augustine, *De civitate dei*, 18.52, pp. 835–6.

27 Peter Classen, "*Res Gestae*, Universal History, Apocalypse – Visions of Past and Future," in *Renaissance and Renewal in the Twelfth Century*, edited by Robert L. Benson and Giles Constable, 387–417 (Cambridge, MA: Harvard University Press, 1982), 403–14; Marjorie Reeves, *The Influence of Prophecy in the Later Middle Ages – A Study in Joachimism* (Oxford: Clarendon Press, 1969), 16–27.

28 Otto of Freising, *The Two Cities: a Chronicle of Universal History [Chronica]*, translated by C. C. Mierow (New York: Columbia University Press, 1928), 6.23, p. 384; 3.prol., p. 218.

29 Augustine, *De civitate dei*, 19.6, pp. 859–61.

30 Ibid., 21.7, p. 978.

31 Otto of Freising, *Chronicle*, 8.4, p. 460; 8.19, p. 478; 8.34, p. 511; 8.35, pp. 513–14.

32 Otto of Freising, *Chronicle*, Ep.ded., p. 90.

33 Orderic Vitalis, *The Ecclesiastical History of Orderic Vitalis*, 3.prol., p. 833.

34 Otto of Freising, *Chronicle*, prol., p. 96.

35 Boethius, *Consolation of Philosophy*, 3.5, p. 251; 4.6, pp. 365–7.

36 Isidore of Seville, *Etymologies*, 8.7, 18.45.

37 Seneca, *On Consolation to Polybius*, in *Moral Essays*, translated by J. W. Basore, Loeb Classical Library (Cambridge, MA: Harvard University Press, 1932), 1.4, p. 359.

38 Rufinus of Aquileia, *Ecclesiastical History*, translated by W. H. Fremantle, A Select Library of Nicene and Post-Nicene Fathers (Oxford: Parker and Co., 1892), 10.pref., p. 565.

39 Macrobius, *Saturnalia*, translated by P. V. Davies (New York: Columbia University Press, 1969), 7.1.18–19, pp. 443–4.

40 Vergil, *Aeneid*, translated by H. Rushton Fairclough, revised by G. P. Goold, 2 vols., Loeb Classical Library (Cambridge, MA: Harvard University Press, 2000).

41 Orosius, *The Seven Books of History*, 1.203, p. 255; 6.377, p. 533.

42 Orosius, *The Seven Books of History*, 4.prol., pp. 121–2; 5.24, p. 227; 7.22, p. 317.

43 Otto of Freising, *Chronicle*, 5.prol., p. 324; 5.9, p. 338.

44 Otto of Freising, *Chronicle*, 2.prol., p. 153; Ep.ded., p. 89.

45 Otto of Freising, *The Deeds of Frederick Barbarossa [Gesta Frederici]*, trans. C. C. Mierow (New York: Columbia University Press, 1953), 1.47, p. 79.

46 Otto of Freising, *Gesta Frederici*, prol., p. 24.

47 Hans-Werner Goetz, "The Concept of Time in the Historiography of the Eleventh and Twelfth Centuries," in *Medieval Concepts of the Past: Ritual, Memory, Historiography*, edited by Gerd Althoff, Johannes Fried, and Patrick J. Geary, 139–65 (Cambridge: Cambridge University Press, 2002).

48 Otto of Freising, *Gesta Frederici*, 1.4, p. 31.

49 Roger Ray, "Medieval Historiography through the Twelfth Century: Problems and Progress of Research," *Viator* 5 (1974): 33–59.

50 Cicero, *De Oratore*, translated by E. Sutton and H. Rackham, Loeb Classical Library (Cambridge, MA: Harvard University Press, 1948), 2.15.62, pp. 243–5.

51 *Proverbia Sententiaeque Latinitatis Medii Aevi*, edited by H. Walther (Göttingen: Vandenhoeck & Ruprecht, 1963–1967), 1:1067.

52 Valerius Maximus, *Memorable Doings and Sayings [Facta et Dicta Memorabilia]*, translated by D. R. Shackleton Bailey, 2 vols., Loeb Classical Library (Cambridge, MA: Harvard University Press, 2000).

53 Wipo, *Deeds of Conrad II*, in *Imperial Lives and Letters of the Eleventh Century*, translated by Theodor E. Mommsen and Karl F. Morrison, edited by Robert L. Benson (New York: Columbia University Press, 2000), prol., p. 54.

54 Paschasius Radbertus, *Epitaphium Arsenii'*, in *Charlemagne's Cousins: Contemporary Lives of Adalard and Wala*, translated, introduction, and notes by Allen Cabaniss (Syracuse, NY: Syracuse University Press, 1967), 83–204.

55 Tuomas M. S. Lehtonen and Päivi Mehtonen, eds., *Historia: The Concept and Genres in the Middle Ages* (Helsinki: Societas Scientiarum Fennica, 2000).

56 Isidore, *Etymologiae*, 1.41–2, p. 67.

57 Cicero, *On Invention [De Inventione]*, trans. H. M. Hubbell, Loeb Classical Library (Cambridge, MA: Harvard University Press, 1949), 1.19.27, p. 55; Vincent of Beauvais, *Speculum Maius* (Graz: Akademische Druck- u. Verlaganstalt, 1964–1965), 6.21, p. 181.

58 Cicero, *Topica*, 1.8, p. 387.

59 *Rhetorica ad Herennium*, translated by H. Caplan, Loeb Classical Library (Cambridge, MA: Harvard University Press, 1954), 4.55.68–9: 405–9; Quintilian, *Institutio Oratoria*, translated by H. E. Butler, 4 vols., Loeb Classical Library (Cambridge, MA: Harvard University Press, 1920–1922), 4.2.63–5: 85.

60 Isidore, *Etymologiae* 1.41.1–2: 67.

61 John O. Ward, "Classical Rhetoric and the Writing of History in Medieval and Renaissance Culture," in *European History and Its Historians*, edited by Frank MacGregor and Nicholas Wright, 1–10 (Adelaide: Adelaide University Union Press, 1977); Ward, "Some Principles of Rhetorical Historiography in the Twelfth Century," in *Classical Rhetoric and Medieval Historiography*, edited by Ernst Breisach, 103–65 (Kalamazoo, MI: Medieval Institute

Publications, 1985); Matthew Kempshall, *Rhetoric and the Writing of History, 400–1500* (Manchester: Manchester University Press, 2011).

62 *Rhetorica ad Herennium*, 1.3.4, p. 9; emphasis added; Quintilian, *Institutio Oratoria*, 4.2.31, p. 67; John of Garland, *The Parisiana Poetria of John of Garland*, edited and translated by Traugott Lawler (New Haven, CT: Yale University Press, 1974) 4.197–8, p. 67.

63 Augustine, *De doctrina Christiana*, 4.4, p. 197.

64 Augustine, *De doctrina Christiana*, 2.25, p. 103.

65 Augustine, *De doctrina Christiana*, 2.129–39, pp. 116–22.

66 Augustine, *Retractions*, translated by M. I. Bogan, Fathers of the Church 60 (Washington, DC: Catholic University of America Press, 1968), 1.26, p. 117.

67 Macrobius, *Commentary on the Dream of Scipio*, translated by W. H. Stahl (New York: Columbia University Press, 1952), 1.2, pp. 84–5.

68 Isidore, *Etymologies*, 1.44.1–5, p. 67; John of Garland, *Parisiana Poetria*, 5.303–72, pp. 99–103; Vincent of Beauvais, *Speculum maius*, vol. 3: *Speculum doctrinale* (Graz: Akademische Druck- u. Verlaganstalt, 1964–1965), 3.127, p. 297.

69 Päivi Mehtonen, *Old Concepts and New Poetics: Historia, Argumentum and Fabula in the Twelfth- and Thirteenth-Century Latin Poetics of Fiction* (Helsinki: Societas Scientiarum Fennica, 1996).

70 John of Garland, *Parisiana Poetria*, 5.319, p. 100.

71 Traugott Lawler, "The Two Versions of Geoffrey of Vinsauf's *Documentum*," in *The Parisiana Poetria of John of Garland*, edited by and translated by Traugott Lawler, 327–32 (New Haven, CT: Yale University Press, 1974), 331.

72 John of Salisbury, *The Metalogicon of John of Salisbury: A Twelfth-Century Defense of the Verbal and Logical Arts of the Trivium*, translated by D. D. McGarry (Berkeley: University of California Press, 1955), 2.3, p. 79.

73 John of Salisbury, *Metalogicon*, 2.13, p. 105.

74 Aristotle, *Topica*, translated by W. A. Pickard-Cambridge, in *The Complete Works of Aristotle: The Revised Oxford Translation*, edited by J. Barnes (Princeton, NJ: Princeton University Press, 1984) 4.5, p. 212.

75 Hugh of Saint Victor, *De Sacramentis*, 1.10.2, p. 168.

76 William of Newburgh, *The History of English Affairs*, bks. I–II, translated by P. G. Walsh and M. J. Kennedy (Warminster: Aris, 1988, 2007), 1.prol., pp. 26–36.

77 Gervase of Canterbury, *Chronica*, in *The Historical Works of Gervase of Canterbury*, edited by W. Stubbs, vol. 1, 84–594 (London: Longman & Co., 1879–1880), 87–9; cf. Bernard Guenée, "Histoires, annales, chroniques. Essai sur les genres historiques au moyen âge," *Annales* 28 (1973): 997–1016; Guenée, "Histoire et Chronique. Nouvelles réflexions sur les genres historiques au Moyen Age," in *La Chronique et l'Histoire au Moyen Age*, edited by Daniel Poirion, 3–12 (Paris: Presses de l'université de Paris-Sorbonne, 1984).

78 Aristotle, *Nicomachean Ethics*, translated by R. Crisp (Cambridge: Cambridge University Press, 2000), 10.9, pp. 203–4.

79 Albert the Great, *Ethicorum Libri Decem*, in *Opera Omnia*, edited by A. Borgnet (Paris: Ludovicus Vives, 1890–1899), 10.3.3, pp. 639–40.

80 Aristotle, *Poetics*, translated by M. E. Hubbard, in *Classical Literary Criticism*, edited by D. A. Russell and Michael Winterbottom, 51–90 (Oxford: Oxford University Press, 1989), 9, p. 62.

81 Aristotle, *Physics*, 1.1, p. 9.

82 Aristotle, *Metaphysics*, translated by W. D. Ross, in *The Complete Works of Aristotle: The Revised Oxford Translation*, edited by J. Barnes (Princeton, NJ: Princeton University Press, 1984), 1.2, pp. 1553–5.

83   Aristotle, *Problemata*, translated by E. S. Forster, in *The Complete Works of Aristotle: The Revised Oxford Translation*, ed. J. Barnes (Princeton, NJ: Princeton University Press, 1984), 18.3, p. 1427.

84   Thomas Aquinas, *Summa theologiae*, edited and translated by Thomas Gilby (Cambridge: Blackfriars, 1964–1981), 1a.1.2 in 2::11–13; 1a.1.10 in 2:37–9.

85   Vincent of Beauvais, *Speculum Maius*, prol.16, p. 13.

86   Giles of Rome, *De regimine principum*, translated by M. S. Kempshall, in *The Cambridge Translations of Medieval Philosophical Texts, volume 2: Ethics and Political Philosophy*, edited by A. S. McGrade, J. Kilcullen, and M. S. Kempshall (Cambridge: Cambridge University Press, 2001), prol.1, p. 204.

87   Giles of Rome, *De regimine principum*, 2.3.20; 3.2.15.

88   Giles of Rome, *De differentia rhetoricae, ethicae et politicae*, in Gerardo Bruni, "The *De Differentia Rhetoricae, Ethicae et Politicae* of Aegidius Romanus," *The New Scholasticism* 6 (1932): 8.

89   Petrarch, *De viris illustribus*, in B. G. Kohl, "Petrarch's Prefaces to *De Viris Illustribus*," *History and Theory* 13 (1974): 138; Petrarch, *Letters on Familiar Matters [Rerum familiarum libri]*, translated by A. S. Bernardo (Baltimore: Johns Hopkins University Press, 1975–1985), 6.4, pp. 314–17.

90   Coluccio Salutati, *Coluccio Salutati Epistolario*, edited by F. Novati, 4 vols. (Rome: Tipografi del Senato, 1891–1911), 7.11, pp. 289–302.

91   Deborah Mauskopf Deliyannis, ed., *Historiography in the Middle Ages* (Leiden: Brill, 2003).

92   R. W. Southern, "Aspects of the European Tradition of Historical Writing 1–4," *Transactions of the Royal Historical Society* 20–3 (1970–1973): 173–96, 159–79, 159–86, 243–63; Beryl Smalley, *Historians in the Middle Ages* (London: Thames & Hudson, 1974); Bernard Guenée, "Y a-t-il une historiographie médiévale?" *Revue Historique* 258 (1977): 261–75.

93   John O. Ward, "'Chronicle' and 'History': The Medieval Origins of Postmodern Historiographical Practice?," *Parergon* 14 (1997): 102–28; Gabrielle M. Spiegel, *The Past as Text: The Theory and Practice of Medieval Historiography* (Baltimore: Johns Hopkins University Press, 1997).

94   Cf. Hayden White, "The Value of Narrativity in the Representation of Reality," *Critical Inquiry* 7 (1980): 5–27.

BIBLIOGRAPHY

PRIMARY SOURCES

Abelard. *Ethica sive Scito teipsum*. In *Peter Abelard's "Ethics,"* edited by David Luscombe. Oxford: Clarendon Press, 1971.

Abelard and Heloise. *The Letter Collection of Peter Abelard and Heloise*. Edited by David Luscombe. Translated by Betty Radice. Oxford: Oxford University Press, 2013.

Abelard and Heloise. "The Personal Letters between Abelard and Heloise (*Ep* 1–4)." *Mediaeval Studies* 15 (1953): 47–94.

Adam of Bremen. *History of the Archbishops of Hamburg-Bremen*. Translated by Francis Joseph Tschan. New York: Columbia University Press, 1959.

Alan of Lille. *De planctu naturae*. In *Literary Works*, edited and translated by Winthrop Wetherbee, 219–517. Dumbarton Oaks Medieval Library 22. Cambridge, MA: Harvard University Press, 2013.

Albert the Great. *Ethicorum libri decem*. In *Opera omnia*, edited by A. Borgnet. 38 volumes. Paris: Ludovicum Vives, 1890–1899.

Albert the Great. *Summa theologiae*. Volume 33. Paris: Ludovicum Vivès, 1885.

Albert the Great. *Super II sententiarum*. Volume 27. Paris: Ludovicum Vivès, 1884.

Alcuin. *Disputatio de rhetorica et de virtutibus, the Rhetoric of Alcuin and Charlemagne*. Translated by W. S. Howell. Princeton, NJ: Princeton University Press, 1941.

Anselm of Canterbury. *S. Anselmi cantuariensis archiepiscopi opera omnia*, edited by F. S. Schmitt. 5 volumes. Stuttgart: Friedrich Fromann Verlag, 1984.

Anselm of Canterbury. *Prosologion*. Translated by Jasper Hopkins and Herbert Richardson. Minneapolis, MN: Arthur J. Banning Press, 2000.

Aquinas, Thomas. *On Evil*. Translated by Jean Oesterle, in *The Collected Works of St. Thomas Aquinas*. Electronic Edition. Vol. 5 (Charlottesville, VA: InteLex Corp, 1993). Past Masters.

Aquinas, Thomas. *Summa theologiae*. Edited and translated by Thomas Gilby. Cambridge: Blackfriars, 1964–1980.

Aquinas, Thomas. *Summa theologiae*. Translated by Fathers of the English Dominican Province. Notre Dame, IN: Christian Classics, 1981.

Aquinas, Thomas. *Summa theologiae*. Edited by Leonine. Rome, 1888. Available online: http://www.corpusthomisticum.org/sth0000.html (accessed January 31, 2022).

Aquinas, Thomas. *Summa Theologica*. Translated by Fathers of the English Dominican Province. New York: Benziger Brothers, 1946.

Aristotle. *Metaphysics*. Translated by W. D. Ross. In *The Complete Works of Aristotle: The Revised Oxford Translation*, edited by J. Barnes. 2 volumes. Princeton, NJ: Princeton University Press, 1984.

Aristotle. *Nicomachean Ethics*. Translated by R. Crisp. Cambridge: Cambridge University Press, 2000.

Aristotle. *Physics*. Translated by R.Waterfield. Oxford: Oxford University Press, 1996.

Aristotle. *Poetics*. Translated by M. E. Hubbard. In *Classical Literary Criticism*, edited by D.A. Russell and Michael Winterbottom, 51–90. Oxford: Oxford University Press, 1989.

Aristotle. *Problemata*. Translated by E. S. Forster. In *The Complete Works of Aristotle: The Revised Oxford Translation*, edited by J. Barnes. 2 volumes. Princeton, NJ: Princeton University Press, 1984.

Aristotle. *Rhetoric*. In *The Basic Works of Aristotle*, edited by Richard McKeon, translated by W. Rhys Roberts. New York: The Modern Library, 2001.

Aristotle. *Topica*. Translated by W. A. Pickard-Cambridge. In *The Complete Works of Aristotle: The Revised Oxford Translation*, edited by J. Barnes. 2 volumes. Princeton, NJ: Princeton University Press, 1984.

Athanasius. *Life of Antony*. Translated by Carolinne White. In *Early Christian Lives*, 1–70. Harmondsworth: Penguin, 1998.

Augustine. *The Advantage of Believing [De utilitate credendi]*. Translated by Ray Kearney. In *On Christian Belief*, edited by Boniface Ramsey, 116–48. New York: New City Press, 2005.

Augustine. *The City of God*. Translated by William Babcock. Hyde Park, NY: New City Press, 2013.

Augustine. *Confessions*. Translated by Carolyn J.-B.Hammond. Cambridge, MA: Harvard University Press, 2014–2016.

Augustine. *Contra mendacium [To Consentius: Against Lying]*. In *Seventeen Short Treatises*, translated by H. Browne, 426–69. Library of the Fathers 22. Oxford: J. H. Parker, 1847.

Augustine. *De mendacio [On Lying]*. In *Seventeen Short Treatises*, translated by H. Browne, 382–425. Library of the Fathers 22. Oxford: J. H. Parker, 1847.

Augustine. *Letters*. Translated by Wilfrid Parsons. Washington, DC: Catholic University of America Press, 1951–1989.

Augustine. *The Literal Meaning of Genesis*. Translated by J. H. Taylor. *Ancient Christian Writers*, 41–2. New York: Newman Press, 1982.

Augustine. *On Christian Teaching [De doctrina Christiana]*. Edited and translated by R. P. H. Green. Oxford: Clarendon Press, 1995.

Augustine. *On the Free Choice of the Will*. In *On the Free Choice of the Will, On Grace and Free Choice and Other Writings*, edited and translated by Peter King, 3–126. Cambridge: Cambridge University Press, 2010.

Augustine. *Retractions*. Translated by M. I. Bogan. Fathers of the Church 60. Washington, DC: Catholic University of America Press, 1968.

Augustine. *Teaching Christianity*. Translated by Edmund Hill. Hyde Park, NY: New City Press, 1996.

Augustine. *The Trinity [De trinitate]*. Translated by Edmund Hill. New York: New City Press, 1991.

Augustine. *True Religion [De vera religione]*. Translated by Edmund Hill. In *On Christian Belief*, edited by Boniface Ramsey, 29–104. New York: New City Press, 2005.

Aulus Gellius. *Noctes Atticae*. Translated by J. C. Rolfe. Loeb Classical Library. Cambridge, MA: Harvard University Press, 1927.

Bede. *Bede's Ecclesiastical History of England. Revised Translation, with Introduction, Life, and Notes by A. M. Sellar*. London: George Bell and Sons, 1907.

Bede. *A History of the English Church and People*. Translated by Leo Sherley-Price, revised by R. E. Latham. Harmondsworth, UK: Penguin, 1968.

Bede. *De schematibus et tropis*. In *Libri II De Arte Metrica et De Schematibus et Tropis: The Art of Poetry and Rhetoric*, translated by Calvin B. Kendall. Saarbrücken: AQ-Verlag, 1991.

Benedict of Nursia. *The Rule of St. Benedict*. Edited and translated by Bruce L. Venarde. Cambridge, MA: Harvard University Press, 2011.

Bernard of Clairvaux. *Five Books on Consideration: Advice to a Pope*. Translated by John D. Anderson and Elizabeth T. Kennan. Kalamazoo, MI: Cistercian Publications, 1976.

Bernard of Clairvaux. *De gradibus humilitatis et superbiae tractatus*. Paris: J.-P Migne, 1859.

Bernard of Clairvaux. *Letter to William of St. Thierry*. In *Early Medieval Art, 300–1150, Sources and Documents*, translated by G. G. Coulton, edited by Caecilia Davis-Weyer, 168–70. Toronto: University of Toronto Press, 1986.

Bernard Silvestris. *The Commentary on the First Six Books of the Aeneid of Vergil Commonly Attributed to Bernardus Silvestris*. Translated by Earl G. Schreiber and Thomas E. Maresca. Lincoln: University of Nebraska Press, 1979.

Bernard Silvestris. *Cosmographia*. Translated by Winthrop Wetherbee. New York: Columbia University Press, 1973.

Bertran de Born. *The Poems of Bertran de Born*. Edited and translated by William D. Paden Jr., Tilde Sankovitch, and Patricia H. Stäblein. Berkeley: University of California Press, 1986.

Boethius. *In Ciceronis Topica*. Translated by E. Stump. Ithaca, NY: Cornell University Press, 1988.

Boethius. *Consolation of Philosophy*. Translated by S. J. Tester. Loeb Classical Library. Cambridge, MA: Harvard University Press, 1973.

Boethius. *De topicis differentiis*. Translated by E. Stump. Ithaca, NY: Cornell University Press, 1978.

Bonaventure. *Breviloquium*. Translated by E. E. Nemmers. London: B. Herder, 1946.

Bonaventure. *Breviloquium*. Translated by José de Vinck. In *The Works of St. Bonaventure*, volume 2. Patterson, NJ: St. Anthony Guild Press, 1963.

Bonaventure. *The Journey of the Mind to God*. Translated by Philotheus O. F. M. Boehner and Stephen F. Brown. Indianapolis, IN: Hackett, 1993.

Bruni, Leonardo. *History of the Florentine People*. Edited and translated by J. Hankins. 3 volumes. Cambridge, MA: Harvard University Press, 2001–2007.

Calcidius. *On Plato's Timaeus*. Edited and translated by John Magee. Dumbarton Oaks Medieval Library 41. Cambridge, MA: Harvard University Press, 2016.

Cappellanus, Andreas. *The Art of Courtly Love*. Translated by John Jay Parry. New York: Norton, 1969.

Carlyle, Thomas. *Thomas Carlyle: Historical Essays*. Edited by Chris R. Vanden Bossche. Berkeley: University of California Press, 2002.

Cassian. *The Monastic Institutes Consisting of On the Training of a Monk and The Eight Deadly Sins*. Translated by Jerome Gertram. London: The Saint Austin Press, 1999.

Caxton, William. *The Game and Playe of the Chesse*. Edited by Jenny Adams. TEAMS. Kalamazoo, MI: Medieval Institute Publications, 2009.

Chaucer, Geoffrey. "The Franklin's Tale." In *The Riverside Chaucer*, edited by Larry D. Benson. Boston: Houghton Mifflin Co., 1987.

Christine de Pizan. *The Book of the Body Politic*. Edited by Kate Langdon Forhan. Cambridge: Cambridge University Press, 1994.

Christine de Pizan. *The Book of the City of Ladies*. Translated by E. J. Richards. New York: Persea, 1982.

Christine de Pizan. *The Treasury of the City of Ladies*. Translated by Charity Cannon Willard. New York: Bard Hall/Persea, 1989.

Cicero. *On Invention [De Inventione]*. Translated by H. M. Hubbell. Loeb Classical Library. Cambridge, MA: Harvard University Press, 1949.

Cicero. *De officiis*. Edited by Michael Winterbottom. Oxford: Oxford University Press, 1994.

Cicero. *De Oratore*. Translated by E. Sutton and H. Rackham. Loeb Classical Library. Cambridge, MA: Harvard University Press, 1948.

Cicero. *Topica*. Edited and translated by Tobias Reinhardt. Oxford: Oxford University Press, 2006.

Damian, Peter. *Letters 91–120*. Translated by Owen J. Blum. Washington, DC: Catholic University of America Press, 1998.

Dhuoda. *Handbook for Her Warrior Son: Liber manualis*. Edited and translated by Marcelle Thiébaux. Cambridge: Cambridge University Press, 1998.

Einhard. *The Life of Charlemagne*. Translated by Samuel Epes Turner. New York: Harper & Brothers, 1880. Reprint in *Internet History Sourcebook*, New York: Fordham University, 1999.

Eusebius. *The History of the Church from Christ to Constantine*. Translated by G. A. Williamson. Harmondsworth, UK: Penguin, 1965.

Ezzaher, Lahcen Elyazghi, ed. *Three Arabic Treatises on Aristotle's* Rhetoric: *The Commentaries of al-Farabi, Avicenna, and Averroes*. Carbondale: Southern Illinois University Press, 2015.

Fortescue, Sir John. *On the Laws and Governance of England*. Edited by Shelley Lockwood. Cambridge: Cambridge University Press, 1997.

Galbert of Bruges. *The Murder of Charles the Good*. Translated by J. B. Ross. New York: Columbia University Press, 1959.

Gerald of Wales. *The History and Topography of Ireland*. Translated by J. O'Meara. London: Penguin Classics, 1982.

Gershom ben Solomon. *The Gate of Heaven (Shaar ha- Shamayim)*. Edited and translated by F. S. Bodenheimer. Jerusalem: Kiryath Sepher, 1953.

Gervase of Canterbury. *Chronica*. In *The Historical Works of Gervase of Canterbury*, edited by W. Stubbs, volume 1, 84–594. London: Longman & Co., 1879–1880.

Gildas. *The Ruin of Britain, and other works [De Excidio Britanniae]*. Edited and translated by Michael Winterbottom. London: Phillimore, 1978.

Giles of Rome. *De differentia rhetoricae, ethicae et politicae*. In Gerardo Bruni, "The *De Differentia Rhetoricae, Ethicae et Politicae* of Aegidius Romanus," *The New Scholasticism* 6 (1932): 1–18.

Giles of Rome. *De regimine principum*, prologue. Translated by M. S. Kempshall. In *The Cambridge Translations of Medieval Philosophical Texts, volume 2: Ethics and Political Philosophy*, edited by A. S. McGrade, J. Kilcullen, and M. S. Kempshall, 203–12. Cambridge: Cambridge University Press, 2001.

Goldschmidt, Rudolf Carrel, ed. and trans. *Paulinus' Churches at Nola*. Amsterdam: Noord-Hollandische Uitgevers Maatschappig, 1940. Reprinted in *Early Medieval Art 300–1150, Sources and Documents*, edited by Caecilia Davis-Weyer. Toronto: University of Toronto Press, 1986.

Green, Rosalie, T. Julian Brown, and Kenneth Levy. *Herrad of Hohenburg Hortus Deliciarum*. London: The Warburg Institute, 1979.

Gregory I. *Pastoral Care [Regula Pastoralis]*. Translated by Henry Davis, SJ. New York, NJ: Newman Press, 1978.

Gregory of Tours. *History of the Franks*. Translated by Lewis Thorpe. Harmondsworth, UK: Penguin, 1978.

Guibert of Nogent. *Autobiographie*. Edited and translated by Edmond-René Labande. Paris: Belles lettres, 1981.

Guibert of Nogent. *Dei gesta per Francos*. In *The Deeds of God through the Franks*, edited and translated by Robert Levine. Woodbridge, UK: Boydell Press, 1997.

Guibert of Nogent. *Monodies and On the Relics of Saints: The Autobiography and a Manifesto of a French Monk from the Time of the Crusades*. Translated by Joseph McAlhany and Jay Rubenstein. New York: Penguin, 2011.

Guillaume de Berneville. *La vie de siant Gilles*. Edited and translated by Françoise Luarent. Paris: Champion, 2003.

Guillaume de Lorris and Jean de Meun. *The Romance of the Rose*. Translated by Charles Dahlberg. Princeton, NJ: Princeton University Press, 1971.

Henry of Huntingdon. *History of the English [Historia Anglorum]*. Edited and translated by Diana Greenway. Oxford Medieval Texts. Oxford: Oxford University Press, 1996.

Hildegard of Bingen. *Book of Divine Works: With Letters and Songs*. Edited and translated by Matthew Fox. Santa Fe, NM: Bear and Co., 1987.

Hilton, Walter. *Walter Hilton's* Mixed Life *Edited from Lambeth Palace MS 472*. Edited by S. J. Ogilvie-Thomson. Salzburg: Institut für Anglistik und Amerikanistik Universität Salzburg, 1986.

Hrotswitha. *The Plays of Hrotswitha of Gandersheim*. Translated by Lanissa Bonfante. Edited by Robert Chipok. Mundelein, IL: Bolchazy-Carducci Publishers, 2014.

Hugh of Fleury. *Historia ecclesiastica*. PL 163: 821–54.

Hugh of Saint Victor. *Hugonis de Sancto Victore Didascalicon de studio legendi: A Critical Text*. Edited by Charles Henry Buttimer. Washington, DC: Catholic University Press, 1939.

Hugh of Saint Victor. *On the Sacraments of the Christian Faith [De sacramentis Christianae fidei]*. Translated by R. J. Deferrari. Cambridge, MA: Mediaeval Academy of America, 1951.

Hugh of Saint Victor. *Soliloquoy on the Betrothal Gift of the Beloved*. In *On Love: A Selection of Works of Hugh, Adam, Achard, Richard and Godfrey of St. Victor*, translated by Hugh Feiss. Hyde Park, NY: New City Press, 2012.

Ibn Fadlān. *Ibn Fadlān and the Land of Darkness: Arab Travellers in the Far North*. Translated by Paul Lunde and Caroline Stone. London: Penguin Classics, 2012.

Isidore of Seville. *The Etymologies of Isidore of Seville*. Edited and translated by Stephen A. Barney, W. J. Lewis, J. A. Beach, and Oliver Berghof. Cambridge: Cambridge University Press, 2006.

Jerome. Preface to the *Commentary on Matthew*. Fathers of the Church 117. Washington, DC: Catholic University of America Press, 2008.

John of Garland. *The Parisiana Poetria of John of Garland*. Edited and translated by Traugott Lawler. New Haven, CT: Yale University Press, 1974.

John of Salisbury. *The Metalogicon of John of Salisbury: A Twelfth-Century Defense of the Verbal and Logical Arts of the Trivium*. Translated by D. D. McGarry. Berkeley: University of California Press, 1955.

John of Salisbury. *Policraticus: Of the Frivolities of Courtiers and the Footprints of Philosophers*. Edited by Cary J. Nederman. Cambridge: Cambridge University Press, 1990.

Kearns, Conleth, trans. *The Life of Catherine of Siena*. Dublin: Dominican Publications, 1980.

Kempe, Margery. *The Book of Margery Kempe*. Edited by Sanford Brown Meech and Hope Emily Allen. London: Oxford University Press for the Early English Text Society, 1997.

Kilwardby, Robert. *On Time and Imagination [De tempore]*. Edited and translated by A. Broadie. Oxford: Oxford University Press, 1993.

Krapp, G. P. and E. K. Dobbie, eds. *The Exeter Book*. New York: Columbia University Press, 1936.

Latini, Brunetto. *The Book of the Treasure (Li Livres dou Tresor)*. Translated by Spurgeon Baldwin and Paul Barrette. New York: Garland Publishing, 1993.

Latini, Brunetto. *Li Livres dou Tresor*. Edited by Spurgeon Baldwin and Paul Barrette. Tempe: Arizona Center for Medieval and Renaissance Studies, 2003.

Latini, Brunetto. *Il Tesoretto (The Little Treasure)*. Edited and translated by Julia Bolton Holloway. New York: Grand Publishing, 1981.

Life of the Emperor Henry IV. In *Imperial Lives and Letters of the Eleventh Century*, translated by T. E. Mommsen and K. F. Morrison, 101–37. New York: Columbia University Press, 2000.

Lombard, Peter. *Sentences*. Translated by Giulio Silano. Toronto: Pontifical Institute of Mediaeval Studies, 2008.

Machiavelli, Niccolò. *The Prince: Second Edition*. Translated by Harvey Mansfield. Chicago: University of Chicago Press, 1998.

Macrobius. *Commentary on the Dream of Scipio*. Translated by W. H. Stahl. New York: Columbia University Press, 1952.

Macrobius. *Saturnalia*. Translated by P. V. Davies. New York: Columbia University Press, 1969.

Marsiglio of Padua. *Defender of Peace*. Translated by Alan Gewirth. 2nd edition. New York: Columbia University Press, 2000.

Masʿūdī. *From the Meadows of Gold*. Translated by Paul Lunde and Caroline Stone. London: Penguin, 2007.

Montaigne, Michel de. *The Complete Essays*. Translated by M. A. Screech. London: Penguin, 1987.

Oresme, Nicole. *Le livre du ciel et du monde*. Edited by Albert J. Menut and Alexander J. Denomy. Translated by Albert D. Menut. Madison: University of Wisconsin Press, 1968.

Oresme, Nicole. *De moneta*. Edited by Charles Johnson. Edinburgh: Thomas Nelson, 1956.

Orosius. *The Seven Books of History Against the Pagans*. Translated by R. J. Deferrari. The Fathers of the Church 50. Washington, DC: Catholic University of America Press, 1964.

Otto of Freising. *The Deeds of Frederick Barbarossa [Gesta Frederici]*. Translated by C. C. Mierow. New York: Columbia University Press, 1953.

Otto of Freising. *The Two Cities: A Chronicle of Universal History [Chronica]*. Translated by C. C. Mierow. New York: Columbia University Press, 1928.

Peter of Blois. "Epistola XCII." *Patrologia Latina*, 2nd series, vol. 207, edited by J.-P. Migne. Paris: 1904.

Lombard, Peter. *The Sentences, Book 1: The Mystery of the Trinity*. Translated by Giulio Silano. Toronto: Pontifical Institute of Mediaeval Studies, 2007.

Peters, Edward, ed. *The Chronicle of Fulcher of Chartres and Other Source Materials*. 2nd edition. Philadelphia: University of Pennsylvania Press, 1998.

Petrarch. *Letters on Familiar Matters [Rerum familiarum libri]*. Translated by A. S. Bernardo. 3 volumes. Baltimore: Johns Hopkins University Press, 1975–1985.

Petrarch. *De viris illustribus*. In B. G. Kohl, "Petrarch's Prefaces to *De Viris Illustribus*," *History and Theory* 13 (1974): 132–44.

Pliny the Elder. *Natural History: A Selection*. Translated by John F. Healy. New York: Penguin, 2004.

Proverbia sententiaeque latinitatis medii aevi. Edited by H. Walther. 5 volumes. Göttingen: Vandenhoeck & Ruprecht, 1963–1967.

Quintilian. *Institutio Oratoria*. Translated by H. E. Butler. 4 volumes. Loeb Classical Library. Cambridge, MA: Harvard University Press, 1920–1922.

Radbertus, Paschasius. *Epitaphium Arsenii*. In *Charlemagne's Cousins: Contemporary Lives of Adalard and Wala*, translated, introduction, and notes by Allen Cabaniss. Syracuse, NY: Syracuse University Press, 1967.

Rhetorica ad Herennium. Translated by H. Caplan. Loeb Classical Library. Cambridge, MA: Harvard University Press, 1954.

Rousseau, Jean-Jacques. *Confessions*. Translated by J. M. Cohen. London: Penguin, 1953.

Rufinus of Aquileia. *Ecclesiastical History*. Translated by W. H. Fremantle. A Select Library of Nicene and Post-Nicene Fathers. Oxford: Parker and Co., 1892.

Salutati, Coluccio. *Epistolario di Coluccio Salutati*. Edited by F. Novati. 4 volumes. Rome: Tipografi del Senato, 1891–1911.

Searby, Denis and Bridget Morris, trans. *The Revelations of St. Birgitta of Sweden:* Liber caelestis, Volume 3, *Books VI–VII*. Oxford: Oxford University Press, 2012.

Seneca. *On Consolation to Polybius*. In *Moral Essays*, translated by J. W. Basore, 356–415. Loeb Classical Library. Cambridge, MA: Harvard University Press, 1932.

Smith, Adam. *An Inquiry into the Nature and Causes of the Wealth of Nations*. Edited by R. H. Campbell and A. S. Skinner. Oxford: Clarendon Press, 1976.

Tacitus. *Histories*. Translated by C. H. Moore. Loeb Classical Library. Cambridge, MA: Harvard University Press, 1925.

Talbot, C. H., ed. and trans. *The Anglo-Saxon Missionaries in Germany, Being the Lives of SS. Willibrord, Boniface, Leoba and Lebuin together with the Hodoepericon of St. Willibald and a Selection from the Correspondence of St. Boniface*. London: Sheed and Ward, 1954.

Tugwell, Simon, ed. *Early Dominicans: Selected Writings*. Mahwah, NJ: Paulist Press, 1982.

Valerius Maximus. *Memorable Doings and Sayings [Facta et Dicta Memorabilia]*. Translated by D. R. Shackleton Bailey. 2 volumes. Loeb Classical Library. Cambridge, MA: Harvard University Press, 2000.

Vergil. *Aeneid*. Translated by H. Rushton Fairclough. Revised by G. P. Goold. 2 volumes. Loeb Classical Library. Cambridge, MA: Harvard University Press, 2000.

Vergil. *Georgics*. Translated by H. Rushton Fairclough. Revised by G. P. Goold. Loeb Classical Library. Cambridge, MA: Harvard University Press, 2000.

Vincent of Beauvais. *Speculum maius*. 4 volumes. Graz: Akademische Druck- u. Verlaganstalt, 1964–1965.

Vitalis, Orderic. *The Ecclesiastical History of Orderic Vitalis [Historia Ecclesiastica]*. Edited and translated by M. Chibnall. 6 volumes. Oxford Medieval Texts. Oxford: Clarendon Press, 1980.

Vives, Juan Luis. *The Passions of the Soul: The Third Book of De Anima et Vita*. Translated by Carlos G. Noreña. Lewiston: Edwin Mellen Press, 1990.

Watson, Nicholas and Jacqueline Jenkins, eds. *The Writings of Julian of Norwich: A Vision Showed to a Devout Woman and A Revelation of Love*. University Park: Pennsylvania State University Press, 2006.

William of Conches. *A Dialogue on Natural Philosophy (Dragmaticon Philosophiae)*. Translated by Italo Ronca and Matthew Curr. Notre Dame, IN: University of Notre Dame Press, 1997.

William of Newburgh. *The History of English Affairs*, books I–II. Translated by P. G. Walsh and M. J. Kennedy. Warminster: Aris, 1988, 2007.

William of Ockham. *De connexione virtutum*. In *Ockham on the Virtues*, edited and translated by Rega Wood. West Lafayette, IN: Purdue University Press, 1997.

William of Pagula. *The Mirror of King Edward III*, in *Political Thought in Early Fourteenth-Century England*. Edited by Cary J. Nederman. Tempe: Arizona Center for Medieval and Renaissance Studies, 2002.

Wipo. *Deeds of Conrad II*. In *Imperial Lives and Letters of the Eleventh Century*, translated by Theodor E. Mommsen and Karl F. Morrison, edited by Robert L. Benson, 52–100. New York: Columbia University Press, 2000.

SECONDARY SOURCES

Abulafia, Anna S. *Christians and Jews in the Twelfth-Century Renaissance*. London: Routledge, 1995.

Aertsen, Jan A., Kent Emery Jr., and Andreas Speer, eds. *Nach der Verurteilung von 1277: Philosophie und Theologie an der Universität von Paris im letzen Viertel des 13. Jahrhunderts. Studien und Texte*. Berlin: Walter de Gruyter, 2001.

Allen, Judson Boyce. *The Ethical Poetic of the Later Middle Ages: A Decorum of Convenient Distinction*. Toronto: University of Toronto Press, 1982.

Allen, S. J. and Emilie Amt, eds. *The Crusades: A Reader*. Toronto: University of Toronto Press, 2010.

Althusser, Louis. "Ideology and Ideological State Apparatuses (Notes Toward an Investigation)." In *Lenin and Philosophy and Other Essays*, translated by Ben Brewster, 123–73. London: New Left Books, 1971.

Appleby, Joyce Oldham. *Economic Thought and Ideology in Seventeenth-Century England*. Princeton, NJ: Princeton University Press, 1978.

Arnold, John H. *Belief and Unbelief in Medieval Europe*. London: Hodder Arnold, 2005.

The Art of Medieval Spain, A.D. 500–1200. Exhibition Catalog. New York: Metropolitan Museum of Art, 1993.

Ashworth, E. J. *Language and Logic in the Post-Medieval Period*. Dordrecht & Boston: D. Reidel Publishing Company, 1974.

Aubert, Marcel, Louis Grodecki, Jean Lafond, and Jean Verrier. *Les Vitraux de Notre-Dame et de la Sainte-Chapelle de Paris*. Corpus Vitrearum Media Aevi. Paris: Caisse Nationale De Monument Historiques, 1959.

Aurell, Martin and Catalina Girbea. *Chevalerie et christianisme aux XIIe et XIIIe siècles*. Rennes: Presses Universitaires de Rennes, 2011.

Azinfar, Fatemeh Chehregosha. *Atheism in the Medieval Islamic and European World: The Influence of Persian and Arabic Ideas of Doubt and Skepticism on Medieval European Literary Thought*. Bethesda, MD: Ibex Publishers, 2008.

Bagliani, Agostino, Jean-Michel Spieser, and Jean Wirth, eds. *Le Portrait: la représentation de l'individu*. Florence: SISMEL, Edizioni del Galluzzo, 2007.

Bagnoli, Martina, Holger A. Klein, C. Griffith Mann, and James Robinson. *Treasures of Heaven: Saints, Relics and Devotion in Medieval Europe*. New Haven, CT: Yale University Press, 2010.

Balace, Sophie, et al. *Une Renaissance, L'art entre Flandre et Champagne*. Exhibition Catalog. Saint-Omer: Musée de l'hôtel Sandelin, 2013.

Baldwin, John W. *Masters, Princes and Merchants: The Social Views of Peter the Chanter and His Circle*. 2 volumes. Princeton, NJ: Princeton University Press, 1970.

Baldwin, John W. *Medieval Theories of the Just Price: Romanists, Canonists, and Theologians in the Twelfth and Thirteenth Centuries*. Transactions of the American Philosophical Society 49, pt. 4. Philadelphia: American Philosophical Society, 1959.

Bang, Peter Fibiger and Dariusz Kołodziejczyk. *Universal Empire: A Comparative Approach to Imperial Culture and Representation in Eurasian History*. Cambridge: Cambridge University Press, 2012.

Barber, Richard. *Bestiary: Being an English Version of the Bodleian Library, Oxford M.S. Bodley 764*. London: Folio Society, 1992.

Beagon, Mary. *Roman Nature: The Thought of Pliny the Elder*. Oxford: Clarendon Press, 1992.

Beagon, Mary. "Situating Nature's Wonders in Pliny's Natural History." In *Vita Vigilia Est: Essays in Honour of Barbara Levick*, edited by E. Bispham and G. Rowe, 19–40. Bulletin of the Institute of Classical Studies Supplement 100. London: Institute of Classical Studies, 2007.

Beagon, Mary. "Variations on a Theme: Isidore and Pliny on Human and Human-Instigated Anomaly." In *Isidore of Seville and his Reception in the Early Middle Ages: Transmitting and Transforming Knowledge*, edited by Andy Fear and Jamie Wood, 57–74. Late Antique and Early Medieval Iberia 2. Amsterdam: Amsterdam University Press, 2016.

Beckwith, Christopher I. *Warriors of the Cloisters: The Central Asian Origins of Science in the Medieval World*. Princeton, NJ: Princeton University Press, 2012.

Bedos-Rezak, Brigitte Miriam. "Medieval Identity: A Sign and a Concept." *American Historical Review* 105 (2000): 1489–533.

Benton, John F. "The Personality of Guibert of Nogent." *Psychoanalytic Review* 57 (1970/1): 563–86.

Bianchi, Luca. *Censure et liberté intellectuelle à l'Université de Paris: XIIIe–XIVe siècles*. Paris: Les Belles Lettres, 1999.

Biller, Peter. "Confession in the Middle Ages: Introduction." In *Handling Sin: Confession in the Middle Ages*, edited by Peter Biller and A. J. Minnis, 3–33. York: York Medieval Press, 1998.

Black, Deborah L. *Logic and Aristotle's Rhetoric and Poetics in Medieval Arabic Philosophy*. Leiden: Brill, 1990.

Bloomfield, Morton. *The Seven Deadly Sins: An Introduction to the History of a Religious Concept, with Special Reference to Medieval English Literature*. East Lansing: Michigan State College Press, 1952.

Blumenberg, Hans. "'Imitation of Nature': Toward a Prehistory of the Idea of Creative Being." [Nachahmung der Natur': Zur Vorgeschichte der Idee des schöpferischen Menschen]. First published in 1957. Translated by Anna Wertz. *Qui Parle* 12, no. 1 (2000): 17–54.

Blumenberg, Hans. *The Legitimacy of the Modern Age*. Cambridge, MA: MIT Press, 1983.

Boas, George. "The Microcosm." In *The History of Ideas: An Introduction*, 212–38. New York: Scribners, 1969.

Bond, Gerald A. *The Loving Subject: Desire, Eloquence, and Power in Romanesque France*. Philadelphia: University of Pennsylvania Press, 1995.

Bonney, Richard S., ed. *State and Fiscal Administration in Europe*. Cambridge: Cambridge University Press, 1995.

Boyle, Leonard. "Innocent III and Vernacular Versions of Scripture." In *The Bible in the Medieval World: Essays in Memory of Beryl Smalley*, edited by Katherine Walsh and Diana Wood, 97–107. Oxford: Basil Blackwell for the Ecclesiastical History Society, 1985.

Boynton, Susan and Diane J. Reilly, eds. *The Practice of the Bible in the Middle Ages: Production, Reception, and Performance in Western Christianity*. New York: Columbia University Press, 2011.

Branner, Robert. "The Painted Medallions in the Sainte-Chapelle, in Paris." *Transactions of the American Philosophical Society* 58, no. 2 (1968): 5–42.

Brooke, John L. *Climate Change and the Course of Global History: A Rough Journey*. Cambridge: Cambridge University Press, 2016.

Brown, Peter. *Augustine of Hippo: A Biography*. Berkeley: University of California Press, 1967.

Brown, Peter. *The Cult of the Saints: Its Rise and Function in Latin Christianity*. Chicago: University of Chicago Press, 1982.

Brown, Peter. *Power and Persuasion in Late Antiquity: Towards a Christian Empire*. Madison: University of Wisconsin Press, 1992.

Brown, Peter. *The Rise of Western Christendom: Triumph and Adversity, A.D. 200–1000*. 2nd edition. Malden, MA: Blackwell Publishing, 2003.

Büntgen, Ulf *et al.* 'Cooling and societal change during the Late Antique Little Ice Age from 536 to around 660 AD', *Nature Geoscience* 9 (2016), 231–236.

Burckhardt, Jacob. *The Civilization of the Renaissance in Italy*. Translated by S. G. C. Middlemore. Vienna: Phaidon Press, 1937.

Burckhardt, Jacob. *The Civilization of the Renaissance in Italy*. Translated by S. G. C. Middlemore. New York: Harper & Brothers, 1958.

Burnett, Charles. *Arabic into Latin in the Middle Ages: The Translators and their Intellectual and Social Context*. Farnham, UK: Ashgate, 2009.

Burnett, Charles. "The Institutional Context of Arabic-Latin Translations of the Middle Ages: A Reassessment of the 'School of Toledo.'" In *Vocabulary of Teaching and Research Between Middle Ages and Renaissance*, edited by Olga Weijers, 214–35. Proceedings of the Colloquium London, Warburg Institute, March 11–12, 1994. Turnhout: Brepols, 1995.

Butler, Judith. *Gender Trouble: Feminism and the Subversion of Identity*. New York: Routledge, 2006.

Bynum, Caroline Walker. "Did the Twelfth Century Discover the Individual?" *Journal of Ecclesiastical History* 31 (1980): 1–17.

Camargo, Martin. "Tria Sunt: The Long and the Short of Geoffrey of Vinsauf's *Documentum de modo et arte dictandi et versificandi.*" *Speculum* 74, no. 4 (1999): 935–55.

Campbell, Jackson J. "Adaptation of Classical Rhetoric in Old English Literature." In *Medieval Eloquence: Studies in the Theory and Practice of Medieval Rhetoric*, edited by James J. Murphy. Berkeley: University of California Press, 1978.

Campbell, Jean C. *The Commonwealth of Nature: Art and Poetic Community in the Age of Dante*. University Park: Pennsylvania State University Press, 2008.

Carmody, Francis J. "Brunetto Latini's *Tresor*: Latin Sources on Natural Science." *Speculum* 12, no. 3 (1937): 359–66.

Carruthers, Mary. *The Book of Memory: A Study of Memory in Medieval Culture*. Cambridge: Cambridge University Press, 1990.

Caviness, Madeline H. "Anchoress, Abbess, and Queen: Donors and Patrons or Intercessors and Matrons?" In *The Cultural Patronage of Medieval Women*, edited by June Hall McCash, 105–54. Athens: University of Georgia Press, 1996.

Chenu, M.-D. *Nature, Man, and Society in the Twelfth Century; Essays on New Theological Perspectives in the Latin West*. Translated by Jerome Taylor and Lester K. Little. Chicago: University of Chicago Press, 1968.

Classen, Peter. "*Res Gestae*, Universal History, Apocalypse – Visions of Past and Future." In *Renaissance and Renewal in the Twelfth Century*, edited by Robert L. Benson and Giles Constable, 387–417. Cambridge, MA: Harvard University Press, 1982.

Cohen, Adam S. "The Multisensory Haggadah." In *Les Cinq Sens au Moyen Âge*, edited by Éric Palazzo, 305–31. Paris: Éditions Cerf, 2016.

Cohen, Meredith. "An Indulgence for the Visitor: The Public at the Sainte-Chapelle of Paris." *Speculum* 83, no. 4 (2008): 840–83.

Cohen, Meredith. *The Sainte-Chapelle and the Construction of Sacral Monarchy: Royal Architecture in Thirteenth-Century Paris*. Cambridge: Cambridge University Press, 2015.

Cole, Andrew and D. Vance Smith, eds. *The Legitimacy of the Middle Ages*. Durham, NC: Duke University Press, 2010.

Coleman, Janet. *Ancient and Medieval Memories – Studies in the Reconstruction of the Past*. Cambridge: Cambridge University Press, 1992.

Colish, Marcia. *Mirror of Language: A Study in the Medieval Theory of Knowledge.* Lincoln: University of Nebraska Press, 1983.

Colish, Marcia. "Systematic Theology and Theological Renewal in the Twelfth Century." *Journal of Medieval and Renaissance Studies* 18, no. 2 (1988): 135–56.

Conger, George Perrigo. *Theories of Macrocosms and Microcosms in the History of Philosophy.* New York: Russell and Russell, 1967.

Connolly, Daniel K. "Imagined Pilgrimage in the Itinerary Maps of Matthew Paris." *Art Bulletin* 81, no. 4 (1999): 598–622.

Constable, Giles. "Opposition to Pilgrimage in the Middle Ages." *Studia Gratiana* 19 (1976): 125–46.

Constable, Giles. *Three Studies in Medieval Religious and Social Thought: The Interpretation of Mary and Martha, The Ideal of the Imitation of Christ, The Orders of Society.* Cambridge: Cambridge University Press, 1995.

Contreni, John J. "Learning for God: Education in the Carolingian Age." *Journal of Medieval Latin,* 24 (2014): 89–129.

Coolman, Boyd Taylor. "Hugh of St. Victor on 'Jesus Wept': Compassion as Ideal *Humanitas.*" *Theological Studies* 69 (2008): 528–56.

Coolman, Boyd Taylor. "The Medieval Affective Dionysian Tradition." *Modern Theology* 24, no. 4 (2008): 615–32.

Copeland, Rita. *Rhetoric, Hermeneutics, and Translation in the Middle Ages: Academic Traditions and Vernacular Texts.* Cambridge: Cambridge University Press, 1991.

Copeland, Rita and Ineke Sluiter. *Medieval Grammar and Rhetoric: Language Arts and Literary Theory, AD 300–1475.* Oxford: Oxford University Press, 2009.

Courtenay, William J. *Capacity and Volition: A History of the Distinction of Absolute and Ordained Power.* Bergamo: P. Lubrina, 1990.

Courtenay, William J. "Nature and the Natural in Twelfth-Century Thought." In *Covenant and Causality in Medieval Thought: Studies in Philosophy, Theology, and Economic Practice,* ch. 3. London: Variorum Reprints, 1984.

Cowdrey, H. E. J. *The Cluniacs and the Gregorian Reform.* Oxford: Clarendon Press, 1970.

Crane, Susan. *The Performance of Self: Ritual, Clothing, and Identity during the Hundred Years War.* Philadelphia: University of Pennsylvania Press, 2002.

Crane, Thomas Frederick, ed. *The Exempla or Illustrative Stories from the* Sermones vulgares *of Jacques de Vitry.* New York: Burt Franklin, 1940.

Dailey, Patricia. "Riddles, Wonder and Responsiveness in Anglo-Saxon Literature." In *The Cambridge History of Early Medieval English Literature,* edited by Clare A. Lees, 451–74. Cambridge: Cambridge University Press, 2013.

Dale, Thomas E. A. "The Portrait as Imprinted Image and the Concept of the Individual in the Romanesque Period." In *Le Portrait: la représentation de l'individu,* edited by Agostino Paravicini Bagliani, Jean-Michel Spieser, and Jean Wirth, 95–116. Florence: SISMEL, Edizioni del Galluzzo, 2007.

Danblon, Emmanuelle. "The Reason of Rhetoric." *Philosophy and Rhetoric* 46, no. 4 (2013): 493–507.

Davis, James. *Medieval Market Morality.* Cambridge: Cambridge University Press, 2012.

Davis, Kathleen. *Periodization and Sovereignty: How Ideas of Feudalism and Secularization Govern the Politics of Time.* Philadelphia: University of Pennsylvania Press, 2008.

Davis, Kathleen and Michael Puett. "Periodization and 'The Medieval Globe': A Conversation." *The Medieval Globe* 2, no. 1 (2015): 1–14.

Davis-Weyer, Caecilia. *Early Medieval Art 300–1150, Sources and Documents.* Toronto: University of Toronto Press, 1986.

Day, John. *The Medieval Market Economy*. Oxford: Oxford University Press, 1987.

De Hamel, Christopher. *A History of Illuminated Manuscripts*. 2nd edition. London: Phaidon, 2006.

Deliyannis, Deborah Mauskopf, ed. *Historiography in the Middle Ages*. Leiden: Brill, 2003.

Denery, Dallas G., II. "The Appearance of Reality: Peter Aureol and the Experience of Perceptual Error." *Franciscan Studies* 55 (1998): 27–52.

Denery, Dallas G., II. *Seeing and Being Seen in the Later Medieval World: Optics, Theology, and Religious Life*. New York: Cambridge University Press, 2005.

Di Cosmo, Nicola. *Empires and Exchanges in Eurasian Late Antiquity: Rome, China, Iran, and the Steppe, ca. 250–750*. Cambridge: Cambridge University Press, 2018.

Diedrichs, Christof L. *Vom Glauben zum Sehen: Die Sichtbarkeit der Reliquie im Reliquiar; Ein Beitrag zur Geschichte des Sehens*. Berlin: Weissensee Verlag, 2001.

Dod, Bernard G. "Aristoteles Latinus." In *The Cambridge History of Later Medieval Philosophy*, edited by Norman Kretzmann, Anthony Kenny, Jan Pinborg, and Eleonore Stump, 45–79. Cambridge: Cambridge University Press, 1982.

Dodwell, Charles R. *The Pictorial Arts of the West, 800–1200*. New Haven, CT: Yale University Press, 1993.

Doody, Aude. *Pliny's Encyclopedia: The Reception of the Natural History*. Cambridge: Cambridge University Press, 2010.

Dronke, Peter. "Bernard Silvestris, Natura, and Personification." *Journal of the Warburg and Courtauld Institutes* 43 (1980): 16–31.

Dronke, Peter. *Poetic Individuality in the Middle Ages: New Departures in Poetry, 1000–1150*. Oxford: Clarendon, 1970.

Drwenski, Matt and David Eaton. "Class Warfare: Changes to the AP World History Course." *Perspectives on History*, June 15, 2018.

Duby, Georges. *The Early Growth of the European Economy*. Translated by Howard B. Clarke. Ithaca, NY: Cornell University Press, 1974.

Dupré, Louis. *Passage to Modernity: An Essay in the Hermeneutics of Nature and Culture*. New Haven, CT: Yale University Press, 1993.

Dutton, Paul Edward. *The Glosae super Platonem of Bernard of Chartres*. Studies and Texts 107. Toronto: Pontifical Institute of Mediaeval Studies, 1991.

Economou, George. *The Goddess Natura in Medieval Literature*. Cambridge, MA: Harvard University Press, 1972.

Elliott, Dyan. *Proving Woman: Female Spirituality and Inquisitional Culture in the Later Middle Ages*. Princeton, NJ: Princeton University Press, 2004.

Elliott, Dyan. "Review of Susan Crane, *The Performance of Self*." *Journal of English and Germanic Philology* 103 (2004): 401–3.

Elliott, Dyan. *Spiritual Marriage: Sexual Abstinence in Medieval Wedlock*. Princeton, NJ: Princeton University Press, 1993.

Evergates, Theodore. *Marie of France: Countess of Champagne, 1145–1198*. Philadelphia: University of Pennsylvania Press, 2019.

Fear, Andrew. "Putting the Pieces Back Together: Isidore's *De natura rerum*." In *Isidore of Seville and his Reception in the Early Middle Ages: Transmitting and Transforming Knowledge*, edited by Andrew Fear and Jamie Wood, 75–92. Late Antique and Early Medieval Iberia 2. Amsterdam: Amsterdam University Press, 2016.

Ferguson, Wallace K. *The Renaissance in Historical Thought: Five Centuries of Interpretation*. Boston: Houghton Mifflin, 1948.

Fletcher, Richard. *The Conversion of Europe: From Paganism to Christianity 371–1386 AD*. London: Fontana Press, 1998.

Foucault, Michel. *The History of Sexuality, Volume 1: An Introduction.* Translated Robert Hurley. New York: Vintage Books, 1990.

Franklin-Brown, Mary. *Reading the World: Encyclopedic Writing in the Scholastic Age.* Chicago: University of Chicago Press, 2012.

Franzén, Carin. "The Legacy of Courtly Love and Feminine Position." In *(Re-)Contextualizing Literary and Cultural History: The Representation of the Past in Literary and Material Culture,* edited by Elisabeth Wåghäll Nivre, Beate Schirrmacher, and Claudia Egere, 93–114. Stockholm: Acta Universitatis Stockholmiensis, 2013.

Freudenthal, Gad. "The Aim and Structure of Gershom ben Solomon's Sha'ar ha-shamayim." *Zutot* 14, no. 1 (2017): 49–63.

Frojmovic, Eva and Catherine E. Karkov, eds. *Postcolonising the Medieval Image.* New York: Routledge, 2017.

Fulton, Rachel. *From Judgment to Passion: Devotion to Christ and the Virgin Mary, 800–1200.* New York: Columbia University Press, 2002.

Funkenstein, Amos. *Theology and the Scientific Imagination from the Middle Ages to the Seventeenth Century.* Princeton, NJ: Princeton University Press, 1986.

Geary, Patrick. *Before France and Germany: The Creation and Transformation of the Merovingian World.* New York: Oxford University Press, 1988.

Gelber, Hester. *It Could Have Been Otherwise: Contingency and Necessity in Dominican Theology at Oxford, 1300–1350.* Leiden: Brill, 2004.

George, Philippe. "Un reliquaire, 'souvenir' du pèlerinage des Liégeois à Compostelle en 1056 (?), provenant du trésor de Saint-Jacques et conservé au Musée d'art religieux et d'art mosan à Liège." *Revue belge d'archéologie et d'histoire de l'art* 57 (1988): 5–21.

Gillespie, Michael Allen. *The Theological Origins of Modernity.* Chicago: University of Chicago Press, 2008.

Gittes, K. S. *Framing the* Canterbury Tales: *Chaucer and the Medieval Frame Narrative Tradition.* New York: Greenwood Press, 1991.

Glacken, Clarence J. *Traces on the Rhodian Shore: Nature and Culture in Western Thought from Ancient Times to the End of the Eighteenth Century.* Berkeley: University of California Press, 1967.

Goetz, Hans-Werner. "The Concept of Time in the Historiography of the Eleventh and Twelfth Centuries." In *Medieval Concepts of the Past: Ritual, Memory, Historiography,* edited by Gerd Althoff, Johannes Fried, and Patrick J. Geary, 139–65. Cambridge: Cambridge University Press, 2002.

Gouiran, Gérard. "Bertran de Born: troubadour de la violence?" In *La violence dans le monde médiéval,* 235–51. Aix-en-Provence: Publications du CUER MA, 1994.

Grant, Edward. *The Foundations of Modern Science in the Middle Ages: Their Religious, Institutional, and Intellectual Contexts.* Cambridge: Cambridge University Press, 1996.

Grant, Edward. *God and Reason in the Middle Ages.* Cambridge: Cambridge University Press, 2001.

Grant, Edward, ed. *A Source Book in Medieval Science.* Cambridge, MA: Harvard University Press, 1974.

Green, Richard Firth. *Elf Queens and Holy Friars: Fairy Beliefs and the Medieval Church.* Philadelphia: University of Pennsylvania Press, 2016.

Greenfield, Concetta C. *Humanist and Scholastic Poetics.* Lewisberg, PA: Bucknell University Press, 1981.

Gregory, Brad S. *The Unintended Reformation: How a Religious Revolution Secularized Society.* Cambridge, MA: Harvard University Press, 2012.

Griffiths, Fiona J. *The Garden of Delights: Reform and Renaissance for Women in the Twelfth Century*. Philadelphia: University of Pennsylvania Press, 2006.

Guenée, Bernard. "Histoires, annales, chroniques. Essai sur les genres historiques au moyen âge." *Annales* 28 (1973): 997–1016.

Guenée, Bernard. "Histoire et Chronique. Nouvelles réflexions sur les genres historiques au Moyen Age." In *La Chronique et l'Histoire au Moyen Age*, edited by Daniel Poirion, 3–12. Paris: Presses de l'université de Paris-Sorbonne, 1984.

Guenée, Bernard. *Histoire et culture historique dans l'Occident medieval*. Paris: Aubier Montaigne, 1980.

Guenée, Bernard. "Y a-t-il une historiographie médiévale?" *Revue Historique* 258 (1977): 261–75.

Gutas, Dimitri. *Greek Thought, Arabic Culture: The Graeco-Arabic Translation Movement in Baghdad and Early 'Abbāsid Society (2nd–4th/8th–10th Centuries)*. London: Routledge, 1998.

Hahn, Cynthia. "The Meaning of Early Medieval Treasuries." In *Reliquiare im Mittelalter*, edited by Bruno Reudenbach and Gia Toussaint, 1–20. Hamburger Forschungen zur Kunstgeschichte 5. Berlin: Akademie Verlag, 2005.

Hahn, Cynthia. *Strange Beauty: Issues in the Making and Meaning of Reliquaries, 400–circa 1204*. University Park: Pennsylvania State University Press, 2012.

Haidu, Peter. *The Subject Medieval/Modern: Text and Governance in the Middle Ages*. Stanford, CA: Stanford University Press, 2004.

Hallam, H. E. *Rural England (1066–1348)*. Hassocks, UK: Harvester Press, 1981.

Haren, Michael. "Confession, Social Ethics and Social Discipline in the *Memoriale Presbiterorum*." In *Handling Sin: Confession in the Middle Ages*, edited by Peter Biller and A. J. Minnis, 109–22. York: York Medieval Press, 1998.

Haren, Michael. "The Interrogatories for Officials, Lawyers, and Secular Estates of the *Memoriale Presbiterorum*." In *Handling Sin: Confession in the Middle Ages*, edited by Peter Biller and A. J. Minnis, 123–64. York: York Medieval Press, 1998.

Harkins, Franklin T. *Reading and the Work of Restoration: History and Scripture in the Work of Hugh of St. Victor*. Toronto: Pontifical Institute of Mediaeval Studies, 2009.

Harper, Kyle. *The Fate of Rome: Climate, Disease, and the End of an Empire*. Princeton, NJ: Princeton University Press, 2017.

Haraway, Donna. *Staying with the trouble: making kin in the Chthulucene*. Durham: Duke University Press, 2016.

Harris, Julie Ann. "Love in the Land of Goshen: Haggadah, History, and the Making of British Library MS Oriental 2737." *Gesta* 52, no. 2 (2013): 161–80.

Haskins, Charles Homer. *The Renaissance of the Twelfth Century*. Cambridge, MA: Harvard University Press, 1955.

Head, Thomas. "Art and Artifice in Ottonian Trier." *Gesta* 36, no. 1 (1997): 65–82.

Heller-Roazen, Daniel. *Fortune's Faces: The* Roman de la Rose *and the Poetics of Contingency*. Baltimore: Johns Hopkins University Press, 2003.

Hissette, Roland. *Enquête sur les 219 articles condamnés à Paris le 7 mars 1277*. Louvain: Publications Universitaires, 1977.

Hoffman, Eva. "Pathways of Portability: Islamic and Christian Interchange from the Tenth to the Twelfth Century." *Art History* 24, no. 1 (2001): 17–50.

Hoffman, Robert. *An Environmental History of Medieval Europe* (Cambridge: Cambridge University Press, 2014).

Holkot, Robert. *Seeing the Future Clearly: Questions on Future Contingents*. Edited by Katherine H. Tachau and Paul A. Streveler. Toronto: Pontifical Institute of Mediaeval Studies, 1995.

Hollingworth, Miles. *Saint Augustine of Hippo: An Intellectual Biography*. Oxford: Oxford University Press, 2013.

Horkheimer, Max and Theodor W. Adorno. *Dialectic of Enlightenment: Philosophical Fragments*. Stanford: Stanford University Press, 2002.

Hudson, Anne. *The Premature Reformation: Wycliffite Texts and Lollard History*. Oxford: Clarendon Press, 1988.

Huizinga, Johan. *The Waning of the Middle Ages: A Study of the Forms of Life, Thought, and Art in France and the Netherlands in the XIVth and XVth Centuries*. London: E. Arnold, 1924.

Hutchison, Terence. *Before Adam Smith: The Emergence of Political Economy, 1662–1776*. Oxford: Blackwell, 1988.

Hyde, J. K. *Society and Politics in Medieval Italy: The Evolution of Civil Life, 1000–1350*. New York: St. Martin's Press, 1973.

Inglis, Erik. "Gothic Architecture and a Scholastic: Jean de Jandun's 'Tractatus de laudibus Parisius' (1323)." *Gesta* 42, no. 1 (2003): 63–85.

Innes, Matthew. "The Classical Tradition in the Carolingian Renaissance: Ninth-Century Encounters with Suetonius." *International Journal of the Classical Tradition* 3, no. 3 (1997): 265–82.

Irvine, M. *The Making of Textual Culture: "Grammatica" and Literary Theory, 350–1100*. Cambridge: Cambridge University Press, 1994.

Iwanczak, Wojciech. "Miles Christi: the Medieval Ideal of Knighthood." *Journal of the Australian Early Medieval Association* 8 (2012): 77–92.

Izdebski, Adam and Michael Mulryan (eds). *Environment and society in the long late antiquity*. Leiden: Brill, 2019.

Jaeger, C. Stephen. *The Envy of Angels: Cathedral Schools and Social Ideals in Medieval Europe, 950–1200*. Philadelphia: University of Pennsylvania Press, 1994.

Jardine, Lisa. "Humanstic Logic." In *Cambridge History of Renaissance Philosophy*, edited by Charles B. Schmitt, Quentin Skinner, Eckhard Kessler, and Jill Kraye, 173–98. Cambridge: Cambridge University Press, 1988.

Jehl, Rainer. "*Acedia* and Burnout Syndrome: From an Occupational Vice of Early Monks to a Psychological Concept in Secularized Professional Life." In *In the Garden of Evil: The Vices and Culture in the Middle Ages*, edited Richard Newhauser, 455–76. Toronto: Pontifical Institute of Mediaeval Studies, 2005.

Johnson, Monte Ransome. *Aristotle on Teleology*. Oxford Aristotle Studies. Oxford: Clarendon Press, 2005.

Jordan, Alyce. *Visualizing Kingship in the Windows of the Sainte-Chapelle*. Turnhout: Brepols, 2002.

Jordheim, Helga. "Against Periodization: Kosseleck's Theory of Multiple Temporalities." *History and Theory* 51, no. 2 (2012): 151–71.

Kahsnitz, Rainer. *Carved Splendor: Late Gothic Altarpieces in Southern Germany, Austria and South Tyrol*. Los Angeles: J. Paul Getty Museum, 2006.

Karkov, Catherine E. *The Art of Anglo-Saxon England*. Woodbridge, UK: Boydell, 2011.

Kay, Sarah. *Courtly Contradictions: The Emergence of the Literary Object in the Twelfth Century*. Stanford, CA: Stanford University Press, 2001.

Kay, Sarah. *Subjectivity in Troubadour Poetry*. Cambridge: Cambridge University Press, 1990.

Kelly, Douglas. "Love, Reason, and Debatable Opinion." In *Christine De Pizan's Changing Opinion: A Quest for Certainty in the Midst of Chaos*, 107–41. Woodbridge, UK: Boydell and Brewer, 2007.

Kempshall, Matthew. *Rhetoric and the Writing of History, 400–1500*. Manchester: Manchester University Press, 2011.

Kennedy, George A. *Classical Rhetoric and its Christian and Secular Tradition*. Chapel Hill: University of North Carolina Press, 1999.

Kieckhefer, Richard. *Magic in the Middle Ages*. Cambridge: Cambridge University Press, 1989.

König, Jason and Tim Whitmarsh, eds. *Ordering Knowledge in the Roman Empire*. Cambridge: Cambridge University Press, 2007.

Koselleck, Reinhart. *Futures Past: On the Semantics of Historical Time*. Translated by Keith Tribe. Cambridge, MA: MIT Press, 1985.

Kratz, Dennis M. *The Romances of Alexander*. New York: Garland Publishing, 1991.

Kristeller, Paul Oskar. *Renaissance Thought: The Classic, Scholastic, and Humanistic Strains*. New York: Harper & Brothers, 1961.

Krueger, Derek. *Liturgical Subjects: Christian Ritual, Biblical Narrative, and the Formation of the Self in Byzantium*. Philadelphia: University of Pennsylvania Press, 2014.

Kudrycz, Walter. *The Historical Present: Medievalism and Modernity*. London: Bloomsbury, 2011.

Lambertini, Roberto. "Wealth and Money according to Giles of Rome." In *Reichtum im späten Mittelalter: politische Theorie, ethische Norm, soziale Akzeptanz*, edited by Peter Hesse and Petra Schulte, 39–53. Stuttgart: Franz Steiner Verlag, 2015.

Lang, Helen. *Aristotle's "Physics" and Its Medieval Varieties*. Albany: State University of New York Press, 1992.

Langholm, Odd. *Economics in the Medieval Schools: Wealth, Exchange, Value, Money and Usury according to the Paris Theological Tradition, 1200–1350*. Leiden: E. J. Brill, 1992.

Langholm, Odd. *The Legacy of Scholasticism in Economic Thought: Antecedents of Choice and Power*. Cambridge: Cambridge University Press, 1998.

Lawler, Traugott. "The Two Versions of Geoffrey of Vinsauf's *Documentum*." In *The Parisiana Poetria of John of Garland*, edited and translated by Traugott Lawler, 327–32. New Haven, CT: Yale University Press, 1974.

Leclercq, Jean. *The Love of Learning and the Desire for God: A Study of Monastic Culture*. Translated by Catharine Mishrahi. New York: Fordham University Press, 1982.

Leclercq, Jean. "Monachisme et peregrination du IXe au XIIe siècle." *Studia Monastica* 3 (1961): 33–52.

Leff, M. C. "Boethius' *De differentiis topicis*, Book IV." In *Medieval Eloquence: Studies in the Theory and Practice of Medieval Rhetoric*, edited by James J. Murphy, 3–24. Berkeley: University of California Press, 1978.

Le Goff, Jacques. "Trades and Professions as Represented in Medieval Confessors' Manuals." In *Time, Work and Culture in the Middle Ages*, translated by Arthur Goldhammer, 107–21. Chicago: University of Chicago Press, 1990.

Lehtonen, Tuomas M. S. and Päivi Mehtonen, eds. *Historia: The Concept and Genres in the Middle Ages*. Helsinki: Societas Scientiarum Fennica, 2000.

Lerer, Seth. "Humanism, Philology, and the Medievalist." *Postmedieval* 5 (2014): 502–16.

Levinas, Emmanuel. *Totality and Infinity: An Essay on Exteriority*. Translated by Alphonso Lingis. Pittsburgh: Duquesne University Press, 1981.

Lewis, C. S. *The Allegory of Love*. New York: Oxford University Press, 1956.

Lindberg, David C. *The Beginnings of Western Science: The European Scientific Tradition in Philosophical, Religious, and Institutional Context, 600 B.C. to A.D. 1450*. Chicago: University of Chicago Press, 2008.

Lindberg, David C. "Roger Bacon's Theory of the Rainbow." *Isis* 57, no. 2 (1966): 235–48.

Lindberg, David C. "The Transmission of Greek and Arabic Learning to the West." In *Science in the Middle Ages*, edited by David C. Lindberg, 52–90. Chicago: University of Chicago Press, 1978.

Little, Lester K. *Religious Poverty and the Property Economy in Medieval Europe*. Ithaca, NY: Cornell University Press, 1978.

Lopez, Robert S. *The Commercial Revolution of the Middle Ages 950–1350*. Cambridge: Cambridge University Press, 1976.

Löwith, Karl. *Meaning in History: The Theological Implications of the Philosophy of History*. Chicago: University of Chicago Press, 1949.

Lynch, K. L. *Chaucer's Philosophical Visions*. Rochester, NY: D. S. Brewer, 2000.

MacDonald, Scott. "Late Medieval Ethics." In *A History of Western Ethics*, edited by Lawrence C. Becker and Charlotte B. Becker, 52–9. New York: Garland Publishing, 1992.

MacIntyre, Alasdair. *After Virtue: A Study in Moral Theory*. Notre Dame, IN: University of Notre Dame Press, 1981.

MacIntyre, Alasdair. *Whose Justice? Which Rationality?* Notre Dame, IN: University of Notre Dame Press, 1988.

Mack, Peter. "Humanist Rhetoric and Dialectic." In *Cambridge Companion to Renaissance Humanism*, edited by Jill Kraye, 82–99. Cambridge: Cambridge University Press, 1996.

Mallette, Karla. "Beyond Mimesis: Aristotle's *Poetics* in the Medieval Mediterranean." *PMLA* 124, no. 2 (2009): 583–91.

Mann, Michael. *The Sources of Social Power, Volume 1: A History of Power from the Beginning to AD 1760*. 2nd edition. Cambridge: Cambridge University Press, 2012.

Mann, Nicholas. "The Origins of Humanism." In *Cambridge Companion to Renaissance Humanism*, edited by Jill Kraye, 1–19. Cambridge: Cambridge University Press, 1996.

Marenbon, John. *Early Medieval Philosophy (480–1150): An Introduction*. 2nd edition. London: Routledge Press, 1988.

Marenbon, John. *Pagans and Philosophers: The Problem of Paganism from Augustine to Leibniz*. Princeton, NJ: Princeton University Press, 2015.

Marenbon, John. *The Philosophy of Peter Abelard*. Cambridge: Cambridge University Press, 1997.

Markus, R. A. *Saeculum – History and Society in the Theology of Augustine*. Cambridge: Cambridge University Press, 1970.

Martin, Therese, ed. *Reassessing the Roles of Women as "Makers" of Medieval Art and Architecture*. 2 volumes. Boston: Brill, 2012.

Martindale, Andrew. *Heroes, Ancestors, Relatives and the Birth of the Portrait*. Maarssen, the Netherlands: SDU Publishers, 1988.

McCormick, Michael, et al. "Climate Change during and after the Roman Empire: Reconstructing the Past from Scientific and Historical Evidence." *Journal of Interdisciplinary History* 43, no. 2 (2012): 169–220.

McEvoy, James. *Robert Grosseteste*. Great Medieval Thinkers. New York: Oxford University Press, 2000.

McGinn, Bernard. *The Flowering of Mysticism: Men and Women in the New Mysticism (1200–1350)*. New York: The Crossroad Publishing Company, 1998.

McGinn, Bernard. *The Growth of Mysticism*. New York: The Crossroad Publishing Company, 1994.

McKeon, Richard. "Rhetoric in the Middle Ages." In *Critics and Criticism*, edited by R. S. Crane, 260–96. Chicago: University of Chicago Press, 1952.

McLaughlin, M. L. "Humanist Concepts of the Renaissance and Middle Ages in the Tre- and Quattrocentro." *Renaissance Studies* 2, no. 2 (1988): 131–42.

McLaughlin, Mary Martin and Bonnie Wheeler, ed. and trans. *The Letters of Heloise and Abelard: A Translation of their Collected Correspondence and Related Writings*. Basingstoke, UK: Palgrave Macmillan, 2009.

McLuhen, Marshall. *Understanding Media: The Extensions of Man*. New York: McGraw-Hill, 1964.

McNally, David. *Political Economy and the Rise of Capitalism*. Berkeley: University of California Press, 1988.

Mehtonen, Päivi. *Old Concepts and New Poetics: Historia, Argumentum and Fabula in the Twelfth- and Thirteenth-Century Latin Poetics of Fiction*. Helsinki: Societas Scientiarum Fennica, 1996.

Metaxas, Eric. *Martin Luther: The Man Who Rediscovered God and Changed the World*. New York City: Viking, 2017.

Minnis, A. J., A. B. Scott, and David Wallace, eds. *Medieval Literary Theory and Criticism, c.1100–c.1375*. Oxford: Clarendon Press, 1988.

Mitchell, J. Allan. "Romancing Ethics in Boethius, Chaucer, and Levinas: Fortune, Moral Luck, and Erotic Adventure." *Comparative Literature* 57, no. 2 (2005): 101–16.

Moore, Robert I. *The First European Revolution, c. 970–1215*. Oxford: Blackwell, 2000.

Morey, James H. "Peter Comestor, Biblical Paraphrase, and the Medieval Popular Bible." *Speculum* 68, no. 1 (1993): 6–35.

Morris, Colin. *The Discovery of the Individual, 1050–1200*. Toronto: University of Toronto Press, 1987.

Muessig, Carolyn. "Learning and Mentoring in the Twelfth Century: Hildegard of Bingen and Herrad of Landsberg." In *Medieval Monastic Education*, edited by George Ferzoco and Carolyn Muessig, 87–104. London: Leicester University Press, 2001.

Murphy, James J. "Rhetoric in Fourteenth-Century Oxford." *Medium Aevum* 34 (1965): 1–20.

Murphy, James J. *Rhetoric in the Middle Ages: A History of Rhetorical Theory from Saint Augustine to the Renaissance*. Berkeley: University of California Press, 1974.

Murphy, James J. *Three Medieval Rhetorical Arts*. Tempe: Arizona Center for Medieval and Renaissance Studies, 2001.

Murphy, Trevor M. *Pliny the Elder's Natural History: The Empire in the Encyclopedia*. Oxford: Oxford University Press, 2004.

Nancy, Jean-Luc. *Ego sum: Corpus, Anima, Fabula*. Translated by Marie-Eve Morin. New York: Fordham University Press, 2016.

Nauta, Lodi. "The *Consolation*: The Latin Commentary Tradition, 800–1700." In *The Cambridge Companion to Boethius*, edited by John Marenbon, 255–78. Cambridge: Cambridge University Press, 2009.

Nederman, Cary. "Aristotelianism and the Origins of 'Political Science' in the Twelfth Century." *Journal of the History of Ideas* 52 (1991): 179–94.

Nederman, Cary. "Empire and the Historiography of European Political Thought: Marsiglio of Padua, Nicolas of Cusa, and the Medieval/Modern Divide." *Journal of the History of Ideas* 66, no. 1 (2005): 1–15.

Newhauser, Richard. "Preaching the 'Contrary Virtues.'" *Mediaeval Studies* 70 (2008): 135–62.

Newman, Barbara. *God and the Goddesses: Vision, Poetry, and Belief in the Middle Ages*. Philadelphia: University of Pennsylvania Press, 2002.

Nolan, Kathleen. *Queens in Stone and Silver: The Creation of a Visual Imagery of Queenship in Capetian France*. New York: Palgrave Macmillan, 2009.

Normore, Calvin. "Some Aspects of Ockham's Logic." In *The Cambridge Companion to Ockham*, edited by Paul Vincent Spade, 31–52. Cambridge: Cambridge University Press, 1999.

Novikoff, Alex. *The Medieval Culture of Disputation: Pedagogy, Practice, and Performance*. Philadelphia: University of Pennsylvania Press, 2013.

Oberman, Heiko. *The Harvest of Medieval Theology: Gabriel Biel and Late Medieval Nominalism*. Cambridge, MA: Harvard University Press, 1963.

Olsen, Alexandra H. and Burton Raffel. *Poems and Prose from the Old English*. New Haven, CT: Yale University Press, 1998.

Ovitt, George Jr. *The Restoration of Perfection: Labor and Technology in Medieval Culture*. New Brunswick, NJ: Rutgers University Press, 1987.

Palmer, James. "Defining Paganism in the Carolingian World." *Early Medieval Europe* 15, no. 4 (2007): 402–25.

Paravicini Bagliani, Agostino. *The Pope's Body*. Translated by David S. Peterson. Chicago: University of Chicago Press, 2000.

Pasnau, Robert. *Thomas Aquinas on Human Nature: A Philosophical Study of Summa Theologiae 1a 75–89*. Cambridge: Cambridge University Press, 2002.

Pearsall, Derek. *Old English and Middle English Poetry*. London: Routledge & Kegan Paul, 1977.

Pedersen, Olaf. *The Book of Nature*. Notre Dame, IN: University of Notre Dame Press, 1992.

Pennock, Caroline Dodds and Amanda Power. "Globalising Cosmologies." *Past and Present* 238 (2018): 88–115.

Phelan, Owen M. "New Insights, Old Texts: Clerical Formation and the Carolingian Renewal in Hrabanus Maurus." *Traditio* 71 (2017): 63–89.

Piron, Sylvain. *L'Occupation du monde*. Brussels: Zones Sensibiles, 2018.

Pollard, John Graham. "The *pecia* System in the Medieval Universities." In *Medieval Scribes, Manuscripts & Libraries: Essays Presented to N.R. Ker*, edited by Malcolm B. Parkes and Andrew G. Watson, 145–61. London: Scolar Press, 1978.

Pollman, Karla and Willemien Otten, eds. *The Oxford Guide to the Historical Reception of Augustine*. Oxford: Oxford University Press, 2013.

Power, Amanda. *Roger Bacon and the Defence of Christendom*. Cambridge: Cambridge University Press, 2012.

Prill, Paul E. "Rhetoric and Poetics in the Early Middle Ages." *Rhetorica* 5, no. 2 (1987): 129–47.

Rasmussen, Ann Marie. "The Female Figures in Gottfried's *Tristan and Isolde*." In *A Companion to Gottfried von Strassburg's* Tristan, edited by Will Hasty, 137–58. Rochester, NY: Camden House, 2003.

Ray, Roger. "Medieval Historiography through the Twelfth Century: Problems and Progress of Research." *Viator* 5 (1974): 33–59.

Rebillard, Éric. *Christians and Their Many Identities in Late Antiquity, North Africa, 200–450 CE*. Ithaca, NY: Cornell University Press, 2012.

Reddy, William. *The Making of Romantic Love: Longing and Sexuality in Europe, South Asia, and Japan 900–1200 CE*. Chicago: University of Chicago Press, 2012.

Reeves, Marjorie. *The Influence of Prophecy in the Later Middle Ages – A Study in Joachimism*. Oxford: Clarendon Press, 1969.

Renn, Jürgen, ed. *The Globalization of Knowledge in History: Based on the 97th Dahlem Workshop*. Berlin: Edition Open Access, 2007.

Reudenbach, Bruno. "Reliquien von Orten: ein frühchristliches Reliquiar als Gedächtnisort." In *Reliquiare im Mittelalter*, edited by Bruno Reudenbach and Gia Toussaint, 21–41. Hamburger Forschungen zur Kunstgeschichte 5. Berlin: Akademie Verlag, 2005.

Reynolds, Susan. *Kingdoms and Communities in Western Europe, 900–1300*. 2nd edition. Oxford: Oxford University Press, 1997.

Riché, Pierre. *Écoles et enseignement dans le Haut Moyen Âge: Fin du Ve siècle–milieu du XIe siècle*. Paris: Picard, 1989.

Ritchey, Sara. "Rethinking the Twelfth-Century Discovery of Nature." *Journal of Medieval and Early Modern Studies* 39, no. 2 (2009): 225–55.

Robertson, Durant, Jr. "The Concept of Courtly Love as an Impediment to the Understanding of Medieval Texts." In *Essays in Medieval Culture*, 257–72. Princeton, NJ: Princeton University Press, 1980.

Robertson, Kellie. *Nature Speaks: Medieval Literature and Aristotelian Philosophy*. Philadelphia: University of Pennsylvania, 2017.

Rodriguez, Jarbel, ed. *Muslim and Christian Contact in the Middle Ages: A Reader*. Toronto: University of Toronto Press, 2005.

de Roover, Raymond. *Business, Banking, and Economic Thought in Late Medieval and Early Modern Europe*. Edited by Julius Kirshner. Chicago: University of Chicago Press, 1974.

Rosenfeld, Jessica. "Compassionate Conversions: Gower's *Confessio Amantis* and the Problem of Envy." *Journal of Medieval and Early Modern Studies* 42, no. 1 (2012): 83–105.

Rosier-Catach, Irène. "Prata rident." In *Langages et philosophie: hommage à Jean Jolivet*, edited by Alain de Libera, Abdelali Elamrani-Jamal, and Alain Galonnier, 156–76. Paris: Vrin, 1997.

Rubenstein, Jay. *Guibert of Nogent: Portrait of a Medieval Mind*. New York: Routledge, 2002.

Rubin, Miri. *Emotion and Devotion: The Meaning of Mary in Medieval Religious Cultures*. Budapest: Central European University Press, 2009.

Savage, Anne and Nicholas Watson, eds. *Anchoritic Spirituality: Ancrene Wisse and Associated Works*. New York: Paulist Press, 1991.

Saxon, Elizabeth. "Carolingian, Ottonian and Romanesque Art and the Eucharist." In *A Companion to the Eucharist in the Middle Ages*, edited by Ian Levy, Gary Macy, and Kristen Van Ausdall, 251–324. Leiden: Brill, 2012.

Sayers, Jane. *Innocent III: Leader of Europe, 1198–1216*. New York: Longman, 1994.

Schapiro, Meyer. "On the Aesthetic Attitude in Romanesque Art." In *Romanesque Art, Selected Papers*, edited by Meyer Schapiro, 1–27. London: Chatto & Windus, 1993.

Schumpeter, Joseph A. *History of Economic Analysis*. New York: Oxford University Press, 1954.

Scott, James C. *Against the Grain: A Deep History of the Earliest States*. New Haven, CT: Yale University Press, 2017.

Scott, James C. *The Art of Not Being Governed: An Anarchist History of Upland Southeast Asia*. New Haven, CT: Yale University Press, 2009.

Shalem, Avinoam. *Islam Christianized: Islamic Portable Objects in the Medieval Churches of the Latin West*. Ars Faciendi. Beiträge und Studien zur Kunstgeschichte, 7. Frankfurt: Peter Lang, 1996.

Simons, Walter. *Cities of Ladies: Beguine Communities in the Medieval Low Countries, 1200–1565*. Philadelphia: University of Pennsylvania Press, 2003.

Skemer, Don C. *Binding Words: Textual Amulets in the Middle Ages*. University Park: Pennsylvania State Press, 2006.

Smalley, Beryl. *Historians in the Middle Ages*. London: Thames & Hudson, 1974.

Smith, D. Vance. *The Book of the Incipit: Beginnings in the Fourteenth Century*. Minneapolis: University of Minnesota Press, 2001.

Somfai, Anna. "The Eleventh-Century Shift in the Reception of Plato's 'Timaeus' and Calcidius's 'Commentary.'" *Journal of the Warburg and Courtauld Institutes* 65 (2002): 1–21.

Southern, R. W. "Aspects of the European Tradition of Historical Writing: 1. The Classical Tradition from Einhard to Geoffrey of Monmouth." *Transactions of the Royal Historical Society* 20 (1970): 173–96.

Southern, R. W. "Aspects of the European Tradition of Historical Writing: 2. Hugh of St.Victor and the Idea of Historical Development." *Transactions of the Royal Historical Society* 21 (1971): 159–79.

Southern, R. W. "Aspects of the European Tradition of Historical Writing: 3. History as Prophecy." *Transactions of the Royal Historical Society* 22 (1972): 159–86.

Southern, R. W. "Aspects of the European Tradition of Historical Writing: 4. The Sense of the Past." *Transactions of the Royal Historical Society* 23 (1973): 243–63.

Southern, R. W. *Saint Anselm and His Biographer: A Study of Monastic Life and Thought, 1059–c. 1130.* Cambridge: Cambridge University Press, 1963.

Southern, R. W. *Western Society and the Church in the Middle Ages.* London: Penguin, 1970.

Speer, Andreas. "The Discovery of Nature: The Contribution of the Chartrians to Twelfth-Century Attempts to Found a Scientia Naturalis." *Traditio* 52 (1997): 135–51.

Spiegel, Gabrielle M. *The Past as Text: The Theory and Practice of Medieval Historiography.* Baltimore: Johns Hopkins University Press, 1997.

Stock, Brian. *The Implications of Literacy: Written Language and Models of Interpretation in the Eleventh and Twelfth Centuries.* Princeton, NJ: Princeton University Press, 1983.

Stock, Brian. *Listening for the Text: On the Uses of the Past.* Baltimore: Johns Hopkins University Press, 1990.

Stock, Brian. *Myth and Science in the Twelfth Century; a Study of Bernard Silvester.* Princeton, NJ: Princeton University Press, 1972.

Stock, Brian. "The Self and Literary Experience in Late Antiquity and the Middle Ages." *New Literary History* 25 (1994): 839–52.

Straw, Carole. "Gregory, Cassian and the Cardinal Vices." In *In the Garden of Evil: The Vices and Culture in the Middle Ages*, edited by Richard Newhauser, 59–73. Toronto: Pontifical Institute of Mediaeval Studies, 2005.

Sullivan, Richard. "Changing Perspectives on the Middle Ages." *Centennial Review* 28, no. 2 (1984): 77–99.

Sweeney, Eileen C. *Anselm of Canterbury and the Desire for the Word.* Washington, DC: Catholic University of America Press, 2012.

Sweeney, Eileen C. "Aquinas on Vice and Sin." In *The Ethics of Aquinas*, edited by Stephen J. Pope, 151–68. Washington, DC: Georgetown University Press, 2002.

Sweeney, Eileen C. "Literary Forms of Medieval Philosophy." In *The Stanford Encyclopedia of Philosophy*, edited by Edward N. Zalta. Summer edition, 2019. Available online: https://plato.stanford.edu/archives/sum2019/entries/medieval-literary (accessed January 31, 2022).

Sweeney, Eileen C. *Logic, Theology and Poetry in Boethius, Abelard, and Alan of Lille: Words in the Absence of Things.* London: Palgrave Macmillan, 2006.

Sweeney, Eileen C. "Sin and Grace." In *Cambridge Companion to Medieval Ethics*, edited by Thomas Williams, 348–72. New York: Cambridge University Press, 2018.

Tachau, Katherine. "Logic's God and the Natural Order in Late Medieval Oxford: The Teaching of Robert Holcot." *Annals of Science* 53 (1996): 235–67.

Tanner, Norman P., ed. *Decrees of the Ecumenical Councils, Volume 1.* London: Sheed and Ward; Washington, DC: Georgetown University Press, 1990.

Taylor, Charles. *A Secular Age.* Cambridge, MA: The Bellknap Press of Harvard University Press, 2007.

Thijssen, J. M. M. H. *Censure and Heresy at the University of Paris, 1200–1400*. Philadelphia: University of Pennsylvania Press, 1998.

Thonemann, Peter. "Phrygia: An Anarchist History, 950 BC–AD 100." In *Roman Phrygia: Culture and Society*, edited by Peter Thonemann, 1–40. Cambridge: Cambridge University Press, 2013.

Thorndike, Lynn. "Newness and Craving for Novelty in Seventeenth-Century Science and Medicine." *Journal of the History of Ideas* 12, no. 4 (1951): 584–98.

Thuillat, Jean-Pierre. *Bertran de Born: histoire et légende*. Périgueux: Fanlac, 2009.

Tin, Louis-Georges. *L'invention de la culture hétérosexuelle*. Paris: Autrement, 2008.

Trexler, Richard C. *Public Life in Renaissance Florence*. New York: Academic Press, 1980.

Urbano, Arthur, Jr. "'Read It Also to the Gentiles': The Displacement and Recasting of the Philosopher in the *Vita Antonii*." *Church History* 77, no. 4 (2008): 877–914.

Vagelpohl, Uwe. "The User-Friendly Galen: Ḥunayn ibn Isḥāq and the Adaptation of Greek Medicine for a New Audience." In *Greek Medical Literature and its Readers From Hippocrates to Islam and Byzantium*, edited by Petros Bouras-Vallianatos and Sophia Xenophontos, 113–30. London: Routledge, 2017.

Vance, Eugene. *From Topic to Tale: Logic and Narrativity in the Middle Ages*. Minneapolis: University of Minnesota Press, 1987.

Van Engen, John H., ed. *Learning Institutionalized: Teaching in the Medieval University*. Notre Dame, IN: University of Notre Dame Press, 2000.

Van Engen, John H. *Sisters and Brothers of the Common Life: The Devotio Moderna and the World of the Later Middle Ages*. Philadelphia: University of Pennsylvania Press, 2014.

Vauchez, André. *The Laity in the Middle Ages: Religious Beliefs and Devotional Practices*. Edited by Daniel E. Bornstein. Translated by Margery J. Schneider. Notre Dame, IN: University of Notre Dame Press, 1993.

Vecchio, Silvana. "The Seven Deadly Sins Between Pastoral Care and Scholastic Theology: The *Summa de viciis* of John of Rupella." In *In the Garden of Evil: The Vices and Culture in the Middle Ages*, translated by Helen Took, edited by Richard Newhauser, 104–27. Toronto: Pontifical Institute of Mediaeval Studies, 2005.

Wallace-Hadrill, Andrew. "Pliny the Elder and Man's Unnatural History." *Greece & Rome* 37, no. 1 (1990): 80–96.

Wallace-Hadrill, J. M. *The Frankish Church*. Oxford: Clarendon Press, 1983.

Ward-Perkins, Bryan. *The fall of Rome and the end of civilization*. Oxford: Oxford University Press, 2005.

Ward, John O. "Classical Rhetoric and the Writing of History in Medieval and Renaissance Culture." In *European History and Its Historians*, edited by Frank MacGregor and Nicholas Wright, 1–10. Adelaide: Adelaide University Union Press, 1977.

Ward, John O. "From Antiquity to the Renaissance: Glosses and Commentaries on Cicero's *Rhetorica*." In *Medieval Eloquence: Studies in the Theory and Practice of Medieval Rhetoric*, edited by James J. Murphy. Berkeley: University of California Press, 1978.

Ward, John O. "Some Principles of Rhetorical Historiography in the Twelfth Century." In *Classical Rhetoric and Medieval Historiography*, edited by Ernst Breisach, 103–65. Kalamazoo, MI: Medieval Institute Publications, 1985.

Ward, John O. "'Chronicle' and 'History': The Medieval Origins of Postmodern Historiographical Practice?" *Parergon* 14 (1997): 102–28.

Warren, Nancy Bradley. "In Praise of Messiness, or What is Gained by Losing Strong Periodization." *Journal for Early Modern Cultural Studies* 13, no. 3 (2018): 138–43.

Waters, Claire M. *Translating* Clergie: *Status, Education, and Salvation in Thirteenth-Century Vernacular Texts*. Philadelphia: University of Pennsylvania Press, 2016.

Wei, Ian. *Intellectual Culture in Medieval Paris: Theologians and the University, c. 1100–1330*. Cambridge: Cambridge University Press, 2012.

Weisheipl, James A. "Classification of the Sciences in Medieval Thought." *Medieval Studies* 27 (1965): 54–90.

Weiss, Daniel. "Architectural Symbolism and the Decoration of the Ste.-Chapelle." *Art Bulletin* 77, no. 2 (1995): 308–20.

Wenzel, Siegfried. "'Acedia' 700–1200." *Traditio* 22 (1966): 73–102.

Wenzel, Siegfried, ed. *Fasciculus Morum: A Fourteenth-Century Preacher's Handbook*. University Park: Pennsylvania State University Press, 1989.

Westermann-Angerhausen, Hiltrud. *Goldschmiedearbeiten der Trierer Egbertwerkstatt*. Trier: Spee-Verlag, 1973.

White, Hayden. "The Value of Narrativity in the Representation of Reality." *Critical Inquiry* 7 (1980): 5–27.

Wickham, Chris. *Framing the Early Middle Ages: Europe and the Mediterranean 400–800*. Oxford: Oxford University Press, 2005.

Wickham, Chris. *The Inheritance of Rome: A History of Europe from 400 to 1000*. London: Penguin Books, 2009.

Wieruszowski, Helene. *Politics and Culture in Medieval Spain and Italy*. Rome: Edizioni di storia e letteratura, 1971.

Willard, Charity Cannon. *Christine de Pizan: Her Life and Her Works*. New York: Persea, 1984.

Williams, James B. "Working for Reform: *Acedia*, Benedict of Aniane and the Transformation of Working Culture in Carolingian Monasticism." In *Sin in Medieval and Early Modern Culture*, edited by Richard G. Newhauser and Susan J. Ridyard, 19–42. York: York Medieval Press, 2012.

Williams, Steven J. *The Secret of Secrets: The Scholarly Career of a Pseudo-Aristotelian Text in the Latin Middle Ages*. Ann Arbor: University of Michigan Press, 2003.

Willoughby, Harold R. "The Distinctive Sources of Palestinian Pilgrimage Iconography." *Journal of Biblical Literature* 74, no. 2 (1955): 61–8.

Wolf, Kenneth Baxter. *The Life and Afterlife of St. Elizabeth of Hungary: Testimony from her Canonization Hearings*. Oxford: Oxford University Press, 2010.

Wood, Diana. *Medieval Economic Thought*. Cambridge: Cambridge University Press, 2002.

Wood, Neal. *The Foundations of Political Economy*. Berkeley: University of California Press, 1994.

Wood, Rega. "The Influence of Arabic Aristotelianism on Scholastic Natural Philosophy." In *The Cambridge History of Medieval Philosophy*, edited by R. Pasnau and C. Van Dyke, 247–66. Cambridge: Cambridge University Press, 2009.

Woods, Marjorie Curry. "Chaucer the Rhetorician: Criseyde and Her Family." *The Chaucer Review* 20, no. 1 (1985): 28–39.

Wright, Georgia Sommers. "The Reinvention of the Portrait Likeness in the Fourteenth Century." *Gesta* 39, no. 2 (2000): 117–34.

Yerushalmi, Yosef Hayim. *Zakhor—Jewish History and Jewish Memory*. Seattle: University of Washington Press, 1982.

Zink, Michel. *La prédication en langue romane avant 1300*. Paris: Honoré Champion, 1982.

Zizek, Slavoj. *The Metastases of Enjoyment: Six Essays on Woman and Causality*. London: Verso, 1994.

CONTRIBUTORS

Karen Bollermann is an independent scholar residing in College Station, Texas, USA. She is coauthor of *Thomas Becket: An Intimate Biography* and has published articles in medieval studies journals, including *Viator*, *Journal of Medieval History*, and *Mediaevistik*. She is engaged in continuing research on Old and Middle English literature, as well as twelfth-century English political and intellectual history.

Dallas G. Denery II is Professor of History at Bowdoin College, USA, specializing in the intellectual and religious history of medieval and early modern Europe. He is the author of *The Devil Wins: A History of Lying from the Garden of Eden to the Enlightenment* (2015) and *Seeing and Being Seen in the Late Medieval World: Optics, Theology and Religious Life* (2005). His latest project, *Everything is Wrong!*, considers what egregiously bad histories can teach us about the nature and purpose of history.

Mary Franklin-Brown is University Lecturer in Medieval French and Occitan Studies at Christ's College, University of Cambridge, UK. Her research covers medieval writing in French, Occitan, Latin, and Catalan. She interprets this literature through the dual lenses of medieval philosophy and current critical thought, and she also takes account of the material transmission of texts through performance or manuscript copy. She is the author of *Reading the World: Encyclopedic Writing of the Scholastic Age* (2012).

Heidi C. Gearhart is Assistant Professor of History and Art History at George Mason University, USA. Her research focuses on sacred arts and manuscripts, artists, and medieval art theory, and she is especially interested in issues of memory, craft, and manufacture. She is the author of *Theophilus and the Theory and Practice of Medieval Art* (2017).

Matthew Kempshall is Cliff Davies Fellow and Clarendon Associate Professor in History at Wadham College, University of Oxford, UK. His research and publications center on the transmission and transformation of aspects of the classical tradition within medieval and early Renaissance Europe. He is the author of *The Common Good in Late Medieval Political Thought* (1999), and *Rhetoric and the Writing of History, 400–1500* (2011).

Cary J. Nederman is Professor of Political Science Texas A&M University, USA. His research concentrates on the history of Western political thought, with a specialization in Greek, Roman, and early European ideas up to the seventeenth century. He focuses on the relationship between historical traditions and contemporary theoretical concerns, focusing especially on early European political thought from 1100 to 1500. He has also published in the field of comparative political thought. He is the author or editor of more than twenty books, including *Inventing Modernity in Medieval European Thought, ca. 1100–ca. 1450* (2018) and *Religion, Power and Resistance from the Eleventh to the*

Sixteenth Centuries: Playing the Heresy Card (2015). His next book, entitled *The Rack and the Chains*, continues his interest in Machiavelli's thought.

Amanda Power is Associate Professor in History at St Catherine's College, University of Oxford, UK. At Oxford, Dr. Power has been involved in developing the field of global medieval history, and new approaches to historical study that speak to the concerns of the mounting climate and environmental crisis. Her focus is on religion, power, and intellectual life in medieval Europe and she is the author of *Roger Bacon and the Defence of Christendom* (2012). She is involved in a series of projects that ask about the future of the Humanities and Social Sciences in the politically, economically, and ecologically unstable period that we are now entering. She is currently working on a book called *Medieval Histories of the Anthropocene*, and co-editing (with Ian Forrest and Minoru Ozawa) *Medieval Zomias: Alternative Global Histories*.

Kellie Robertson is Professor of English and Comparative Literature at the University of Maryland, USA. She is the author of *Nature Speaks: Medieval Literature and Aristotelian Philosophy* (2017). Her current book project is entitled *Yesterday's Weather: A Prehistory of Climate Change*. This study examines how medieval and early modern societies depicted the shock of the natural disaster and how such representations continue to influence the stories we tell ourselves about climate today.

Eileen C. Sweeney is Professor of Philosophy at Boston College, USA. Her research interests include medieval philosophy, the philosophy of language, and theories of the passions. She is the author of *Words in the Absence of Things: Logic, Theology and Poetry in Boethius, Abelard and Alan of Lille* (2006), and *Anselm of Canterbury and the Desire for the Word* (2012). Her current projects are on the liberal arts and science in the Middle Ages, and the history of the passions from the Medieval to the Modern period.

Claire M. Waters is Professor of English at University of California Davis, USA. Her work focuses on medieval religious literature and culture, from saints' lives and preaching to doctrinal handbooks and miracles of the Virgin Mary, with a particular interest in the relationship between teachers and learners, between the audiences of sermons and religious writings and the creators of those works. She is the author of *Angel and Earthly Creatures: Preaching, Performance, and Gender in the Later Middle Ages* (2004) and *Translating Clergie: Status, Education, and Salvation in Thirteenth-Century Vernacular Texts* (2016).

Wesley Chihyung Yu is Associate Professor of English and Director of Studies for English at Mount Holyoke College, USA. He specializes in the literature of the Middle Ages with emphases in medieval rhetoric, logic, and early poetics. He is currently completing a book manuscript that examines medieval theories of argumentation, focusing on the influence of argument on vernacular poetic composition and development between the eighth and fourteenth centuries.

INDEX